NUMERICAL METHODS IN FINANCE

GERAD 25th Anniversary Series

- **Essays and Surveys in Global Optimization**
  Charles Audet, Pierre Hansen, and Gilles Savard, editors
- **Graph Theory and Combinatorial Optimization**
  David Avis, Alain Hertz, and Odile Marcotte, editors
- **Numerical Methods in Finance**
  Hatem Ben-Ameur and Michèle Breton, editors
- **Analysis, Control and Optimization of Complex Dynamic Systems**
  El-Kébir Boukas and Roland Malhamé, editors
- **Column Generation**
  Guy Desaulniers, Jacques Desrosiers, and Marius M. Solomon, editors
- **Statistical Modeling and Analysis for Complex Data Problems**
  Pierre Duchesne and Bruno Rémillard, editors
- **Performance Evaluation and Planning Methods for the Next Generation Internet**
  André Girard, Brunilde Sansò, and Félisa Vázquez-Abad, editors
- **Dynamic Games: Theory and Applications**
  Alain Haurie and Georges Zaccour, editors
- **Logistics Systems: Design and Optimization**
  André Langevin and Diane Riopel, editors
- **Energy and Environment**
  Richard Loulou, Jean-Philippe Waaub, and Georges Zaccour, editors

NUMERICAL METHODS IN FINANCE

Edited by
MICHÈLE BRETON
GERAD and HEC Montréal

HATEM BEN-AMEUR
GERAD and HEC Montréal

Springer

ISBN 978-1-4419-3773-5 e-ISBN 978-0-387-25118-9

Printed in the United States of America.

9 8 7 6 5 4 3 2 1

springeronline.com

Foreword

GERAD celebrates this year its 25th anniversary. The Center was created in 1980 by a small group of professors and researchers of HEC Montréal, McGill University and of the École Polytechnique de Montréal. GERAD's activities achieved sufficient scope to justify its conversion in June 1988 into a Joint Research Centre of HEC Montréal, the École Polytechnique de Montréal and McGill University. In 1996, the Université du Québec à Montréal joined these three institutions. GERAD has fifty members (professors), more than twenty research associates and post doctoral students and more than two hundreds master and Ph.D. students.

GERAD is a multi-university center and a vital forum for the development of operations research. Its mission is defined around the following four complementarily objectives:

- The original and expert contribution to all research fields in GERAD's area of expertise;
- The dissemination of research results in the best scientific outlets as well as in the society in general;
- The training of graduate students and post doctoral researchers;
- The contribution to the economic community by solving important problems and providing transferable tools.

GERAD's research thrusts and fields of expertise are as follows:

- Development of mathematical analysis tools and techniques to solve the complex problems that arise in management sciences and engineering;
- Development of algorithms to resolve such problems efficiently;
- Application of these techniques and tools to problems posed in related disciplines, such as statistics, financial engineering, game theory and artificial intelligence;
- Application of advanced tools to optimization and planning of large technical and economic systems, such as energy systems, transportation/communication networks, and production systems;
- Integration of scientific findings into software, expert systems and decision-support systems that can be used by industry.

One of the marking events of the celebrations of the 25th anniversary of GERAD is the publication of ten volumes covering most of the Center's research areas of expertise. The list follows: **Essays and Surveys in Global Optimization**, edited by C. Audet, P. Hansen and G. Savard; **Graph Theory and Combinatorial Optimization**, edited by D. Avis, A. Hertz and O. Marcotte; **Numerical Methods in Finance**, edited by H. Ben-Ameur and M. Breton; **Analysis, Control and Optimization of Complex Dynamic Systems**, edited by E.K. Boukas and R. Malhamé; **Column Generation**, edited by G. Desaulniers, J. Desrosiers and M.M. Solomon; **Statistical Modeling and Analysis for Complex Data Problems**, edited by P. Duchesne and B. Rémillard; **Performance Evaluation and Planning Methods for the Next Generation Internet**, edited by A. Girard, B. Sansò and F. Vázquez-Abad; **Dynamic Games: Theory and Applications**, edited by A. Haurie and G. Zaccour; **Logistics Systems: Design and Optimization**, edited by A. Langevin and D. Riopel; **Energy and Environment**, edited by R. Loulou, J.-P. Waaub and G. Zaccour.

I would like to express my gratitude to the Editors of the ten volumes, to the authors who accepted with great enthusiasm to submit their work and to the reviewers for their benevolent work and timely response. I would also like to thank Mrs. Nicole Paradis, Francine Benoît and Louise Letendre and Mr. André Montpetit for their excellent editing work.

The GERAD group has earned its reputation as a worldwide leader in its field. This is certainly due to the enthusiasm and motivation of GERAD's researchers and students, but also to the funding and the infrastructures available. I would like to seize the opportunity to thank the organizations that, from the beginning, believed in the potential and the value of GERAD and have supported it over the years. These are HEC Montréal, École Polytechnique de Montréal, McGill University, Université du Québec à Montréal and, of course, the Natural Sciences and Engineering Research Council of Canada (NSERC) and the Fonds québécois de la recherche sur la nature et les technologies (FQRNT).

Georges Zaccour
Director of GERAD

Avant-propos

Le Groupe d'études et de recherche en analyse des décisions (GERAD) fête cette année son vingt-cinquième anniversaire. Fondé en 1980 par une poignée de professeurs et chercheurs de HEC Montréal engagés dans des recherches en équipe avec des collègues de l'Université McGill et de l'École Polytechnique de Montréal, le Centre comporte maintenant une cinquantaine de membres, plus d'une vingtaine de professionnels de recherche et stagiaires post-doctoraux et plus de 200 étudiants des cycles supérieurs. Les activités du GERAD ont pris suffisamment d'ampleur pour justifier en juin 1988 sa transformation en un Centre de recherche conjoint de HEC Montréal, de l'École Polytechnique de Montréal et de l'Université McGill. En 1996, l'Université du Québec à Montréal s'est jointe à ces institutions pour parrainer le GERAD.

Le GERAD est un regroupement de chercheurs autour de la discipline de la recherche opérationnelle. Sa mission s'articule autour des objectifs complémentaires suivants :

- la contribution originale et experte dans tous les axes de recherche de ses champs de compétence;
- la diffusion des résultats dans les plus grandes revues du domaine ainsi qu'auprès des différents publics qui forment l'environnement du Centre;
- la formation d'étudiants des cycles supérieurs et de stagiaires post-doctoraux;
- la contribution à la communauté économique à travers la résolution de problèmes et le développement de coffres d'outils transférables.

Les principaux axes de recherche du GERAD, en allant du plus théorique au plus appliqué, sont les suivants :

- le développement d'outils et de techniques d'analyse mathématiques de la recherche opérationnelle pour la résolution de problèmes complexes qui se posent dans les sciences de la gestion et du génie;
- la confection d'algorithmes permettant la résolution efficace de ces problèmes;
- l'application de ces outils à des problèmes posés dans des disciplines connexes à la recherche opérationnelle telles que la statistique, l'ingénierie financière, la théorie des jeux et l'intelligence artificielle;
- l'application de ces outils à l'optimisation et à la planification de grands systèmes technico-économiques comme les systèmes énergétiques, les réseaux de télécommunication et de transport, la logistique et la distributique dans les industries manufacturières et de service;

- l'intégration des résultats scientifiques dans des logiciels, des systèmes experts et dans des systèmes d'aide à la décision transférables à l'industrie.

Le fait marquant des célébrations du 25e du GERAD est la publication de dix volumes couvrant les champs d'expertise du Centre. La liste suit : **Essays and Surveys in Global Optimization**, édité par C. Audet, P. Hansen et G. Savard ; **Graph Theory and Combinatorial Optimization**, édité par D. Avis, A. Hertz et O. Marcotte ; **Numerical Methods in Finance**, édité par H. Ben-Ameur et M. Breton ; **Analysis, Control and Optimization of Complex Dynamic Systems**, édité par E.K. Boukas et R. Malhamé ; **Column Generation**, édité par G. Desaulniers, J. Desrosiers et M.M. Solomon ; **Statistical Modeling and Analysis for Complex Data Problems**, édité par P. Duchesne et B. Rémillard ; **Performance Evaluation and Planning Methods for the Next Generation Internet**, édité par A. Girard, B. Sansò et F. Vázquez-Abad ; **Dynamic Games : Theory and Applications**, édité par A. Haurie et G. Zaccour ; **Logistics Systems : Design and Optimization**, édité par A. Langevin et D. Riopel ; **Energy and Environment**, édité par R. Loulou, J.-P. Waaub et G. Zaccour.

Je voudrais remercier très sincèrement les éditeurs de ces volumes, les nombreux auteurs qui ont très volontiers répondu à l'invitation des éditeurs à soumettre leurs travaux, et les évaluateurs pour leur bénévolat et ponctualité. Je voudrais aussi remercier Mmes Nicole Paradis, Francine Benoît et Louise Letendre ainsi que M. André Montpetit pour leur travail expert d'édition.

La place de premier plan qu'occupe le GERAD sur l'échiquier mondial est certes due à la passion qui anime ses chercheurs et ses étudiants, mais aussi au financement et à l'infrastructure disponibles. Je voudrais profiter de cette occasion pour remercier les organisations qui ont cru dès le départ au potentiel et la valeur du GERAD et nous ont soutenus durant ces années. Il s'agit de HEC Montréal, l'École Polytechnique de Montréal, l'Université McGill, l'Université du Québec à Montréal et, bien sûr, le Conseil de recherche en sciences naturelles et en génie du Canada (CRSNG) et le Fonds québécois de la recherche sur la nature et les technologies (FQRNT).

Georges Zaccour
Directeur du GERAD

Contents

Foreword v

Avant-propos vii

Contributing Authors xi

Preface xiii

1
Corporate Debt Valuation: The Structural Approach 1
P. François

2
Bessel Processes and Asian Options 35
D. Dufresne

3
Dynamic Management of Portfolios with Transaction Costs under Tychastic Uncertainty 59
J.-P. Aubin, D. Pujal, and P. Saint-Pierre

4
The Robust Control Approach to Option Pricing and Interval Models: An Overview 91
P. Bernhard

5
A Finite Element Method for Two Factor Convertible Bonds 109
J. de Frutos

6
On Numerical Methods and the Valuation of American Options 129
M. Bellalah

7
Valuing American Contingent Claims when Time to Maturity is Uncertain 143
T. Berrada

8
Foreign Direct Investment: The Incentive to Expropriate and the Cost of Expropriation Risk 159
E. Clark

9
Exact Multivariate Tests of Asset Pricing Models with Stable Asymmetric Distributions 173
M.-C. Beaulieu, J.-M. Dufour, and L. Khalaf

10
A Stochastic Discount Factor-Based Approach for Fixed-income Mutual Fund Performance Evaluation 193
M.A. Ayadi and L. Kryzanowski

11
Portfolio Selection with Skewness 227
P. Boyle and B. Ding

12
Continuous Min-Max Approach for Single Period Portfolio Selection Problem 241
N. Gülpınar and B. Rustem

Contributing Authors

JEAN-PIERRE AUBIN
Université Paris-Dauphine, France
jean-pierre.aubin@viab.dauphine.fr

MOHAMED A. AYADI
Brock University, Canada
mayadi@brocku.ca

MARIE-CLAUDE BEAULIEU
Université Laval, Canada
marie-claude.beaulieu@fas.ulaval.ca

MONDHER BELLALAH
Université de Cergy et ESG Group, France
mondher.bellalah@eco.u-cergy.fr

PIERRE BERNHARD
Université de Nice – Sophia Antipolis, France
pierre.bernhard@unice.fr

TONY BERRADA
HEC Montréal, Canada
tony.berrada@hec.ca

PHELIM BOYLE
University of Waterloo, Canada
pboyle@uwaterloo.ca

EPHRAIM CLARK
Middlesex University, UK
e.clark@mdx.ac.uk

BRIAN DING
Toronto Dominion Bank, Canada
brian.ding@td.com

JEAN-MARIE DUFOUR
Université de Montréal, Canada
jean.marie.dufour@umontreal.ca

DANIEL DUFRESNE
University of Melbourne, Australia
dufresne@unimelb.edu.au

PASCAL FRANÇOIS
HEC Montréal, Canada
pascal.francois@hec.ca

JAVIER DE FRUTOS
University of Valladolid, Spain
frutos@mac.cie.uva.es

NALAN GÜLPINAR
Imperial College London, England
ng2@doc.ic.ac.uk

LYNDA KHALAF
Université Laval, Canada
lynda.khalaf@ecn.ulaval.ca

LAWRENCE KRYZANOWSKI
Concordia University, Canada
lkryzan@vax2.concordia.ca

DOMINIQUE PUJAL
Université Paris-Dauphine, France
dominique.pujal@dauphine.fr

BERÇ RUSTEM
Imperial College London, England
br@doc.ic.ac.uk

PATRICK SAINT-PIERRE
Université Paris-Dauphine, France
patrick.saint@dauphine.fr

Preface

This volume collects twelve chapters dealing with a wide range of topics in numerical finance. It is divided in three parts. The first part contains surveys and tutorial contributions, reviewing the current state of the art in diverse mathematical methods and models and their applications in finance. The second part examines asset pricing, proposing numerical methods and specific applications. Finally, the third part deals with asset portfolios, presenting methods for efficiency testing, performance evaluation and optimal selection, with empirical experiments.

Part I

In Chapter 1, P. François presents a survey of the major models of the structural approach for the valuation of corporate debt in a continuous-time arbitrage-free economy. Numerous models are presented, including endogenous capital structure, discrete coupon payments, flow-based state variables, interest rate risk, strategic debt service and advanced default rules. Finally, the author presents an assessment of the performance of these structural models in capturing the empirical patterns of the term structure of credit spread.

Chapter 2 prepared by D. Dufresne is a concise account of the connection between Bessel processes and the integral of geometric Brownian motion. The main motivation for the study of this integral is the pricing of Asian options. The author reviews the definition and properties of Bessel processes. The expressions for the density function of the integral and of the Laplace transform for Asian option prices are given. Some new derivations and alternative proofs for these results are also presented.

Chapter 3, by J.-P. Aubin, D. Pujal and P. Saint-Pierre, presents the main results of the viability/capturability approach for the valuation and hedging of contingent claims with transaction costs in the tychastic control framework (or dynamic game against nature). A viability/capturability algorithm is proposed, and it is shown that this provides both the value of the contingent claim and the hedging portfolio. An outline of the viability/capturability strategy establishing these results is subsequently provided.

In Chapter 4, P. Bernhard presents an overview of the robust control approach to option pricing and hedging, based on an interval model for security prices. This approach does not assume a probabilistic knowledge of market prices behaviour. The theory developed allows for continuous or discrete trading for hedging options, while taking transaction costs into account. A numerical algorithm implementing the theory and efficiently computing option prices is also provided.

Part II

Chapter 5, by J. de Frutos, presents a finite element method for pricing two-factor bonds with conversion, call and put embedded options. The method decouples the state and temporal discretizations, thus allowing the use of efficient numerical procedures for each one of the decoupled problems. Numerical experiments are presented, showing stability and accuracy.

In Chapter 6, M. Bellalah proposes a finite difference method for the valuation of index options, where the index price volatility has two components, one of which is specific and the other is related to the interest rate volatility. An extension of the Alternating Direction Implicit numerical scheme is proposed. Numerical illustrations are provided, showing the impact of interest rate volatility on early exercise of American options.

Chapter 7 by T. Berrada studies American options with uncertain maturities. The author shows how to use the exercise premium decomposition to value such options by a backward integral equation. Two application examples are presented: real options to invest in projects and employee stock options. Numerical illustrations in both cases show the effect of stochastic maturity on the optimal exercise boundary.

In Chapter 8, E. Clark uses an American option framework to study the expropriation decision by a host country, in order to estimate the expropriation risk in foreign direct investment projects. The model is used to illustrate the impact of incomplete information about the expropriation costs on the valuation of foreign direct investment projects.

Part III

Chapter 9, prepared by M.-C. Beaulieu, J.-M. Dufour and L. Khalaf, propose exact inference procedures for asset pricing models. The statistical approach presented allows for possibly asymmetric, heavy tailed distributions, based on Monte-Carlo test techniques. The methods proposed are applied to a mean-variance efficiency problem using portfolio returns of the NYSE and show significant goodness-of-fit improvement over standard distribution frameworks.

In Chapter 10, M. Ayadi and L. Kryzanowski use a general asset pricing framework to evaluate the performance of actively managed fixed-income mutual fund portfolios. Their approach is independent of asset-pricing models and distributional assumptions. Applying this to Canadian fixed-income mutual funds, they find that the measured unconditional performance of fund managers is negative.

In Chapter 11, P. Boyle and B. Ding propose a linear approximation for the third moment of a portfolio in a mean-absolute deviation-skewness approach for portfolio optimization. Their model can be used to obtain a high skewness and a relatively lower variance, while keeping the expected return fixed, with respect to a base portfolio. The model is then used to analyse the potential for put options to increase the skewness of portfolios. Numerical experiments use historical data from the Toronto Stock Exchange.

Chapter 12, by N. Gülpınar and B. Rustem, presents a continuous min-max approach for single-period portfolio selection in a mean-variance context. The optimization is performed assuming a range of expected returns and various covariance scenarios. The optimal investment strategy is robust in the sense that it has the best lower bound performance. Computational experiments using historical prices of FTSE stocks are provided, and illustrate the robustness of the min-max strategy.

Acknowledgements

The Editors would like to express their gratitude to the authors for their contributions and timely responses to their comments and suggestions. They also wish to thank Francine Benoît, André Montpetit and Nicole Paradis for their expert editing of the volume.

HATEM BEN-AMEUR
MICHÈLE BRETON

Chapter 1

CORPORATE DEBT VALUATION: THE STRUCTURAL APPROACH

Pascal François

Abstract This chapter surveys the contingent claims literature on the valuation of corporate debt. Model summaries are presented in a continuous-time arbitrage-free economy. After a review of the basic model, I extend the approach to models with an endogenous capital structure, discrete coupon payments, flow-based state variables, interest rate risk, strategic debt service, and more advanced default rules. Finally, I assess the empirical performance of structural models in light of the latest tests available.

1. Introduction

The purpose of this chapter is to review the structural models for valuing corporate straight debt. Beyond the scope of this survey are the reduced-form models of credit risk[1] as well as the structural models for vulnerable securities and for risky bonds with option-like provisions.[2] Earlier reviews of this literature may be found in Cooper and Martin (1996); Bielecki and Rutkowski (2002) and Lando (2004). This survey covers several topics that were previously hardly surveyed (in particular Sections 5, 7, 8, and 9). Model summaries are presented in a continuous-time arbitrage-free economy. Adaptations to the binomial setting may be found in Garbade (2001).

In Section 2, I present the basic model (valuation of finite-maturity corporate debt with a continuous coupon and an exogenous default

[1]See for instance Jarrow and Turnbull (1995); Jarrow et al. (1997); Duffie and Singleton (1999) or Madan and Unal (2000).

[2]See, e.g., Klein (1996); Rich (1996), and Cao and Wei (2001) for vulnerable options, Ho and Singer (1984) for bonds with a sinking-fund provision, Ingersoll (1977) and Brennan and Schwartz (1980) for convertibles, and Acharya and Carpenter (2002) for callables.

threshold). Then I extend the approach to models with an endogenous capital structure (Section 3), discrete coupon payments (Section 4), flow-based state variables (Section 5), interest rate risk (Section 6), strategic debt service (Section 7), and more advanced default rules (Section 8). In Section 9, I discuss the empirical efficacy of structural models measured by their ability to reproduce observed patterns of term structure of credit spreads. I conclude in Section 10.

2. The basic model

2.1 Contingent claims pricing assumptions

Throughout I consider a firm with equity and debt outstanding. This version of the basic model was initially derived by Merton (1974) in the set-up defined by Black and Scholes (1973). It relies on the following assumptions

1 The assets of the firm are continuously traded in an arbitrage-free and complete market. Uncertainty is represented by the filtered probability space $(\Omega, \mathcal{F}, \mathbb{P})$ where $\mathbb{P}$ stands for the historical probability measure. From Harrison and Pliska (1981) we have that there exists a unique probability measure $\mathbb{Q}$, equivalent to $\mathbb{P}$, under which asset prices discounted at the risk-free rate are martingales.

2 The term structure of interest rates is flat. The constant r denotes the instantaneous risk-free rate (this assumption is relaxed in Section 6).

3 Once debt is issued, the capital structure of the firm remains unchanged (this assumption is relaxed in Section 3.3).

4 The value of the firm assets $V(t)$ is independent of the firm capital structure and, under $\mathbb{Q}$, it is driven by the geometric Brownian motion

$$\frac{dV(t)}{V(t)} = (r - \delta)\, dt + \sigma\, dz_t$$

where δ and σ are two constants and $(z_t)_{t \geq 0}$ is a standard Brownian motion. This equation states that the instantaneous return on the firm assets is r and that a proportion δ of assets is continuously paid out to claimholders. Firm business risk is captured by $(z_t)_{t \geq 0}$, and the risk-neutral firm profitability is Gaussian with mean r and standard deviation σ. Other possible state variables are examined in Section 5. Other dynamics for $V(t)$ are possible,[3] but the pricing technique remains the same.

[3]Mason and Bhattacharya (1981) postulate a pure jump process for the value of assets. Zhou (2001a) investigates the jump-diffusion case.

Absent market frictions such as taxes, bankruptcy costs or informational asymmetry costs, assumption 4 is consistent with the Modigliani–Miller paradigm. In this framework, the value of the firm assets is identical to the total value of the firm and Merton (1977) shows that capital structure irrelevance still holds in the presence of costless default risk. This setup can however be extended to situations where optimal debt level matters. In that case, the total value of the firm is $V(t)$ net of the present value of market frictions.

The debt contract is a bond with nominal M and maturity T (possibly infinite) paying a continuous coupon c. Let $D(t, V)$ denote the value of the bond. According to the structural approach of credit risk, $D(t, V)$ is a claim contingent to the value of the firm assets. In the absence of arbitrage, it verifies

$$rD\,dt = c\,dt + E_{\mathbb{Q}}(dD)$$

where $E_{\mathbb{Q}}(\cdot)$ denotes the expectation operator under $\mathbb{Q}$. Using Itô's lemma, we obtain the following PDE for D

$$rD = c + (r - \delta)VD_V + \tfrac{1}{2}\sigma^2V^2D_{VV} + D_t \tag{1.1}$$

where D_x stands for the partial derivative of D with respect to x.

To account for the presence of default risk in corporate debt contracts, two types of boundary conditions are typically attached to the former PDE. The first condition ensures that in case of no default, the debtholder receives the contractual payments. Let T_d denote the random default date. The no-default condition associated to the debt contract defined above may be written as

$$D(T, V) = M \cdot 1_{T_d > T},$$

where 1_ω stands for the indicator function of the event ω.

The second condition characterizes default. This event is fully described by its timing and its magnitude. In the structural approach, the timing of default is modeled as the *first hitting time* of the state variable to a given level. Let $V_d(t)$ denote the default threshold. The default date T_d may be written as

$$T_d = \inf\{t \geq 0 : V(t) = V_d(t)\}.$$

The magnitude of default represents the loss in debt value following the default event. Formally, we have that

$$D(T_d, V_d) = \Psi(V_d)$$

where $\Psi(\cdot)$ is the function relating the remaining debt value to the firm asset value at the time of default.

2.2 Default magnitude

The function $\Psi(\cdot)$ depends on three key factors:

1. The nature of the claim held by debtholders after default. If default leads to immediate liquidation, the remaining assets of the firm are sold and debtholders share the proceeds. In that case debt value may be considered as a fraction of $V_d(t)$, where the proportional loss reflects the discount caused by fire asset sales and/or by the inefficient piecewise reallocation of assets.[4] If default leads to the firm reorganization, the debtholders obtain a new claim whose value may be defined as a fraction of the initially promised nominal M (aka the recovery rate) or as a fraction of the equivalent risk-free bond with same nominal and maturity. Altman and Kishore (1996) provide extensive evidence on recovery rates.
2. The total costs associated to the event of default. One can distinguish direct costs (induced by the procedure resolving financial distress) from indirect costs (induced by foregone investment opportunities). Again, if default is assumed to lead to immediate liquidation, it is convenient to express these costs as a fraction of the remaining assets.[5]
3. In case default is resolved through the legal bankruptcy procedure, the *absolute priority rule* (APR) states that debtholders have highest priority to recover their claims. In practice however, equityholders may bypass debtholders and perceive some of the proceeds of the firm liquidation. Franks and Torous (1989) and Eberhart et al. (1990) provide evidence of very frequent (but relatively small) deviations from the APR in the US bankruptcy procedure.

To account for all these factors, we denote by α the total proportional costs of default and by γ the proportional deviation from the APR (calculated from the value of remaining assets *net of default costs*).

---

[4] Liquidation costs may be calculated as the firm's going concern value minus its liquidation value, divided by its going concern value. Using this definition, Alderson and Betker (1995) and Gilson (1997) report liquidation costs equal to 36.5% and 45.5% for the median firm in their samples.

[5] Empirical studies by Warner (1977); Weiss (1990), and Betker (1997) report costs of financial distress between 3% and 7.5% of firm value one year before default. Bris et al. (2004) find that bankruptcy costs are very heterogeneous and sensitive to measurement method.

2.3 Exogenous default threshold

Firm asset value follows a geometric Brownian motion and can therefore be written as

$$V(t) = V \exp\left[\left(r - \delta - \frac{\sigma^2}{2}\right)t + \sigma z_t\right].$$

The default threshold under consideration is exogenous with exponential shape $V_d(t) = V_d \exp(\lambda t)$ and terminal point $V_d(T) = M$. Default occurs the first time before T we have

$$z_t = \frac{1}{\sigma}\ln\frac{V_d}{V} - \left(\frac{r - \delta - \lambda}{\sigma} - \frac{\sigma}{2}\right)t,$$

or otherwise if

$$z_T = \frac{1}{\sigma}\ln\frac{M}{V} - \left(\frac{r - \delta}{\sigma} - \frac{\sigma}{2}\right)T.$$

Knowing the distribution of $(z_t)_{t\geq 0}$, one obtains the following result.

PROPOSITION 1.1 *Consider a corporate bond with maturity T, nominal M and continuous coupon c. The issuer is a firm whose asset value follow a geometric Brownian motion with volatility σ. The default threshold starts at V_d, grows exponentially at rate λ and jumps at level M upon maturity. In case of default, a fraction α of remaining assets is lost as third party costs and an additional fraction γ accrues to equityholders. Initial bond value is given by*

$$\begin{aligned}
D = {} & Me^{-rT}\left[\Phi(d_1) - \left(\frac{V_d}{V}\right)^{2R/\sigma^2-1}\Phi(d_2)\right] + \chi V e^{-\delta T}\left(\Phi(d_3) - \Phi(d_4)\right) \\
& + \chi V e^{-\delta T}\left(\frac{V_d}{V}\right)^{2R/\sigma^2+1}\left(\Phi(d_5) - \Phi(d_6)\right) \\
& + \chi V\left[\left(\frac{V_d}{V}\right)^{(R+\sigma^2/2+\rho)/\sigma^2}\Phi(d_7) + \left(\frac{V_d}{V}\right)^{(R+\sigma^2/2-\rho)/\sigma^2}\Phi(d_8)\right] \\
& + \frac{c}{r}\left[1 - \left(\frac{V_d}{V}\right)^{(R-\sigma^2/2+\rho)/\sigma^2}\Phi(d_7) - \left(\frac{V_d}{V}\right)^{(R-\sigma^2/2-\rho)/\sigma^2}\Phi(d_8)\right] \\
& - \frac{c}{r}e^{-rT}\left[\Phi(d_9) - \left(\frac{V_d}{V}\right)^{2R/\sigma^2-1}\Phi(d_{10})\right],
\end{aligned}$$

where δ is the firm payout rate, r is the constant risk-free rate and

$$R = r - \delta - \lambda$$

$$\rho = \sqrt{\left(r - \delta - \lambda - \frac{\sigma^2}{2}\right)^2 + 2\sigma^2 r}$$

$$\chi = (1-\gamma)(1-\alpha)$$

$$d_1 = \frac{1}{\sigma\sqrt{T}}\left(\ln\frac{V}{M}+\left(r-\delta-\frac{\sigma^2}{2}\right)T\right) \qquad d_6 = \frac{1}{\sigma\sqrt{T}}\left(\ln\frac{V_d}{V}+\left(R+\frac{\sigma^2}{2}\right)T\right)$$

$$d_2 = \frac{1}{\sigma\sqrt{T}}\left(\ln\frac{V_d^2}{MV}+\left(R-\frac{\sigma^2}{2}\right)T\right) \qquad d_7 = \frac{1}{\sigma\sqrt{T}}\left(\ln\frac{V_d}{V}+\rho T\right)$$

$$d_3 = \frac{1}{\sigma\sqrt{T}}\left(\ln\frac{V}{V_d}+\left(R+\frac{\sigma^2}{2}\right)T\right) \qquad d_8 = \frac{1}{\sigma\sqrt{T}}\left(\ln\frac{V_d}{V}-\rho T\right)$$

$$d_4 = d_1+\sigma\sqrt{T} \qquad d_9 = d_3-\sigma\sqrt{T}$$

$$d_5 = d_2+\sigma\sqrt{T} \qquad d_{10} = d_6-\sigma\sqrt{T}$$

and $\Phi(\cdot)$ is the cumulative normal distribution function.

Proposition 1.1 embeds as special cases the pricing formulae by Black and Cox (1976) (when $c = 0$ and $\chi = 1$, that is a discount bond with no costs of financial distress nor deviations from the APR), by Leland and Toft (1996) (when the exogenous default threshold is a constant ($\lambda = 0$)), and by Merton (1974) (the exogenous default threshold is zero).

From the Feynman–Kac representation theorem, Proposition 1.1 (and subsequent results) may either be obtained by solving PDE (1.1) with appropriate boundary conditions, or by applying the martingale property of discounted prices under the risk-neutral probability measure. Ericsson and Reneby (1998) emphasize the modularity of the latter methodology. The time-t value $x(t)$ of any claim on V promising a single payoff at date T can be written as

$$x(t) = E_{\mathbb{Q}}\left(x(T)\exp\left(-\int_t^T r(u)\,du\right)\right).$$

Corporate debt can then be decomposed into such claims that are valued as building blocks of the whole contract.

3. Debt pricing and capital structure

Since the structural approach links the value of corporate securities to an economic fundamental related to firm value, it has by construction a balance-sheet view of the firm and is therefore well suited to connect the issue of pricing risky debt to the capital structure decision. This connection provides a natural way to endogenize the decision to default: The optimal amount of debt is chosen in order to maximize the value of the firm, and, based on this amount, shareholders select the default threshold that maximizes equity value.

3.1 Infinite maturity debt

The default threshold V_d can be endogenized as shareholders' choice to maximize equity value. If debt is a perpetuity, the PDE for D can be written as

$$rD = c + (r - \delta)VD_V + \tfrac{1}{2}\sigma^2 V^2 D_{VV} \tag{1.2}$$

with boundary conditions:

1 When $V = V_d$, the firm is immediately liquidated[6] and creditors take possession of the residual assets net of costs of default and deviations from the APR

$$D(V_d) = (1 - \gamma)(1 - \alpha)V_d,$$

2 As $V \to \infty$, debt value converges to that of the risk-free perpetuity

$$\lim_{V \to +\infty} D(V) = \frac{c}{r}.$$

The PDE (1.2) with the above conditions admits the following closed-form solution

$$D(V) = \frac{c}{r} + \left[(1 - \gamma)(1 - \alpha)V_d - \frac{c}{r}\right]\left(\frac{V_d}{V}\right)^{\xi}$$

with

$$\xi = \frac{r - \delta - \sigma^2/2}{\sigma^2} + \sqrt{\left(\frac{r - \delta - \sigma^2/2}{\sigma^2}\right)^2 + \frac{2r}{\sigma^2}}.$$

Equity value, denoted by $S(V)$, is now determined as the residual claim value on the firm, i.e.,

$$S(V) = v(V) - D(V)$$

where $v(V)$ denotes the firm value.

Leland (1994) proposes to rely on the static trade-off capital structure theory to determine firm value. In this framework, v equals the value of

[6] In practice, resolution of financial distress may take on several forms other than liquidation. In Section 8, we study other types of default rules.

the firm's assets (V) plus the tax advantage of debt (TB(V)) minus the present value of bankruptcy costs (BC(V)). Both TB(V) and BC(V) obey the same PDE (1.2) and their corresponding boundary conditions are respectively:

$$\mathrm{TB}(V_d) = 0 \qquad \lim_{V\to\infty} \mathrm{TB}(V) = \tau\frac{c}{r},$$
$$\mathrm{BC}(V_d) = \alpha V_d \qquad \lim_{V\to\infty} \mathrm{BC}(V) = 0,$$

where τ stands for the corporate tax rate.

Solving for TB(V) and BC(V) yields firm value and equity value is given by

$$S(V) = V - (1-\tau)\frac{c}{r} + \left[(1-\tau)\frac{c}{r} - (1-\gamma(1-\alpha))V_d\right]\left(\frac{V_d}{V}\right)^{\xi}.$$

Shareholders' optimal default rule is then obtained using the following smooth pasting condition:

$$\left.\frac{\partial S}{\partial V}\right|_{V=V_d} = \gamma(1-\alpha),$$

which yields

$$V_d = \frac{\xi}{(\xi+1)}\frac{(1-\tau)c}{[1-\gamma(1-\alpha)]r}.$$

The endogenous default threshold is interpreted as the value of the option to wait for defaulting $\left(\xi/(\xi+1)\right)$ times the opportunity cost of servicing the debt.

3.2 Finite maturity debt with stationary capital structure

Leland and Toft (1996) examine a firm with a debt service that is invariant through time, which allows for a constant default threshold. The firm constant debt level is M. For each period, M/T units of bonds are issued with maturity T while a fraction M/T of former bonds is reimbursed. This roll over strategy maintains the debt service at a constant level $C + M/T$ where C denotes the sum of all coupons.

The value of a *single* bond issue with nominal m and continuous coupon c is given by (for clarity of exposition, we set $\gamma = 0$):

$$d(V, V_d, T) = \int_0^T e^{-rs}c(1-F(s))\,ds + e^{-rT}m(1-F(T))$$
$$+ \int_0^T e^{-rs}(1-\alpha)V_d f(s)\,ds,$$

where $f(t)$ and $F(t)$ stand for the density and the cumulative distribution function of the default date T_d respectively.

From Proposition 1.1, we get

$$\begin{aligned} d(V, V_d, T) = \frac{c}{r} &+ \left((1-\alpha)V_d - \frac{c}{r}\right)\left(\frac{V_d}{V}\right)^{(r-\delta-\sigma^2/2+\rho)/\sigma^2} \Phi(d_7) \\ &+ \left((1-\alpha)V_d - \frac{c}{r}\right)\left(\frac{V_d}{V}\right)^{(r-\delta-\sigma^2/2-\rho)/\sigma^2} \Phi(d_8) \\ &+ \left(m - \frac{c}{r}\right)e^{-rT}\left[\Phi(d_9) - \left(\frac{V_d}{V}\right)^{2(r-\delta)/\sigma^2-1} \Phi(d_{10})\right]. \end{aligned}$$

Total debt is the sum of all bond issues with nominal $M = mT$ and coupon $C = cT$. Its value $D(V, V_d, T)$ is given by

$$D(V, V_d, T) = \int_0^T d(V, V_d, t)\, dt,$$

and Leland and Toft (1996) obtain

$$\begin{aligned} D(V, V_d, T) = \frac{C}{r} + \left(M - \frac{C}{r}\right)\left(\frac{1-e^{-rT}}{rT} - I(T)\right) \\ + \left((1-\alpha)V_d - \frac{C}{r}\right)J(T) \end{aligned}$$

with

$$\begin{aligned} I(T) = \frac{1}{rT}\left[\left(\frac{V_d}{V}\right)^{(r-\delta-\sigma^2/2+\rho)/\sigma^2} \Phi(d_7) + \left(\frac{V_d}{V}\right)^{(r-\delta-\sigma^2/2-\rho)/\sigma^2} \Phi(d_8)\right] \\ - \frac{e^{-rT}}{rT}\left[\Phi(-d_9) + \left(\frac{V_d}{V}\right)^{2(r-\delta)/\sigma^2-1} \Phi(d_{10})\right], \end{aligned}$$

and

$$\begin{aligned} J(T) = \frac{\sigma}{\rho\sqrt{T}}\left(\frac{V_d}{V}\right)^{(r-\delta-\sigma^2/2+\rho)/\sigma^2} \Phi(d_7)d_7 \\ - \frac{\sigma}{\rho\sqrt{T}}\left(\frac{V_d}{V}\right)^{(r-\delta-\sigma^2/2-\rho)/\sigma^2} \Phi(d_8)d_8. \end{aligned}$$

Equity value, $S(V, V_d, T)$, is again obtained as the difference between firm value and total debt value. Since capital structure is stationary, the tax advantage of debt as well as the present value of bankruptcy costs are computed over an infinite horizon, that is they both obey PDE (1.2). Which yields

$$S(V, V_d, T) = V + \tau\frac{C}{r}\left[1 - \left(\frac{V_d}{V}\right)^{\xi}\right] - \alpha V_d\left(\frac{V_d}{V}\right)^{\xi} - D(V, V_d, T).$$

The smooth pasting condition on $S(V, V_d, T)$ yields the endogenous default threshold

$$V_d = \frac{C(A/rT - B)/r - AM/rT - \tau C\xi/r}{1 + \alpha\xi - (1-\alpha)B}$$

with

$$\begin{aligned}
A = & \left[\frac{2(r-\delta)}{\sigma^2} - 1\right]e^{-rT}\Phi\left(\frac{(r-\delta)}{\sigma}\sqrt{T} - \frac{\sigma}{2}\sqrt{T}\right) - 2\frac{\rho}{\sigma^2}\Phi\left(\frac{\rho}{\sigma}\sqrt{T}\right)\\
& - \frac{2}{\sigma\sqrt{T}}\phi\left(\frac{\rho}{\sigma}\sqrt{T}\right) + \frac{2e^{-rT}}{\sigma\sqrt{T}}\phi\left(\frac{(r-\delta)}{\sigma}\sqrt{T} - \frac{\sigma}{2}\sqrt{T}\right)\\
& + \frac{\rho}{\sigma^2} - \frac{2(r-\delta)}{\sigma^2} + 1,\\
B = & -\left(\frac{2\rho}{\sigma^2} + \frac{2}{\rho T}\right)\Phi\left(\frac{\rho}{\sigma}\sqrt{T}\right) - \frac{2}{\sigma\sqrt{T}}\phi\left(\frac{\rho}{\sigma}\sqrt{T}\right) + \frac{\rho}{\sigma^2}\\
& - \frac{2(r-\delta)}{\sigma^2} + 1 + \frac{1}{\rho T},
\end{aligned}$$

where $\phi(\cdot)$ denotes the normal density function.

3.3 Dynamic capital structure

In models presented in Sections 3.1 and 3.2, the optimal capital structure is determined at initial date and the level of debt is not changed subsequently. In practice, firms have the flexibility to adjust their level of debt to current economic conditions. In the Fischer et al. (1989) model, the value of firm assets V is assumed to follow a geometric Brownian motion and, for a fixed face value of debt M, so does the value-to-debt ratio $y = V/M$. Debt value D and equity value S obey a PDE similar to (1.2) adjusted for a simple tax regime where τ_c is the corporate tax rate and τ_p is the tax rate on income revenues, that is

$$\begin{aligned}
r(1-\tau_p)D &= \widehat{\mu}yD_y + \tfrac{1}{2}\sigma^2y^2D_{yy} + (1-\tau_p)iM\\
r(1-\tau_p)S &= \widehat{\mu}yS_y + \tfrac{1}{2}\sigma^2y^2S_{yy} - (1-\tau_c)iM,
\end{aligned}$$

where $\widehat{\mu}$ stands for the risk-adjusted expected return on the firm's assets (yet to be characterized).

The firm may recapitalize and issue additional debt when its value-to-debt ratio reaches an upper bound $\overline{y}$. Recapitalization induces a proportional cost k, hence firm value must verify

$$v(\overline{y}, M) = v\left(y_0, \frac{\overline{y}}{y_0}M\right) - k\frac{\overline{y}}{y_0}M,$$

where y_0 stands for the initial value-to-debt ratio. Similarly, the firm may reduce its level of debt when its value-to-debt ratio reaches an lower bound $\underline{y}$. However, this debt reduction is possible provided the firm is not already in bankruptcy. Denoting by α the proportional bankruptcy costs, the value of the firm at the lower recapitalization level $v\left(\underline{y}, M\right)$ is given by

$$\begin{cases} \max\left[v\left(y_0, \frac{\underline{y}}{y_0}M\right) - k\frac{\underline{y}}{y_0}M - \alpha M, 0\right], \\ \qquad\qquad\qquad\qquad \text{if } v\left(y_0, \frac{\underline{y}}{y_0}M\right) - k\frac{\underline{y}}{y_0}M < M, \\ v\left(y_0, \frac{\underline{y}}{y_0}M\right) - k\frac{\underline{y}}{y_0}M, \quad \text{otherwise.} \end{cases}$$

In the absence of arbitrage, firm value just after recapitalization equals the value of assets plus recapitalization costs, hence

$$v(y, M) = yM + kM.$$

In particular, at the recapitalization bounds, this yields

$$\begin{aligned} v\left(y_0, \frac{\overline{y}}{y_0}M\right) &= \overline{y}M + k\frac{\overline{y}}{y_0}M \\ v\left(y_0, \frac{\underline{y}}{y_0}M\right) &= \underline{y}M + k\frac{\underline{y}}{y_0}M. \end{aligned}$$

Combining with the expressions for $v(\overline{y}, M)$ and $v(\underline{y}, M)$, we get

$$\begin{aligned} v(\overline{y}, M) &= \overline{y}M \\ v(\underline{y}, M) &= \begin{cases} \max[(\underline{y} - \alpha)M, 0], & \text{if } \underline{y} < 1 \\ \underline{y}M, & \text{otherwise.} \end{cases} \end{aligned}$$

Debt value is retrieved as the difference between firm value and equity value. Assuming debt is issued and callable at par, this yields

$$\begin{aligned} D(\overline{y}, M) &= M \\ D(\underline{y}, M) &= \begin{cases} \max[(\underline{y} - \alpha)M, 0], & \text{if } \underline{y} < 1, \\ M, & \text{otherwise,} \end{cases} \end{aligned}$$

and these expressions are used as boundary conditions to solve the PDE for debt value. Fischer et al. (1989) obtain

$$D(y, M) = D_1 y^{m_1} + D_2 y^{m_2} + \frac{iM}{r},$$

where

$$\begin{aligned}
D_1 &= \frac{M}{\Delta}\left\{\left(1-\frac{i}{r}\right)\underline{y}^{m_2} - \left[(\underline{y}-\alpha)^+ - \frac{i}{r}\right]\overline{y}^{m_2}\right\}\\
D_2 &= \frac{M}{\Delta}\left\{\left[(\underline{y}-\alpha)^+ - \frac{i}{r}\right]\overline{y}^{m_1} - \left(1-\frac{i}{r}\right)\underline{y}^{m_1}\right\}\\
\Delta &= \overline{y}^{m_1}\underline{y}^{m_2} - \overline{y}^{m_2}\underline{y}^{m_1}\\
m_1 &= \frac{1}{2} - \frac{\widehat{\mu}}{\sigma^2} + \sqrt{\left(\frac{1}{2} - \frac{\widehat{\mu}}{\sigma^2}\right)^2 + \frac{2r(1-\tau_p)}{\sigma^2}}\\
m_2 &= \frac{1}{2} - \frac{\widehat{\mu}}{\sigma^2} - \sqrt{\left(\frac{1}{2} - \frac{\widehat{\mu}}{\sigma^2}\right)^2 + \frac{2r(1-\tau_p)}{\sigma^2}}.
\end{aligned}$$

To characterize the optimal recapitalization policy, Fischer et al. (1989) define the advantage of leverage as

$$\delta = r(1-\tau_p) - \widehat{\mu}.$$

The equilibrium is found by maximizing firm value net of recapitalization costs, that is

$$\max_{\overline{y},\underline{y},M,i} v(y_0, M, \overline{y}, \underline{y}) - kM$$

subject to

$$\begin{aligned}
v(y_0, M, \overline{y}, \underline{y}) &= y_0 M + kM\\
\left.\frac{\partial S(y, M, \overline{y}, \underline{y})}{\partial y}\right|_{y=\underline{y}} &\geq 0\\
S(y_0, M, \overline{y}, \underline{y}) &= M
\end{aligned}$$

The first condition is a no-arbitrage condition, the second one is the smooth-pasting condition preserving the limited liability property of equity, and the third one states that debt is initially issued at par. Solving this program yields the initial optimal leverage (M), the optimal recapitalization policy ($\overline{y}$ and $\underline{y}$) as well as the risk-adjusted expected return on the firm's assets $\widehat{\mu}$ and the coupon rate i.

The basic model is extended in several directions. Leland (1998) examines the case of finite-maturity debt in a framework similar to that of

Leland and Toft (1996) with a possibility to call the debt at some upper boundary for asset value (downside restructuring is not addressed). Goldstein et al. (2001) and Dangl and Zechner (2004) also value corporate debt within a dynamic capital structure model. Because they use a different underlying state variable, we shall review their approach in Section 5. Ju et al. (2003) build a model of dynamic recapitalization within the static trade-off capital structure framework (i.e., the optimal amount of debt results from trading off the tax advantage with expected bankruptcy costs) at the cost of assuming an exogenous exponential default boundary.

4. Discrete coupon payments

In practice, coupons are paid annually or semi-annually and the continuous coupon assumption may not be appropriate. Geske (1977) extends the basic model to the case of a discrete coupon-bearing debt. Debt service is a sequence of coupon payments $\{C_{t_i}, i = 1, \ldots, n\}$ to be paid at date t_i (with $t_n = T$). At date t_{n-1}, debt is zero-coupon and may be priced with Merton's (1974) formula:

$$D(t_{n-1}) = C_{t_n} e^{-r(t_n - t_{n-1})} \Phi(d_1) + V(t_{n-1}) e^{-\delta(t_n - t_{n-1})} [1 - \Phi(d_4)].$$

At date t_{n-2}, there are two debt payments remaining. If $V(t_{n-1}) > V_d(t_{n-1})$, debtholders receive $C_{t_{n-1}} + D(t_{n-1})$. Otherwise, they get the residual value of assets $V_b(t_{n-1})$ (for simplicity, we set $\alpha = 0$). Which yields

$$\begin{aligned} D(t_{n-2}) = {} & C_{t_n} e^{-r(t_n - t_{n-2})} \Phi_2(h_{n-1}, h_n, \theta) + C_{t_{n-1}} e^{-r(t_{n-1} - t_{n-2})} \Phi(h_{n-1}) \\ & + [1 - \Phi_2(h_{n-1} + \sigma\sqrt{t_n - t_{n-1}}, h_n + \sigma\sqrt{t_n - t_{n-2}}, \theta)] \\ & \times V(t_{n-2}) e^{-\delta(t_n - t_{n-2})} \end{aligned}$$

with

$$\begin{aligned} h_n &= \frac{1}{\sigma\sqrt{T - t_{n-2}}} \left[\ln \frac{V(t_{n-2})}{C_{t_n}} + \left(r - \delta - \frac{\sigma^2}{2} \right) (T - t_{n-2}) \right] \\ h_{n-1} &= \frac{1}{\sigma\sqrt{T - t_{n-1}}} \left[\ln \frac{V(t_{n-2})}{V_d(t_{n-1})} + \left(r - \delta - \frac{\sigma^2}{2} \right) (T - t_{n-1}) \right] \\ \theta &= \sqrt{\frac{t_{n-1} - t_{n-2}}{T - t_{n-2}}} \end{aligned}$$

and $\Phi_2(\cdot)$ stands for the bivariate cumulative normal distribution function.

Pursuing the same analysis recursively, Geske (1977) obtains the following result.

PROPOSITION 1.2 *Consider a corporate bond with maturity T, and n coupons $\{C_{t_i}\}$ to be paid at dates $\{t_i\}$ $(i = 1, \ldots, n)$. The issuer is a firm whose asset value follow a geometric Brownian motion with volatility σ. The default threshold is a collection of default points $V_b(t_i)$ at each date t_i. Initial bond value is given by*

$$D = Ve^{-\delta T}[1 - \Phi_n(h_i + \sigma\sqrt{t_i}, \{\theta_{ij}\})] + \sum_{i=1}^{n} C_{t_i} e^{-rt_i} \Phi_i(h_i, \{\theta_{ij}\})$$

with, for all $i = 1, \ldots, n$ and $j = 1, \ldots, n$

$$h_i = \frac{1}{\sigma\sqrt{t_i}}\left[\ln\frac{V}{V_d(t_i)} + \left(r - \delta - \frac{\sigma^2}{2}\right)t_i\right], \quad \theta_{ij} = \sqrt{\frac{t_i}{t_j}} \quad \forall (i,j)\ i < j$$

and $\Phi_i(\cdot)$ is the multivariate cumulative normal distribution function of dimension i.

Geske (1977) proposes the following rule for endogenizing the default points $V_b(t_i)$. Shareholders are not allowed to liquidate more than a fraction δ of the assets to finance the coupon payments. Beyond this level, they have to issue equity. Hence, the default point is the level of asset value at which equity value net of asset sales is sufficient to pay the coupon, that is $V_b(t_i)$ is the value of $V(t_i)$ inferred from

$$S(t_i) = C_{t_i} - \delta V(t_i).$$

At this level, equity value is nil once debt service is paid. The following recursive procedure can therefore be implemented:

- At date T, the default point is M. One computes $D(t_{n-1})$ and $S(t_{n-1}) = V(t_{n-1}) - D(t_{n-1})$,
- One infers $V_b(t_{n-1})$ from equation $S(t_{n-1}) = C_{t_{n-1}} - \delta V(t_{n-1})$,
- One computes $D(t_{n-2})$ and $S(t_{n-2}) = V(t_{n-2}) - D(t_{n-2})$,

... and further on until date 0.

5. Flow-based models

Although most structural models of corporate debt rely on the value of the firm's assets, contingent claims pricing does not require any formal identification of the state variable. According to Long (1974), contingent claims models could therefore relate the price of debt to *any* variable, in the absence of any economic justification. In response to this criticism,

Merton (1977) argues that contingent claims analysis only allows for valuing underlying corporate securities for a given state variable. However, the specification of the state variable is a modelling choice, and does not invalidate the methodology.

Because the value of the firm's assets may be difficult to observe, some structural models such as Mello and Parsons (1992); Fries et al. (1997) or Mella-Barral and Tychon (1999) propose alternative specifications for the state variable. Possible candidates are the firm's operating cash flow (directly inferred from income statement data) or the market price of the firm's output (e.g., the oil industry). Goldstein et al. (2001) propose a contingent claims model of the levered firm using EBIT as the state variable. This choice allows them to treat all contingent claimants (shareholders, creditors, and the government) in a consistent manner. In particular, the debt tax shield is analyzed as a reduction of outflow of funds (and not an inflow of funds in traditional models). An implication is that equity value is predicted to be decreasing with the tax rate.

Suppose EBIT, denoted by $(x_t)_{t\geq 0}$, follows a geometric Brownian motion with drift μ and volatility σ. Using the standard arbitrage argument, debt value is still given by

$$D(x, x_d, c) = \frac{c}{r} + \left(L - \frac{c}{r}\right)\left(\frac{x}{x_d}\right)^{-\lambda},$$

where x_d denotes the default threshold, L is the exogenous liquidation value, and

$$\lambda = \frac{\mu - \sigma^2/2}{\sigma^2} + \sqrt{\left(\frac{\mu - \sigma^2/2}{\sigma^2}\right)^2 + \frac{2r}{\sigma^2}}.$$

In the EBIT-based model, equity value is the after-tax sum of all future discounted cash flows and is given by

$$\begin{aligned} S(x, x_d, c) &= (1-\tau)E_{\mathbb{Q}}\left[\int_0^{T_d} (x_s - c)e^{-rs}\, ds\right] \\ &= (1-\tau)\left(\frac{x}{r-\mu} - \frac{c}{r}\right) - (1-\tau)\left(\frac{x_d}{r-\mu} - \frac{c}{r}\right)\left(\frac{x}{x_d}\right)^{-\lambda}. \end{aligned}$$

The smooth pasting condition on equity value yields the optimal default threshold

$$x_d = \frac{\lambda}{\lambda+1}\frac{c(r-\mu)}{r}.$$

The optimal coupon is obtained so as to maximize equity value plus debt value, that is

$$c^* = \arg\max_c [D(x, x_d, c) + S(x, x_d, c)],$$

which yields

$$c^* = \left(\frac{\tau}{\tau + \alpha\lambda}\right)^{-\lambda} \frac{rx}{r-\mu}\frac{\lambda+1}{\lambda}.$$

Goldstein et al. (2001) extend this model to the cases in which (i) the tax structure is more sophisticated, and (ii) the firm may dynamically adjust its capital structure.

6. Interest rate risk

6.1 The Gaussian framework

Let $(r_t)_{t\geq 0}$ denote the stochastic process for the instantaneous risk-free rate. In this subsection, we assume $(r_t)_{t\geq 0}$ is a Gaussian mean-reverting process and we analyze corporate debt in the Vasicek (1977) term structure model. Specifically, we have under $\mathbb{Q}$

$$dr = \kappa(\zeta - r)\,dt + \sigma_r\,dW_t,$$

where κ, ζ and σ_r are three constants, and $(W_t)_{t\geq 0}$ is a standard Brownian motion with ρ its correlation coefficient with $(z_t)_{t\geq 0}$.

In this setup, time-t prices of discount bonds with nominal 1 and maturity T, denoted by $P(t,T)$, are available in closed-form (see Vasicek, 1977). Also, discount bond price volatility is given by

$$\sigma_p(t,T) = \frac{\sigma_r}{\kappa}(1 - e^{-\kappa(T-t)}).$$

Consider a firm financed with equity and a zero-coupon bond with face value M and maturity T. As a direct extension of the exponential default barrier proposed by Black and Cox (1976), we assume shareholders adopt the following default rule:

$$V_d(t) = \lambda M P(t,T),$$

where λ is the constant reflecting the fraction of discounted debt nominal covered by assets upon default. When $V = V_d$, debtholders get

$$D(V_d, t) = \beta M P(t,T),$$

that is, they lose a fraction $\beta/\lambda < 1$ of the value of residual assets.

This framework is first introduced by Briys and de Varenne (1997) for pricing corporate discount bonds. François and Hübner (2004) extend their analysis to multiple coupon-bearing debt issues (with different maturities and priorities) and to credit derivatives.

PROPOSITION 1.3 *Consider a firm defaulting as soon as the value of its assets (driven by a geometric Brownian motion) is only worth a fraction λ of the discounted value of debt principal. In a stochastic interest rate environment where the instantaneous spot rate follows an Ornstein-Uhlenbeck process, the value of the coupon-bearing bond with nominal M and maturity T is given by*

$$\begin{aligned} D(V,c) &= MP(0,T)\mathcal{N}(u_2) + V\mathcal{N}(-u_1) + \lambda MP(0,T)\mathcal{N}(-u_6) \\ &\quad - \frac{V}{\lambda}\mathcal{N}(-u_5) - \left(1 - \frac{\beta}{\lambda}\right)[\lambda MP(0,T)\mathcal{N}(u_3) + V\mathcal{N}(u_4)] \\ &\quad + \sum_{i=1}^{n} cP(0,t_i)\left(\mathcal{N}(-d_1^i) - \frac{V}{\lambda\Phi}\mathcal{N}(d_2^i)\right) \end{aligned}$$

with

$$u_1 = \frac{1}{s(0,T)}\left[\ln\frac{V}{MP(0,T)} + \frac{s^2(0,T)}{2}\right] \qquad u_2 = u_1 - s(0,T)$$

$$u_3 = \frac{1}{s(0,T)}\left[\ln\frac{\lambda MP(0,T)}{V} + \frac{s^2(0,T)}{2}\right] \qquad u_4 = u_3 - s(0,T)$$

$$u_5 = \frac{1}{s(0,T)}\left[\ln\frac{V}{\lambda^2 MP(0,T)} + \frac{s^2(0,T)}{2}\right] \qquad u_6 = u_5 - s(0,T)$$

and

$$s^2(t,T) = \int_t^T \left[(\rho\sigma + \sigma_p(v,T))^2 + (1-\rho^2)\sigma^2\right] dv.$$

If default can only occur at maturity, Proposition 1.3 collapses to

$$D(V) = MP(0,T)\mathcal{N}(u_2) + V\mathcal{N}(-u_1),$$

which is the extension of Merton's (1974) result, provided by Shimko et al. (1993).

In the same context, Longstaff and Schwartz (1995) propose to evaluate the corporate discount bond with a constant (exogenous) default threshold. In such a modelling however, the state variable growing at the risk-neutral drift moves away from the default state, thereby inducing a decreasing trend for the firm's leverage. To account for a stationary leverage ratio, Collin-Dufresne and Goldstein (2001) assume the risk-neutral dynamics of the log-default boundary $(k_t)_{t\geq 0}$ is given by

$$dk_t = \lambda(y_t - v - \phi(r_t - \zeta) - k_t)\,dt$$

where $y_t = \ln V_t$ and λ, v, and ϕ are three positive constants. These dynamics capture the mean-reverting behavior of the default threshold, indicating that the firm aims at maintaining its leverage ratio at a target level. It also accounts for a negative correlation between debt issuance and the level of interest rates.

Upon default (whether before or at maturity), the corporate discount bond is assumed to pay a fraction $(1-\alpha)$ of its nominal M *at maturity.* Hence

$$\begin{aligned} D(V, r_0) &= M \cdot E_{\mathbb{Q}}\left[\left(\exp - \int_0^T r_u \, du\right)(1 - \alpha \cdot 1_{T_d<T})\right] \\ &= M \cdot P(0,T)\left(1 - \alpha \mathbb{Q}^T(T_d < T)\right), \end{aligned}$$

where $\mathbb{Q}^T(T_d < T)$ denotes the probability of default before T under the T-forward neutral measure. There is no closed-form expression for this probability but Collin-Dufresne and Goldstein (2001) propose the following discretization algorithm

$$\mathbb{Q}^T(T_d < T) = \sum_{j=1}^{n_T} \sum_{i=1}^{n_r} q\,(r_i, t_j)$$

where time and $r-$space are discretized into n_T and n_r equal intervals respectively. For the sake of brevity, the complex expression for $q(r_i, t_j)$ is not reported but it is available in Collin-Dufresne and Goldstein (2001).

6.2 The Cox – Ingersoll – Ross framework

In this section, we assume $(r_t)_{t\geq 0}$ is a square-root process as in the Cox et al. (1985) term structure model. Specifically, we have under $\mathbb{Q}$

$$dr = \kappa(\zeta - r)\, dt + \sigma_r \sqrt{r}\, dW_t,$$

where ρ still denotes the correlation coefficient between $(W_t)_{t\geq 0}$ and $(z_t)_{t\geq 0}$. Again, prices of discount bonds $P(t,T)$ are available in closed-form.

In this setup, the no-arbitrage value of the corporate bond with nominal M, maturity T and continuous coupon c satisfies the following PDE

$$\begin{aligned} rD = c + (r - \delta)VD_V + \tfrac{1}{2}\sigma^2 V^2 D_{VV} + D_t \\ + \kappa(\zeta - r)D_r + \frac{1}{2}\sigma_r^2 r D_{rr} + \rho\sigma\sigma_r\sqrt{r}VD_{rV}, \end{aligned}$$

which is PDE (1.1) plus three additional terms accounting for interest rate risk.

Kim et al. (1993) numerically solve this PDE with the following boundary conditions

$$D(t, V_d) = \min[\beta M P(t,T,c); V_d],$$
$$D(T) = \min(V(T), M),$$
$$\lim_{V\to\infty} D(V,t,T,c) = P(t,T,c),$$

where $P(t,T,c) = c\int_t^T P(t,s)\,ds$ is the value of the coupon-bearing government bond. The first equation is an early default condition: Upon default, debtholders receive a fraction β of the equivalent risk-free bond, provided this recovery value does not exceed that of the remaining assets. The second equation is Merton's (1974) default-at-maturity condition. The third equation ensures that the corporate bond value converges to the value of the equivalent risk-free bond when asset value goes to infinity.

Kim et al. (1993) rely on an exogenous default threshold but propose to define it as a cash flow constraint. Specifically, default occurs as soon as the firm's payout does not cover the debt service, i.e., $V_d = c/\delta$. The PDE is solved using the alternating directions implicit scheme.

Cathcart and El Jahel (1998) use a similar framework but rely on some "signalling" state variable. They posit that this variable follows a geometric Brownian motion but, since it does not represent the value of a traded asset, its risk-neutral drift is assumed to be a constant m. In addition, the dynamics of this state variable is supposed to be uncorrelated with the instantaneous interest rate process. In this context, the PDE satisfied by the value of corporate discount bond simplifies to

$$rD = mVD_V + \tfrac{1}{2}\sigma^2V^2D_{VV} + D_t + \kappa(\zeta - r)D_r + \tfrac{1}{2}\sigma_r^2 rD_{rr}.$$

Assuming that upon default, bondholders get a fraction $(1-\alpha)$ of the equivalent risk-free bond (this assumption is similar to that in Collin-Dufresne and Goldstein, 2001), Cathcart and El Jahel (1998) look for a solution of the form

$$D = M \cdot P(0,T)\big(1 - \alpha\mathbb{Q}^T(T_d < T)\big),$$

where $\mathbb{Q}^T(T_d < T)$ is the forward neutral default probability.

Cathcart and El Jahel (1998) propose to evaluate this probability by inverting a Laplace transform. However, since in this setup default risk and interest rate risk are independent, the forward neutral and the risk neutral default probabilities are the same. Using this argument, Moraux (2004) shows that, since default is described by the first hitting time of a geometric Brownian motion to a fixed barrier, $\mathbb{Q}^T(T_d < T)$ admits an analytical solution (Saà-Requejo and Santa-Clara, 1999, make a similar observation).

6.3 Stochastic interest rate and default barrier

Nielsen et al. (1993) propose a more general approach where (i) the state variable follows a geometric Brownian motion, (ii) the instantaneous risk-free rate follows a Vasicek process, and (iii) the exogenous default threshold is stochastic. Saà-Requejo and Santa-Clara (1999) extend their work to any single-factor interest rate model. The default threshold obeys the following stochastic differential equation

$$\frac{dV_d}{V_d} = (r_t - \delta_d)\, dt + \sigma_{rd}\, dW_t + \sigma_{Vd}\, dz_t.$$

Default occurs the first time when the state variable hits V_d that can be seen as the market value of the firm's total liabilities (the parameter δ_d stands for the payout rate to debtholders).

7. Strategic debt service

In the previous sections, it was implicitly assumed that claimholders stick to the terms of their initial contracts. In particular, shareholders' decision to default is based on their ability to pay the debt along the schedule initially contracted. When default is costly however, there is scope for renegotiation. The reason is that debtholders are willing to avoid the default state (since they bear the default costs), so shareholders can make strategic debt service every time the firm is close enough to bankruptcy and the threat of default gets credible. Models with strategic debt service should therefore result in riskier debt compared to models which do not take into account any coupon renegotiation.

Anderson and Sundaresan (1996) (and Anderson et al., 1996, for a continuous time version of the model) price discount and coupon-bearing debt in a binomial setting where all the bargaining power is in the hands of shareholders. In a parallel work, Mella-Barral and Perraudin (1997) examine perpetuities in the case where shareholders or debtholders can make take-it-or-leave-it offers. Fan and Sundaresan (2000) and François and Morellec (2004) extend the renegotiation process to a more general game where the surplus is shared according to a Nash bargaining solution.

Let V_R denote the threshold at which shareholders start making strategic debt service, and $\eta \in [0, 1]$ denote their bargaining power. When V reaches V_R, claimholders bargain over the sharing rule $\theta \in [0, 1]$ of firm value $v(V_R)$. Absent deviations from the APR, the Nash solution to the bargaining game is characterized by

$$\theta^* = \arg\max\{[\theta v(V_R)]^\eta [(1-\theta)v(V_R) - (1-\alpha)V_R]^{1-\eta}\},$$

which yields

$$\theta^* = \eta\left[1 - \frac{(1-\alpha)V_R}{v(V_R)}\right].$$

Debt subject to strategic debt service now promises the following payments: initial coupon c when $V > V_R$, and reduced coupon c' when $V \leq V_R$.[7] In this setup, the value of a perpetuity is given by

$$D(V) = \frac{c}{r} - \frac{c}{r}\left(\frac{V_R}{V}\right)^\xi + (1-\eta\alpha)V_R\left(\frac{V_R}{V}\right)^\xi + (1-\eta)\frac{\tau c}{r}\frac{\xi}{2\rho}\left(\frac{V_R}{V}\right)^\xi$$

where ρ is defined as in Proposition 1.1. The optimal renegotiation threshold is

$$V_R = \frac{\xi}{\xi+1}\frac{c[1-\tau+\eta\tau(\xi/2\rho)]}{r(1-\eta\alpha)}.$$

The setup may be applied to finite maturity debt. In that case, the valuation problem admits no analytical solution. Anderson and Tu (1998) show how models with strategic debt service can be solved numerically.

Strategic debt service models tend to generate higher credit spreads than traditional models since bondholders anticipate the opportunistic behavior of shareholders and reflect the associated wealth extraction in the pricing of corporate debt. However, Acharya et al. (2002) argue that when an active cash management is taken into account, shareholders use retained earnings as precautionary savings which reduce the probability of financial distress and hence the scope of default threats. The net impact of strategic debt service on credit spreads is therefore a question still open to debate.

8. More advanced default rules

In standard contingent claims model, default is assimilated with liquidation. This is a restrictive assumption however, since financial distress is often resolved through a restructuring process in which all stakeholders renegotiate their claims to keep the company as a going concern. Reorganization of the firm may be undertaken through a *private workout*, that is, an out-of-Court process, or through a *bankruptcy procedure*. The consequences of default are in particular strongly determined by

[7]It should be noted that such a model precludes the possibility of liquidation since creditors will always be better off accepting the strategic debt service.

the country's legal system (see, e.g., White, 1996, for an international comparison). Evidence in the U.S. suggests that liquidation of big firms is a somewhat rare event that occurs only when all the reorganization options have expired.[8]

Franks and Torous (1989) and Longstaff (1990) model Chapter 11 as the right to extend once the maturity of debt. Clearly, this right is valuable to shareholders as they may postpone the liquidation date. Consequently, credit spreads on corporate discount bonds increase with the length of the extension privilege. In practice however, firms may enter into and emerge from financial distress several times before being eventually liquidated.

To account for a more accurate description of the bankruptcy procedure and its impact on corporate debt valuation, François and Morellec (2004) model the liquidation date as a stopping time based on the excursion of the state variable below the default threshold. Let θ denote the time allowed by the Court for claimholders to renegotiate a reorganization plan every time the firm defaults (i.e., V hits V_d). In this setup, corporate securities can be priced as infinitely-lived Parisian options on the assets of the firm. In particular, the value of the defaultable perpetuity is given by

$$D(\theta, c) = \frac{c}{r}\left[1 - \left(\frac{V}{V_d}\right)^{-\xi}\right] + (1-\alpha)V_d\left(\frac{V}{V_d}\right)^{-\xi} + (1-\eta)R(\theta)\left(\frac{V}{V_d}\right)^{-\xi},$$

where $\eta \in [0, 1]$ is shareholders' bargaining power, $R(\theta)$ is the renegotiation surplus at the time of default that satisfies

$$R(\theta) = \alpha V_d(1 - C(\theta)) - \frac{\varphi}{\delta}(\delta A(\theta) - C(\theta))V_d + \frac{\tau c}{r}(1 - B(\theta)),$$

with φ the proportional costs incurred in financial distress, and

$$A(\theta) = \frac{1}{\lambda}\left(\frac{1}{\lambda + b + \sigma} + \frac{1}{\lambda - b - \sigma}\frac{\Phi(-\lambda\sqrt{\theta})}{\Phi(\lambda\sqrt{\theta})}\right),$$

$$B(\theta) = \frac{\lambda - b}{2\lambda} + \frac{\lambda + b}{2\lambda}\frac{\Phi(-\lambda\sqrt{\theta})}{\Phi(\lambda\sqrt{\theta})},$$

$$C(\theta) = \frac{\Phi(-(\sigma + b)\sqrt{\theta})}{\Phi(\lambda\sqrt{\theta})},$$

[8]Gilson et al. (1990) and Weiss (1990) find that around 5% of firms in their sample are eventually liquidated under Chapter 7 (ruling the liquidation procedure in the U.S. Bankruptcy Code) after filing Chapter 11 (ruling the reorganization procedure in the U.S. Bankruptcy Code).

with

$$b = \frac{r - \delta - \sigma^2/2}{\sigma}, \quad \lambda = \sqrt{2r + b^2}, \quad \Phi(x) = 1 + x\sqrt{2\pi}\exp\left(\frac{x^2}{2}\right)\mathcal{N}(x).$$

As in Leland (1994), the default threshold V_d and the coupon c are endogenously determined as the values maximizing shareholder's equity value ex post and firm value ex ante respectively.

Moraux (2003) extends the Black and Cox (1976) framework by considering two stylized bankruptcy procedures in which the firm is liquidated according to (i) the *consecutive* time spent in default (as in François and Morellec, 2004) or (ii) the *cumulative* time spent in default.[9] Moraux (2003) claims that these two procedures induce a lower and an upper boundary for the real-life liquidation stopping time. Consequently, they can be used to interpolate the values of corporate securities under the existing bankruptcy procedure. Using previous results on occupation time derivatives (see Hugonnier, 1999), Moraux (2003) obtains semi-analytical expressions for finite-maturity debt (including senior, junior and convertible debt). The solution only requires the inversion of a Laplace transform that can be performed with a Gaussian quadrature technique.

As a further step to describe the liquidation criterion in a bankruptcy procedure, Galai et al. (2003) model the liquidation stopping time as a function of the cumulative time spent in default and the severity of distress (measured by the cumulated area between the default threshold and the sample path of the state variable). They account for the "memory" of the Court by allowing for different weights to the past default periods. Their parametric approach enables them to embed the François and Morellec (2004) and the Moraux (2003) bankruptcy procedures. However, implementing their model heavily relies on the calibration of hardly observable parameters.

In Chen (2003), the firm chooses between three default strategies: (i) to directly file for Chapter 11 (thereby avoiding the private workout), (ii) to make a strategic debt service (without Chapter 11 protection), or (iii) to start serving strategic debt and then to file for Chapter 11. The level of informational asymmetry regarding the firm's profitability determines the default strategy and impacts on the credit risk premium.

[9] When liquidation depends on the cumulative time spent in default, corporate securities can be priced as so-called "parasian" options on the assets of the firm. Using this liquidation criterion, Yu (2003) evaluates corporate debt in a Cox – Ingersoll – Ross interest rate framework.

9. Empirical performance

Models of corporate bond valuation are commonly tested in their ability to replicate observed patterns in the term structure of credit spreads. It is important to note however that only a *fraction* of the observed spread is attributable to credit risk. Fisher (1959) points out that corporate bond spreads reflect the sum of all priced factors in which corporate and Treasury bonds differ. Among these are mainly the risk of default, but also liquidity and tax effects should be taken into account. In their empirical study, Elton et al. (2001) find that the expected default loss accounts for no more than 25% of the corporate bond spread. Huang and Huang (2003) find that credit risk explains around 20% of the total spread for investment grade bonds but this fraction increases as bond quality deteriorates.

In this section, we shall first describe the known patterns of the term structure of credit spreads, namely its magnitude and its shape. Then, we shall review the extent to which structural models capture these patterns.

9.1 Magnitude and shape of the term structure of credit spreads

In Table 1.1 below, I report the findings of several empirical studies on the U.S. bond market. The table displays different periods of observation and allows for a distinction between AAA and investment grade bonds. Information on minimum, maximum and average spreads (for all maturities) is reported when available. As expected, credit spreads (measured in basis points) vary with macroeconomic cycles and credit ratings.

Early studies of credit spreads by Fisher (1959) and Johnson (1967) analyzed yield spreads using coupon-bearing bonds with sometimes embedded options. A more formal comparison of spreads, using zero-coupon bond prices, is made by Sarig and Warga (1989). They document that the term structure of credit spreads can take on three different shapes:

- decreasing for low credit quality bonds,
- humped (with a peak around the $2-3$ year maturity) for medium credit quality bonds,
- increasing for high credit quality bonds.

Recent evidence however suggests that the shape of the term structure of credit spreads can sometimes differ from these three dominant shapes. Wei and Guo (1997) document N-shaped term structures on the Eurodollar market and on the U.S. certificates of deposits market

Table 1.1. Credit spreads reported by several empirical studies of the U.S. bond market

Study	Period	Rating	Min. (bps)	Max. (bps)	Average (bps)
Litterman and Iben (1991)	1986 – 1990	Aaa	17	70	
		Aa	30	75	
		A	50	104	
		Baa	88	170	
Kim et al. (1993)	1926 – 1986	Aaa	15	215	77
		Baa	51	787	198
Longstaff and Schwartz (1995)	1977 – 1992	Aaa			70
		Aa			80
		A			126
		Baa			175
Duffee (1998)	1985 – 1995	Aaa	67	79	
		Aa	69	91	
		A	93	118	
		Baa	142	184	
Elton et al. (2001)	1987 – 1996	Aa	41	67	
		A	62	96	
		Baa	117	134	
Huang and Huang (2003)	1973 – 1993	Aaa			63
		Aa			91
		A			123
		Baa			194
		Ba			320
		B			470

in 1992. Helwege and Turner (1999) report an upward sloping term structure for speculative grade bonds.

9.2 Structural models and observed credit spreads

Merton (1974) and Pitts and Selby (1983) have formally demonstrated that any structural model can generate increasing, decreasing and humped term structures of credit spreads. In most cases however, the decreasing shape can only be generated for unrealistic leverage ratios. In addition, many contingent claims models induce a humped (or decreasing) term structure for speculative grade bonds. Collin-Dufresne and

Goldstein (2001) show however that accounting for a stationary leverage ratio helps reconcile with Helwege and Turner's (1999) evidence. The N-shape is still another puzzle for the structural approach.

Furthermore, contingent claims models are often criticized for their inability to account for term structures that *do not* converge to zero as time to maturity goes to zero. In structural models indeed, default is a predictable stopping time: Over an infinitesimal time interval, the probability that the state variable hits the default threshold converges to zero. In practice, bond markets seem to price credit risk as if default could suddenly happen as a surprise even for very short maturities. In other words, very short defaultable bonds still exhibit a risk premium.

The structural approach brings two types of answers to this criticism. First, incomplete information in a structural model may help explain the "surprise" effect on short-term credit spreads. Duffie and Lando (2001) build a framework in which investors only observe the process

$$\widehat{V}_t = V_t \exp(U_t),$$

where $(V_t)_{t\geq 0}$ is the fundamental state variable and $(U_t)_{t\geq 0}$ is a random noise. This perturbation accounts for the hectic arrival of information (through periodic accounting reports and sporadic financial news). In such a model, very short spreads are not zero since investors are aware that the pricing of a risky bond could be updated by a last-minute piece of information. Giesecke (2003) extends this approach by introducing incomplete information also on the issuer's default threshold.

A second answer is that the credit spread is, as we mentioned before, only a fraction of the total yield spread. Very short term bonds may therefore exhibit a premium, not due to credit risk but to another source of risk, namely liquidity risk. This is the argument put forward by Ericsson and Renault (2003). In a contingent claims model that combines credit and liquidity risks, they obtain that the term structure of liquidity premia is decreasing, and analyze the interaction between the credit and liquidity factors on the total spread.

Beyond the shape of the term structure, the structural approach is also challenged for the magnitude of spreads. Early tests of the Merton's (1974) formula by Jones et al. (1984); Ogden (1987) and Franks and Torous (1989) reveal that the basic model with realistic input parameters generates spreads that are too low. Again, it can be argued that only part of the observed spread is attributable to credit risk. Nevertheless, numerous efforts were attempted to correct for this bias. For instance, models with endogenous capital structure as well as strategic debt service models have shown that the structural approach is able to generate credit spreads of comparable magnitudes as those observed for corporate bond yield spreads.

More recent studies have tested the empirical performance of some of the most advanced structural models and their results are mixed. Anderson and Sundaresan (2000) test a structural model that embeds those of Merton (1974); Leland (1994) and Anderson and Sundaresan (1996). They obtain a rather good fit for yield spreads inferred from an aggregate time series of US bond prices, and for historical default probabilities reported by Moody's, over the 1970 – 1996 period. Eom et al. (2004) test the models of Merton (1974); Geske (1977); Longstaff and Schwartz (1995); Leland and Toft (1996) and Collin-Dufresne and Goldstein (2001). Their sample contains 182 bonds over the 1986 – 1997 period. Their main finding is that structural models do not systematically underprice credit risk (which was the conclusion of early tests of Merton's (1974) model). However, they question the accuracy of structural models and find in particular that the pricing bias is often correlated with the credit quality of the bond.

More supportive conclusions are found in Huang and Huang (2003) and Ericsson and Reneby (2004). Huang and Huang (2003) show that if structural models are calibrated to match historical default experience data (both default frequencies and loss rates given default), then a large class of them can generate consistent credit spreads. Ericsson and Reneby (2004) claim that the poor empirical performance previously attributed to structural models stems from an inaccurate method of parameter estimation. By contrast, they show that when the value and the volatility of the state variable is estimated using a maximum likelihood approach, then the implementation of the Merton (1974); Leland and Toft (1996) and Briys and de Varenne (1997) models yields more satisfactory results.

10. Conclusion

This survey has presented the major developments of the structural approach for pricing corporate bonds. Although theoretical contributions have explored various aspects of credit risk, the controversial conclusions reached by empirical tests suggest that a lot of research effort needs to be done. I shall only suggest some possible avenues.

Structural models value public bonds and private loans in the same manner. For valuation purposes, the placement of a debt issue should be taken into account. Hackbarth et al. (2003) is a first attempt in this direction.

The interplay between debt valuation and the capital structure decision is far from being fully understood. Most models with an endogenous capital structure rely on the static trade-off theory of capital structure. Mello and Parsons (1992) quantify the agency costs of debt but such an analysis could be extended to other informational costs that might impact on the credit risk premium.

Most structural models focus on a firm-level analysis. Perhaps one of the biggest challenges that structural models will have to face, is their adaptation to a bond portfolio context, which raises two fundamental issues. The first one is the modelling of default correlations (see Zhou, 2001b). The other issue is to determine ultimately whether credit risk is diversifiable or not. In investigating the determinants of credit spread changes, Collin-Dufresne et al. (2001) find that these changes are not driven by firm-specific factors, but rather by an aggregate factor common to all corporate bonds. This result contradicts the standard framework of structural models and calls for analyzing credit risk in combination with market risk in a general equilibrium model.

Acknowledgments This article is a revised and updated version of the working paper entitled "Bond Evaluation with Default Risk: A Review of the Continuous Time Approach" Working paper ESSEC 97034. I have benefited from comments by Philippe Arztner, Bernard Dumas, Patrick Navatte, Patrice Poncet and Roland Portait. Financial support from SSHRC, IFM2, and FQRSC is gratefully acknowledged.

References

Acharya, V. and Carpenter, J. (2002). Corporate bond valuation and hedging with stochastic interest rates and endogenous bankruptcy. *Review of Financial Studies*, 15:1355 – 1383.

Acharya, V., Huang, J., Subrahmanyam, M., and Sundaram, R. (2002). *When Does Strategic Debt Service Matter?* Working paper, Stern School of Business, New York University.

Alderson, M. and Betker, B. (1995). Liquidation costs and capital structure. *Journal of Financial Economics*, 39:45 – 69.

Altman, E. and Kishore, V. (1996). Almost everything you wanted to know about recoveries on defaulted bonds. *Financial Analysts Journal*, 52:57 – 64.

Anderson, R. and Sundaresan, S. (1996). The design and valuation of debt contracts. *Review of Financial Studies*, 9:37 – 68.

Anderson, R. and Sundaresan, S. (2000). A comparative study of structural models of corporate bond yields: An exploratory investigation. *Journal of Banking and Finance*, 24:255 – 269.

Anderson, R., Sundaresan, S., and Tychon, P. (1996). Strategic analysis of contingent claims. *European Economic Review*, 40:871 – 881.

Anderson, R. and Tu, C. (1998). Numerical analysis of strategic contingent claims models. *Journal of Computational Economics*, 11:3 – 19.

Betker, B. (1997). The administrative costs of debt restructurings: Some recent evidence. *Financial Management*, 26:56 – 68.

Bielecki, T. and Rutkowski, M. (2002). *Credit Risk: Modeling, Valuation and Hedging. Springer Finance*, Springer, New York.

Black, F. and Cox, J. (1976). Valuing corporate securities: Some effects of bond indenture provisions. *Journal of Finance*, 31:351 – 367.

Black, F. and Scholes, M. (1973). The pricing of options and corporate liabilities. *Journal of Political Economy*, 81:637 – 654.

Brennan, M. and Schwartz, E. (1980). Analyzing convertible bonds. *Journal of Financial and Quantitative Analysis*, 15:907 – 929.

Bris, A., Welch, I., and Zhu, N. (2004). *The Costs of Bankruptcy: Chapter 7 Cash Auctions vs. Chapter 11 Bargaining.* Working paper, Yale School of Management.

Briys, E. and de Varenne, F. (1997). Valuing risky fixed rate debt: An extension. *Journal of Financial and Quantitative Analysis*, 32:239 – 248.

Cao, M. and Wei, J. (2001). Vulnerable options, risky corporate bond and credit spread. *Journal of Futures Markets*, 21:301 – 327.

Cathcart, L. and El Jahel, L. (1998). Valuation of defaultable bonds. *Journal of Fixed Income*, 8:65 – 78.

Chen, N. (2003). *Asymmetric Information, the Choice of Financial Distress Resolution and Implications for Corporate Debt Pricing.* Working paper, Columbia University.

Collin-Dufresne, P., and Goldstein, R. (2001). Do credit spreads reflect stationary leverage ratios? *Journal of Finance*, 56:1929 – 1957.

Collin-Dufresne, P., Goldstein, R., and Martin, S. (2001) The determinants of credit spread changes. *Journal of Finance*, 56:2177 – 2207.

Cooper, I.A. and Martin, M. (1996). Default risk and derivative products. *Applied Mathematical Finance*, 3:53 – 74.

Cox, J., Ingersoll, J., and Ross, S. (1985). A theory of the term structure of interest rates. *Econometrica*, 53:385 – 407.

Dangl, T. and Zechner, J. (2004). Credit risk and dynamic capital structure. Forthcoming in *Journal of Financial Institutions.*

Duffee, G. (1998). The relation between Treasury yields and corporate bond yield spreads. *Journal of Finance*, 53:2225 – 2241.

Duffie, D. and Lando, D. (2001). Term structures of credit spreads with incomplete accounting information. *Econometrica*, 69:633 – 664.

Duffie, D. and Singleton, K. (1999). Modeling term structures of defaultable bonds. *Review of Financial Studies*, 12:687 – 720.

Eberhart, A.C., Moore, W.T., and Roenfeldt, R.L. (1990). Security pricing and deviations from the absolute priority rule in bankruptcy proceedings. *Journal of Finance*, 45:1457 – 1469.

Elton, E., Gruber, M., Agrawal, D., and Mann, C. (2001). Explaining the rate spread on corporate bonds. *Journal of Finance*, 56:247 – 277.

Eom, Y.H., Helwege, J., and Huang, J. (2004). Structural models of corporate bond pricing: An empirical analysis. *Review of Financial Studies*, 17:499 – 544.

Ericsson, J. and Renault, O. (2003). *Liquidity and Credit Risk.* Working paper, McGill University.

Ericsson, J. and Reneby, J. (1998). A framework for valuing corporate securities. *Applied Mathematical Finance*, 5:1 – 21.

Ericsson, J. and Reneby, J. (2004). Estimating structural bond pricing models. Forthcoming in *Journal of Business.*

Fan, H. and Sundaresan, S. (2000). Debt valuation, renegotiation, and optimal dividend policy. *Review of Financial Studies*, 13:1057 – 1099.

Fischer, E., Heinkel, R., and Zechner, J. (1989). Dynamic capital structure choice: Theory and tests. *Journal of Finance*, 44:19 – 40.

Fisher, L. (1959). Determinants of risk premium on corporate bonds. *Journal of Political Economy*, 68:217 – 237.

François, P. and Hübner, G. (2004). Credit derivatives with multiple debt issues. *Journal of Banking and Finance*, 28:997 – 1021.

François, P. and Morellec, E. (2004). Capital structure and asset prices: Some effects of bankruptcy procedures. *Journal of Business*, 78:387 – 411.

Franks, J. and Torous, W. (1989). An empirical investigation of U.S. firms in reorganization. *Journal of Finance*, 44:747 – 769.

Fries, S., Miller, M., and Perraudin, W. (1997). Debt in industry equilibrium. *Review of Financial Studies*, 10:39 – 67.

Galai, D., Raviv, A., and Wiener, Z. (2003). *Liquidation Triggers and the Valuation of Equity and Debt.* Working paper, The Hebrew University Business School.

Garbade, K. (2001). *Pricing Corporate Securities as Contingent Claims.* The MIT Press, Cambridge, MA.

Geske, R. (1977). The valuation of corporate liabilities as compound options. *Journal of Financial and Quantitative Analysis*, 12:541 – 552.

Giesecke, K. (2003). *Default and Information.* Working paper, Cornell University.

Gilson, S. (1997). Transactions costs and capital structure choice: Evidence from financially distressed firms. *Journal of Finance*, 52:161–196.

Gilson, S., John, K., and Lang, L. (1990). Troubled debt restructurings: An empirical study of private reorganization of firms in default. *Journal of Financial Economics*, 27:315 – 353.

Goldstein, R., Ju, N., and Leland, H. (2001). An EBIT-based model of dynamic capital structure. *Journal of Business*, 74:483 – 512.

Hackbarth, D., Hennessy, C., and Leland, H. (2003). *The Optimal Mix of Bank and Market Debt: An Asset Pricing Approach.* Working paper, Haas School of Business, University of California Berkeley.

Harrison, M. and Pliska, S. (1981). Martingales and stochastic integrals in the theory of continuous trading. *Stochastic Processes and their Applications*, 11:215 – 260.

Helwege, J. and Turner, C. (1999). The slope of the credit yield curve for speculative-grade issuers. *Journal of Finance*, 54:1869 – 1884.

Ho, T. and Singer, R. (1984). The value of corporate debt with a sinking-fund provision. *Journal of Business*, 57:315 – 336.

Huang, J. and Huang, M. (2003). *How Much of the Corporate-Treasury Yield Spread Is Due to Credit Risk?* Working paper, Stern School of Business, New York University.

Hugonnier, J. (1999). The Feynman – Kac formula and pricing occupation time derivatives. *International Journal of Theoretical and Applied Finance*, 2:153 – 178 .

Ingersoll, J. (1977). A contingent-claims valuation of convertible securities. *Journal of Financial Economics*, 4:289 – 322.

Jarrow, R., Lando, D., and Turnbull, S. (1997). A Markov model for the term structure of credit risk spreads. *Review of Financial Studies*, 10:481 – 523.

Jarrow, R. and Turnbull, S. (1995). Pricing derivatives on financial securities subject to credit risk. *Journal of Finance*, 50:53 – 85.

Johnson, R. (1967). Term structures of corporate bond yields as a function of risk of default. *Journal of Finance*, 22:313 – 345.

Jones, E., Mason, S., and Rosenfeld, E. (1984). Contingent claims analysis of corporate capital structures: An empirical investigation. *Journal of Finance*, 39:611 – 627.

Ju, N., Parrino, R., Poteshman, A., and Weisbach, M. (2003). *Horses and Rabbits? Optimal Dynamic Capital Structure from Shareholder and Manager Perspectives.* Working paper, University of Maryland.

Kim, I.J., Ramaswamy, K., and Sundaresan, S. (1993). Does default risk in coupons affect the valuation of corporate bonds? A contingent claims model. *Financial Management*, 22:117 – 131.

Klein, P. (1996). Pricing Black – Scholes options with correlated credit risk. *Journal of Banking and Finance*, 20:1211 – 1229.

Lando, D. (2004). *Credit Risk Modeling. Princeton Series in Finance*, Princeton University Press, Princeton, NJ.

Leland, H. (1994). Corporate debt value, bond covenants, and optimal capital structure. *Journal of Finance*, 49:1213 – 1252.

Leland, H. (1998). Agency costs, risk management, and capital structure. *Journal of Finance*, 53:1213 – 1243.

Leland, H. and Toft, K.B. (1996). Optimal capital structure, endogenous bankruptcy, and the term structure of credit spreads. *Journal of Finance*, 51:987 – 1019.

Litterman, R., and Iben, T. (1991). Corporate bond valuation and the term structure of credit spreads. *Journal of Portfolio Management*, Spring:52 – 64.

Long, J.B. (1974). Discussion. *Journal of Finance*, 29:485 – 488.

Longstaff, F. (1990). Pricing options with extendible maturities: Analysis and applications. *Journal of Finance*, 45:935 – 957.

Longstaff, F. and Schwartz, E. (1995). A simple approach to valuing risky fixed and floating rate debt. *Journal of Finance*, 50:789 – 819.

Madan, D. and Unal, H. (2000). A two-factor hazard rate model for pricing risky debt and the term structure of credit spreads. *Journal of Financial and Quantitative Analysis*, 35:43 – 65.

Mason, S. and Bhattacharya, S. (1981). Risky debt, jump processes, and safety covenants. *Journal of Financial Economics*, 9:281 – 307.

Mella-Barral, P. and Perraudin, W. (1997). Strategic debt service. *Journal of Finance*, 52:531 – 556.

Mella-Barral, P. and Tychon, P. (1999). Default risk in asset pricing. *Finance*, 20:7 – 22.

Mello, A. and Parsons, J. (1992). Measuring the agency costs of debt. *Journal of Finance*, 47:1887 – 1904.

Merton, R.C. (1974). On the pricing of corporate debt: The risk structure of interest rates. *Journal of Finance*, 29:449 – 470.

Merton, R.C. (1977). On the pricing of contingent claims and the Modigliani – Miller theorem. *Journal of Financial Economics*, 5:241 – 249.

Moraux, F. (2003). *Valuing Corporate Securities in Presence of Bankruptcy Procedures.* Working paper, Université de Rennes 1.

Moraux, F. (2004). A closed-form solution for pricing defaultable bonds. *Finance Research Letters*, 1:135 – 142.

Nielsen, L., Saà-Requejo, J., and Santa-Clara, P. (1993). *Default Risk and Interest Rate Risk: The Term Structure of Default Spreads.* Working paper, INSEAD.

Ogden, J.P. (1987). Determinants of the ratings and yields on corporate bonds: Tests of the contingent-claims model. *Journal of Financial*

Research, 10:329 – 339.

Pitts, C. and Selby, M. (1983). The pricing of corporate debt: A further note. *Journal of Finance*, 38:1311 – 1313.

Rich, D. The valuation and behaviour of Black – Scholes options subject to intertemporal default risk. *Review of Derivatives Research*, 1:25 – 59.

Saá-Requejo, J. and Santa-Clara, P. (1999). *Bond Pricing with Default Risk.* Working paper, University of California Los Angeles.

Sarig, O. and Warga, A. (1989). Some empirical estimates of the risk structure of interest rates. *Journal of Finance*, 44:1351 – 1360.

Shimko, D., Tejima, N., and Van Deventer, D. (1993). The pricing of risky debt when interest rates are stochastic. *Journal of Fixed Income*, 3:58 – 65.

Vasicek, O. (1977). An equilibrium characterization of the term structure. *Journal of Financial Economics*, 5:177 – 188.

Warner, J. (1977). Bankruptcy costs: Some evidence. *Journal of Finance*, 3:337 – 347.

Wei, D. and Guo, D. (1997). Pricing risky debt: An empirical comparison of the Longstaff and Schwartz and Merton models. *Journal of Fixed Income*, 7:8 – 28.

Weiss, L. (1990). Bankruptcy resolution: Direct costs and violation of priority of claims. *Journal of Financial Economics*, 27:285 – 314.

White, M. (1996). The costs of corporate bankruptcy: A U.S. – European comparison. In: J. Bhandari and L. Weiss (eds), *Corporate Bankruptcy: Economic and Legal Perspectives*, Cambridge University Press, Cambridge.

Yu, L. (2003). *Pricing Credit Risk as Parasian Options with Stochastic Recovery Rate of Corporate Bonds.* Working paper, Manchester Business School.

Zhou, C. (2001a). The term structure of credit spreads with jump risk. *Journal of Banking and Finance*, 25:2015 – 2040.

Zhou, C. (2001b). An analysis of default correlations and multiple defaults. *Review of Financial Studies*, 14:555 – 576.

Chapter 2

BESSEL PROCESSES AND ASIAN OPTIONS

Daniel Dufresne

Abstract The goal of this chapter is to give a concise account of the connection between Bessel processes and the integral of geometric Brownian motion. The latter appears in the pricing of Asian options. Bessel processes are defined and some of their properties are given. The known expressions for the probability density function of the integral of geometric Brownian motion are stated, and other related results are given, in particular the Geman and Yor (1993) Laplace transform for Asian option prices.

1. Introduction

In several papers, Marc Yor has described and applied the properties of Bessel processes that relate to the integral of geometric Brownian motion (called "IGBM" in the sequel). The goal of this chapter is to give a concise account of the connection between Bessel processes and IGBM. From the point of view of financial mathematics, the main motivation for the study of IGBM is the pricing of Asian options. Some of the most important results about pricing of Asian options will be given, in particular the Geman – Yor formula for the Laplace transform of Asian option prices and the four known expressions for the probability density function ("PDF" in the sequel) of IGBM. Specialists will not find much that is new, with the possible exception of a somewhat different derivation of the law of IGBM sampled at an exponential time (Section 3). Also, a known result is stated and proved again, namely that the Geman – Yor transform for Asian options is valid for all drifts, not only nonnegative ones; this is in response to Carr and Schröder (2003), who noticed that the proof in Geman and Yor (1993) covered only non-negative drifts, and extended the original proof to all drifts. Section 3 shows that there is a much simpler approach, which had already been pointed out (perhaps too briefly) in Dufresne (2000, Section 1), and also in Donati-Martin et al. (2001).

Section 2 defines Bessel processes and gives some of their properties. Section 3 describes the relation between IGBM and Asian options, and then shows how time-reversal can be applied to IGBM. A first expression for the PDF of IGBM is given. This expression goes back to Wong (1964), but was apparently unknown in financial mathematics until quite recently. Section 4 uses the link between geometric Brownian motion and Bessel processes (Lamperti's relation) to derive the law of IGBM at an independent exponential time. Some applications of this result are mentioned: (i) a second expression for the PDF of IGBM; (ii) a relationship between IGBM with opposite drifts; (iii) the Geman-Yor formula for the Laplace transform of Asian option prices; (iv) an extension of Pitman's $2M - X$ theorem. In Section 5 formulas for the reciprocal moments of IGBM and two other expressions for the PDF of IGBM are given.

Vocabulary and notation

"Brownian motion" means "standard Brownian motion" (i.e., drift 0, variance t in one dimension; vector of independent one-dimensional standard Brownian motions in higher dimensions). Equality of probability distributions is denoted "$\stackrel{\mathrm{d}}{=}$."

a.s.	almost surely (same as "with probability one")
A_t	$= A_t^{(0)} = \int_0^t e^{2B_s}\,ds$
$A_t^{(\nu)}$	$= \int_0^t e^{2(\nu t + B_s)}\,ds$
B_t	Brownian motion
B_t^i	ith component of vector of Brownian motions
$B_t^{(\nu)}$	$= \nu t + B_t$: Brownian motion with drift ν
$\mathrm{BES}^\delta(x)$	δ-dimensional Bessel process starting from x
$\mathrm{BES}^{(\nu)}(x)$	Bessel process of index ν starting from x (same as $\mathrm{BES}^\delta(x)$ if $\nu = \delta/2 - 1$)
$\mathrm{BESQ}^\delta(x)$	δ-dimensional squared Bessel process starting from x
$\mathrm{BESQ}^{(\nu)}(x)$	squared Bessel process of index ν starting from x (same as $\mathrm{BESQ}^\delta(x)$ if $\nu = \delta/2 - 1$)
BM	1-dimensional Brownian motion starting from 0
BM^δ	δ-dimensional Brownian motion starting from 0
$\mathrm{BM}^\delta(x)$	δ-dimensional Brownian motion starting from x
$f_t^\delta(x, y)$	transition density function of $\mathrm{BESQ}^\delta(x)$

${}_1F_1(a,b;z)$	$= \sum_{n=0}^{\infty} \frac{(a)_n}{(b)_n} \frac{z^n}{n!}$: confluent hypergeometric function
${}_2F_1(a,b,c;z)$	$= \sum_{n=0}^{\infty} \frac{(a)_n (b)_n}{(c)_n} \frac{z^n}{n!}$: (Gauss) hypergeometric function
$g_\nu(t,x)$	PDF of $A_t^{(\nu)}$
$H_\nu(z)$	$= \frac{2^\nu \Gamma(\frac{1}{2})}{\Gamma([1-\nu]/2)} {}_1F_1\left(-\frac{\nu}{2}, \frac{1}{2}; z^2\right) + \frac{2^\nu \Gamma(-\frac{1}{2})}{\Gamma(-\nu/2)} z {}_1F_1\left(\frac{1-\nu}{2}, \frac{3}{2}; z^2\right)$: Hermite function
$I_\nu(z)$	$= \sum_{n=0}^{\infty} \frac{(z/2)^{\nu+2n}}{n!\Gamma(n+\nu+1)}$: modified Bessel function of the first kind of order ν
$K_\nu(z)$	$= \frac{\pi}{2} \frac{I_{-\nu}(z) - I_\nu(z)}{\sin \nu z}$: Macdonald's function of order ν
$L_n^a(z)$	Laguerre polynomial
$p_t^{(\nu)}(x,y)$	transition density function of Bessel process of index ν starting from x
S_λ	exponential random variable, with PDF $\lambda e^{-\lambda t} \mathbf{1}_{\{t>0\}}$
T_u	t such that $A_t^{(\nu)} = u$
$W_{a,b}(z)$	Whittaker function
ρ_t	a Bessel process
ρ_t^2	squared Bessel process

2. Bessel processes: definition, some fundamental results

The quadratic variation of a stochastic process is used below. For a continuous process X which can be expressed as $C + M$, where C has bounded variation and M is a local martingale (X is then a continuous semimartingale), the quadratic variation of X, also called the "bracket of X", is

$$\langle X, X \rangle_t = \lim_{\max_i |t_{i+1} - t_i| \to 0} \sum_{i=0}^{n-1} (M_{t_{i+1}} - M_{t_i})^2,$$

where $0 = t_0 < t_1 < \cdots < t_n = t$. The quadratic covariation (or "bracket") of two processes X and Y is defined as

$$\langle X, Y \rangle_t = \tfrac{1}{4}(\langle X+Y, X+Y \rangle_t - \langle X-Y, X-Y \rangle_t).$$

This definition implies that $\langle \cdot, \cdot \rangle_t$ is symmetric and linear in each argument:

$$\langle X,Y\rangle = \langle Y,X\rangle, \quad \langle \alpha_1 X^{(1)} + \alpha_2 X^{(2)}, Y\rangle_t = \alpha_1\langle X^{(1)},Y\rangle_t + \alpha_2\langle X^{(2)},Y\rangle_t$$

for all $\alpha_1, \alpha_2 \in \mathbb{R}$. If X and Y have Itô differentials

$$dX = a_X\,dt + \sigma_X\,dB, \quad dY = a_Y\,dt + \sigma_Y\,dB,$$

then

$$\langle X,Y\rangle_t = \int_0^t \sigma_X(s)\sigma_Y(s)\,ds.$$

The definition of quadratic covariation given above implies that the bracket of two independent Brownian motions is 0. (For more details on quadratic variation, see Revuz and Yor (1999, pp. 120 – 128) and Protter (1990, pp. 58, 98).)

We will also use Itô's formula: if $X^{(1)},\dots,X^{(n)}$ have Itô differentials, and if $F(X^{(1)},\dots,X^{(n)})$ is a function with continuous second-order partial derivatives in an open set which comprises all the possible values of $X^{(1)},\dots,X^{(n)}$, then

$$dF(X^{(1)},\dots,X^{(n)}) = \sum_{i=1}^{n} F_{x_i}\,dX^{(i)} + \frac{1}{2}\sum_{i,j=1}^{n} F_{x_i x_j}\,d\langle X^{(i)},X^{(j)}\rangle_t.$$

The following facts regarding Bessel processes are taken from Revuz and Yor (1999, Chapter XI). We first define the squared Bessel processes for integer dimensions. We write $X = \{X_t; t \geq 0\} \sim BM^\delta(x)$ if X is δ-dimensional Brownian motion starting at $x \in \mathbb{R}^\delta$. Let $B = (B^1,\dots,B^\delta) \sim \mathrm{BM}^\delta(x)$, and define $\rho = |B|$. Then Itô's formula implies

$$\rho_t^2 = \rho_0^2 + 2\sum_{i=1}^{\delta}\int_0^t B_s^i\,dB_s^i + \delta t.$$

(Here $\rho_0^2 = |x|^2$.) Next, define a new one-dimensional process β as follows:

$$\beta_t = \sum_{i=1}^{\delta}\int_0^t \left(\frac{B_s^i}{\rho_s}\right) dB_s^i.$$

For $\delta \geq 1$, the set $\{s : \rho_s = 0\}$ has Lebesgue measure 0, and $|B_s^i/\rho_s| \leq 1$, so the division by ρ_s above causes no problem. We now appeal to a classical result due to Lévy:

If X is a continuous local martingale with respect to a filtration $\{\mathcal{F}_t\}$ with $X_0 = 0$ and $\langle X,X\rangle_t = t$ for all $t \geq 0$, then it is a $\{\mathcal{F}_t\}$-Brownian motion.

A simple calculation shows that $\langle\beta,\beta\rangle_t = t$, and thus β is Brownian motion:

$$\langle\beta,\beta\rangle_t = \sum_{i=1}^{t} \int_0^t \frac{(B_s^i)^2}{\rho_s^2}\, ds = \int_0^t \frac{\rho_s^2}{\rho_s^2}\, ds = t.$$

We may thus rewrite the stochastic differential of ρ^2 as

$$\rho_t^2 = \rho_0^2 + 2\int_0^t \rho_s\, d\beta_s + \delta t, \qquad \delta = 1, 2, \ldots$$

The Bessel processes are extended to other $\delta \geq 0$ as follows. For $x \in \mathbb{R}_+$, consider the stochastic differential equation ("SDE" in the sequel)

$$Z_t = x + 2\int_0^t \sqrt{|Z_s|}\, d\beta_s + \delta t.$$

General theorems ensure that this SDE has a unique strong solution for any $x \geq 0$, $\delta \geq 0$. There are also comparison theorems which say that, since the solution of the equation when $\delta = x = 0$ is $Z_t = 0$ for all $t \geq 0$, then $Z_t \geq 0$ in all cases where $\delta, x \geq 0$. The solution of this SDE will be said to have "dimension" parameter δ, even when δ is not an integer.

Definition Let $x, \delta \geq 0$. The unique strong solution of

$$Z_t = x + 2\int_0^t \sqrt{Z_s}\, d\beta_s + \delta t$$

is called the *squared Bessel process of dimension* δ started at x. The *index* of the process is $\nu = \delta/2 - 1$. The notation is either $Z \sim \mathrm{BESQ}^\delta(x)$ or $Z \sim \mathrm{BESQ}^{(\nu)}(x)$. The probability law of this process on the set of continuous functions will be denoted Q_x^δ or $\mathrm{Q}_x^{(\nu)}$.

(**N.B.** The meaning of the index of a Bessel process will soon become clear.) It is convenient to write $\mathrm{Q}_x^\delta(F(X))$ for $\mathrm{E}\,F(\rho^2)$, when $\rho^2 \sim \mathrm{BESQ}^\delta(x)$. (Here X_t represents the t-coordinate of a sample path of ρ^2, and F is a functional of the process, for example

$$F(X) = X_{t_1} + X_{t_2}^2 \quad \text{or} \quad F(X) = \int_0^1 g(X_t)\, dt.)$$

Additivity property of the squared Bessel process laws When δ_1, δ_2 are integers, it is easy to see that the sum of two independent $\mathrm{BESQ}^{\delta_i}(x_i)$, $i = 1, 2$ must be $\mathrm{BESQ}^{\delta_1+\delta_2}(x_1 + x_2)$: simply represent the processes as

$$B_1^2 + \cdots + B_{\delta_1}^2 \quad \text{and} \quad B_{\delta_{i+1}}^2 + \cdots + B_{\delta_1+\delta_2}^2,$$

respectively, where $B_1, \ldots, B_{\delta_1+\delta_2}$ are independent one-dimensional Brownian motions. Many proofs of properties of Bessel processes become much simpler by using the fact that this additivity property remains valid when the dimensions of the Bessel processes are not both integers. The proof is as follows. Suppose $\beta^{(1)}$, $\beta^{(2)}$ are two independent Brownian motions, and that

$$dX_t^{(i)} = 2\sqrt{X_t^{(i)}}\, d\beta_t^{(i)} + \delta_i\, dt, \quad \delta_i, X_0^{(i)} \geq 0, \; i = 1, 2.$$

The processes $X^{(1)}$, $X^{(2)}$ are then independent. Define $X = X^{(1)} + X^{(2)}$. Let $\beta^{(3)}$ be a third independent Brownian motion and define a new process

$$\beta_t = \int_0^t \mathbf{1}_{\{X_s>0\}} \left[\sqrt{\frac{X_s^{(1)}}{X_s}}\, d\beta_s^{(1)} + \sqrt{\frac{X_s^{(2)}}{X_s}} \right] d\beta_s^{(2)} + \int_0^t \mathbf{1}_{\{X_s=0\}}\, d\beta_s^{(3)}.$$

Then $\langle \beta, \beta \rangle_t = t$, β is Brownian motion and

$$dX_t = 2\sqrt{X_t}\, d\beta_t + (\delta_1 + \delta_2)\, dt,$$

which mean that $X \sim \mathrm{BESQ}^{\delta_1+\delta_2}(x_1 + x_2)$. This may be written more succinctly as

$$\mathrm{Q}_{x_1}^{\delta_1} * \mathrm{Q}_{x_2}^{\delta_1} = \mathrm{Q}_{x_1+x_2}^{\delta_1+\delta_2}, \quad \delta_i, x_i \geq 0, \; i = 1, 2.$$

Scaling property of BESQ One-dimensional Brownian motion has the familiar scaling property, which says that if $\{B_t; t \geq 0\}$ is Brownian motion, then so is $\{cB_{t/c^2}; t \geq 0\}$. This carries over immediately to the square of Brownian motion, and then to sums of independent squared Brownian motions. The same scaling property also holds for arbitrary BESQ processes: for any $c > 0$,

$$\{X_t; t \geq 0\} \sim \mathrm{BESQ}^{\delta}(x) \quad \text{implies} \quad \{cX_{t/c}; t \geq 0\} \sim \mathrm{BESQ}^{\delta}(cx).$$

The distribution of ρ_t^2 If $\rho^2 \sim \mathrm{BESQ}^{\delta}(x)$, then

$$\mathrm{E}\, e^{-\lambda \rho_t^2} = \mathrm{Q}_x^{\delta}(e^{-\lambda X_t}) = \phi(x, \delta).$$

The additivity property of squared Bessel processes implies that

$$\phi(x_1 + x_2, \delta_1 + \delta_2) \;=\; \phi(x_1, \delta_1)\phi(x_2, \delta_2) \quad \text{for all } x_1, x_2, \delta_1, \delta_2 \geq 0.$$

In particular, this implies $\phi(x_1 + x_2, 0) = \phi(x_1, 0)\phi(x_2, 0)$; given that $\phi(0, 0) = 1$, we find that $\phi(x) = A^x$ for some $A > 0$. The same reasoning leads to $\phi(0,\delta) = C^\delta$ for some $C > 0$. Since $\phi(x,\delta) = \phi(x,0)\phi(0,\delta)$, we get

$$\phi(x,\delta) = A^x C^\delta.$$

In order to find A and C, suppose $\{B_t; t \geq 0\}$ is $\mathrm{BM}^1(\sqrt{x})$ and calculate

$$\phi(x,1) = \mathrm{E}\, e^{-\lambda B_t^2} = \frac{1}{(1+2\lambda t)^{1/2}} e^{-\lambda x/(1+2\lambda t)}.$$

This implies that, in general,

$$\phi(x,\delta) = \frac{1}{(1+2\lambda t)^{\delta/2}} e^{-\lambda x/(1+2\lambda t)}.$$

When $x = 0$ and $\delta > 0$, the exponential disappears from this expression, and ρ_t^2 has a gamma distribution with PDF

$$f_t^\delta(0,y) = \frac{y^{\delta/2-1}}{(2t)^{\delta/2}\Gamma(\delta/2)} e^{-y/2t} \mathbf{1}_{\{y>0\}}.$$

When $x, \delta > 0$, the exponential factor in the Laplace transform above corresponds to a compound Poisson/Exponential distribution:

$$e^{-\lambda x/(1+2\lambda t)} = \exp\left[\frac{x}{2t}(M(\lambda) - 1)\right], \quad M(\lambda) = \frac{1}{(1+2\lambda t)},$$

and thus

$$\mathrm{E}\, e^{-\lambda \rho_t^2} = e^{-x/2t} \sum_{n=0}^{\infty} \frac{x^n}{(2t)^n n!} M(\lambda)^{n+\delta/2}.$$

The PDF of ρ_t^2 can thus be found by summing the densities of the $\mathbf{Gamma}(n + \delta/2, 1/2t)$ which appear when inverting this expression term by term:

$$f_t^\delta(x,y) = \sum_{n=0}^{\infty} \frac{x^n y^{\delta/2+n-1}}{n!\Gamma(\delta/2+n)(2t)^{\delta/2+2n}} e^{-(x+y)/2t}.$$

Next, the reason for the name "Bessel" process, as well as for the definition of the "index" of the process are finally given: recall the "modified Bessel function of the first kind of order ν"

$$I_\nu(z) = \sum_{n=0}^{\infty} \frac{(z/2)^{\nu+2n}}{n!\Gamma(n+\nu+1)}, \quad \nu, z \in \mathbb{C}.$$

Then

$$f_t^\delta(x,y) = \frac{1}{2t}\left(\frac{y}{x}\right)^{\nu/2} e^{-(x+y)/2t} I_\nu\left(\frac{\sqrt{xy}}{t}\right) \mathbf{1}_{\{y>0\}}, \quad \nu = \frac{\delta}{2} - 1.$$

The case $x > 0$, $\delta = 0$ is special, because the distribution of ρ_t^2 is then compound Poisson/Exponential with no independent gamma component added, and so there is a positive probability that $\rho_t^2 = 0$. A slight modification of the above calculation yields the probability mass at the origin and the density of the continuous part of the distribution:

$$\mathrm{P}(\rho_t^2 = 0) = e^{-x/2t}$$

$$\mathrm{P}(\rho_t^2 \in dy) = \frac{1}{2t}\left(\frac{y}{x}\right)^{-1/2} e^{-(x+y)/2t} I_1\left(\frac{\sqrt{xy}}{t}\right) \mathbf{1}_{\{y>0\}}\, dy.$$

Behaviour of trajectories of squared Bessel processes We have just seen that there is a positive probability that $\rho_t^2 = 0$ if, and only if, $\delta = 0$. This is related to the following facts about the trajectories of BESQ^δ (see Revuz and Yor, 1999, Chapter XI, for more details):

(i) for $\delta = 0$, the point $x = 0$ is absorbing (after it reaches 0, the process will stay there forever);
(ii) for $0 < \delta < 2$, the point $x = 0$ is reflecting (the process inmmediately moves away from 0);
(iii) for $\delta \le 1$, the point $x = 0$ is reached a.s.;
(iv) for $\delta \ge 2$, the point $x = 0$ is unattainable.

DEFINITION For $x \ge 0$, the square root of $\mathrm{BESQ}^\delta(x^2)$ is called the Bessel process of dimension δ started at x, denoted $\mathrm{BES}^\delta(x)$ or $\mathrm{BES}^{(\nu)}(x)$.

When $x > 0$ and $\delta \ge 2$ the point 0 is unattainable, and we may apply Itô's formula, with $\rho = \sqrt{\rho^2}$, to find that BES^δ satisfies the SDE

$$\rho_t = x + \beta_t + \frac{\delta - 1}{2}\int_0^t \frac{ds}{\rho_s} = x + \beta_t + (\nu + \tfrac{1}{2})\int_0^t \frac{ds}{\rho_s}.$$

For $\delta < 2$, the squared Bessel process reaches 0, and thus the conditions needed to apply Itô's formula are not satisfied; see Revuz and Yor (1999, pp. 446, 451). In the sequel we will restrict our attention to Bessel processes of order greater than or equal to 2.

3. A functional of Brownian motion: the integral of geometric Brownian motion

Motivation: Asian options In the Black – Scholes framework, let r be the risk-free rate of interest, $t \in [0, T]$, $B \sim \mathrm{BM}$, and

$$dS_t = \mu S_t\, dt + \sigma S_t\, dB_t.$$

Asian (or average) options have payoffs which involve some average of the prices of the risky asset S. For instance, an Asian call option would have a payoff such as

$$\left(\frac{1}{N}\sum_{i=1}^{N} S_{t_i} - K\right)_+, \quad \text{where } 0 \le t_1 < t_2 < \cdots < t_N \le T.$$

The no-arbitrage theory of derivative pricing says that, in this model, the price of a European option is the expected discounted value of the payoff under the risk-free measure. A problem arises with Asian options because the distribution of the sum in this expression does not have a simple form, which implies numerical difficulties in computing the N-fold integral which gives the price of the option. Various approximations exist, but few error bounds are available; even simulation is not very efficient (Vázquez-Abad and Dufresne, 1998; Su and Fu, 2000).

If the average contains enough prices, and if they are computed at evenly spread time points, then the discrete average above is very close to the continuous average

$$\frac{1}{T}\int_0^T S_u\,du = \frac{S_0}{T}\int_0^T e^{(r-\sigma^2/2)u+\sigma\widetilde{B}_u}\,du.$$

(Here $\widetilde{B}$ is BM under the equivalent martingale measure.) There are three parameters in the above integral, r, σ and T. By the scaling property of Brownian motion, we can fix one of the parameters. Marc Yor chose to set $\sigma = 2$ (for reasons which will become apparent later), and thus define

$$A_t^{(\nu)} = \int_0^t e^{2(\nu s + B_s)}\,ds, \quad B \sim \mathrm{BM}.$$

(We will also write $A_t = A_t^{(0)}$.) The conversion rule is

$$\int_0^T e^{\mu s+\sigma B_s} \overset{\mathrm{d}}{=} \frac{4}{\sigma^2}A_t^{(\nu)}, \quad t = \frac{\sigma^2 T}{4}, \ \nu = \frac{2\mu}{\sigma^2}.$$

(**N.B.** In the case where $\mu = r - \sigma^2/2$, it can be seen that the normalized drift ν can be positive or negative, large or small.)

Geman and Yor (1993) appear to have been the first to study the pricing of continuous-average Asian options, though the process $A_t^{(\nu)}$ had been studied before, as the integral of geometric Brownian motion occurs in various contexts.

Moments The law of $A_t^{(\nu)}$ has all moments finite; this is because

$$te^{-2t\nu_- + 2\underline{B}_t} \le A_t^{(\nu)} \le te^{2t\nu_+ + 2\overline{B}_t},$$

where $\underline{B}$ and $\overline{B}$ are respectively the running minimum and maximum of B. All moments (positive or negative) of the variables on either sides of the inequality are finite, and so

$$\mathrm{E}(A_t^{(\nu)})^r < \infty \quad \forall r \in \mathbb{R}.$$

Dufresne (1989) and Yor (1992a) independently derived the general expression for $\mathrm{E}(A_t^{(\nu)})^n$, but it has since been found (Yor, 2001, p. 54) that the following formula had appeared in a paper about an astronomical model, see Ramakrishnan (1954): for $n = 1, 2, \ldots,$

$$\mathrm{E}(A_t^{(\nu)})^n = \sum_{k=0}^{n} b_{n,k} e^{a_k t}, \quad a_k = 2k\nu + 2k^2, \; b_{n,k} = n! \Big/ \prod_{\substack{j=0 \\ j \neq k}}^{n} (a_j - a_k).$$

These moments can be found directly or by using time reversal (see below)

REMARK *By the scaling property of Brownian motion, the above formula also gives*

$$\mathrm{E}\left(\int_0^T e^{\mu s + \sigma B_s}\, ds\right)^n, \quad n = 1, 2 \ldots$$

Time reversal The following result (Dufresne, 1989) has been extended to Lévy processes by Carmona et al. (1997):

For each fixed $t > 0$,

$$Y_t^{(\nu)} \stackrel{\text{def}}{=} \int_0^t e^{2[(t-s) + B_t - B_s]}\, ds \stackrel{\text{d}}{=} A_t^{(\nu)}.$$

To prove this, note that the two continuous processes

$$U = \{B_s; 0 \le s \le t\}, \quad V = \{B_t - B_{t-s}; 0 \le s \le t\}$$

have the same finite-dimensional distributions, and thus have the same law (as random elements of $C[0,t]$). Define a functional $I \colon C[0,t] \to \mathbb{R}$ by

$$I(x) = \int_0^t e^{2(\nu s + x_s)}\, ds.$$

Then $I(U)$ and $I(V)$ have the same distribution, which means that

$$\int_0^t e^{2(\nu s+B_s)}\,ds \overset{\mathrm{d}}{=} \int_0^t e^{2(\nu s+B_t-B_{t-s})}\,ds = \int_0^t e^{2[(t-u)+B_t-B_u]}\,du.$$

By Itô's formula,

$$dY_t^{(\nu)} = [2(\nu+1)Y_t^{(\nu)}+1]dt + 2Y_t^{(\nu)}\,dB_t.$$

This SDE yields ordinary differential equations for the moments of $Y_t^{(\nu)}$. Moreover, the PDE associated with this diffusion may be solved, to give the eigenfunction expansion for the PDF of $Y_t^{(\nu)}$. This was done by Wong (1964). Monthus and Comtet (1994) write the eigenfunction expansion as

$$\begin{aligned} &g_\nu(t,x) \\ &= e^{-1/2x}\Bigg[2\sum_{0\le n<-\nu/2} e^{2tn(\nu+n)}\frac{(-1)^{n+1}(\nu+2n)}{\Gamma(1-\nu-n)}\left(\frac{1}{2x}\right)^{1-\nu-n} L_n^{-\nu-2n}\left(\frac{1}{2x}\right) \\ &\qquad + \frac{1}{2\pi^2}\int_0^\infty ds\, e^{-t(\nu^2+s^2)/2} s\sinh(\pi s)\left|\Gamma\left(\frac{\nu+is}{2}\right)\right|^2 \\ &\qquad\qquad \times\left(\frac{1}{2x}\right)^{(1-\nu)/2} W_{(1-\nu)/2,is/2}\left(\frac{1}{2x}\right)\Bigg], \end{aligned}$$

where $W_{a,b}$ is Whittaker's function. Details about eigenfunction expansions for Asian options may be found in Linetsky (2001).

4. The law of $A_t^{(\nu)}$ at an independent exponential time

One of the classical tools of probability theory is the *resolvent*: given a process $\{X_t; t\ge 0\}$, this is the application which associates to a function f the integral

$$\mathrm{E}\int_0^\infty e^{-\lambda t} f(X_t)\,dt.$$

This is of course a Laplace transform in the time parameter t. A very well known example is Brownian motion starting at x, for which

$$\int_0^\infty e^{-\lambda t} f(B_t)\,dt = \int_{-\infty}^\infty \frac{1}{\sqrt{2\lambda}} e^{-\sqrt{2\lambda}|y-x|} f(y)\,dy.$$

Here the function $(1/\sqrt{2\lambda})e^{-\sqrt{2\lambda}|y-x|}$ is the density of the resolvent. An equivalent way of viewing the resolvent is to think of it as

$$\frac{1}{\lambda}\mathrm{E}\,f(X_{S_\lambda}),$$

where $S_\lambda \sim$ **Exponential**(λ) is independent of $\{X_t; t \geq 0\}$. Finding the density of the resolvent is then equivalent to finding the distribution of X_{S_λ}. From what was said above, the PDF of B_{S_λ} is $(\sqrt{2\lambda}/2)e^{-\sqrt{2\lambda}|y-x|}$, or, said another way, $B_{S_\lambda} - x \sim$ **DoubleExponential**$(\sqrt{2\lambda})$.

The distribution of $A^{(\nu)}_{S_\lambda}$ was found by Marc Yor. The derivation below is a little different from the original papers (Yor 1992a,b; Yor 2001, Chapter 6); other derivations may be found in Donati-Martin et al. (2001) and Dufresne (2001b). Here is the main result of this section (Yor, 1992a):

*The distribution of $A^{(\nu)}_{S_\lambda}$ is the same as that of $B/2G$, where B and G are independent, $B \sim$ **Beta**$(1, \alpha)$, $G \sim$ **Gamma**$(\beta, 1)$, with*

$$\alpha = \frac{\gamma + \nu}{2}, \quad \beta = \frac{\gamma - \nu}{2}, \quad \gamma = \sqrt{2\lambda + \nu^2}.$$

The proof presented below rests on a relationship between geometric Brownian motion and Bessel processes, due to Lamperti (1972) (see Revuz and Yor, 1999, p. 452). Two other required results are, first, that the transition density of the $BES^{(\nu)}(x)$ is

$$p_t^{(\nu)}(x, y) = \frac{y}{t}\left(\frac{y}{x}\right)^{\nu} e^{-(x^2+y^2)/2t} I_\nu\left(\frac{xy}{t}\right) \mathbf{1}_{\{y>0\}}, \quad x, t > 0, \ \nu \geq 0.$$

and, second, that for $\rho \sim BES^{(0)}(x)$,

$$\mathrm{E}\left(e^{-v^2 \int_0^t ds/\rho_s^2} \mid \rho_t = r\right) = \frac{I_{|v|}(rx/t)}{I_0(rx/t)} \quad \forall\, v \in \mathbb{R}.$$

The first result is a direct consequence of the expression previously given for $f_t^\delta(x, y)$, while the second one follows from Girsanov's Theorem (Revuz and Yor 1999, p. 450; Yor 1992a). Only the case $\nu = 0$ is needed in the sequel.

First, let us state and prove the result due to Lamperti:

Let $B \sim$ BM, $\delta \geq 2$ and $\nu = \delta/2 - 1$. There exists $\rho \sim$ BES$^\delta(1)$ such that

$$e^{\nu t + B_t} = \rho_{A_t^{(\nu)}}, \quad A_t^{(\nu)} = \int_0^t e^{2(\nu s + B_s)}\, ds.$$

To prove the existence of such a ρ, observe that the process $A_t^{(\nu)}$ is continuous and strictly increasing in $t \geq 0$, $A_0^{(\nu)} = 0$, and, since $\nu \geq 0$, $\lim_{t\to\infty} A_t^{(\nu)} = \infty$. Hence, for any $u \geq 0$, one may define variable T_u by

$$A_{T_u}^{(\nu)} = u.$$

Differentiating each side with respect to u yields

$$\frac{dT_u}{du} = e^{-2(\nu s+B_s)}\Big|_{s=T_u}.$$

By Itô's formula,

$$e^{\nu t+B_t} = 1 + \left(\nu + \frac{1}{2}\right)\int_0^t e^{\nu s+B_s}\,ds + M_t, \quad M_t = \int_0^t e^{\nu s+B_s}\,dB_s$$

which implies

$$e^{\nu T_u+B_{T_u}} = 1 + \left(\nu + \frac{1}{2}\right)\int_0^{T_u} e^{\nu s+B_s}\,ds + \beta_u, \quad \beta_u = M_{T_u}.$$

The process M is a continuous martingale, $\langle M, M\rangle_t = A_t^{(\nu)}$, and $\langle M, M\rangle_\infty = \infty$. We may then use the well-known result, due to Dambis, Dubins, and Schwarz (see Revuz and Yor, 1999, p. 181), which says that if these conditions hold then M is a time-transformed Brownian motion, as the process $\{\beta_u; u \geq 0\}$ is Brownian motion and $M_t = \beta_{\langle M,M\rangle_t}$ for $t \geq 0$. (The filtrations of the Brownian motions B and β are however different.)

Moreover, from the formula for dT_u/du, we also find

$$\int_0^{T_u} e^{\nu s+B_s}\,ds = \int_0^u e^{\nu T_y+B_{T_y}}\,dT_y = \int_0^u \frac{dy}{e^{\nu T_y+B_{T_y}}}.$$

Hence, if we define $\rho_u = e^{\nu T_u+B_{T_u}}$, then

$$\rho_u = 1 + \left(\nu + \frac{1}{2}\right)\int_0^u \frac{dy}{\rho_y} + \beta_u,$$

which means that $\rho \sim \mathrm{BES}^{(\nu)}(1)$. Lamperti's relation is proved.

Next, let us derive the law of $A_{S_\lambda}^{(\nu)}$.

Step 1. First, find the joint law of $(e^{B_{S_\lambda}^{(\nu)}}, A_{S_\lambda}^{(\nu)})$. The idea is to look for a function $h(\cdot,\cdot)$ such that for any non-negative functions f, g,

$$\mathrm{E}[f(e^{B_{S_\lambda}^{(\nu)}})g(A_{S_\lambda}^{(\nu)})] = \iint f(x)g(y)h(x,y)\,dx\,dy.$$

The function $h(\cdot,\cdot)$ is then the PDF of $(e^{B_{S_\lambda}^{(\nu)}}, A_{S_\lambda}^{(\nu)})$.

By the Cameron–Martin theorem,

$$\mathrm{E}[f(e^{B_t^{(\nu)}})g(A_t^{(\nu)})] = e^{-\nu^2 t/2}\,\mathrm{E}[e^{\nu B_t} f(e^{B_t})g(A_t)],$$

and so

$$\mathrm{E}[f(e^{B^{(\nu)}_{S_\lambda}})g(A^{(\nu)}_{S_\lambda})] = \lambda\,\mathrm{E}\int_0^\infty e^{-\gamma^2 t/2} e^{\nu B_t} f(e^{B_t}) g(A_t)\,dt$$
$$= \lambda\,\mathrm{E}\int_0^\infty e^{-\gamma^2 T_u/2} e^{\nu B_{T_u}} f(e^{B_{T_u}}) g(A_{T_u})\,dT_u.$$

As we have seen before, $A^{(\nu)}_{T_u} = u$, and $\{\rho_u = e^{B_{T_u}}; u \geq 0\}$ is $\mathrm{BES}^{(0)}(1)$, so the last expression is equal to

$$\lambda\,\mathrm{E}\int_0^\infty e^{-\gamma^2 T_u/2} \rho_u^\nu f(\rho_u) g(u)\,dT_u$$
$$= \lambda\,\mathrm{E}\int_0^\infty e^{-(\gamma^2/2)\int_0^u ds/\rho_s^2} \rho_u^{\nu-2} f(\rho_u) g(u)\,du,$$

where we have used $dT_u/du = e^{-2B_{T_u}} = \rho_u^{-2}$.

Next, by conditioning on ρ_u,

$$\mathrm{E}\big[e^{-(\gamma^2/2)\int_0^u ds/\rho_s^2} \rho_u^{\nu-2} f(\rho_u)\big] = \mathrm{E}\big\{f(\rho_u)\rho_u^{\nu-2}\,\mathrm{E}\big[e^{-(\gamma^2/2)\int_0^u ds/\rho_s^2} \mid \rho_u\big]\big\}$$
$$= \mathrm{E}\left[f(\rho_u)\rho^{\nu-2}\frac{I_\gamma(\rho_u/u)}{I_0(\rho_u/u)}\right]$$
$$= \int_0^\infty f(r) r^{\nu-2}\frac{I_\gamma(r/u)}{I_0(r/u)} p_u^{(0)}(1,r)\,dr$$
$$= \frac{1}{u}\int_0^\infty f(r) r^{\nu-1} e^{-(1+r^2)/2u} I_\gamma\left(\frac{r}{u}\right) dr.$$

Hence,

$$\mathrm{E}[f(e^{B^{(\nu)}_{S_\lambda}})g(A^{(\nu)}_{S_\lambda})] = \int_0^\infty\int_0^\infty f(r) g(u) \frac{\lambda}{u} r^{\nu-1} e^{-(1+r^2)/2u} I_\gamma\left(\frac{r}{u}\right) dr\,du$$

and the joint distribution we are seeking is

$$\mathrm{P}\left(e^{B^{(\nu)}_{S_\lambda}} \in dr, A^{(\nu)}_{S_\lambda} \in du\right) = \frac{\lambda}{u} r^{\nu-1} e^{-(1+r^2)/2u} I_\gamma\left(\frac{r}{u}\right) dr\,du\,\mathbf{1}_{\{r,u>0\}}$$
$$= \lambda r^{\nu-2-\gamma} p_u^{(\gamma)}(1,r)\,dr\,du\,\mathbf{1}_{\{r>0\}}.$$

Step 2. From the preceding formula, we can find the PDF of $A^{(\nu)}_{S_\lambda}$ by integrating out r. This may be achieved by expressing the Bessel function as a series and then integrating term by term. Thus

$$\mathrm{P}\left(A_{S_\lambda}^{(\nu)} \in du\right) = \lambda(2u)^{(\nu-\gamma)/2-1}\frac{\Gamma([\nu+\gamma]/2)}{\Gamma(\gamma+1)}e^{-1/2u}\,{}_1F_1\left(\frac{\nu+\gamma}{2},\gamma+1,\frac{1}{2u}\right).$$

From the formula $e^{-z}{}_1F_1(a,b;z) = {}_1F_1(b-a,b;-z)$, this can be rewritten as

$$\mathrm{P}\left(A_{S_\lambda}^{(\nu)} \in du\right) = \lambda(2u)^{(\nu-\gamma)/2-1}\frac{\Gamma([\nu+\gamma]/2)}{\Gamma(\gamma+1)}\,{}_1F_1\left(\frac{\gamma-\nu}{2}+1,\gamma+1,-\frac{1}{2u}\right).$$

Now, if $B \sim \mathbf{Beta}(c,d)$ and $G \sim \mathbf{Gamma}(f,1)$ are independent, then, by conditioning on B, the PDF of B/G is seen to be

$$g(x) = \frac{x^{-f-1}\Gamma(c+d)}{\Gamma(c)\Gamma(d)\Gamma(f)}\int_0^1 e^{-y/x}y^{c+f-1}(1-y)^{d-1}\,dy\,\mathbf{1}_{\{x>0\}}.$$

From the well-known integral formula for confluent hypergeometric functions (Lebedev, 1972, p. 266),

$${}_1F_1(a,b;z) = \frac{\Gamma(b)}{\Gamma(a)\Gamma(b-a)}\int_0^1 e^{zt}t^{a-1}(1-t)^{b-a-1}\,dt, \quad \operatorname{Re} b > \operatorname{Re} a > 0,$$

the PDF of B/G can also be expressed as

$$g(x) = \frac{x^{-f-1}\Gamma(c+d)\Gamma(c+f)}{\Gamma(c)\Gamma(f)\Gamma(c+d+f)}\,{}_1F_1\left(c+f, c+d+f; -\frac{1}{x}\right)\mathbf{1}_{\{x>0\}}.$$

From this formula, it can be seen that the law of $A_{S_\lambda}^{(\nu)}$ is that of the ratio of a beta variable to an independent gamma variable, with the parameters given in the statement of the theorem.

We now turn to some applications of Yor's theorem.

Application 1: A second expression for the PDF of $A_t^{(\nu)}$ Based on the law of $A_{S_\lambda}^{(\nu)}$, Yor (1992a) found that

$$\begin{aligned}\mathrm{P}\left(A_t^{(\nu)} \in du \,\middle|\, B_t + \nu t = x\right) &= a_t(x,u)\,du \\ &= \frac{\sqrt{2\pi t}}{u}\,e^{x^2/2t-(1+e^{2x})/2u}\theta_{e^x/u}(t)\,du,\end{aligned}$$

where

$$\theta_r(t) = \frac{re^{\pi^2/2t}}{\sqrt{2\pi^3 t}}\int_0^\infty \exp\left(-\frac{y^2}{2t}\right)\exp(-r\cosh y)(\sinh y)\sin\left(\frac{\pi y}{t}\right)dy.$$

This means that the PDF of $A_t^{(\nu)}$ is the integral of $a_t(\cdot,u)$ times the normal density function with mean νt and variance t. The PDF is thus a double integral, with the function $\sin(\pi y/t)$ making the computation possibly more difficult when t is small.

Application 2: A relationship between $A_t^{(\nu)}$ and $A_t^{(-\nu)}$ The appearance of beta and gamma distributions in the law of $A_{S_\lambda}^{(\nu)}$ makes it possible to apply the following result (Dufresne, 1998):

*If all the variables below are independent, with $B_{r,s} \sim$ **Beta**(r,s), $G_r \sim$ **Gamma**$(r,1)$, $a,b,c > 0$, then*

$$\frac{G_a}{B_{b,a+c}} + G'_c \stackrel{\mathrm{d}}{=} \frac{G_{a+c}}{B_{b,a}}.$$

This identity implies the following result, but only for fixed t (Dufresne, 2001a); the more general result for processses was proved by Matsumoto and Yor (2001a).

*If $G_\nu \sim$ **Gamma**$(\nu,1)$ is independent of $\{A_t^{(\nu)}; t \geq 0\}$, then the proceses below have the same law:*

$$\left\{\frac{1}{2A_t^{(\nu)}} + G_\nu; t \geq 0\right\} \stackrel{\mathrm{d}}{=} \left\{\frac{1}{2A_t^{(-\nu)}}; t \geq 0\right\}.$$

The next result (Dufresne, 1990) was originally obtained by very different means, and has other proofs as well, but it is perhaps easiest to view it as a corollary of the relationship between IGBMs of different drifts: since $A_\infty^{(\nu)} = \infty$ when $\nu \geq 0$, we find

For any $\nu > 0$,

$$\frac{1}{2A_\infty^{(-\nu)}} \sim \mathbf{Gamma}(\nu, 1).$$

N.B. From the scaling property of Brownian motion, this is the same as

$$\frac{2}{\sigma^2}\left(\int_0^\infty e^{-\mu t + \sigma B_t}\, dt\right)^{-1} \sim \mathbf{Gamma}\left(\frac{2\mu}{\sigma^2}, 1\right) \quad \forall\, \mu, \sigma > 0.$$

Application 3: A formula for Asian options Geman and Yor (1993) derived the Laplace transform (in the time parameter) for continuous-averaging Asian option prices. The result was first proved directly from the connection between Bessel processes and IGBM and apparently only allowed $\nu \geq 0$, though both sides of the formula could easily be seen to be analytic in ν, which implies that the result holds for all ν. However, a much simpler proof is obtained (Dufresne, 2000, p. 409) if we take the law of $A_{S_\lambda}^{(\nu)}$ as given, and this shorter proof works for all ν. (Carr and Schröder (2003) extend the original proof in Geman and Yor (1993) to $\nu \in \mathbb{R}$.) Finally, observe that the Laplace transform below is in fact equivalent to Yor's theorem about the law of $A^{(\nu)}_{S_\lambda}$, because the function

$$k \to \mathrm{E}(X-k)_+ = \int_k^\infty \mathrm{P}(X>x)\,dx, \quad k \geq 0,$$

uniquely determines the distribution of a non-negative variable X. Here is the result by Geman and Yor (1993):

For all $\nu \in \mathbb{R}$, $q>0$, $\lambda > 2(\nu+1)$,

$$\int_0^\infty e^{-\lambda t}\,\mathrm{E}[(A_t^{(\nu)}-q)_+]\,dt = \frac{(2q)^{1-\beta}}{2\lambda(\alpha+1)\Gamma(\beta)}\int_0^1 u^{\beta-2}(1-u)^{\alpha+1}e^{-u/2q}\,du.$$

This formula is obtained by noting that its left hand side equals

$$\begin{aligned}
&\frac{1}{2}\int_0^\infty e^{-\lambda t}\,\mathrm{E}(2A_t^{(\nu)}-2q)_+\,dt \\
&\qquad = \frac{1}{2\lambda}\,\mathrm{E}(2A^{(\nu)}_{T_\lambda}-2q)_+ = \frac{1}{2\lambda}\,\mathrm{E}\left(\frac{B_{1,\alpha}}{G_\beta}-2q\right)_+ \\
&\qquad = -\frac{1}{2\lambda}\int_0^1\int_0^{u/2q}\left(\frac{u}{x}-2q\right)\frac{x^{\beta-1}}{\Gamma(\beta)}e^{-x}\,dx\,d_u(1-u)^\alpha \\
&\qquad = -\frac{1}{2\lambda(\alpha+1)\Gamma(\beta)}\int_0^1\int_0^{u/2q} x^{\beta-2}e^{-x}\,dx\,d_u\,(1-u)^{\alpha+1}.
\end{aligned}$$

A further integration by parts yields the result.

From the usual integral expression for the confluent hypergeometric function (noted previously), the formula in Theorem 2 is seen to be the same as

$$\begin{aligned}
&\int_0^\infty e^{-\lambda t}\,\mathrm{E}(A_t^\nu - q)_+\,dt \\
&\qquad = \frac{(2q)^{1-\beta}\Gamma(\alpha+1)}{2\lambda(\beta-1)\Gamma(\alpha+\beta+1)}\,{}_1F_1\left(\beta-1,\alpha+\beta+1,-\frac{1}{2q}\right).
\end{aligned}$$

The latter formula was pointed out by Donati-Martin et al. (2001).

An alternative expression for the Laplace transform of $\mathrm{E}(A_t^\nu - q)_+$ can be found in Schröder (1999); an explicit integral expression for $\mathrm{E}(A_t^\nu - q)_+$ is given in Schröder (2002).

Application 4: An extension of Pitman's $2M-X$ theorem The relationship between $A_t^{(\nu)}$ and $A_t^{(-\nu)}$ is one of the tools used to derive a generalization of Pitman's $2M-X$ theorem (Revuz and Yor 1999, p. 253; Matsumoto and Yor 1999, 2000, 2001b):

For $\nu \in \mathbb{R}$ and $c > 0$, the process

$$\left\{c\log\left(\int_0^t e^{2B_s^{(\nu)}/c}\,ds\right) - B_t^{(\nu)} - c\log(c^2); t \geq 0\right\}$$

is a diffusion process with infinitesimal generator

$$\frac{1}{2}\frac{d^2}{dx^2} + b^{\nu,c}(x)\frac{d}{dx}, \quad b^{\nu,c}(x) = \frac{d}{dx}\log K_{\nu c}(e^{-x/c}).$$

As $c \to 0+$, the process above tends to $\{2M_t^{(\nu)} - B_t^{(\nu)}; t \geq 0\}$ and $b^{\nu,c}(x)$ tends to $\nu\coth(\nu x)$, where $M^{(\nu)}$ is the runing maximum of $B^{(\nu)}$, which relate to the original results by Pitman and by Rogers and Pitman.

5. Another expression for the PDF of $A_t^{(\nu)}$

The moments $\mathrm{E}(A_t^{(\nu)})^r$ can be found by inverting

$$\mathrm{E}(A_{S_\lambda}^{(\nu)})^r = \mathrm{E}\left(\frac{B_{1,\alpha}}{2G_\beta}\right) = \frac{2^{-t}\Gamma(t+1)\Gamma(\alpha+1)\Gamma(\beta-t)}{\Gamma(\alpha+t+1)\Gamma(\beta)},$$

where $\alpha = \frac{1}{2}(\nu + \sqrt{2\lambda+\nu^2})$ and $\beta = \alpha - \nu$ are as before. This yields (Dufresne, 2000):

For all $\nu \in \mathbb{R}$ and $r > -\frac{3}{2}$,

$$\begin{aligned}
\mathrm{E}(A_t^{(\nu)})^r &= \frac{e^{-\nu^2 t/2}}{\sqrt{2\pi t^3}}\int_0^\infty y e^{-y^2/2t}\psi_\nu(r,y)\,dy \\
\psi_\nu(r,y) &= \frac{\Gamma(1+r)}{\Gamma(2+2r)}e^{-\nu y}(1-e^{-2y})^{1+2r} \\
&\qquad \times {}_2F_1(\nu+1+2r, 1+r, 2+2r; 1-e^{-2y}) \\
\psi_\nu(-1,y) &= \frac{\cosh[(\nu-1)y]}{\sinh(y)}.
\end{aligned}$$

Schröder (2000) has shown that the integral moments of $1/A_t^{(\nu)}$ may alternatively be expressed as theta integrals: for $n = 1, 2, \ldots,$

$$\mathrm{E}(A_t^{(\nu)})^{-n} = e^{-\nu^2/2}\sum_{k=1}^{n} a_{n,k}\,T_k(t)$$

with

$$T_k(t) = 2^{-3/2}\int_0^\infty \vartheta\left(\frac{\nu}{2} \mid y\right)\frac{y^{k-1}}{(yt+\frac{1}{2})^{k+1/2}}\,dy,$$

where ϑ is Riemann's theta function.

It is easy to see that $\mathrm{E}\exp(sA_t^{(\nu)}) = \infty$ for all $s > 0$, and it has been proved that the distribution of $A_t^{(\nu)}$ is not determined by its moments (Hörfelt, 2004); this makes sense intuitively, as the same situation prevails for the lognormal distribution. By contrast, and a little surprisingly, $\mathrm{E}\exp(s/2A_t^{(\nu)}) < \infty$ if $s < 1$ (Dufresne, 2001b). This implies that the distribution of $1/A_t^{(\nu)}$ is determined by its moments. These facts suggest there might be some advantage in concentrating on $1/A_t^{(\nu)}$, rather than on $A_t^{(\nu)}$. It can be shown (Dufresne, 2000) that the PDF of $A_t^{(\nu)}$ can be expressed as a Laguerre series in which the weights are combinations of the moments of $1/A_t^{(\nu)}$: a third expression for the PDF of $A_t^{(\nu)}$ is

$$g_\nu(t,x) = 2^{-b-1}c^{a+1}x^{-b-2}e^{-c/2x}\sum_{n=0}^{\infty} a_n(t)L_n^a(c/2x),$$

where $a > -1$, $b \in \mathbb{R}$, $0 < c < e^{-\nu_- t}$, and

$$\begin{aligned} a_n(t) &= \frac{n!}{\Gamma(n+a+1)}\,\mathrm{E}\,L_n^a\left(\frac{c}{2A_t^{(\nu)}}\right) \\ &= \sum_{k=0}^{n}\frac{n!(-c)^k}{\Gamma(k+a+1)k!(n-k)!}\,\mathrm{E}(2A_t^{(\nu)})^{-(a-b+k)}. \end{aligned}$$

Similar series are given in Dufresne (2000) for Asian option prices. The Laguerre series are further improved by Schröder (2000).

The hypergeometric PDE The appearance of hypergeometric functions is not fortuitous, as the next result shows (Dufresne, 2001b):

Let $h^{\nu,r}(s,t) := e^{\nu^2 t/2}\,\mathrm{E}(A_t^{(\nu)})^{-r}e^{s/2A_t^{(\nu)}}$. *Then* $h = h^{\nu,r}$ *satisfies the PDE*

$$-\tfrac{1}{2}h_t = -\tfrac{1}{4}(\nu-2r)^2h + [r + (\nu - 2r - 1)s]h_s + s(1-s)h_{ss},$$

(subscripts indicate partial derivatives).

The right hand side is the Gauss hypergeometric operator. Properties of the law of $A_t^{(\nu)}$ may be obtained from this PDE; we cite two: a relation between $A_t^{(\nu)}$ for different drifts ν, and a fourth expression for the density of $1/A_t^{(\nu)}$.

For all $\mu, r \in \mathbb{R}$, $\Re(s) < 1$, $t > 0$,

$$h^{\mu,r}(s,t) = (1-s)^{\mu-r}h^{2r-\mu,r}(s,t).$$

This property includes $1/2A_t^{(\mu)} + G_\mu \stackrel{\mathrm{d}}{=} 1/2A_t^{(-\mu)}$ as a particular case.

Let $\nu \in \mathbb{R}$, $t, x > 0$ and

$$q(y,t) = \frac{e^{\pi^2/8t - y^2/2t}}{\pi\sqrt{2t}} \cosh y.$$

The PDF of $1/(2A_t^{(\nu)})$ is $g_\nu(t,x) = e^{-\nu^2 t/2}\tilde{g}_\nu(t,x)$ with

$$\tilde{g}_\nu(t,x) = 2^{-\nu}x^{-(\nu+1)/2}\int_{-\infty}^{\infty} e^{-x\cosh^2 y} q(y,t)\cos\left(\frac{\pi}{2}\left(\frac{y}{t}-\nu\right)\right) \times H_\nu(\sqrt{x}\sinh y)\,dy.$$

Here H_ν is the Hermite function (a generalization of the Hermite polynomials, see Lebedev (1972, Chapter 10)). An interesting aspect of this expression is that it boils down to a single integral when $\nu = 0, 1, 2, \ldots$. Other equivalent expressions are:

(a) If $\nu \neq -1, -3, \ldots$:

$$\begin{aligned}
&\tilde{g}_\nu(t,x)\\
&= 2x^{-(\nu+1)/2}e^{-x}\frac{\Gamma([\nu+1]/2)}{\Gamma(\frac{1}{2})}\int_0^{\infty} q(y,t)\cos\left(\frac{\pi y}{2t}\right)\int_0^{\infty} q(y,t)\cos\left(\frac{\pi y}{2t}\right)\\
&\qquad \times {}_1F_1\left(\frac{\nu+1}{2},\frac{1}{2};-x\sinh^2 y\right)dy\\
&= 2x^{-(\nu+1)/2}\frac{\Gamma([\nu+1]/2)}{\Gamma(\frac{1}{2})}\int_0^{\infty} e^{-x\cosh^2 y}q(y,t)\cos\left(\frac{\pi y}{2t}\right)\\
&\qquad \times {}_1F_1\left(-\frac{\nu}{2},\frac{1}{2};x\sinh^2 yt\right)dy.
\end{aligned}$$

(b) If $\nu \neq -2, -4, \ldots$:

$$\begin{aligned}
&\tilde{g}_\nu(t,x)\\
&= 2x^{-\nu/2}e^{-x}\frac{\Gamma(\nu/2+1)}{\Gamma(\frac{3}{2})}\int_0^{\infty} q(y,t)\sinh y\sin\left(\frac{\pi y}{2t}\right)\\
&\qquad \times {}_1F_1\left(\frac{\nu}{2}+1,\frac{3}{2};-x\sinh^2 y\right)dy\\
&= 2x^{-\nu/2}\frac{\Gamma(\nu/2+1)}{\Gamma(\frac{3}{2})}\int_0^{\infty} e^{-x\cosh^2 y}q(y,t)\sinh y\sin\left(\frac{\pi y}{2t}\right)\\
&\qquad \times {}_1F_1\left(\frac{1-\nu}{2},\frac{3}{2};x\sinh^2 y\right)dy.
\end{aligned}$$

References

Carmona, P., Petit, F., and Yor, M. (1997). On the distribution and asymptotic results for exponential functionals of Lévy processes. In: *Exponential Functionals and Principal Values Related to Brownian Motion*, pp. 73 – 121. Biblioteca de la Revista Matemática Iberoamericana, Madrid.

Carr, P. and Schröder, M. (2003). *Bessel Processes, the Integral of Geometric Brownian Motion, and Asian Options.* Working paper, University of Mannheim.

Donati-Martin, C., Ghomrasni, R., and Yor, M. (2001). On certain Markov processes attached to exponential functionals of Brownian motion; application to Asian options. *Revista Matematica Iberoamericana*, 17:179 – 193.

Dufresne, D. (1989). Weak convergence of random growth processes with applications to insurance. *Insurance: Mathematics and Economics*, 8:187 – 201.

Dufresne, D. (1990). The distribution of a perpetuity, with applications to risk theory and pension funding. *Scandinavian Actuarial Journal*, 1990:39 – 79.

Dufresne, D. (1998). Algebraic properties of beta and gamma distributions, and applications. *Advances in Applied Mathematics*, 20:285 – 299.

Dufresne, D. (2000). Laguerre series for Asian and other options. *Mathematical Finance*, 10:407 – 428.

Dufresne, D. (2001a). An affine property of the reciprocal Asian process. *Osaka Journal of Mathematics*, 38:379 – 381.

Dufresne, D. (2001b). The integral of geometric Brownian motion. *Advances in Applied Probability*, 33:223 – 241.

Geman, H. and Yor, M. (1993). Bessel processes, Asian options and perpetuities. *Mathematical Finance*, 3:349 – 375.

Hörfelt, P. (2004) *The Integral of a Geometric Brownian Motion is Indeterminate by Its Moments.* Working paper. Fraunhofer – Chalmers Research Centre for Industrial Mathematics, Göteborg, Sweden.

Lamperti, J.W. (1972). Semi-stable Markov processes. *Zeitschrift für Wahrscheinlichkeitstheorie und Verwandte Gebiete*, 22:205 – 225.

Lebedev, N.N. (1972). *Special Functions and their Applications.* Dover, New York.

Linetsky, V. (2001). *Spectral Expansions for Asian (Average Price) Options.* Working paper, Department of Industrial Engineering and Management Sciences, Northwestern University.

Matsumoto, H. and Yor, M. (1999). A version of Pitman's $2M - X$ theorem for geometric Brownian motions. *Comptes Rendus de l'Académie des Sciences. Série I*, 328:1067–1074.

Matsumoto, H. and Yor, M. (2000). An analogue of Pitman's $2M - X$ theorem for exponential Wiener functionals. Part I: A time-inversion approach. *Nagoya Mathematical Journal*, 159:125–166.

Matsumoto, H. and Yor, M. (2001a). A relationship between Brownian motions with opposite drifts via certain enlargments of the Brownian filtration. *Osaka Journal of Mathematics*, 38:383–398.

Matsumoto, H. and Yor, M. (2001b). An analogue of Pitman's $2M - X$ theorem for exponential Wiener functionals. Part II: The role of the generalized inverse Gaussian laws. *Nagoya Mathematical Journal*, 162:65–86.

Monthus, C. and Comtet, A. (1994). On the flux in a one-dimensional disordered system. *Journal de Physique. I*, 4:635–653.

Protter, P. (1990). *Stochastic Integration and Differential Equations: A New Approach.* Springer-Verlag, New York.

Ramakrishnan, A. (1954). A stochastic model of a fluctuating density field. *The Astrophysical Journal* 119:682–685.

Revuz, D. and Yor, M. (1999) *Continuous Martingales and Brownian Motion* (Third Edition). Springer-Verlag, Berlin.

Schröder, M. (1999). *On the Valuation of Arithmetic-Average Asian Options: Integral Representations.* Working paper, University of Mannheim.

Schröder, M. (2000). *On the Valuation of Arithmetic-Average Asian Options: Laguerre Series and Theta Integrals.* Working paper, University of Mannheim.

Schröder, M. (2002). *Analytical Ramifications of Derivatives Valuation: Asian Options and Special Functions.* Working paper, University of Mannheim.

Su, Y. and Fu, M.C. (2000). Importance sampling in derivative securities pricing. *Proceedings of the 2000 Winter Simulation Conference*, pp. 587–596.

Vázquez-Abad, F. and Dufresne, D. (1998). Accelerated simulation for pricing Asian options. *Winter Simulation Conference Proceedings*, pp. 1493–1500.

Wong, E. (1964). The construction of a class of stationary Markoff processes. In: Bellman, R. (ed.), *Sixteenth Symposium in Applied Mathematics — Stochatic Processess in Mathematical Physics and Engineering*, pp. 264–276. American Mathematical Society, Providence, RI.

Yor, M. (1992a). On some exponential functionals of Brownian motion. *Advances in Applied Probability*, 24:509 – 531.

Yor, M. (1992b). Sur les lois des fonctionnelles exponentielles du mouvement brownien, considérées en certains instants aléatoires. *Comptes Rendus de l'Académie des Sciences. Série I. Mathématique*, 314:951 – 956.

Yor, M. (2001) *Exponential Functionals of Brownian Motion and Related Processes.* Springer-Verlag, New York.

Chapter 3

DYNAMIC MANAGEMENT OF PORTFOLIOS WITH TRANSACTION COSTS UNDER TYCHASTIC UNCERTAINTY

Jean-Pierre Aubin
Dominique Pujal
Patrick Saint-Pierre

Abstract We use in this chapter the viability/capturability approach for studying the problem of dynamic valuation and management of a portfolio with transaction costs in the framework of tychastic control systems (or dynamical games against nature) instead of stochastic control systems. Indeed, the very definition of the guaranteed valuation set can be formulated directly in terms of guaranteed viable-capture basin of a dynamical game.

Hence, we shall "compute" the guaranteed viable-capture basin and find a formula for the valuation function involving an underlying criterion, use the tangential properties of such basins for proving that the valuation function is a solution to Hamilton-Jacobi-Isaacs partial differential equations. We then derive a dynamical feedback providing an adjustment law regulating the evolution of the portfolios obeying viability constraints until it achieves the given objective in finite time. We shall show that the Pujal – Saint-Pierre viability/capturability algorithm applied to this specific case provides both the valuation function and the associated portfolios.

Outline The first section is an introduction stating the problem and describing the main results presented. It is intended to readers who are not interested in the mathematical technicalities of the viability approach to financial dynamic valuation and management problems. The second section outlines the viability/capturability strategy for sketching the proofs of the main results

1. Introduction and survey of the main results

1.1 Statement of the problems

We shall describe the main results of this chapter in the framework of the dynamic valuation and management of a portfolio replicating European, American or Kairotic options (options exercised at the first instant when the value of the portfolio is above the contingent value), postponing the general case in the next section.

Let $n+1$ financial assets $i = 0, 1, \ldots, n$, the first one being non-risky (a *bond*) and the n other ones being risky assets (*stocks*).

The components of the variable $x := (x_0, x_1, \ldots, x_n) \in \mathbb{R}^{n+1}$ are the price of the non risky asset (*bond*), labelled $i = 0$, and the prices of the n risky assets (*stocks*), labelled $i = 1, \ldots, n$, usually denoted by $S := (S_0, S_1, \ldots, S_n)$ in the financial literature. A *portfolio* is an element

$$p := (p_0, p_1, \ldots, p_n) \in \mathbb{R}^{n+1}$$

describing the number of shares of assets $i = 0, 1, \ldots, n$. The associated *capital* (or the value of the portfolio) y, usually denoted by W in the financial literature,[1] can be written

$$y := \langle p, x \rangle = \sum_{i=0}^{n} p_i x_i.$$

Assume that

(1) the uncertain evolution of prices $x(t) \in \mathbb{R}^{n+1}$ of financial assets is known, rather, forecasted,

(2) *constraints*

  (a) $p(t) \in D\big(t, x(t)\big)$ on the portfolios $p(t)$,

  (b) $p'(t) \in P\big(t, x(t), p(t)\big)$ on the velocities $p'(t)$ of portfolios $p(t) \in \mathbb{R}^{n+1}$ (describing *transaction costs*, for instance)

are given (*constraints* on the portfolio can be integrated in the constraints on their velocities by setting $P(t,x,p) = \emptyset$ whenever $p \notin D(t,x)$).

Let us consider a given *time-independent function* $\mathbf{u} : \mathbb{R}^{n+1} \mapsto \mathbb{R} \cup \{+\infty\}$, called the *contingent claim*, and an *exercise time* T. The general

[1] In several financial studies, a *policy (of capital allocation)* is an element $\pi := (\pi_0, \pi_1, \ldots, \pi_n)$ where the component π_i defined by $p_i x_i = \pi_i \langle p, x \rangle$ denotes the proportion of the capital allocated to asset i are used as variables. They are defined naturally only when the capital $y := \langle p, x \rangle$ is strictly positive. We shall not use this definition because *imposing constraints on the actual number of shares of assets seems to us more realistic than imposing constraints on the proportions of shares.*

problem of dynamic portfolio management is to *find an evolution law of the portfolio $p(\cdot)$ such that, whatever the uncertain evolution of the prices, one of the following option rules*[2] is satisfied: We require that for the *exercise time* T, the option is exercised

$$\begin{cases} \text{(i)} & \text{at } \textit{exercise time } T\text{:} \\ & \displaystyle\sum_{i=0}^{n} p_i(T)x_i(T) \geq \mathbf{u}(x(T)) \qquad \text{(European Option)} \\ \text{(ii)} & \text{at any time during the whole } \textit{exercise period } [0,T]\text{:} \\ & \forall t \in [0,T],\ \displaystyle\sum_{i=0}^{n} p_i(t)x_i(t) \geq \mathbf{u}(x(t)) \quad \text{(American Option)} \\ \text{(iii)} & \text{at the first opportune time (kairos) } t^* \in [0,T]\text{:} \\ & \exists t^* \in [0,T] \text{ such that } \displaystyle\sum_{i=0}^{n} p_i(t^*)x_i(t^*) \geq \mathbf{u}(x(t^*)) \\ & \qquad \text{(Kairotic Option)} \end{cases} \tag{3.1}$$

Our ultimate goal is to construct

(1) the **valuation function** $(T,x,p) \mapsto V^\sharp(T,x,p) \in \mathbb{R} \cup \{+\infty\}$ associating with the exercise time T, the initial price x of the shares and the initial portfolio the smallest initial capital $V^\sharp(T,x,p)$ guaranteeing that one of the above rules is satisfied whatever the uncertainty
(2) and above all, **the regulation map** $\Gamma : \mathbb{R}_+ \times \mathbb{R}^{n+1} \times \mathbb{R}^{n+1} \rightsquigarrow \mathbb{R}^{n+1}$ providing the a posteriori *adjustment law*

$$p'(t) \in \Gamma(T-t, x(t), p(t))$$

governing the evolution of the portfolio necessary to solve the given management problem whatever the uncertainty.

We shall answer these questions by solving a whole family of rules containing as particular cases the three rules (3.1), use the "epigraphical approach" to transform the inequalities involved in the above rules as a viability/capturability problem and then, use some results of viability theory not only for theoretical results, but also to design algorithms providing the valuation function and the regulation map, bypassing the numerical computation of solutions to analogues of Black and Scholes partial differential equations.

[2]These rules are applied in finance theory for determining the portfolios replicating options when the function $\mathbf{u}$ is regarded as a claim function.

1.2 Underlying viability/capturability problem

Indeed, in order to treat the three rules (3.1) as particular cases of a more general framework, we introduce two nonnegative extended functions (functions taking infinite values) **b** (constraint function) and **c** (objective function) satisfying

$$\forall(t,x,p) \in \mathbb{R}_+ \times \mathbb{R}_+^{n+1} \times \mathbb{R}^{n+1}, \quad 0 \leq \mathbf{b}(t,x,p) \leq \mathbf{c}(t,x,p) \leq +\infty$$

and

$$\forall p \notin D(b,x), \quad \mathbf{b}(t,x,p) = +\infty.$$

For example, we can associate with the initial function **u** the extended function $\mathbf{u}_\infty$ defined by

$$\mathbf{u}_\infty(t,x,p) := \begin{cases} \mathbf{u}(x,p) & \text{if } t = 0 \\ +\infty & \text{if not} \end{cases} \tag{3.2}$$

and introduce the extended function **0** defined by

$$\mathbf{0}(t,x,p) = \begin{cases} 0 & \text{if } t \geq 0, \\ +\infty & \text{if not.} \end{cases}$$

We replace the requirements (3.1) by the family of rules

$$\begin{cases} \text{(i)} \ \ \forall t \in [0,t^*], y(t) \geq \mathbf{b}(T-t, x(t), p(t)) & \text{(dynamical constraint)} \\ \text{(ii)} \ y(t^*) \geq \mathbf{c}(T-t^*, x(t^*), p(t^*)) & \text{(final objective)} \end{cases} \tag{3.3}$$

associated with pairs of extended functions $(\mathbf{b},\mathbf{c})$.

Since extended functions can take infinite values, we are able to acclimate many examples. In particular, *the three rules* (3.1) *associated with a same function* $\mathbf{u}$: $\mathbb{R}^{n+1} \times \mathbb{R}^{n+1} \mapsto \mathbb{R} \cup \{+\infty\}$ *can be written in the form* (3.3) *by adequate choices of pairs* $(\mathbf{b},\mathbf{c})$ *of functions associated with* $\mathbf{u}$:

$$\begin{cases} \text{(i)} \ \displaystyle\sum_{i=0}^{n} p_i(T)x_i(T) \geq \mathbf{u}(x(T)) & \text{(European Option)} \\ \quad \text{by taking } \mathbf{b}(t,x,p) := \mathbf{0}(t,x,p) \text{ and } \mathbf{c}(t,x,p) = \mathbf{u}_\infty(t,x,p) & \\ \text{(ii)} \ \forall t \in [0,T], \displaystyle\sum_{i=0}^{n} p_i(t)x_i(t) \geq \mathbf{u}(x(t)) & \text{(American Option)} \\ \quad \text{by taking } \mathbf{b}(t,x,p) := \mathbf{u}(x,p) \text{ and } \mathbf{c}(t,x,p) := \mathbf{u}_\infty(t,x,p) & \\ \text{(iii)} \ \exists t^* \in [0,T] \text{ such that } \displaystyle\sum_{i=0}^{n} p_i(t^*)x_i(t^*) \geq \mathbf{u}(x(t^*)) & \text{(Kairotic Option)} \\ \quad \text{by taking } \mathbf{b}(t,x,p) := \mathbf{0}(t,x,p) \text{ and } \mathbf{c}(t,x,p) = \mathbf{u}(x,p) & \end{cases} \tag{3.4}$$

The case of prescribed time is obtained in the following way:

LEMMA 3.1 *Problems with prescribed final time (as in portfolios replicating European and American options) are obtained with objective functions satisfying the condition*

$$\forall t > 0, \quad \mathbf{c}(t, x, p) := +\infty.$$

In this case, $t^* = T$ and condition (3.3) boils down to

$$\begin{cases} \text{(i)} \ \ \forall t \in [0, T], \ \ y(t) \geq b\big(T - t, x(t), p(t)\big) \\ \text{(ii)} \ \ y(T) \geq c\big(0, x(T), p(T)\big). \end{cases}$$

Proof. Indeed, since $y(t^*)$ is finite and since $\mathbf{c}\big(T - t^*, x(t^*), p(t^*)\big)$ is infinite whenever $T - t^* > 0$, we infer from inequality (3.3)(ii) that $T - t^*$ must be equal to 0. □

DEFINITION 3.1 *The* epigraph *of an extended function* $\mathbf{v}: \mathbb{R}_+ \times X \times X \mapsto \mathbb{R}_+ \cup \{+\infty\}$ *is defined by*

$$\mathcal{E}p(\mathbf{v}) := \{(x, \lambda) \in X \times \mathbb{R} \mid \mathbf{v}(x) \leq \lambda\}.$$

We recall that *an extended function* $\mathbf{v}$ *is convex (resp. positively homogeneous) if and only if its epigraph is convex (resp. a cone)* and that the epigraph of $\mathbf{v}$ is closed if and only if $\mathbf{v}$ is lower semicontinuous:

$$\forall x \in X, \mathbf{v}(x) = \liminf_{y \to x} \mathbf{v}(y).$$

We can translate the viability/capturability conditions (3.3) in the following geometric form:

LEMMA 3.2 *An evolution $t \mapsto \big(T - t, x(t), p(t)\big)$ satisfies viability/capturability conditions* (3.3) *if and only if it is* viable *in the epigraph $\mathcal{E}p(\mathbf{b})$ until it* captures *the target $\mathcal{E}p(\mathbf{c})$: This means that there exists a finite time $t^\star \geq 0$ such that*

$$\begin{cases} \text{(i)} \ \ \big(T - t^\star, x(t^\star), p(t^\star), y(t^\star)\big) \in \mathcal{E}p(\mathbf{c}) \\ \text{(ii)} \ \forall t \in [0, t^\star], \ \ (T - t, x(t), p(t), y(t)) \in \mathcal{E}p(\mathbf{b}). \end{cases} \tag{3.5}$$

The reformulation of the rules (3.3) describing the nature of the financial problem in this framework allows us to use viability theory: In a nutshell, we shall prove that once the dynamics governing the evolutions of prices and portfolios are given, the epigraphs of the "valuation function" of the portfolio is the "capture basin" of the target (epigraph

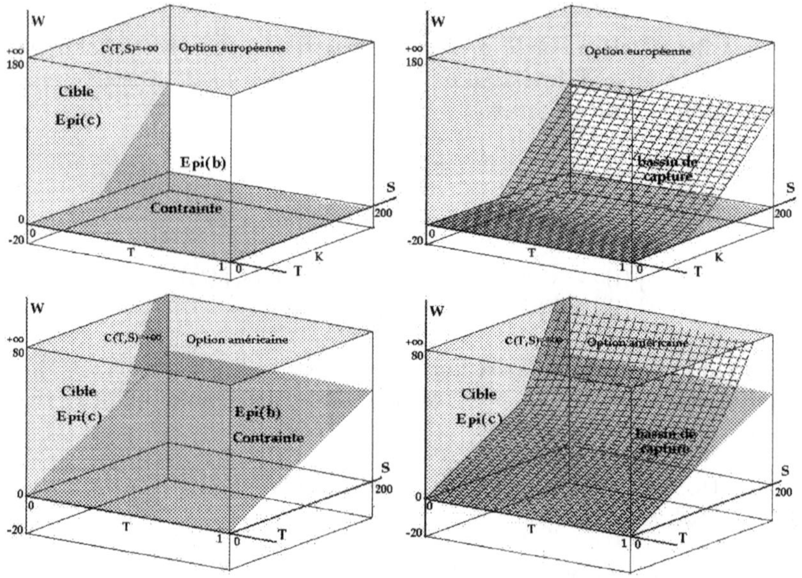

Figure 3.1. Epigraphs of Valuation Functions of portfolios are capture basin of a target (epigraph of function) viable in a constrained set (epigraph of another function $c\colon \mathbb{R}_+ \times X \times X \mapsto \mathbb{R}_+ \cup \{+\infty\}$) viable in a constrained set (epigraph of another function $b\colon \mathbb{R}_+ \times X \times X \mapsto \mathbb{R}_+ \cup \{+\infty\}$) satisfying $\forall (t,x) \in \mathbb{R}_+ \times X$, $0 \le \mathbf{b}(t,x) \le \mathbf{c}(t,x) \le +\infty$ This illustrated here in the case of European and American Options without transaction costs.

of a function $c\colon \mathbb{R}_+ \times X \times X \mapsto \mathbb{R}_+ \cup \{+\infty\}$) viable in a constrained environment (epigraph of another function $b : \mathbb{R}_+ \times X \times X \mapsto \mathbb{R}_+ \cup \{+\infty\}$) satisfying

$$\forall (t,x) \in \mathbb{R}_+ \times X, \quad 0 \le \mathbf{b}(t,x) \le \mathbf{c}(t,x) \le +\infty.$$

The terms "valuation function" and "capture basin" will be defined in due time. The "epigraphical approach" consisting in using the properties of the epigraphs of a function was proposed by J.-J. Moreau and R.T. Rockafellar in convex analysis in the early 1960's,[3] and has been used in optimal control by H. Frankowska in a series of papers Frankowska (1989, 1993) and Aubin and Frankowska (1996) for studying the value function of optimal control problems and characterize it as generalized

[3]see for instance Aubin and Frankowska (1990) and Rockafellar and Wets (1997) among many other references.

solution (episolutions and/or viscosity solutions) of (first-order) Hamilton–Jacobi–Bellman equations, in Aubin (1981); Aubin and Cellina (1984); Aubin (1986, 1991) for characterizing and constructing Lyapunov functions, in Cardaliaguet (1994, 1996, 2000) for characterizing the minimal time function, in Pujal (2000) in finance and other authors since. This is this approach that we adopt and adapt here, since the concepts of "capturability of a target" and of "viability" of a constrained set allows us to study this problem under a new light (see for instance Aubin (1991) and Aubin (1997) for economic applications) for studying the evolution of the state of a tychastic control system subjected to viability constraints in control theory and in tychastic control systems — or dynamical games against nature or robust control (see Quincampoix, 1992; Cardaliaguet, 1994, 1996, 2000; Cardaliaguet et al., 1999. Numerical algorithms for finding viability kernels have been designed in Saint-Pierre, 1994 and adapted to our type of problems in Pujal, 2000 and Pujal and Saint-Pierre, 2001).

1.3 The dynamics

1.3.1 Dynamics of prices. As in papers Bernhard (2000b,c, 2002); Pujal (2000) and Pujal and Saint-Pierre (2001) that appeared simultaneously and independently at the end of the year 2000, as well as earlier contributions Olsder (1999); Runggaldier (2000), the evolution of the prices is governed by

$$\forall i = 1, \ldots, n, \; x_i'(t) = x_i(t)\rho_i\big(x(t), v(t)\big) \qquad \text{where } v(t) \in Q(t, x(t), p(t)) \subset \mathbb{R}^m$$

where the set-valued map $Q: \mathbb{R}_+ \times \mathbb{R}^{n+1} \times \mathbb{R}^{n+1} \rightsquigarrow \mathbb{R}^m$, the *tychastic map* associating with any triple (t, x, p) a set of elements $v \in Q(t, x, p)$ regarded as *tyches (or perturbations, disturbances)*, one of the Greek words encapsulating the concept of chance, personified by the Goddess Tyche. The size of the tychastic map represents a kind of "tychastic volatility", called *"versatility"*.

The tychastic map (that could be a fuzzy subset, as it is advocated in Aubin and Dordan, 1996) provides an alternative mathematical translation of evolution under uncertainty parallel to the usual mathematical translation by a diffusion in the framework of stochastic differential equations. The size of the subsets $Q(t, x, p)$ captures mathematically the concept of "tychastic versatility" — instead of "stochastic volatility": The larger the subsets $Q(t, x, p)$, the more "tychastic" the system.

Controlling a system for solving a problem (such as viability, capturability, intertemporal optimality) whatever the perturbation is the branch

Charles (Sanders) Peirce (1839 – 1914) introduced the concept of *tychastic evolution* in a paper published in 1893 under the title *evolutionary love.*
"Three modes of evolution have thus been brought before us: evolution by fortuitous variation, evolution by mechanical necessity, and evolution by creative love. We may term them tychastic evolution, or tychasm, anancastic evolution, or anancasm, and agapastic evolution, or agapasm." In this paper, Peirce associates the concept of *anancastic evolution* with the Greek concept of necessity, *ananke*, anticipating the "chance and necessity" framework that motivated viability theory. Peirce was a logician and a prolific and profound philosopher interested in evolution theory after Charles Darwin and Herbert Spencer (1820-1903), introduced many concepts, such as *abduction* ("process of thought capable of producing no conclusion more definite than a conjecture") and *semiotics* (the "general science of the nature of signs").

State-dependent uncertainty can also be translated mathematically by parameters on which actors, agents, decision makers, etc. have no controls. These parameters are often perturbations, disturbances (as in "robust control" or "differential games against nature") or more generally, *tyches* (meaning "chance" in classical Greek, from the Goddess Tyche) ranging over a state-dependent *tychastic map.* They could be called "random variables" if this vocabulary were not already confiscated by probabilists. This is why we borrow the term of *tychastic evolution* to Charles Peirce who introduced it in a paper published in 1893 under the title *evolutionary love.* One can prove that stochastic viability is a (very) particular case of tychastic viability. The size of the tychastic map captures mathematically the concept of *"versatility (tychastic volatility)"*— instead of "(stochastic) volatility": *The larger the graph of the tychastic map, the more "versatile" the system.*

of dynamical games (dynamical games against nature) known among control specialists as "robust control", that we propose to call "tychastic control" in contrast to "stochastic control," where such properties must be satisfied "almost surely."

However, these apparently different two choices sharing a same philosophy can be reconciled, since there is a deep link between tychastic and stochastic problems for viability/capturability issues. Indeed, thanks to the equivalence formulas between Itô and Stratonovitch stochastic integrals and to the Strook and Varadhan "Support Theorem" (see for instance Doss, 1977), and under convenient assumptions, stochastic viability problems are equivalent to invariance problems for tychastic systems (see Aubin and Doss, 2001). By the way, this is in this framework of invariance under tychastic systems associated with stochastic problems that stochastic invariance issues in mathematical finance are studied (Bjork, 1998; Filipovic, 1999; Jachimiak, 1996; Milian, 1995, 1997, 1998; Tessitore and Zabczyk, 1998; Zabczyk, 1996, 1999, etc.).

1.3.2 Dynamics of portfolios. From the view point of a manager, a *strategy* or a *decision* can be regarded as the velocity $p'(t)$ of his/her portfolio, describing how and how fast he/she modifies the portfolio.

We assume that the available velocities $p'(t) = u(t)$ of the portfolios, chosen as control $u(t)$, range over a subset $P(t, x(t), p(t))$, where the set-valued map $P\colon \mathbb{R}_+ \times \mathbb{R}^{n+1} \times \mathbb{R}^{n+1} \rightsquigarrow \mathbb{R}^m$ is regarded as a *cybernetic map*.[4] Observe that this map encapsulates time/price-dependent constraints on portfolios translated by the condition $p(t) \in D(t, x(t))$ where

$$D(t,x) := \{p \text{ such that } P(t,x,p) \neq \emptyset\}.$$

For instance, *transaction costs*, balancing the variations resulting from the buy/sell operations on the bond and on the risky asset, can be taken into account in the definition of the set-valued map P, that can take the

[4]In tychastic control problems, we have two kinds of uncertainties, one described by the set-valued map Q, describing tychastic uncertainty, and the one described by the set-valued map P, encapsulating the concept of *cybernetic uncertainty*, providing a set of *available regulation parameters (regulons)*, the size of it describing the *"redundancy"* of the cybernetic map. The larger the cybernetic map P, the more redundant is the system to find a regulation regulon or a control to satisfy a given property whatever the perturbation in Q. In some sense, the "cybernetic map" P is an antidote to cure the negative effects of unknown tyches provided by the tychastic map Q. Redundancy compensates for versatility ... or plain ignorance

form

$$P(t,x,p) := \begin{cases} \{u \in \mathbb{R}^{n+1} \mid |u_i| \le \gamma_i \text{ and} \\ \quad \sum_{i=1}^{n} (u_i x_i + \delta_i(|u_i|, x_i)) = 0\} & \text{if } p \in D(t,x) \\ \emptyset & \text{if not.} \end{cases}$$

where the functions δ_i are the transaction cost functions and bounds γ_i on the rates of exchanges of shares describe some inertia in the transaction. Other behavioral constraints can be taken into account in the cybernetic map.

The self-financing assumption meaning that it is forbidden to borrow external income to modify the capital of the portfolio, i.e., that the capital of portfolio can change only by financing it with revenues obtained by selling and buying assets (case when $\delta_i = 0$ and $\gamma_i = \infty$) is described by

$$P(t,x,p) = \{u \in \mathbb{R}^{n+1} | \langle u, x\rangle = 0\}.$$

In this case, there is no constraint on the norm of the velocities of the prices, that can be as large as wanted, as long as $\langle u, x\rangle = 0$, and the influence of the velocity $p'(t)$ disappears from the dynamics of the capital. We are in the simpler case case studied by Pujal (2000); Pujal and Saint-Pierre (2001).

1.3.3 Dynamics of capital. Knowing the tychastic evolution of prices and the contingent evolution of portfolios describing the behavioral rule of the investor, we deduce the evolution of the capital:

$$\begin{cases} y'(t) = \langle p(t), x'(t)\rangle + \langle p'(t), x(t)\rangle \\ = \sum_{i=0}^{n} p_i(t) x_i(t) \rho_i(x(t), v(t)) + \langle u(t), x(t)\rangle \\ = y(t)\rho_0(x(t)) - \sum_{i=1}^{n} p_i(t) x_i(t) (\rho_0(x_0(t)) - \rho_i(x(t), v(t))) + \langle u(t), x(t)\rangle. \end{cases}$$

1.4 Dynamic management and valuation of the portfolio

We choose any one of the rule (3.1), or, more generally, (3.3). Our ultimate goal is to construct the **the valuation function** $(T, x, p) \mapsto V^\sharp(T, x, p) \in \mathbb{R} \cup \{+\infty\}$ and above all, **the regulation map** $\Gamma : \mathbb{R}_+ \times \mathbb{R}^{n+1} \times \mathbb{R}^{n+1} \rightsquigarrow \mathbb{R}^{n+1}$ and differential inclusion

$$p'(t) \in \Gamma(T - t, x(t), p(t))$$

governing the evolution of the portfolio under tychastic uncertainty:

1 **The Valuation Function** $(T, x, p) \mapsto V^\sharp(T, x, p) \in \mathbb{R} \cup \{+\infty\}$, defined in the following way:

DEFINITION 3.2 *Let us associate with any exercise time T the tychastic system*

$$\begin{cases} (i) & \forall i = 0, \ldots, n, x_i'(t) = x_i(t)\rho_i(x(t), v(t)) \\ (ii) & p'(t) = u(t) \\ (iii) & y'(t) = \sum_{i=0}^{n} p_i(t)x_i(t)\rho_i(x(t), v(t)) + \langle u(t), x(t)\rangle \\ & \quad \textit{where } u(t) \in P(T-t, x(t), p(t)) \\ & \qquad \textit{and } v(t) \in Q(T-t, x(t), p(t)) \end{cases} \tag{3.6}$$

governing the evolution of the prices, the portfolio and the capital and parameterized by controls $u(\cdot)$ and tyches $v(\cdot)$. The problems are:

(a) *find the* guaranteed valuation *subset $\mathcal{V}^\sharp \subset \mathbb{R}_+ \times \mathbb{R}^{n+1} \times \mathbb{R}^{n+1} \times \mathbb{R}_+$ of (T, x, p, y) made of the exercise time T, the initial price x, the initial portfolio p and the initial capital y such that there exists a dynamical feedback $(t, x, p) \mapsto \widetilde{u}(t, x, p) \in P(t, x, p)$ such that, for all evolutions of tyches $t \in [0, T] \mapsto v(t) \in Q(t, x(t)), p(t)$, for all solutions to differential equation*

$$\begin{cases} (i) & \forall i = 0, \ldots, n, x_i'(t) = x_i(t)\rho_i(x(t), v(t)) \\ (ii) & p'(t) = \widetilde{u}(T-t, x(t), p(t)) \\ (iii) & y'(t) = \sum_{i=0}^{n} p_i(t)x_i(t)\rho_i(x(t), v(t)) \\ & \quad + \langle \widetilde{u}(T-t, x(t), p(t)), x(t)\rangle \\ & \quad \textit{where } v(t) \in Q(T-t, x(t), p(t)) \end{cases} \tag{3.7}$$

satisfying $x(0) = x$, $p(0) = p$, $y(0) = y$, there exists a time $t^* \in [0, T]$ such that the chosen condition (3.3) is satisfied,

(b) *associate with any exercise time T, initial price x and any portfolio p the smallest capital $V^\sharp(T, x, p)$:*

$$V^\sharp(T, x, p) := \inf_{(T,x,p,y) \in \mathcal{V}^\sharp} y. \tag{3.8}$$

The function $(T, x, p) \mapsto V^\sharp(T, x, p)$ is called the guaranteed valuation function *of the portfolio, i.e., the minimal initial capital y satisfying the two constraints (3.3).*

(c) *Knowing this function, associate the cheapest capital*

$$V_0^\sharp(T,x) := \inf_{p\in D(T,x)} V^\sharp(T,x,p)$$

in terms of the exercise time and the initial price only.

2 **The Regulation Map** $\Gamma : \mathbb{R}_+ \times \mathbb{R}^{n+1} \times \mathbb{R}^{n+1} \rightsquigarrow \mathbb{R}^{n+1}$ containing all the dynamical feedbacks

$$\widetilde{u}(t,x,p) \in \Gamma(t,x,p)$$

governing the evolutions of portfolios through system (3.7)(ii): $p'(t) = \widetilde{u}(T-t, x(t), p(t))$ satisfying the chosen rule (3.3) whatever the tyches $v(t) \in Q(T-t, x(t), p(t))$.

1.5 A numerical example

Even before explaining how the answers to these questions are obtained through the properties of guaranteed capture basins provided by viability theory, we now adapt to the case of transaction costs the *Basin Capture Algorithm* designed for evaluating options in the case of self-financed portfolio without transaction costs in Pujal and Saint-Pierre (2001) and Pujal (2000).

For these numerical applications we only consider the case $n = 1$ of a single risky asset. We drop the index 1 mentioning the risky asset. Let $x_K > 0$ be the exercise price and $\overline{p}$ the maximal amount of shares of the risky asset. We take

$$D(t,x) := \begin{cases} [0,\overline{p}] & \text{if } x \in [0, 2x_K] \\ \emptyset & \text{if } x \notin [0, 2x_K] \end{cases}$$

The simplest example of tychastic map is obtained when we take $\rho(x,v) := (\rho + v)x$ and $Q(t,x,p) := [-\tau, +\tau]$, where $\tau \geq 0$ describes some measure of versatility (tychastic volatility).

We also assume that $r := \rho_0(x_0)$ is a constant interest rate of the bond and that there are no transaction costs on the bond ($\delta_0 = 0$). The evolutions of the price of the bound and of the shares of the bond are independent of the evolutions of the prices and shares of risky assets and of the capital y, that are governed by the tychastic control system of 3 equations (instead of 5 equations)

$$\begin{cases} (i) & x'(t) = x(t)(\rho + v(t)) \\ (ii) & p'(t) = u(t) \\ (iii) & y'(t) = y(t)r - p(t)x(t)(r - (\rho + v(t))) - \delta|u(t)|x(t) \\ & \quad \text{where } x(t) \in [0, 2x_K], p(t) \in [0, \overline{p}], |u(t)| \leq \gamma \\ & \qquad\qquad\qquad\qquad \text{and } v(t) \in [-\tau, +\tau] \end{cases} \tag{3.9}$$

We take the classical contingent claim function: $\mathbf{u}(x_0, x) := \max(0, x - x_K)$. We restrict our numerical examples to the European Options (see Pujal, 2000 and Pujal and Saint-Pierre, 2001 for other kinds of options in the self-financing case).

We apply the Capture Basin Algorithm in the case of portfolio with transaction costs replicating an European Option in the following cases:

- $T = 1$, $x_K = 100$, $\tau := 0.3$, $r = 0$, $\rho = 0.1$.

- $\delta \in \{0.00, 0.01, 0.02, 0.03, 0.04, 0.05, 0.06, 0.07, 0.08, 0.09, 0.10\}$, (rate of transaction cost)

The graphs of the approximations of the regulation map $(t, x, p) \mapsto \Gamma(t, x, p)$ are represented in Figure 3.2 for several values of t.

In Figures 3.3 and 3.4, valuation functions $(x, p) \mapsto V^\sharp(T, x, p)$ are computed for different values of T. Each graph, corresponding to a given discrete exercise time, provides the value of the option when the price of the risky asset is x and the number of shares of this asset in the portfolio is p. They are represented separately in Figure 3.3 (for case $\delta = 1\%$) and superimposed on each other in Figure 3.4 (with a high value of the transaction cost δ for a better view).

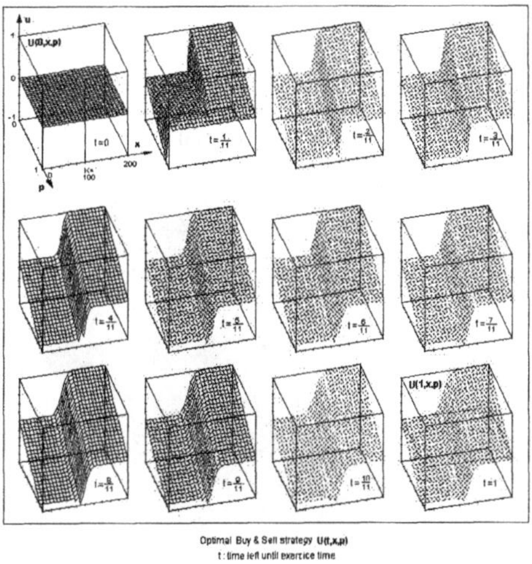

Figure 3.2. $(t, x, p) \mapsto \Gamma(t, x, p)$ providing the discrete *adjustment law* $p'(t) \in \Gamma(T - t, x(t), p(t))$ providing the variations of the amount of shares of the risky asset in the replicating portfolio. We observe that when $t = T$ is the exercise time, then $p'(t) = 0$ and no transaction can occur at that time, naturally. We observe that $p'(t) \leq 0$ for prices well below the exercise price and that $p'(t) \geq 0$ for prices well above the exercise price.

Figure 3.5 shows the graph of the valuation function $(x,p) \mapsto V^\sharp(T,x,p)$ and the graph of the minimal capital valuation $x \mapsto V_0^\sharp(T,x) := \inf_{p\in[0,\overline{p}]} V^\sharp(T,x,p)$ that is projected in the plane (x,y) in Figure 3.6.

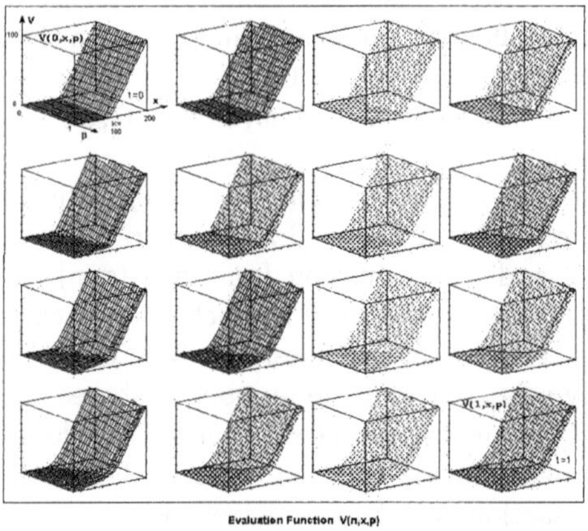

Figure 3.3. Valuation functions $(x,p) \mapsto V^\sharp(T,x,p)$ are computed for different values of T ($\delta = 1\%$).

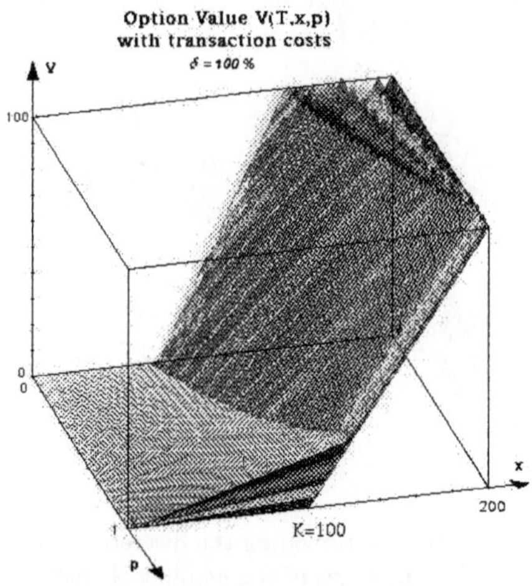

Figure 3.4. Superimposed valuation functions $(x,p) \mapsto V^\sharp(T,x,p)$ are computed for different values of T ((with a high value of the transaction cost δ for a better view)).

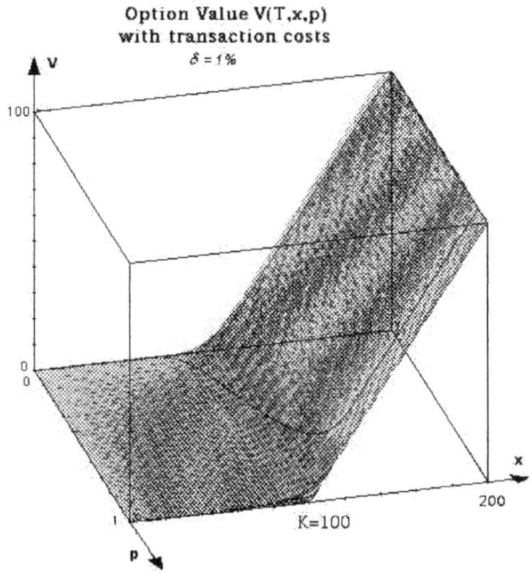

Figure 3.5. This is the graph of $(x,p) \mapsto V^\sharp(T,x,p)$ for $\delta = 1\%$. The graph of the minimal capital valuation function $x \mapsto V_0^\sharp(T,x) := \inf_{p\in[0,\overline{p}]} V^\sharp(T,x,p)$ is represented.

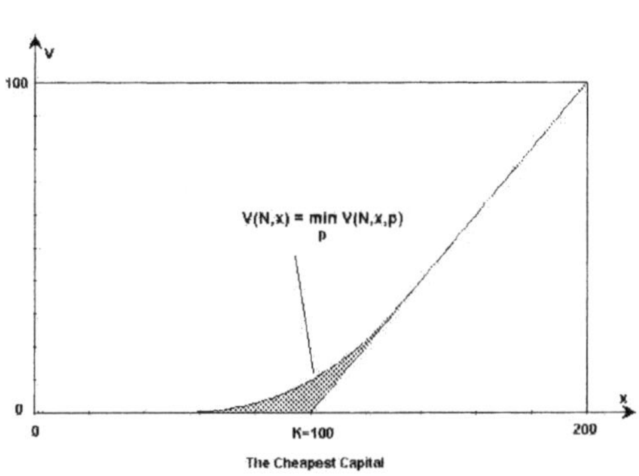

Figure 3.6. Graph of the minimal capital valuation function $x \mapsto V_0^\sharp(T,x)$.

1.6 Hamilton-Jacobi inequalities and regulation maps

Establishing partial differential equations à la Black and Scholes is no longer the starting point of the model, but a property of the valuation function that is derived according to the viability/capturability story we told above. This partial differential equation is only useful for defining analytically the dynamics Γ of the adjustment law, because we do not need it for computing it by the Capture Basin Algorithm. Since the capture basin and the viability kernel algorithms allow us to compute numerically the valuation function and the evolution of the portfolio, we do not need any longer to solve numerically this type of partial differential equations.

The valuation function $V^\sharp$ is actually a solution $\mathbf{v}$ to the nonlinear Hamilton-Jacobi-Isaacs partial differential equation

$$-\frac{\partial \mathbf{v}(t,x,p)}{\partial t} + \inf_{u\in P(t,x,p)} \sum_{i=0}^{n} \left(\frac{\partial \mathbf{v}(t,x,p)}{\partial p_i} - x_i \right) u_i + \sup_{v\in Q(t,x,p)} \left(\sum_{i=0}^{n} \left(\frac{\partial \mathbf{v}(t,x,p)}{\partial x_i} - p_i \right) x_i \rho_i(x,v) \right) = 0$$

satisfying the initial condition

$$\mathbf{v}(0,x) = \mathbf{u}(x)$$

on the subset

$$\Omega_{(\mathbf{b},\mathbf{c})}(\mathbf{v}) := \{(t,x,p) \in \mathbb{R}_+ \times \mathbb{R}^{n+1} \times \mathbb{R}^{n+1} \text{ such that } \mathbf{b}(t,x,p) \leq \mathbf{v}(t,x,p) < \mathbf{c}(t,x,p)\}$$

which depends of the unknown function[5] $\mathbf{v}$.

For instance, these subsets boil down to

1 **European Case:**

$$\Omega_{(\mathbf{0},\mathbf{u}_\infty)}(\mathbf{v}) := \{(t,x,p) | t > 0 \text{ and } \mathbf{v}(t,x,p) \geq 0\}$$

2 **American Case**

$$\Omega_{(\mathbf{u},\mathbf{u}\infty)}(\mathbf{v}) := \{(t,x,p) | t > 0 \text{ and } \mathbf{v}(t,x,p) \geq \mathbf{u}(x)\}$$

---

[5] In this case, such problems are called *variational inequalities* (see for instance Bensoussan and Lions, 1982).

3 Kairotic Case

$$\Omega_{(\mathbf{0},\mathbf{u})}(\mathbf{v}) := \{(t,x,p) | t > 0 \text{ and } \mathbf{u}(x) > \mathbf{v}(t,x,p) \geq 0\}$$

Knowing the derivatives of the guaranteed valuation function $V^\sharp$, we derive the regulation map Γ, equal to

$$\begin{cases} \Gamma(t,x,p) := \Big\{ u \in P(t,x,p) \text{ such that} \\ \quad -\frac{\partial V^\sharp(t,x,p)}{\partial t} + \sum_{i=0}^{n} \left(\frac{\partial V^\sharp(t,x,p)}{\partial p_i} - x_i \right) u_i \\ \quad + \sup_{v \in Q(t,x,p)} \left(\sum_{i=0}^{n} \left(\frac{\partial V^\sharp(t,x,p)}{\partial x_i} - p_i \right) x_i \rho_i(x,v) \right) = 0 \Big\}. \end{cases}$$

Actually, the solution of the above partial differential equation is taken in the "contingent sense", or, by duality, in the "viscosity sense", as it is explained later.

Example. Let us consider the simplest case of tychastic uncertainty:

$$\forall i = 1, \ldots, n, \rho_i(x,v) := \rho_i(x) + v_i \text{ where} v_i \in [-\tau_i, +\tau_i]$$

where τ_i denotes the *versatility (tychastic volatility)* of the ith asset.

In this case, the above Hamilton-Jacobi-Isaacs partial differential equation can be written in the form

$$\begin{cases} -\frac{\partial \mathbf{v}(t,x,p)}{\partial t} + \inf_{u \in P(t,x,p)} \sum_{i=0}^{n} \left(\frac{\partial \mathbf{v}(t,x,p)}{\partial p_i} - x_i \right) u_i \\ \sum_{i=0}^{n} \left(\frac{\partial \mathbf{v}(t,x,p)}{\partial x_i} - p_i \right) x_i \rho_i(x) + \sum_{i=1}^{n} \tau_i x_i \left| \frac{\partial \mathbf{v}(t,x,p)}{\partial x_i} - p_i \right| = 0. \end{cases}$$

Remark. Letting the tychastic volatilities grow to ∞. When the tychastic volatilities $\tau_i \to +\infty$, we obtain (formally) that

$$\forall i = 1, \ldots, n, p_i = \frac{\partial \mathbf{v}(t,x,p)}{\partial x_i}$$

a formula familiar in the finance literature under the name of "Greeks". Writing

$$p_0 x_0 = \mathbf{v}(t,x,p) - \sum_{i=1}^{n} p_i x_i = \mathbf{v}(t,x,p) - \sum_{i=1}^{n} \frac{\partial \mathbf{v}(t,x,p)}{\partial x_i} x_i$$

the above partial differential equation boils down to

$$\left\{\begin{array}{l} -\dfrac{\partial \mathbf{v}(t,x,p)}{\partial t} + \inf_{u\in P(t,x,p)} \sum_{i=0}^{n} \left(\dfrac{\partial \mathbf{v}(t,x,p)}{\partial p_i} - x_i\right) u_i \\ +\rho_0(x_0) \sum_{i=0}^{n} \dfrac{\partial \mathbf{v}(t,x,p)}{\partial x_i} x_i - \rho_0(x_0)\mathbf{v}(t,x,p) = 0. \end{array}\right.$$

This is (in the case with transaction costs) the first-order partial differential equation derived by Pierre Bernhard (under the name of the "naive theory") in Bernhard (2000b,c) in the "Black and Scholes style". It is obtained when the uncertainties are maximal ($\tau_i = +\infty$), through a limiting procedure of the case when the tychastic uncertainty is limited in the sense that the tyches are bounded.

1.7 Analytical formulas for the valuation functions

We shall first provide a formula for the valuation function that states that it is the valuation function of a two person dynamical game:

We associate with the contingent claim function $\mathbf{u}$ the functional

$$\left\{\begin{array}{l} J_{\mathbf{u}}(t;(x(\cdot),p(\cdot),v(\cdot));\widetilde{u})(T,x,p) := e^{-\int_0^t \rho_0(x_0(s))ds}\mathbf{u}(x(t),p(t)) \\ + \displaystyle\int_0^t e^{-\int_0^\tau \rho_0(x_0(s))ds} \left(\sum_{i=0}^{n} p_i(\tau)x_i(\tau)(\rho_0(x_0(\tau)) - \rho_i(x_i(\tau),v(\tau)))\right. \\ \qquad\qquad \left. -\langle \widetilde{u}(T-\tau,x(\tau)),x(\tau)\rangle \right) d\tau. \end{array}\right.$$

We set

$$\left\{\begin{array}{l} I_{\mathbf{0}}(t;(x(\cdot),p(\cdot),v(\cdot));\widetilde{u})(t,x,p) := \\ \sup_{r\in[0,t]} \displaystyle\int_0^r e^{-\int_0^\tau \rho_0(x_0(s))ds} \left(\sum_{i=0}^{n} p_i(\tau)x_i(\tau)(\rho_0(x_0(\tau)) - \rho_i(x_i(\tau),v(\tau)))\right. \\ \qquad\qquad \left. -\langle \widetilde{u}(T-\tau,x(\tau)),x(\tau)\rangle \right) d\tau. \end{array}\right.$$

We shall associate with it and with each of the three rules of the game the three corresponding valuation functions:

1 **European Options**: We obtain

$$\left\{\begin{array}{l} V^{\sharp}_{(\mathbf{0},\mathbf{u}_\infty)}(T,x,p) = \inf_{\widetilde{u}(\cdot)\in P(t,x,p)} \sup_{(x(\cdot),p(\cdot),v(\cdot))\in\mathcal{C}_{\widetilde{u}}(x,p)} \\ \max\left[J_{\mathbf{u}}(T;(x(\cdot),p(\cdot),v(\cdot));\widetilde{u})(T,x,p),\right. \\ \qquad\qquad \left. I_{\mathbf{0}}(T;(x(\cdot),p(\cdot),v(\cdot));\widetilde{u})(T,x,p)\right]. \end{array}\right. \tag{3.10}$$

2 **American Options**: We obtain

$$\left\{\begin{array}{l} V^{\sharp}_{(\mathbf{u},\mathbf{u}_{\infty})}(T,x,p) = \inf_{\widetilde{u}(\cdot)\in P(t,x,p)} \sup_{(x(\cdot),p(\cdot),v(\cdot))\in\mathcal{C}_{\widetilde{u}}(x,p)} \\ \sup_{t\in[0,T]} \max\big[J_{\mathbf{u}}(t;(x(\cdot),p(\cdot),v(\cdot));\widetilde{u})(T,x,p), \\ \qquad\qquad I_{\mathbf{0}}(t;(x(\cdot),p(\cdot),v(\cdot));\widetilde{u})(T,x,p)\big]. \end{array}\right. \tag{3.11}$$

3 **Kairotic Options**: We obtain

$$\left\{\begin{array}{l} V^{\sharp}_{(\mathbf{0},\mathbf{u})}(T,x,p) = \inf_{\widetilde{u}(\cdot)\in P(t,x,p)} \sup_{(x(\cdot),p(\cdot),v(\cdot))\in\mathcal{C}_{\widetilde{u}}(x,p)} \\ \inf_{t\in[0,T]} \max\big[J_{\mathbf{u}}(t;(x(\cdot),p(\cdot),v(\cdot));\widetilde{u})(T,x,p), \\ \qquad\qquad I_{\mathbf{0}}(t;(x(\cdot),p(\cdot),v(\cdot));\widetilde{u})(T,x,p)\big]. \end{array}\right. \tag{3.12}$$

2. The viability/capturability strategy

We shall prove that the *epigraph* of the guaranteed valuation function is the guaranteed viable-capture basin of a target viable in a constrained set under an auxiliary dynamical game that we shall construct. Both the target and the constrained sets are epigraphs of functions associated with the contingent claim function **u** and one of the three rules (European, American, Kairotic) we have singled-out. Once this task is completed, we can

1 Gather the properties of guaranteed capture basins of targets under tychastic control systems at this general level, and in particular, study the tangential conditions enjoyed by the guaranteed viable-capture basins,
2 Adapt the Capture Basin Algorithm for *computing numerically* the (epigraph of) the guaranteed valuation function and the (graph of) the regulation map, by discretizing the problem and by using algorithms devised in Saint-Pierre (1994); Pujal and Saint-Pierre (2001) and Pujal (2000).
3 And use set-valued analysis and nonsmooth analysis for *translating* the general results of guaranteed viable-capture basins to the corresponding results on our option dynamic valuation and management problem, in particular translating tangential conditions to give a meaning to the concept of a generalized solution (Frankowska's episolutions or, by duality, viscosity solutions) to Hamilton-Jacobi-Isaacs variational inequalities.

The approach we propose distinguishes clearly the rules of the games, such as the rules (3.1), which appear in the target and the constrained set of the auxiliary problem, from the nature of the dynamics governing the evolution of the prices. The choice of these dynamics predicting or extrapolating the dynamics of the prices is another problem that we do not address here.

However, our hope is to adapt the viability/capturability strategy we adopt here to other kinds of dynamics whenever it has not be done yet:

1 *Discrete stochastic evolutions.* This viability/capturability approach has already be used by J. Zabczyk for European and American options in the framework of discrete stochastic models under the name of controllability and strong controllability (Zabczyk, 1996, 1999)

2 *Continuous stochastic evolutions.* The capturability approach has already been used by Soner and Touzi for European options in the framework of stochastic control problems under the name of stochastic targets (Soner and Touzi, 1998, 2000, 2005). However, *option pricing with transaction costs* to quote Soner et al. (1995) presents difficulties in the stochastic case.
Viability and Invariance Theorems have been adapted to the stochastic case, as in Aubin and Da Prato (1995, 1998); Aubin et al. (2000); Aubin and Doss (2001); Da Prato and Frankowska (1994, 2001, 2004); Bardi and Goatin (1997, 1998); Buckdahn et al. (2000, 1997, 1998a,b); Gautier and Thibault (1993); Kisielewicz (1995), etc.

3 *History dependent (path dependent) evolutions.* They involve the case when the evolution of financial asset prices is governed by an history dependent (path dependent) dynamical system as a prediction mechanism. For instance, Aubin and Haddad (2002) studies the dynamical valuation and management of a portfolio (replicating for instance European, American and other options) depending upon such a prediction mechanism (instead of an uncertain evolution of prices, stochastic or tychastic), using in particular results of Haddad (1981a,b,c), partly presented in Chapter 12 of Aubin (1991). The valuation functionals are solutions of kinds of Hamilton-Jacobi equations involving "Clio derivatives" of functionals (on the history of an evolution),

4 *Impulse tychastic evolutions*, allowing to take into account payments of dividends using results of Aubin (1999, 2000a,b); Aubin and Haddad (2001a,b); Aubin et al. (2002) in impulse control and hybrid systems (see for instance Bensoussan and Menaldi, 1997; Saint-Pierre, 2005, and, in the stochastic case, Zabczyk, 1973, among many other references).

In this chapter, we shall treat only the tychastic control approach and answer two types of questions:

1 Provide a formula of the valuation function and *uncover* the underlying criterion to be optimized in a tychastic way.

2 Prove that the valuation function is the solution of Hamilton-Jacobi-Isaacs variational inequalities and derive the adjustment law.

2.1 Introducing auxiliary tychastic systems

We observe that the evolution of $(T-t, x(t), p(t), y(t))$ made up of the backward time $\tau(t) := T - t$, of prices $x(t)$ of the shares, of portfolios $p(t)$ and of the capital $y(t)$ is governed by the tychastic system

$$\left\{ \begin{array}{ll} (i) & \tau'(t) = -1 \\ (ii) & \forall i = 0, \ldots, n, x_i'(t) = x_i(t)\rho_i(x(t), v(t)) \\ (iii) & p'(t) = u(t) \\ (iv) & y'(t) = \sum_{i=0}^{n} p_i(t)x_i(t)\rho_i(x(t), v(t)) + \langle u(t), x(t) \rangle \\ & \quad \text{where } u(t) \in P(x(t), p(t)) \text{ and } v(t) \in Q(x(t)) \end{array} \right. \tag{3.13}$$

starting at (T, x, p, y). We summarize it in the form of the tychastic system

$$\left\{ \begin{array}{ll} (i) & z'(t) \in g(z(t), u(t), v(t)) \\ (ii) & u(t) \in P(z(t)) \text{ and } v(t) \in Q(z(t)) \end{array} \right.$$

where $z := (\tau, x, p, y) \in \mathbb{R} \times \mathbb{R}^{n+1} \times \mathbb{R}^{n+1} \times \mathbb{R}$, where the map $g : \mathbb{R} \times \mathbb{R}^{n+1} \times \mathbb{R}^{n+1} \times \mathbb{R} \rightsquigarrow \mathbb{R} \times \mathbb{R}^{n+1} \times \mathbb{R}^{n+1} \times \mathbb{R}$ is defined by $g(z, u, v)$

$$= \left(-1, x_i(t)\rho_i(x(t), v(t)), u, \sum_{i=0}^{n} p_i(t)x_i(t)\rho_i(x(t), v(t)) + \langle u(t), x(t) \rangle \right)$$

where u ranges over $P(z) := P(t, x, p)$ and v over $Q(z) := Q(t, x, p)$.

We say that a selection $z \mapsto \widetilde{u}(z) \in P(z)$ is a *feedback*, regarded as a strategy. One associates with such a feedback chosen by the manager or the player the evolutions governed by the perturbed differential equation

$$z'(t) = g(z(t), \widetilde{u}(z(t)), v(t))$$

starting at time 0 at z.

2.2 Introducing guaranteed capture basins

We now define the guaranteed viable-capture basin that is involved in the definition of guaranteed valuation subsets.

DEFINITION 3.3 *Let K and $C \subset K$ be two subsets of Z.*

The guaranteed viable-capture basin *of the target C viable in K is the set of elements $z \in K$ such that there exists a continuous feedback*

$\widetilde{u}(z) \in P(z)$ such that for every $v(\cdot) \in Q(z(\cdot))$, for every solutions $z(\cdot)$ to $z' = g(z, \widetilde{u}(z), v)$, there exists $t^* \in \mathbb{R}_+$ such that the viability/capturability conditions

$$\begin{cases} (i) & \forall t \in [0, t^*], \quad z(t) \in K \\ (ii) & \qquad\qquad\quad\; z(t^*) \in C \end{cases}$$

are satisfied.

We thus observe that

PROPOSITION 3.1 *The guaranteed valuation subset $\mathcal{V}^{\sharp}_{(\mathbf{b},\mathbf{c})}$ defined in Definition 3.3 is related to the guaranteed viable-capture basin under the tychastic system (3.13) of the epigraph of the objective function* $\mathbf{c}$ *viable in the epigraph of the constraint function* $\mathbf{b}$.

The characterization of this subset and the study of its properties are one of the major topics of the viability approach to dynamical games theory that we summarize in the two next sections.

2.3 Analytical formula of the valuation function

We set $\mathbf{l}(x, p, u, v) := -\sum_{i=0}^{n} p_i x_i \rho_i(x, v) - \langle u, x \rangle$ and we obtain

$$\begin{cases} J_{\mathbf{c}}(t; (x(\cdot), p(\cdot), v(\cdot)); \widetilde{u})(T, x, p) := \mathbf{c}(T - t, x(t), p(t)) \\ + \displaystyle\int_0^t \Bigg(\sum_{i=0}^{n} p_i(\tau) x_i(\tau) \rho_i(x_i(\tau), v(\tau)) \\ \qquad\qquad - \langle \widetilde{u}(T - \tau, x(\tau), p(\tau)), v(\tau))), x(\tau) \rangle \Bigg) d\tau. \end{cases}$$

We shall associate with it three pairs of time-dependent functions $(\mathbf{b}, \mathbf{c})$ and obtain three different valuation functions of portfolios duplicating European, American options and first time options:

1 *European case*: We take $\mathbf{b}(t, x, p) := 0$ and $\mathbf{c}(t, x, p) := \mathbf{u}_\infty(t, x, p)$. In this case, we obtain

$$V^{\sharp}_{(\mathbf{0},\mathbf{u}_\infty)}(T, x, p) := \inf_{\widetilde{u}(t,x,p) \in P(t,x,p)} \sup_{(x(\cdot),p(\cdot),v(\cdot)) \in \mathcal{C}_{\widetilde{u}}(x,p)} J_{\mathbf{u}}(T; (x(\cdot), p(\cdot), v(\cdot)); \widetilde{u})(x, p).$$

2 *American case*: We take $\mathbf{b}(t, x, p) := \mathbf{u}(x, p)$ and $\mathbf{c}(t, x, p) := \mathbf{u}_\infty(t, x, p)$. In this case, we obtain

$$V^{\sharp}_{(\mathbf{u},\mathbf{u}_\infty)}(T, x, p) := \inf_{\widetilde{u}(x) \in P(x,p)} \sup_{(x(\cdot),p(\cdot),v(\cdot)) \in \mathcal{C}_{\widetilde{u}}(x,p)} \sup_{t \in [0,T]} J_{\mathbf{u}}(t; (x(\cdot), p(\cdot), v(\cdot)); \widetilde{u})(x, p).$$

3 *Kairotic case*: We assume that $\mathbf{l} \geq 0$ and we take $\mathbf{b}(t,x,p) := 0$ and $\mathbf{c}(t,x,p) = \mathbf{u}(x,p)$. In this case, we obtain

$$V^{\sharp}_{(\mathbf{0},\mathbf{u})}(T,x,p) := \inf_{\widetilde{u}(x)\in P(x,p)} \sup_{(x(\cdot),p(\cdot),v(\cdot))\in\mathcal{C}_{\widetilde{u}}(x,p)} \inf_{t\in[0,T]} J_{\mathbf{u}}(t;(x(\cdot),p(\cdot),v(\cdot));\widetilde{u})(x,p).$$

We have to compute the functionals $J_{\mathbf{u}}$, $J_{\mathbf{u}_\infty}$, $\mathbf{I_0}$ and $\mathbf{I_u}$ to obtain our three formulas.

First, we observe that for $\mathbf{c}(t,x,p) := \mathbf{u}(x,p)$,

$$\begin{cases} J_{\mathbf{u}}(t;(x(\cdot),p(\cdot),v(\cdot));\widetilde{u})(T,x,p) := \mathbf{u}(x(t),p(t)) \\ + \displaystyle\int_0^t \left(\sum_{i=0}^n p_i(\tau)x_i(\tau)\rho_i(x_i(\tau),v(\tau)) \right. \\ \qquad \left. -\langle \widetilde{u}(T-\tau,x(\tau),p(\tau)),v(\tau))),x(\tau)\rangle \right) d\tau. \end{cases}$$

Second, when we take $\mathbf{c}(t,x,p) := \mathbf{u}_\infty(t,x,p)$ that takes infinite values for $t>0$, we observe that

$$J_{\mathbf{u}_\infty}(t;(x(\cdot),p(\cdot),v(\cdot));\widetilde{u})(T,x,p) := \begin{cases} J_{\mathbf{u}}(T;(x(\cdot),p(\cdot),v(\cdot));\widetilde{u})(T,x,p) & \text{if } t=T \\ +\infty & \text{if } t\in[0,T[\end{cases}$$

so that

$$\inf_{t\in[0,T]} J_{\mathbf{u}_\infty}(t;(x(\cdot),p(\cdot),v(\cdot));\widetilde{u})(T,x,p) := J_{\mathbf{u}}(T;(x(\cdot),p(\cdot),v(\cdot));\widetilde{u})(T,x,p).$$

Third, when $\mathbf{b}=0$, we observe that

$$J_{\mathbf{0}}(t;(x(\cdot),p(\cdot),v(\cdot));\widetilde{u})(T,x,p) = \int_0^t \mathbf{l}(x(\tau),p(\tau),\widetilde{u}(x(\tau),p(\tau)),v(\tau))d\tau$$

so that,

$$\begin{cases} I_{\mathbf{0}}(t;(x(\cdot),p(\cdot),v(\cdot));\widetilde{u})(T,x,p) \\ = \sup_{s\in[0,t]} \int_0^s \mathbf{l}(x(\tau),p(\tau),\widetilde{u}(x(\tau),p(\tau)),v(\tau))d\tau. \end{cases}$$

Finally, when $\mathbf{b}(t,x,p) = \mathbf{u}(x,p)$, we observe that

$$\begin{cases} I_{\mathbf{u}}(t;(x(\cdot),p(\cdot),v(\cdot));\widetilde{u})(T,x,p) \\ = \displaystyle\sup_{s\in[0,t]} \left(\mathbf{u}(x(t),p(t)) + \int_0^s \mathbf{l}(x(\tau), \right. \\ \qquad \left. p(\tau),\widetilde{u}(T-\tau,x(\tau),p(\tau)),v(\tau))d\tau \right). \end{cases}$$

2.4 Black and Scholes type variational inequalities

Let us associate with a nonnegative extended function $\mathbf{v}$ the subset

$$\Omega_{(\mathbf{b},\mathbf{c})}(\mathbf{v}) := \{(t,x,p) \in \mathbb{R}_+ \times \mathbb{R}^{n+1} \times \mathbb{R}^{n+1} \text{ such that}$$
$$\mathbf{b}(t,x,p) \leq \mathbf{v}(t,x,p) < \mathbf{c}(t,x,p)\}$$

which depends of the function $\mathbf{v}$.

Example. When for all $t > 0$, $\mathbf{c}(t,x,p) := +\infty$, and when $\mathbf{b}(0,x,p) := \mathbf{c}(0,x,p)$, we observe that

$$\Omega_{(\mathbf{b},\mathbf{c})}(\mathbf{v}) := \{(t,x,p) \in \mathbb{R}_+ \times \mathbb{R}^{n+1} \times \mathbb{R}^{n+1} \text{ such that}$$
$$t > 0 \textit{ and } \mathbf{b}(t,x,p) \leq \mathbf{v}(t,x,p)\} \quad \blacksquare$$

We shall prove that the guaranteed value-function $V^\sharp_{(\mathbf{b},\mathbf{c})}$ is a "contingent" solution $\mathbf{v}$ to the *Hamilton-Jacobi-Isaacs variational inequality*: for every $(t,x,p) \in \Omega_{(\mathbf{b},\mathbf{c})}(\mathbf{v})$,

$$\left\{ \begin{array}{l} \dfrac{\partial \mathbf{v}(t,x,p)}{\partial t} = \inf\limits_{u \in P(x,p)} \left(\displaystyle\sum_{i=0}^{n} \frac{\partial \mathbf{v}(t,x,p)}{\partial p_i} u_i \right. \\ \\ \left. + \sup\limits_{v \in Q(x)} \left(\displaystyle\sum_{i=0}^{n} \frac{\partial \mathbf{v}(t,x,p)}{\partial x_i} x_i \rho_i(x,v) + \mathbf{l}(x,p,u,v) \right) \right). \end{array} \right.$$

This is a *free boundary* problem, well studied in mechanics and physics: the domain $\Omega_{(\mathbf{b},\mathbf{c})}(\mathbf{v})$ on which we look for a solution $\mathbf{v}$ to the Hamilton-Jacobi partial differential equation depends upon the unknown solution $\mathbf{v}$.

Observe that Hamilton-Jacobi partial differential equation itself depends only upon the dynamic of the system (ρ, P, Q) and the map $\mathbf{l}$, whereas the domain $\Omega_{(\mathbf{b},\mathbf{c})}(\mathbf{v})$ depends only upon the pair $(\mathbf{b},\mathbf{c})$ describing the dynamical constraints and the objective. Changing them, the valuation function is a solution of the same Hamilton-Jacobi partial differential equation, but defined on different "free sets" $\Omega_{(\mathbf{b},\mathbf{c})}(\mathbf{v})$ depending on $\mathbf{v}$.

The usefulness and relevance of the Hamilton-Jacobi-Isaacs variational inequality is that it provides the *adjustment law* — through *dynamical feedbacks* — that we are looking for. Indeed, we introduce the *regulation map* Γ associating with any $(t,x,p) \in \mathbb{R}_+ \times \mathbb{R}^{n+1} \times \mathbb{R}^{n+1}$ the subset

$\Gamma(t,x,p)$ of strategies $u \in P(x,p)$ satisfying

$$\left\{\begin{array}{l} \displaystyle\sum_{i=0}^{n} \frac{\partial V^{\sharp}_{(\mathbf{b},\mathbf{c})}(t,x,p)}{\partial p_i} u_i \\ \displaystyle + \sup_{v\in Q(x)} \left(\sum_{i=0}^{n} \frac{\partial V^{\sharp}_{(\mathbf{b},\mathbf{c})}(t,x,p)}{\partial x_i} x_i \rho_i(x,v) + \mathbf{l}(x,p,u,v) \right) \\ \displaystyle \le \frac{\partial V^{\sharp}_{(\mathbf{b},\mathbf{c})}(t,x,p)}{\partial t}. \end{array}\right.$$

The adjustment law states in essence that the evolution of the portfolio allowing to satisfy the viability/capturability conditions (3.3) against all perturbations $v \in Q(t,x,p)$ is governed by the differential inclusion

$$p'(t) \in \Gamma(T-t, x(t), p(t)).$$

Namely, knowing the guaranteed valuation function and its derivatives, a guaranteed solution is obtained in the following way: Starting from x_0 and p_0 such that $\mathbf{b}(T,x_0,p_0) \le V^{\sharp}_{(\mathbf{b},\mathbf{c})}(T,x_0,p_0) < \mathbf{c}(T,x_0,p_0)$, solutions to the new system

$$\left\{\begin{array}{ll} (i) & \forall i = 0,\ldots,n,\ x_i'(t) = x_i(t)\rho_i(x(t),v(t)) \\ (ii) & p'(t) \in \Gamma(T-t, x(t), p(t)) \\ (iii) & y'(t) = -\mathbf{l}(x(t),p(t),u(t),v(t)) \end{array}\right.$$

regulate the guaranteed solutions of the tychastic system until the first time $t^* \in [0,T]$ when

$$V^{\sharp}_{(\mathbf{b},\mathbf{c})}(T-t^*, x(t^*), p(t^*)) = \mathbf{c}(T-t^*, x(t^*), p(t^*)).$$

Setting $\mathbf{l}(x,p,u,v) := -\sum_{i=0}^{n} p_i x_i \rho_i(x,v) - \langle u, x\rangle$, the Hamilton-Jacobi-Isaacs variational inequality becomes: for every $(t,x,p) \in \Omega_{(\mathbf{b},\mathbf{c})}(\mathbf{v})$,

$$-\frac{\partial V^{\sharp}(t,x,p)}{\partial t} + \inf_{u\in P(x,p)} \sum_{i=0}^{n} \left(\frac{\partial V^{\sharp}(t,x,p)}{\partial p_i} - x_i \right) u_i + \sup_{v\in Q(x)} \left(\sum_{i=0}^{n} \left(\frac{\partial V^{\sharp}(t,x,p)}{\partial x_i} - p_i \right) x_i \rho_i(x,v) \right) = 0$$

and the regulation map Γ associates with any $(T,x,p) \in \mathbb{R}_+ \times \mathbb{R}^{n+1} \times \mathbb{R}^{n+1}$ the subset $\Gamma(T,x,p)$ of $u \in P(x,p)$ satisfying

$$\begin{cases} \sum_{i=0}^{n} \left(\frac{\partial V^\sharp(t,x,p)}{\partial p_i} - x_i \right) u_i \\ \qquad\qquad + \sup_{v \in Q(x)} \left(\sum_{i=0}^{n} \left(\frac{\partial V^\sharp(t,x,p)}{\partial x_i} - p_i \right) x_i \rho_i(x,v) \right) \\ \leq \frac{\partial V^\sharp(t,x,p)}{\partial t}. \end{cases}$$

Acknowledgements The authors thank Giuseppe Da Prato, Francine Catté, Halim Doss, Hélène Frankowska, Georges Haddad, Nisard Touzi and Jerzy Zabczyk for many useful discussions and Michèle Breton and Georges Zaccour for inviting them in June 2004 to present these results in the Montréal's GERAD (Groupe d'études et de recherche en analyse des décisions) and Cref (Centre de recherche en e-finance).

This work was supported in part by the European Community's Human Potential Programme under contract HPRN-CT-2002-00281, [Evolution Equations].

References

Aubin, J.-P. (1981). Contingent derivatives of set-valued maps and existence of solutions to nonlinear inclusions and differential inclusions. In: L. Nachbin ed., *Advances in Mathematics, Supplementary studies*, pp. 160–232.

Aubin, J.-P. (1986). A viability approach to Lyapunov's second method. In: A. Kurzhanski and K. Sigmund (eds.), *Dynamical Systems*, Lectures Notes in Economics and Math. Systems, 287:31–38. Springer-Verlag.

Aubin, J.-P. (1991). *Viability Theory.* Birkhäuser, Boston, Basel, Berlin.

Aubin, J.-P. (1997). *Dynamic Economic Theory: A Viability Approach.* Springer-Verlag.

Aubin, J.-P. (1999). *Impulse Differential Inclusions and Hybrid Systems: A Viability Approach.* Lecture Notes, University of California at Berkeley.

Aubin, J.-P. (2000a). Lyapunov Functions for Impulse and Hybrid Control Systems. *Proceedings of the CDC 2000 Conference.*

Aubin, J.-P. (2000b). Optimal impulse control problems and quasi-variational inequalities thirty years later: a viability approach. In: *Contrôle optimal et EDP : Innovations et Applications.* IOS Press.

Aubin, J.-P., Bayen, A., Bonneuil, N., and Saint-Pierre, P. (2005). *Viability, Control and Games: Regulation of Complex Evolutionary Systems Under Uncertainty and Viability Constraints.* Springer-Verlag.

Aubin, J.-P. and Catte, F. (2002). Fixed-Point and Algebraic Properties of Viability Kernels and Capture Basins of Sets. *Set-Valued Analysis*, 10:379–416.

Aubin, J.-P. and Cellina, A. (1984). *Differential Inclusions.* Springer-Verlag.

Aubin, J.-P. and Da Prato, G. (1995). Stochastic Nagumo's viability theorem. *Stochastic Analysis and Applications*, 13:1–11.

Aubin, J.-P. and Da Prato, G. (1998). The viability theorem for stochastic differential inclusions. *Stochastic Analysis and Applications*, 16:1–15

Aubin, J.-P., Da Prato, G., and Frankowska, H. (2000). Stochastic Invariance for differential inclusions. *Set-Valued Analysis*, 8:181–201.

Aubin, J.-P. and Dordan, O. (1996). Fuzzy systems, viability theory and toll sets. In: H. Nguyen (ed.), *Handbook of Fuzzy Systems, Modeling and Control*, pp. 461–488. Kluwer.

Aubin, J.-P. and Doss, H. (2001). Characterization of stochastic viability of any nonsmotth set involving its generalized contingent curvature. *Stochastic Analysis and Applications*, 25:951–981.

Aubin, J.-P. and Frankowska, H. (1990). *Set-Valued Analysis.* Birkhäuser.

Aubin, J.-P. and Frankowska, H. (1996). The viability kernel algorithm for computing value functions of infinite horizon optimal control problems. *J. Math. Anal. Appl.*, 201:555–576.

Aubin, J.-P. and Haddad, G. (2001a). Cadenced runs of impulse and hybrid control systems. *International Journal Robust and Nonlinear Control*, 11:401–415.

Aubin, J.-P. and Haddad, G. (2001b). Path-dependent impulse and hybrid systems. In: Di Benedetto and Sangiovanni-Vincentelli (eds.), *Hybrid Systems: Computation and Control, Proceedings of the HSCC 2001 Conference, LNCS 2034*, pp. 119–132. Springer-Verlag.

Aubin, J.-P. and Haddad, G. (2002). History (path) dependent optimal control and portfolio valuation and management. *Journla of Positivity*, 6:331–358.

Aubin, J.-P., Lygeros, J., Quincampoix, M., Sastry, S., and Seube, N. (2002). Impulse differential inclusions: A viability approach to hybrid systems. *IEEE Transactions on Automatic Control*, 47:2–20.

Bardi, M. and Capuzzo Dolcetta, I. (1998). *Optimal Control and Viscosity Solutions to Hamilton-Jacobi-Bellman Equations.* Birkhäuser.

Bardi, M. and Goatin, P. (1997). *A Dirichlet Type Problem for Nonlinear Degenerate Elliptic Equations Arinsing in Time-Optimal Stochastic Control.* Preprint SISSA 50/97.

Bardi, M. and Goatin, P. (1998). *Invariant sets for controlled degenerate diffusions: a viscosity solution approach.* Preprint Padova 2/98.

Bensoussan, A. and Lions, J.-L. (1982). *Contrôle impulsionnel et inéquations quasi-variationnelles.* Dunod, Paris. (English translation: (1984) *Impulse Control and Quasi-Variational Inequalities*, Gauthier-Villars).

Bensoussan, A. and Menaldi (1997). Hybrid control and dynamic programming. *Dynamics of Continuous, Discrete and Impulse Systems*, 3:395–442.

Bernhard, P. (2000a). Max-Plus algebra and mathematical fear in dynamic optimization. *J. Set-Valued Analysis.*

Bernhard, P. (2000b). Une approche déterministe de l'évaluation des options. In: *Optimal Control and Partial Differential Equations*, IOS Press.

Bernhard, P. (2000c). *A Robust Control Approach to Option Pricing.* Cambridge University Press.

Bernhard, P. (2002). Robust control approach to option pricing, including transaction costs. *Annals of Dynamic Games*

Bjork, T. (1998). *Arbitrage theory in continuous time.* Oxford University Press.

Buckdahn, R., Quincampoix, M., and Rascanu, A. (1997). Propriétés de viabilité pour des équations différentielles stochastiques rétrogrades et applications à des équations auxdérivées partielles. *Comptes-Rendus de l'Académie des Sciences*, 235:1159–1162.

Buckdahn, R., Quincampoix, M., and Rascanu, A. (1998a). *Stochastic Viability for Backward Stochastic Differential Equations and Applications to Partial Differential Equations*, Un. Bretagne Occidentale, 01-1998.

Buckdahn, R., Peng, S., Quincampoix, M., and Rainer, C. (1998b). Existence of stochastic control under state constraints. *Comptes-Rendus de l'Académie des Sciences*, 327:17–22.

Buckdahn, R., Cardaliaguet, P., and Quincampoix, M. (2000). *A representation formula for the mean curvature motion*, UBO 08-2000.

Cardaliaguet, P. (1994). *Domaines dicriminants en jeux différentiels.* Thèse de l'Université de Paris-Dauphine.

Cardaliaguet, P. (1996). A differential game with two players and one target. *SIAM J. Control and Optimization*, 34(4):1441–1460.

Cardaliaguet, P. (2000). Introduction à la théorie des jeux différentiels. Lecture Notes, Université Paris-Dauphine.

Cardaliaguet, P., Quincampoix, M., and Saint-Pierre, P. (1999). Set-valued numerical methods for optimal control and differential games. In: *Stochastic and differential games. Theory and numerical methods, Annals of the International Society of Dynamical Games*, pp. 177–247. Birkhäuser.

Cox, J. and Rubinstein, M. (1985). *Options Market.* Prentice Hall.

Da Prato, G. and Frankowska, H. (1994). A stochastic Filippov theorem. *Stochastic Calculus*, 12:409–426.

Da Prato, G. and Frankowska, H. (2001). Stochastic viability for compact sets in terms of the distance function. *Dynamics Systems Appl.*, 10:177–184.

Da Prato, G. and Frankowska, H. (2004). Invariance of stochastic control systems with deterministic arguments. *J. Differential Equations*, 200:18–52.

Doss, H. (1977). Liens entre équations différentielles stochastiques et ordinaires. *Annales de l'Institute Henri Poincaré, Calcul des Probabilités et Statistique*, 23:99–125.

Filipovic, D. (1999). *Invariant manifolds for weak solutions to stochastic equations.* Preprint.

Frankowska, H. (1989). Optimal trajectories associated to a solution of contingent Hamilton-Jacobi equations. *Applied Mathematics and Optimization*, 19:291–311.

Frankowska, H. (1989). Hamilton-Jacobi equation: viscosity solutions and generalized gradients. *J. of Math. Analysis and Appl.* 141:21–26.

Frankowska, H. (1991). Lower semicontinuous solutions to Hamilton-Jacobi-Bellman equations. In: *Proceedings of 30th CDC Conference, IEEE*, Brighton.

Frankowska, H. (1993). Lower semicontinuous solutions of Hamilton-Jacobi-Bellman equation. *SIAM J. on Control and Optimization.*

Gautier, S. and Thibault, L. (1993). Viability for constrained stochastic differential equations. *Differential Integral Equations*, 6:1395–1414.

Haddad, G. (1981a). Monotone trajectories of differential inclusions with memory. *Isr. J. Math.*, 39:83–100.

Haddad, G. (1981b). Monotone viable trajectories for functional differential inclusions. *J. Diff. Eq.*, 42:1–24.

Haddad, G. (1981c). Topological properties of the set of solutions for functional differential differential inclusions. *Nonlinear Anal. Theory, Meth. Appl.*, 5:1349–1366.

Jachimiak, W. (1996). A note on invariance for semilinear differential equations. *Bull. Pol. Acad. Sc.*, 44:179–183.

Jachimiak, W. (1998). *Stochastic invariance in infinite dimension.* Preprint.

Kisielewicz, M. (1995). Viability theorem for stochastic inclusions. *Discussiones Mathematicae, Differential Inclusions*, 15:61–74.

Milian, A. (1995). Stocastic viability and a comparison theorem. *Colloq. Math.*, 68:297–316.

Milian, A. (1997). Invariance for stochastic equations with regular coefficients. *Stochastic Anal. Appl.*, 15:91–101.

Milian, A. (1998). *Comparison theorems for stochastic evolution equations.* Preprint.

Olsder, G.J. (1999). *Control-theoretic thoughts on option pricing.* Preprint.

Pujal, D. (2000). *Valuation et gestion dynamiques de portefeuilles*, Thèse de l'Université de Paris-Dauphine.

Pujal, D. and Saint-Pierre, P. (2001). *L'algorithme du bassin de capture appliqué pour évaluer des options européennes, américaines ou exotiques.* Preprint.

Quincampoix, M. (1992). Differential inclusions and target problems. *SIAM J. Control and Optimization*, 30:324–335.

Rockafellar, R.T. and Wets, R. (1997). *Variational Analysis.* Springer-Verlag.

Runggaldier, W.J. (2000). Adaptive and robust control peocedures for risk minimization under uncertainty. In: *Optimal Control and Partial Differential Equations*, pp. 511–520. IOS Press.

Saint-Pierre, P. (1994). Approximation of the viability kernel. *Applied Mathematics and Optimisation*, 29:187–209.

Saint-Pierre, P. (2005). Approximation of capture basins for hybrid systems. Preprint.

Soner, H.M., Shreve, S.E., and Cvitanic, J. (1995). There is no trivial hedging for option pricing with transaction costs. *The Annals of Probability*, 5:327-355.

Soner, H.M. and Touzi, N. (1998). Super-replication under Gamma constraints. *SIAM J. Control and Opt.*, 39:73–96.

Soner, H.M. and Touzi, N. (2000). Dynamic programming for a class of control problems. Preprint.

Soner, H.M. and Touzi, N. (2005). Stochastic target problems, dynamical programming and viscosity solutions. Preprint.

Tessitore, G. and Zabczyk, J. (1998). *Comments on transition semigroups and stochastic invariance.* Preprint.

Zabczyk, J. (1973). Optimal control by means of switching. *Studia Matematica*, 65:161–171.

Zabczyk, J. (1992). *Mathematical Control Theory: An Introduction.* Birkhäuser.

Zabczyk, J. (1996). Chance and decision: stochastic control in discrete time. Quaderni, Scuola Normale di Pisa.

Zabczyk, J. (1999). Stochastic invariance and consistency of financial models. Preprint Scuola Normale di Pisa.

Chapter 4

THE ROBUST CONTROL APPROACH TO OPTION PRICING AND INTERVAL MODELS: AN OVERVIEW

Pierre Bernhard

Abstract We give an overview of our work since 2000 on an alternate theory of option pricing and contingent claim hedging based upon the so-called "interval model" of security prices, which let us develop a consistent theory in discrete and continuous trading within the same model, taking transaction costs into account from the start. The interval model rules out crises on the stock market. While Samuelson's model does not, so does in practice Black and Scholes' theory in its assumption of instantaneous, continuous trading. Our theory does not make use of any probabilistic *knowledge* (or rather *assumption*) on market prices. But we show that Black and Scholes theory does not either.

1. Introduction

If a mathematical model can be termed "good" only relatively to a purpose, the classical Samuelson (geometric diffusion) model of stock prices on the market is not good for the purpose of deriving a hedging method and pricing rule for options in the presence of transaction costs (see Soner et al., 1995), nor in discrete trading. For that reason, new approaches have appeared in the work of various authors (McEneaney, 1997; Pujal, 2003; Roorda et al., 2000; Aubin et al., 2005; Dupire, 2003; Roorda et al., 2003; Saint-Pierre, 2004) all based upon the ideas of robust control, and most of them somehow assuming some bounds on how fast prices may evolve.

In these approaches, the critical part of the market model is the set Ω of admissible trajectories. In spite of the choice of name, aimed at recalling that there lie the uncertainties, in these approaches there is no need to endow this set with a probabilistic structure, thus greatly simplifying the model. The intuitive notion of "causal" strategy ("adapted" in the parlance of stochastic theories) will be rendered by the technical apparatus of *non-anticipative strategies*, classical in the theory of differential games and robust control. This lets one formalize the fact that future stock prices are not known by the trader. In some sense, we even give the trader less information on future prices than any stochastic theory, since we do not even let it know a probability law governing future prices.

We review here our own work, most of which uses the so called "interval model" of the market, independently introduced around 1999 by Aubin and Pujal, ourselves and Roorda, Engwerda, and Schumacher, the latter being the inventors of the name we use. This work has sometimes been criticized on the basis of the fact that since it does not make use of any probabilistic knowledge (or *assumptions*) on the market, it cannot capture the essence of the problem. Hence we review also here an earlier work of ours which shows that the celebrated Black and Scholes theory does not either.

On our way, and in particular in Section 4.1 and in the conclusion, we provide some discussions of the relative merits and weaknesses of these two approaches.

2. Dynamics and hedging

2.1 Notations and dynamics

Our notations will be as follows. All the problems we consider will be on a fixed time interval $[0, T]$. There exists a riskless interest rate ρ per unit time, and we shall use the end-value factor

$$R(t) = e^{\rho(t-T)}$$

which can equivalently be thought of as the value of a riskless bond worth one at time T. All monetary values will be expressed in end-time value, so that the riskless rate will disappear from most of the theory.

We shall let $S(t)$ be the price at time t of a specified *underlying* security, and let

$$u(t) = \frac{S(t)}{R(t)}.$$

We shall consider a *hedging portfolio* containing an amount $v(t)$ (in end-time monetary value) of the underlying security, the rest being $y(t)$ riskless bonds, for a total worth (in end-time value) of $w(t) = v(t) + y(t)$.

Transaction amounts will be denoted ξ (see more details below). When transaction costs are present, we shall take them proportional to the amount of the transaction, the proportionality coefficient being

C^+ for a buy of the underlying, and $-C^-$ for a sale. We shall let ε be the sign of the transaction, so that its cost will be $C^\varepsilon\xi$. Closing transactions at exercize time T will bear costs at possibly different rates c^+ and c^-, of absolute value no more than their counterparts C^+ and C^- respectively.

2.1.1 Continuous trading. In the case of continuous trading, in all of our developments but one (Section 3.1.2), $u(\cdot)$ will be absolutely continuous, and we shall let

$$\tau(t) = \frac{\dot{u}(t)}{u(t)}.$$

It is defined for almost all t and measurable, and $u(\cdot)$ is the unique (according to Gronwal's inequality) continuous solution of $u(t) = u(0) + \int_0^t \tau(s)u(s)\,\mathrm{d}s$. So that we may alternatively represent $u(\cdot)$ via $u(0)$ and $\tau(\cdot)$.

We shall let $\xi(t)$ be our rate (in end-time value) of trading, a buy if $\xi(t) > 0$, a sale if $\xi(t) < 0$. We shall also allow for impulsions in $\xi(\cdot)$ at a finite number of time instants t_k, of amplitude ξ_k, all chosen by the trader as part of his control.

We summarize the dynamics as

$$\dot{u} = \tau u, \tag{4.1}$$

$$\dot{v} = \tau v + \xi, \tag{4.2}$$

$$v(t_k^+) = v(t_k) + \xi_k, \tag{4.3}$$

$$\dot{w} = \tau v - C^\varepsilon\xi, \tag{4.4}$$

$$w(t_k^+) = w(t_k) - C^{\varepsilon_k}\xi_k. \tag{4.5}$$

We shall use the fact that the last two equations integrate explicitly as

$$w(t) = w(0) + \int_0^t \big(\tau(s)v(s) - C^\varepsilon\xi(s)\big)\,\mathrm{d}s - \sum_{k|t_k<t} C^{\varepsilon_k}\xi_k. \tag{4.6}$$

2.1.2 Discrete trading. In the case of discrete trading, a time step h is fixed. The trader is constrained to use impulses only, at fixed time instants $t_k = kh$. We write $u(kh) = u(t_k) = u_k$, and similarly for v and w. Let also τ_k be the relative variation of u during the time step $[t_k, t_{k+1}]$:

$$\tau_k = \frac{u_{k+1} - u_k}{u_k},$$

so that again, u_0 and the sequence $\{\tau_k\}$ together define the sequence $\{u_k\}$. Notice however that a non anticipative strategy must make use of strictly past τ_j's to determine ξ_k $(j < k)$.

The dynamics are now

$$u_{k+1} = (1+\tau_k)u_k, \tag{4.7}$$
$$v_{k+1} = (1+\tau_k)(v_k+\xi_k), \tag{4.8}$$
$$w_{k+1} = w_k + \tau_k(v_k+\xi_k) - C^\varepsilon \xi_k, \tag{4.9}$$

Again, the last equation integrates as

$$w_k = w_0 + \sum_{\ell=0}^{k-1}[\tau_\ell(v_\ell+\xi_\ell) - C^\varepsilon \xi_\ell]. \tag{4.10}$$

2.2 Hedging portfolio

2.2.1 Closure. In most of the chapter, except Section 5.4.1, we consider European claims, valued at exercize time T. Let $M(u(T))$ be the amount due by the writer to the buyer according to the contingent claim. It is known to be $M(u) = \max\{0, u-K\}$ for a Call of strike K, and $M(u) = \max\{K-u, 0\}$ for a Put. But other claims may be considered, such as a digital call worth $M(u) = \Upsilon(u-K)$, the Heaviside echelon. Notice however that convexity of M on the one hand, continuity on the other, do make a difference, so that digital calls or puts yield a more complex theory that we shall only allude to here.

The total expense incurred by the writer may be different from $M(u(T))$ due to transaction costs, themselves function of whether the final transaction is in cash or in kind. We discuss here the case of a call, and we consider only positive v's. (We would consider negative v's for a put.)

The auxiliary functions $\breve{v}(u)$ and $\breve{w}(u)$ that we introduce now will serve in Section 4.3 as the final values $\breve{v}(T,u)$ and $\breve{w}(T,u)$ of the functions $\breve{v}(t,u)$ and $\breve{w}(t,u)$.

Closure in cash. We give some details for a call option. The situation for a put is entirely similar. In the case of a closure in cash, the trader will have to trade in all of its underlying stocks, resulting in an added cost of $-c^- v(T)$. (Recall that $c^- \le 0$.) Hence its total closure costs will be $N(u(T), v(T))$ with

$$N(u,v) = M(u) - c^- v.$$

It will be useful to write this in terms of two auxiliary functions $\breve{v}(u)$ and $\breve{w}(u)$, according to the following tables

Call	$u \leq K$	$u \geq K$
$\check{v}(u)$	0	$u/(1+c^-)$
$\check{w}(u)$	0	$u/(1+c^-) - K$

$N(u,v) = \check{w}(u) + c^-(\check{v}(u) - v)$

Put	$u \leq K$	$u \geq K$
$\check{v}(u)$	$-u/(1+c^+)$	0
$\check{w}(u)$	$K - u/(1+c^+)$	0

$N(u,v) = \check{w}(u) + c^+(\check{v}(u) - v)$

(4.11)

Closure in kind. Again we discuss the case of a call. In the case of a closure in kind, if the buyer exercises the option, the trader will have to bring the underlying content in his portfolio to $v(T) = u(T)$ before giving one share of it to the buyer in exchange for K in cash. Let $\eta := \text{sign}(u - v)$. Hence we now get

$$N(u,v) = \max\{u(T) - K + c^\eta(u - v), -c^- v\}.$$

A simple analysis shows that this can be described as follows. Let

Call	$u \leq K/(1+c^+)$	$K/(1+c^+) \leq u \leq K/(1+c^-)$	$K/(1+c^-) \leq u$
$\check{v}(u)$	0	$[(1+c^+)u - K]/(c^+ - c^-)$	u
$\check{w}(u)$	0	$-c^-\check{v}(u)$	$u - K$

Put	$u \leq K/(1+c^+)$	$K/(1+c^+) \leq u \leq K/(1+c^-)$	$K/(1+c^-) \leq u$
$\check{v}(u)$	$-u$	$[K - (1+c^-)u]/(c^- - c^+)$	0
$\check{w}(u)$	$K - u$	$-c^+\check{v}(u)$	0

(4.12)

N is now given in both cases by the unique formula

$$N(u,v) = \check{w}(u) + c^\varepsilon(\check{v}(u) - v), \quad \varepsilon = \text{sign}(\check{v}(u) - v). \tag{4.13}$$

2.2.2 Non-anticipative strategies. Let $\omega \in \Omega$ represent a realization of an uncertain time function, (say the price history of a security), $\omega(t)$ be the information available to the trader from time t on, and $\xi(t)$ be the trader's decision at time t (a transaction level) with $\xi(\cdot) \in \Xi$. A *non-anticipative strategy* is an application from Ω to Ξ such that, if the restrictions of ω_1 and of ω_2 to $[0,t]$ coincide, so do those of $\varphi(\omega_1)$ and of $\varphi(\omega_2)$. In discrete time, we may distinguish strictly non anticipative strategies for which the condition is that $\omega_1(s)$ and $\omega_2(s)$ coincide for $s < t$. In continuous time, where we shall allow Dirac impulses in $\xi(\cdot)$, we must specify that if it contains an impulse at time t, then the impulse is present in the restriction of $\xi(\cdot)$ to $[0,t]$.

Let Ψ be the set of admissible relative rate of change histories $\tau(\cdot)$. We can as well decide that the admissible strategies are non-anticipative maps from $\mathbb{R}^+ \times \Psi$ into Ξ, but now, we must require that if the restrictions of $\tau_1(\cdot)$ and $\tau_2(\cdot)$ to the half-open set $[0,t)$ coincide, then

$\varphi\big(u_0,\tau_1(\cdot)\big)(t) = \varphi\big(u_0,\tau_2(\cdot)\big)(t)$. This is the right definition both in discrete time, because then $\tau(t)$ is an information on $u(t+h)$, and in continuous time because $\tau(\cdot)$ may be discontinuous, and it can be checked that allowing a strategy $\xi(t) = \varphi\big(\tau(t)\big)$ is not only not feasible in practice, it is also no longer a non anticipative strategy in $u(\cdot)$. (It does no longer forbid arbitrages.)

We shall call Φ the set of admissible (non-anticipative) strategies, the context will decide whether from Ω into Ξ or from $\mathbb{R}^+ \times \Psi$ into Ξ.

2.2.3 Hedging.

The aim of a hedging portfolio is to insure that, for all admissible price trajectories,

$$w(T) \geq N(u(T), v(T)). \tag{4.14}$$

Equivalently, this can be written as

$$\sup_{u(\cdot)\in\Omega} [N(u(T), v(T)) - w(T)] \leq 0,$$

We reformulate this using (4.6). Use the representation $\big(u(0), \tau(\cdot)\big)$ of $u(\cdot)$, and fix $u(0)$. We get

$$\sup_{\tau(\cdot)\in\Psi}\left[N\big(u(T),v(T)\big)+\int_0^T(-\tau(s)v(s)+C^{\varepsilon}\xi(s))\,\mathrm{d}s+\sum_k C^{\varepsilon_k}\xi_k\right]\leq w(0),$$

or equivalently with the discrete formula (4.10). We wish $w(0)$ to be as small as possible, so we are lead to the investigation of

$$P(u_0) = \inf_{\varphi\in\Phi}\sup_{\tau\in\Psi}\Bigg[N\big(u(T),v(T)\big) + \int_0^T\big(-\tau(s)v(s) + C^{\varepsilon}\xi(s)\big)\,\mathrm{d}s + \sum_k C^{\varepsilon_k}\xi_k\Bigg]. \tag{4.15}$$

As a matter of fact, the left hand side still depends on $u(0)$. We shall therefore get a price (or *premium*) $w(0) = P(u_0)$, function of $u(0) = u_0$.

In the case of discrete trading, the equivalent formula is (with $Kh{=}T$)

$$P(u_0) = \min_{\varphi\in\Phi}\sup_{\tau\in\Psi}\left[N\big(u_K,v_K\big) + \sum_{k=0}^{K-1}[-\tau_k(v_k+\xi_k) + C^{\varepsilon_k}\xi_k]\right] \tag{4.16}$$

3. Continuous trading, no transaction costs

This section is based upon Bernhard (2001, 2003a).

3.1 A simple theory

The framework here is that of the classical theory. We have $C^+ = C^- = 0$, and closure expenses are just $M\big(u(T)\big)$. In this case, there is no expense in moving money from stocks (i.e., v) to bonds (y), and we may use v as our control and disregard ξ.

In this framework, we achieve (4.14) via the classical device of *replication* for two different models Ω. We find a portfolio and a trading strategy insuring

$$\forall u(\cdot) \in \Omega, \quad w(T) = M\big(u(T)\big).$$

A simple way of doing this is to exhibit a function $W(t,u)$ such that

$$\forall u \in \mathbb{R}^+, \quad W(T,u) = M(u), \tag{4.17}$$

together with a strategy $v = \varphi(t,u)$ such that if one actually implements that strategy with an initial portfolio worth $w(0) = W(0, u(0))$, it results in

$$\forall \tau(\cdot) \in \Psi, \forall t \in [0,T], \quad w(t) = W\big(t, u(t)\big).$$

The way to obtain this is to choose φ in such a way that

$$\forall t \in [0,T], \forall u \in \mathbb{R}^+, \quad \dot{w}(t) = \frac{\mathrm{d}W(t,u(t))}{\mathrm{d}t}.$$

3.1.1 Prices with bounded total variation. Let us choose for Ω continuous functions with bounded total variation. We use the notations of the Stieltjes calculus to get

$$\forall u \in \mathbb{R}^+, \quad \tau v \,\mathrm{d}t = \frac{\partial W}{\partial t}\,\mathrm{d}t + \frac{\partial W}{\partial u}\tau u \,\mathrm{d}t$$

which is achieved choosing

$$\frac{\partial W}{\partial t} = 0, \quad v = u\frac{\partial W}{\partial u}.$$

Hence, $W(t,u) = W(T,u) = M(u)$.

For a simple call, this means that $v = 0$ if $u < K$, $v = 1$ if $u > K$. This is the so called "stop loss" strategy. In that model, the premium is just the parity value $P(u) = M(u)$. (Recall that interest rates have been factored out via the use of end-time values. In current value, this gives $P\big(u(0)\big) = \exp(-\rho T) M(\exp(\rho T)u))$.

3.1.2 Prices with fixed relative quadratic total variation.

Let σ be a fixed positive number. We now choose for Ω the set Ω_σ of continuous functions such that

$$\forall t \in [0,T], \quad \lim_{h\to 0} \sum_{k=0}^{t/h-1} \left(\frac{u((k+1)h)-u(kh)}{u(kh)}\right)^2 = \sigma^2 t.$$

(It should be noticed that the trajectories of the classical Samuelson geometric diffusion model belong almost surely to that set.) These functions have infinite total variation and are nowhere differentiable. But we make use of the following simple form (independently proved in Bernhard, 2003a) of a lemma of Föllner:

LEMMA 4.1 *Let a twice continuously differentiable function $V(t,u)$: $[0,T]\times\mathbb{R}^+ \to \mathbb{R}$ and $u \in \Omega_\sigma$ be such that $\forall t \in [0,T]$, it holds that $(\partial V/\partial u)\big(t,u(t)\big) = 0$, then $t \mapsto V\big(t,u(t)\big)$ is differentiable and satisfies*

$$\frac{\mathrm{d}}{\mathrm{d}t}V(t,u(t)) = \frac{\partial V}{\partial t}(t,u(t)) + \frac{\sigma^2}{2}u(t)^2\frac{\partial^2 V}{\partial u^2}(t,u(t)).$$

We set $v = xu$, so that $w = xu + y$, and let $V(t,u) = W(t,u) - x(t)u - y(t)$. We insure the condition $\partial V/\partial u = 0$ by choosing $x(t) = (\partial W/\partial u)\big(t,u(t)\big)$, and use the fact that $\mathrm{d}w = x\,\mathrm{d}u$ thus $\mathrm{d}x\,u + \mathrm{d}y = 0$ (the *self-financing condition*) to obtain that the condition $\mathrm{d}V/\mathrm{d}t = 0$ is equivalent to

$$\frac{\partial W}{\partial t} + \frac{\sigma^2}{2}u^2\frac{\partial^2 W}{\partial u^2} = 0.$$

Thus, if W satisfies the above equation and the boundary condition (4.17), which together form the celebrated "Black and Scholes equation" (Black and Scholes, 1973), the strategy $v(t) = u(t)(\partial W/\partial u)\big(t,u(t)\big)$ insures that the hedging condition (4.14) be met.

This yields a "light" Black and Scholes theory (see Bernhard, 2003a for more details), and mainly serves the purpose of showing that the said theory does not really make use of any probabilistic assumption on the price trajectories, but only on their regularity. Incidentally, it also answers the question "why is the drift absent from the solution?". Our answer is "because it is absent from the problem statement."

4. Interval model: continuous trading

This section is based upon Bernhard et al. (2002, 2004).

4.1 The interval model

We now introduce the market model that we shall use from now on, in both the continuous trading and the discrete trading theories, which shall merge in a single one.

Let two numbers $\tau^- < 0$ and $\tau^+ > 0$ be given. We choose Ω as follows:

$$\Omega = \{u(\cdot) \text{ absolutely continuous} \mid \\ \forall t_1, t_2 \in [0,T], \quad e^{\tau^-(t_2-t_1)} \le \frac{u(t_2)}{u(t_1)} \le e^{\tau^+(t_2-t_1)}\}. \quad (4.18)$$

An equivalent characterization we shall use in the continuous trading theory is (4.1) together with the condition $\tau \in [\tau^-, \tau^+]$.

Hence we assume that the relative rate of variation of the underlying's price is bounded by a priori bounds. This is a weakness of our theory, since fast variations of the prices are ruled out from the start by the very model we work with, while we know that they do happen in real life.

The geometric diffusion model used by the theory of Black and Scholes does not have that drawback. But it cannot be used to derive a theory of hedging with proportional transaction costs (see Soner et al., 1995) because its trajectories are of unbounded total variation, yielding infinite transaction costs, nor in discrete time, whether with or without transaction costs, because the possible price variation in any finite time interval is unbounded. The fact that the continuous trajectory be of unbounded total variation may be a desirable feature. Anyhow, it is difficult to avoid within a stochastic theory, as it is a consequence of the fact that one needs a process with independent increments to avoid any arbitrage opportunity. The framework of robust control and non-anticipative strategies avoids that problem since we do not need to endow the set of trajectories with a probability which the trader might use to devise an arbitrage.

It should be further emphasized that Black and Scholes' theory suffers its own shortcomings in that it requires a continuous trading with no delay in information use, an unrealistic portfolio model. This is of little consequence as long as the prices do not change too rapidly, but becomes a fundamental limitation of the usefulness of the theory as a guide to managing a hedging portfolio when these sudden changes do happen. Hence in the situations where our market model is violated, so is Black and Scholes' portfolio model.

4.2 Isaacs' equation

We therefore have the following problem to solve. The dynamics are now (4.1) (4.2) (4.3) with $\tau(\cdot) \in \Psi = \{$measurable functions $[0, T] \to [\tau^-, \tau^+]\}$, $\xi(\cdot) \in \Xi$ where it is understood that $\xi(\cdot)$ contains the impulses that cause the jumps (4.3), that is, Ξ is the set of all sums of measurable functions from $[0, T]$ into $\mathbb{R}$ and of finitely many weighted translated Dirac impulses $\xi_k \delta(t - t_k)$.

The problem is to find, if it exists, the non-anticipative strategy $\varphi^* \in \Phi$ that provides the minimum in (4.15).

This is a non-classical differential game in that it features an impulse control, and the corresponding Isaacs quasi variational inequality is further degenerated, as compared to the (control) theory in Bensoussan and Lions (1982), because the cost of jumps has a zero infimum. Yet, we may take advantage of that last fact to transform that game into a classical one in an artificial time (see Joshua's transformation in Bernhard et al., 2002), leading to a differential form of the quasi-variational inequality of the impulse control game, and to the following theorem.

THEOREM 4.1 *The Value function $W(t, u, v)$ of the above game is a viscosity solution of the following differential quasi-variational inequality:*

$$0 = \min\left\{ \frac{\partial W}{\partial t} + \max_{\tau \in [\tau^-, \tau^+]} \tau \left[\frac{\partial W}{\partial u} u + \left(\frac{\partial W}{\partial v} - 1 \right) v \right], \right.$$
$$\left. \frac{\partial W}{\partial v} + C^+, -\left(\frac{\partial W}{\partial v} + C^- \right) \right\}, \tag{4.19}$$

$$W(T, u, v) = N(u, v).$$

This function is further characterized by its rates of growth at infinity in u (one) and v ($-C^+$ at $-\infty$ and $-C^-$ at $+\infty$). Yet, a direct uniqueness proof derived from the theory of viscosity solutions of Isaacs equation is still missing. We rely instead on the fact that the solution we shall exhibit with the representation theorem below is sufficiently regular for the Isaacs-Breakwell theory to apply, the viscosity condition being the modern form of Breakwell's "non leaking corners" (or our corner conditions). (See Bernhard, 1977; Breakwell, 1977.)

In our case, the function N is convex. The following is a consequence of the convergence theorem of the next section (we do not know a direct proof):

THEOREM 4.2 *When the function N is convex, the solution of* (4.19) *is convex in (u, v) for all t.*

This is an interesting property in itself. In addition, we discuss in Bernhard et al. (2002) how this saves much time in the computations of a discretized scheme for numerically solving that equation. Yet the real breakthrough in the numerical computation of that function is given by the following subsection, and the corresponding numerical algorithm that we shall show in the next section.

4.3 A representation theorem

We need to introduce the following notations. Let, for a closure in kind

$$\begin{aligned} q^-(t) &= \max\{(1+c^-)\exp[\tau^-(T-t)]-1, C^-\}, \\ q^+(t) &= \min\{(1+c^+)\exp[\tau^+(T-t)]-1, C^+\}. \end{aligned} \tag{4.20}$$

(For a closure in cash, both q^+ and q^- are constructed with c^- for a call and c^+ for a put instead of c^ε above). We shall refer to both at a time as q^ε, where $\varepsilon = \pm$ is usually the sign of $\check{v} - v$ (see below). Notice that $q^\varepsilon = C^\varepsilon$ for $t \le t_\varepsilon = T - (1/\tau^\varepsilon)\ln[(1+C^\varepsilon)/(1+c^\varepsilon)]$, and increases (for q^+) or decreases (for q^-) towards c^ε as $t \to T$. For any realistic data, t_+ and t_- are very close to T, say one day or less.

Let also

$$\mathcal{S} = \begin{pmatrix} 1 & 0 \\ 1 & 0 \end{pmatrix}, \text{ and } \mathcal{T} = \frac{1}{q^+ - q^-}\begin{pmatrix} \tau^+q^+ - \tau^-q^- & \tau^+ - \tau^- \\ -(\tau^+ - \tau^-)q^+q^- & \tau^-q^+ - \tau^+q^- \end{pmatrix}.$$

We introduce a pair of functions of two variables $\check{v}(t,u)$ and $\check{w}(t,u)$ collectively called

$$\mathcal{V}(t,u) = \begin{pmatrix} \check{v}(t,u) \\ \check{w}(t,u) \end{pmatrix}$$

and defined by the final conditions (4.11) or (4.12), depending on which applies, and the following linear P.D.E.:

$$\frac{\partial \mathcal{V}}{\partial t} + \mathcal{T}\left(\frac{\partial \mathcal{V}}{\partial u}u - \mathcal{S}\mathcal{V}\right) = 0. \tag{4.21}$$

It may be noticed that $\check{v}(t,u)$ and $\check{w}(t,u)$ keep the same form as in (4.11) for $u \notin \left[K\exp\bigl(\tau^+(t-T)\bigr), K\exp\bigl(\tau^-(t-T)\bigr)\right]$ for a closure in cash, or (4.12) and $u \notin \left[(K/1+c^+)\exp\bigl(\tau^+(t-T)\bigr), (K/1+c^-)\exp\bigl(\tau^-(t-T)\bigr)\right]$ for a closure in kind.

We prove in Bernhard et al. (2004) the following representation theorem:

THEOREM 4.3 *The Value function of the game is given by the formula*

$$W(t,u,v) = \check{w}(t,u) + q^\varepsilon(\check{v}(t,u) - v), \qquad \varepsilon = \text{sign}(\check{v}(t,u) - v). \tag{4.22}$$

This formula gives a useful insight into the shape of the value function and the role of the transaction costs. It also is the basis of a fast algorithm to approximate W, that we shall see in the next section. The main point is that we have to compute for each time instant two functions of one variable instead of one function of two variables, a considerable savings if each variable is discretized in a few hundreds to a few thousand points. Moreover, $\check{v}$ plays the role of an "optimal portfolio composition" as the next result shows:

THEOREM 4.4 *The optimal trading strategy is to jump at initial time to* $v = \check{v}\big(0, u(0)\big)$ *and stay at* $v(t) = \check{v}\big(t, u(t)\big)$ *while* $t < t_\varepsilon$*, do nothing if* $t \geq t_\varepsilon$*.*

There, however, lies a difficulty. Staying at $v(t) = \check{v}\big(t, u(t)\big)$ is not possible within our assumptions, because one easily sees that this would entail a strategy of the form $\xi(t) = \varphi\big(t, u(t), v(t), \tau(t)\big)$. But we have emphasized the fact that this is *not* an admissible, non-anticipative, strategy. The solution of that dilemma is provided by the convergence result of the next section which shows that the optimal value in the game above can be approximated arbitrarily well with a non-anticipative (discrete) trading strategy. (The minimum is actually *not* reached in (4.15)).

5. Interval model: Discrete trading

This section is based upon the same references Bernhard et al. (2002, 2004) as the previous one.

5.1 The model

We turn to the more realistic model where trading is restricted to happen at discrete time instants. Let $h > 0$ be our time step. The trader is restricted to jumps of the form (4.3) at predetermined time instants, multiples of h. Let therefore $t_k = kh$, $k \in \mathbb{N}$, $u(t_k) = u_k$ and $v(t_k) = v_k$. The market model Ω translates into

$$e^{\tau^- h} - 1 \leq \frac{u_{k+1} - u_k}{u_k} \leq e^{\tau^+ h} - 1.$$

We shall let $\tau_h^\varepsilon := \exp(\tau^\varepsilon h) - 1$. It should be noted that τ_h^ε converges to 0 as h (it is equivalent to $\tau^\varepsilon h$), instead of as $\sqrt{h}$ in the limiting Cox Ross and Rubinstein theory. This means that we do keep a single market model Ω, while the step size is decreased towards zero, while the classical (and remarkable) limiting process of the Cox Ross and Rubinstein theory towards the Black and Scholes theory entails a continuous change of model.

With these notations, our model is now (4.7)(4.8) with $\tau_k \in [\tau_h^-, \tau_h^+]$, and the non-anticipative strategies are simply of the form $\xi_k = \varphi_k(u_k,$

$u_{k-1},\dots)$. Equivalently, we shall find the optimal strategy in the form $\xi_k = \varphi_k(u_k, v_k)$. And our problem is to find the minimum, together with the minimizing strategy φ^*, in (4.16).

5.2 Isaacs' equation

This problem is now a classical multistage dynamic game, whose value function W^h is given by its Isaacs equation (we again use subscripts for the stage counter, and $Kh = T$):

$$\begin{aligned} W_k^h(u,v) &= \min_{\xi} \max_{\tau\in[\tau_h^-,\tau_h^+]} \big[W_{k+1}^h\big((1+\tau)u,(1+\tau)(v+\xi)\big) \\ &\qquad\qquad - \tau(v+\xi) + C^\varepsilon\xi\big] \qquad (4.23) \\ W_K^h(u,v) &= N(u,v). \end{aligned}$$

It turns out to be useful to notice the following "fractional step" form of the first equation:

$$\begin{aligned} W_{k+\frac{1}{2}}^h(u,v) &= \max_{\tau\in[\tau_h^-,\tau_h^+]} \big[W_{k+1}^h\big((1+\tau)u,(1+\tau)v\big) - \tau v\big], \\ W_k^h(u,v) &= \min_{\xi}[W_{k+\frac{1}{2}}^h(u,v+\xi) + C^\varepsilon\xi]. \end{aligned}$$

This form lets one easily show the following theorem:

THEOREM 4.5 *If the function $v \mapsto N(u,v)$ is convex for all u, so is the function $v \mapsto W_k^h(u,v)$ for all (k,u). If the function $(u,v) \mapsto N(u,v)$ is convex, so is the function $(u,v) \mapsto W_k^h(u,v)$ for all k.*

This theorem in turn is useful to accelerate a numerical algorithm to evaluate the sequence $\{W_k^h\}_k$ and the optimal trading strategy using Isaacs'equation. As a matter off fact, then $\tau \mapsto W_{k+1}\big((1+\tau)u,(1+\tau)v\big)$ is convex, hence its max is reached at an end of the interval $[\tau_h^-,\tau_h^+]$. And the minimization in ξ can also benefit from the convexity, see Bernhard et al. (2002). We do not stress much that fact here because the representation theorem below provides a much faster algorithm when it holds. But an important consequence of the remark concerning the maximum in τ is as follows.

PROPOSITION 4.1 *For a convex claim $M(u)$, the above theory with no transaction costs coincide with the Cox, Ross, and Rubinstein theory (Cox et al., 1979).*

A consequence of that proposition is that, for small transaction costs and small time step, for reasonable values of τ_h^- and τ_h^+, the pricing curve given by our theory will resemble that of Black and Scholes.

The main theorem of our discrete trading theory is the following. Define $W^h(t,u,v)$ as being the linear interpolation in time of the sequence $\{W_k^h(u,v)\}$.

THEOREM 4.6 *The function $W^h(t,u,v)$ converges uniformly on any compact to the function $W(t,u,v)$ (value of the continuous trading problem) when h tends to zero as $h = Tn^{-d}$, $n,d \in \mathbb{N}$, $d \to \infty$.*

As a matter of fact, one easily sees first that the W_k^h are non-negative, and using classical ideas of dynamical games, we see that W^h decreases as d above increases. It therefore has a monotoneous limit. This limit is then shown to be a sufficiently regular viscosity solution of (4.19) using basically the method of Capuzzo Dolcetta (1983), but with many technical details to adapt it to our problem.

The consequence of that theorem is that one can approximate arbitrarily well the value of the continuous trading portfolio with discrete trading, if that trading happens often enough. This is a very desirable feature of any continuous trading theory, since trading has to be discrete in practice, yet it is not enjoyed by the Black and Scholes theory.

5.3 Representation theorem and fast algorithm

Introduce the following recursions. Let

$$q_K^\varepsilon = c^\varepsilon$$

for a closure in kind, or

$$q_K^\varepsilon = c^- \text{ for a Call} \quad \text{and} \quad q_K^\varepsilon = c^+ \text{ for a Put}$$

for a closure in cash, and

$$\begin{aligned} q_{k+1/2}^\varepsilon &= (1+\tau_h^\varepsilon) q_{k+1}^\varepsilon + \tau_h^\varepsilon, \\ q_k^\varepsilon &= \varepsilon \min\{\varepsilon q_{k+1/2}^\varepsilon, \varepsilon C^\varepsilon\}, \end{aligned} \tag{4.24}$$

and let, for every integer ℓ:

$$Q_\ell^\varepsilon = \begin{pmatrix} q_\ell^\varepsilon & 1 \end{pmatrix} \quad \text{and} \quad \mathcal{V}_\ell^h(u) = \begin{pmatrix} \check{v}_\ell^h(u) \\ \check{w}_\ell^h(u) \end{pmatrix}. \tag{4.25}$$

(Notice that then $q_k^\varepsilon = q^\varepsilon(kh)$ as given by (4.20).) Take $\check{v}_K^h(u) = \check{v}(u)$, $\check{w}_K^h(u) = \check{w}(u)$ as given by (4.11) or (4.12) according to which applies, and

$$\mathcal{V}_k^h(u) = \frac{1}{q_{k+1/2}^+ - q_{k+1/2}^-} \times \begin{pmatrix} 1 & -1 \\ -q_{k+1/2}^- & q_{k+1/2}^+ \end{pmatrix} \begin{pmatrix} Q_{k+1}^+ \mathcal{V}_{k+1}^h((1+\tau_h^+)u) \\ Q_{k+1}^- \mathcal{V}_{k+1}^h((1+\tau_h^-)u) \end{pmatrix}. \tag{4.26}$$

It can be checked that this is a consistent finite difference scheme for (4.21).

We claim (proof to appear in Bernhard et al., 2004):

THEOREM 4.7 *The solution of* (4.23) *is given by* (4.24), (4.25), (4.26), *and* (4.11) *or* (4.12), *as*

$$W_k^h(u,v) = \breve{w}_k^h(u) + q_k^\varepsilon(\breve{v}_k^h(u) - v) = Q_k^\varepsilon V_k^h(u) - q_k^\varepsilon v, \quad \varepsilon = \mathrm{sign}(\breve{v}_k^h(u) - v).$$

This theorem is the basis for a fast algorithm to compute the sequence $\{W_k^h\}_k$ and the corresponding minimizing non-anticipative strategy φ^*. And in view of the convergence theorem, it is also an algorithm to approximate the continuous trading limit.

5.4 Extensions

Some extensions of that theory are natural and simple. (Some are difficult such as the case of the digital options which are neither convex nor continuous. We shall report on that case elsewhere.) Let us just show two such extensions.

5.4.1 American options.

Dealing with American options requires that one re-introduces the riskless interest rate ρ. Let

$$\widehat{N}(t,u,v) = \mathrm{e}^{\rho(t-T)} N\big(\mathrm{e}^{\rho(T-t)}u, \mathrm{e}^{\rho(T-t)}v\big),$$

and as usual $\widehat{N}_k^h(u,v) = \widehat{N}(kh,u,v)$. This is the cost to the writer if the buyer exercises the option at time $t < T$. The minimax control problem is now one with stopping time, since the buyer may stop the problem any time. The criterion (4.16) should therefore be replaced by

$$P(u_0) = \inf_{\varphi\in\Phi} \sup_{\tau\in\Psi} \sup_{\ell<K} \left[\widehat{N}_\ell(u_\ell, v_\ell) + \sum_{k=0}^{\ell-1}[-\tau_k(v_k+\xi_k) + C^{\varepsilon_k}\xi_k]\right]. \quad (4.27)$$

It is a classical fact that Isaacs equation is now replaced by a quasi variational inequality

$$W_k^h(u,v) = \max\Big\{\widehat{N}_k^h(u_k,v_k), \min_\xi \max_{\tau\in[\tau_h^-,\tau_h^+]} [W_{k+1}^h((1+\tau)u,(1+\tau)(v+\xi)) - \tau(v+\xi) + C^\varepsilon\xi]\Big\},$$

$$W_K^h(u,v) = N(u,v).$$

Numerically implementing that equation requires adding a single line of code in the implementation of (4.23). As a matter of fact, one computes the $\min_\xi \max_\tau$ exactly in the same fashion, and upon writing it in the table holding W_k^h, compare with $\widehat{N}_k^h$ and keep whichever is larger for W_k^h. And because the maximum of convex functions is convex, we preserve the convexity of W_k^h, and hence the fast computation we derived from it.

We have done very little work with that theory, and do not have a representation theorem comparable to the above one. Whether there is one is an open question. What we did check is the following, which is as in the stochastic theory:

THEOREM 4.8 *It is never advantageous for the buyer to exercise an American call before exercize time.*

5.4.2 Strictly causal strategies. If the trading instants are to be very closely spaced (small h), it may be more realistic to allow the trader to use only u_{k-1} to choose ξ_k. This strictly causal strategy is the equivalent of a predictable strategy in a stochastic framework, as opposed to measurable (only). This is easily done via the following device. Decide that $\xi_k = \varphi(u_k, v_k)$ can be applied only at time $k+1$. (Hence it is the ξ_{k+1} of the previous theory.) Now, this is achieved by changing our dynamic model into

$$v_{k+1} = (1+\tau)v_k + \xi_k$$

instead of (4.8).

Isaacs'equation is changed accordingly. However, it does not easily split into two equations as was done here, hence even the convexity of the resulting value function is not as easy to prove. Again, this has not been investigated so far.

6. Conclusion

The approach of robust control together with the interval model for the market yields a rather comprehensive theory of option pricing. This model has its drawbacks. But it lets us build a consistent theory of discrete and continuous trading option hedging with transaction costs, a feat that the classical stochastic approach with Samuelson's market model can not achieve. Moreover, while the main weakness of the model is in the market model, it should be noted that this model is violated under the same circumstances that cause the portfolio model of Black and Scholes theory to fail.

This is an incomplete market model, which is a serious drawback, because we must therefore resort to super replication instead of exact replication. Whether this leads to unacceptably high prices depends on the choice of interval $[\tau_h^-, \tau_h^+]$, and there is therefore a trade-off to be made between the realism of the market model and the price to pay for that undesirable feature. Yet, the difference in pricing with the Black and Scholes theory, in the case of a convex claim, is not very large, as the comparison with the theory of Cox, Ross, and Rubinstein shows. (And since our pricing is obviously a continuous function of the transaction costs, which are ignored in that comparison.)

A rather unexpected representation theorem yields a fast algorithm to numerically implement the theory, thus approaching in that respect the great simplicity and elegance of Black and Scholes theory.

References

Aubin, J.-P., Pujal, D., and Saint-Pierre, P. (2005). Dynamic management of portfolios with transaction costs under tychastic uncertainty. In this volume.

Bensoussan, A. and Lions, J.L. (1982). *Contrôle impulsionnel et inéquations quasi variationnelles.* Dunod, Paris.

Bernhard, P. (1977). Singular surfaces in differential games: an introduction. In: Haggedorn et al. (eds.), *Differential games and Applications*, pp. 1 – 33. Lecture Notes in Information and Control Sciences, vol. 3. Springer, Berlin.

Bernhard, P. (2001). Une approche déterministe de l'évaluation d'options. In: J-L. Menaldi, E. Roffman, and A. Sulem (eds.), *Optimal Control and Partial Differential Equations*, pp. 511 – 520. IOS Press.

Bernhard, P. (2003a). Robust control approach to option pricing. In: M. Salmon (ed.), *Applications of Robust Decision Theory and Ambiguity in Finance.* City University Press, London.

Bernhard, P. (2003b). An explicit solution of quasi-variational inequality arising in finances. In: 4th ISDG Workshop, pp. 19–21. Goslar, Germany.

Bernhard, P. (2004). A robust control approach to option pricing including transaction costs. In: A. Nowak (ed.), *Annals of the International Society of Dynamic Games*, vol. 7. Birkhäuser.

Bernhard, P., El-Farouq, N., and Thiery, S. (2002). An impulsive differential game arising in finance with interesting singularities. In: *10th International Symposium on Dynamic Games and Applications*, pp. 8 – 11. St. Petersburg, Russia.

Bernhard, P., El-Farouq, N., and Thiery, S. (2005). Discrete and continuous hedging strategies with transaction costs in the interval model. I3S internal report, University of Nice-Sophia Antipolis. Submitted for publication.

Black, F. and Scholes, M. (1973). The pricing of options and corporate liabilities. *Journal of Political Economy*, 81:637 – 659.

Breakwell, J.V. (1977). A lecture on differential games. In Haggedorn et al. (eds.), *Differential games and Applications*, Lecture Notes in Information and Control Sciences, vol. 3. Springer, Berlin.

Capuzzo Dolcetta, I. (1983). On a discrete approximation of the Hamilton – Jacobi equation of dynamic programming. *Applied Mathematics and Optimization*, 10:367 – 377.

Cox, J.C., Ross, S.A., and Rubinstein, M. (1979). Option pricing: A simplified approach. *Journal of Financial Economics*, 7:229–263.

Dupire, B. (2003). *Résultats de dominance.* Seminar at Université de Nice.

McEneaney, W.M. (1997). A robust control framework for option pricing. *Mathematics of Operations Research*, 22:22 – 221.

Pujal, D. (2000). *Évaluation et gestion dynamiques de portefeuilles.* Thesis, Université Paris-Dauphine.

Roorda, B., Engwerda, J., and Schumacher, H. (2000). *Performance of Hedging Strategies in Interval Models.* Preprint.

Roorda, B., Engwerda, J., and Schumacher, H. (2003). *Coherent Acceptability Measures in Multiperiod Models.* Preprint (http://center.uvt.nl/staff/schumach/pub/arch/coh_rev.pdf).

Saint-Pierre, P. (2004). Viable capture basin for studying differential and hybrid games. *International Game Theory Review*, 6:109 – 136.

Soner, H.M., Shreve, S.E., and Cvitanic, J. (1995). There is no nontrivial hedging portfolio for option pricing with transaction costs. *The Annals of Applied Probability*, 5:327–355.

Chapter 5

A FINITE ELEMENT METHOD FOR TWO FACTOR CONVERTIBLE BONDS

Javier de Frutos

Abstract We present a finite element method for the numerical valuation of two factor convertible bonds with call and put embedded options. We use the method of lines to decouple the state variables and the temporal discretizations. The state variables discretization is carried out by means of bilinear finite elements. For the temporal discretization we use an implicit-explicit Runge–Kutta method. Some numerical experiments are presented.

1. Introduction

A wide variety of derivative securities traded in exchange markets such as call or put options on dividend paying stocks, foreign currency options, callable bonds, among others, are American type contracts. An American contract gives the right to exercise and exit the contract at any time before the expiration date specified in the contract. Valuating such contracts is considerably more difficult than the corresponding European contract where the holder can only exercise at expiration. In fact there is no closed form analytical formula for valuing American contracts even in the simpler cases. Numerical methods are thus necessary for pricing those contracts.

In this chapter we are concerned with the problem of pricing convertible bonds with embedded call or put options. A bond is a contract paying a known fixed amount, the principal, at a given date in the future, the maturity. The contract can also pay smaller quantities, the coupons, at specific intervals up to the maturity date. Many contracts incorporate several embedded options such as call, put or conversion features. A callable bond gives the issuer the right to purchase back the bond for a fixed amount, the call price, whereas a putable one gives the holder the right to return the bond to the issuer for a fixed amount, the put price. Convertible bonds add the possibility of exchanging the bond for a fixed number of shares of the issuer. Usually the optional features incorporated in the bond can be exercised at any time during the life of the bond. Such contracts fall into the class of American style derivatives.

A number of methods have been employed for the numerical valuation of bonds with embedded options. Finite difference methods were used for the first time in Brennan and Schwarz (1977). Trinomial trees were later used in Hull and White (1990). A finite volume method with stabilization was used in d'Halluin et al. (2001) whereas in Barone-Adesi et al. (2003) the authors used finite elements coupled with the characteristics method. Recently, in Ben-Ameur et al. (2004) the authors propose a dynamic programing approach which is proved to be a very efficient way to numerically evaluate bonds with embedded call and put options which can be exercised at discrete times. Of course this list of references is not, and cannot be, exhaustive. We refer the interested reader to the references contained in the previously cited papers for a more complete and up-to-date list.

Several diffusion models have been used in the literature to describe the dynamics of the short term risk-free interest rate. In this chapter we use the CIR model (Cox et al., 1985) but the numerical method we present is sufficiently general to be easily applicable to other models as, for example, the Hull and White's model (Hull and White, 1990). In practice the use of a general model can be necessary in order to calibrate the parameters to capture the term structure of interest rate; see for example Barone-Adesi et al. (2003).

The rest of the chapter is organized as follows. In Section 2 we present the valuation problem and its formulation as a set of partial differential inequalities. In Section 3 we present the proposed discretization of the continuous model. We use a penalty formulation to approximate the variational inequalities. We use the method of lines to decouple the discretization into two separate steps, the finite element approximation to the state variable and the temporal discretization by means of an implicit-explicit Runge–Kutta method. The method requires a non linear iteration that is proved to be convergent in a finite number of steps. In Section 4 we present some numerical experiments to illustrate the practical behaviour of the method.

2. The model

The price $V(S,r,t)$ of a convertible bond with maturity date $T>0$, which fromnow on is supposed to be constant, is a measurable function of the underlying stock S, the spot interest rate r and the time $t<T$. Although the price depends also on the maturity T, for the sake of simplicity in the notation we shall not make explicit this dependence. We present the model under the risk-free measure. The dynamics for the stock and interest rate are given by the diffusion processes:

$$dS_t = (r-D)S_t\,dt + \omega_S S_t\,dW_t^1, \tag{5.1}$$

$$dr_t = (a-br_t)\,dt + \omega_r r_t^{1/2}\,dW_t^2, \tag{5.2}$$

where D, a, b, ω_S and ω_r are given constants and W_t^1, W_t^2 are two standard Brownian motions. In addition we suppose that the stock and the short-rate processes are correlated

$$\mathbb{E}(dW_t^1 dW_t^2) = \rho\,dt, \quad -1<\rho<1. \tag{5.3}$$

The contract has the following specifications:

1 Continuous coupon payments. The holder receives coupon payments at rate $\kappa(S,r,t)$.

2 At the expiration date the issuer pays a fixed amount Par, the principal or par value of the bond.

3 Conversion feature. The holder has the right to convert the bond into n units of the stock at any time $t\le T$.

4 Put feature. The holder can put back the bond at any time $t\le T$ for a specified reward $\mathrm{PP}(t)$.

5 Call feature. The issuer can call back the bond paying a specified compensation $\mathrm{CP}(t)$ to the holder.

Elimination of arbitrage opportunities impose the following restrictions on the value of the bond

$$V(S,r,t) \ge \max\big(nS, \mathrm{PP}(t)\big),$$
$$V(S,r,t) \le \mathrm{CP}(t).$$

Given two stopping times σ and ζ we define the reward functional as the expectation at time t, under the risk-free measure, of the future payoff discounted at the risk-free rate, that is

$$\begin{aligned} J_{x,t}(\sigma,\zeta) = \mathbb{E}^{x,t}\bigg(\int_t^{\sigma\wedge\zeta} & e^{-\int_t^u r(X_v,v)dv}\kappa(X_u,u)\,du \\ & + e^{-\int_t^\sigma r(X_u,u)du}\psi_1(X_\sigma,\sigma)\chi_{\sigma<\zeta} \\ & + e^{-\int_t^\zeta r(X_u,u)du}\psi_2(X_\zeta,\zeta)\chi_{\sigma\ge\zeta}\bigg), \end{aligned} \tag{5.4}$$

where $\mathbb{E}^{x,t}$ is the mathematical expectation with respect the probabilistic law of the process given by (5.1) and (5.2) such that $X_t = x$, χ_A is the indicator function of a measurable set A and $\sigma \wedge \zeta = \min(\sigma, \zeta)$. Here, X_t denotes the stochastic vector $X_t = (S_t, r_t)$. The functions ψ_1 and ψ_2 are given by

$$\begin{aligned}\psi_1 &= \mathrm{CP}(t),\\ \psi_2 &= \min\bigl(\max(nS, \mathrm{PP}(t), \mathrm{Par}\,\delta_{t-T}), \mathrm{CP}(t)\bigr),\end{aligned}$$

where δ denotes the Dirac function.

The holder's objective is to maximize $J(x,t)$ choosing ζ whereas the issuer chooses σ to minimize the payoff $J(x,t)$. The problem is to find (σ^*, ζ^*) such that

$$J_{x,t}(\sigma^*, \zeta) \le J_{x,t}(\sigma^*, \zeta^*) \le J_{x,t}(\sigma, \zeta^*). \tag{5.5}$$

The fair value of the bond is then

$$V(x,t) = J_{x,t}(\sigma^*, \zeta^*) = \inf_{\sigma} \sup_{\zeta} J_{x,t}(\sigma, \zeta) = \sup_{\zeta} \inf_{\sigma} J_{x,t}(\sigma, \zeta). \tag{5.6}$$

The value function can be deterministically determined as the solution of the following set of differential inequalities (Friedman, 1976):

$$\begin{aligned}
&\frac{\partial V}{\partial t} - LV - rV + \kappa \ge 0, \qquad \psi_2 < V \le \psi_1, \qquad (S,r) \in \Omega,\\
&\frac{\partial V}{\partial t} - LV - rV + \kappa \le 0, \qquad \psi_2 \le V < \psi_1, \qquad (S,r) \in \Omega,\\
&\frac{\partial V}{\partial t} - LV - rV + \kappa = 0, \qquad \psi_2 < V < \psi_1, \qquad (S,r) \in \Omega,\\
&\qquad V(S,r,T) = \psi_2(S,r), \quad (S,r) \in \Omega,
\end{aligned} \tag{5.7}$$

where $\Omega = (0,\infty) \times (0,\infty)$ and LV denotes the characteristic operator

$$\begin{aligned}LV = -\left(\frac{1}{2}\omega_S^2 S^2 \frac{\partial^2 V}{\partial S^2} + \rho\omega_S\omega_r S r^{1/2} \frac{\partial^2 V}{\partial S \partial r} + \frac{1}{2}\omega_r^2 r \frac{\partial^2 V}{\partial r^2}\right)\\
- \left((r-D)S\frac{\partial V}{\partial S} + (a - br)\frac{\partial V}{\partial r}\right).\end{aligned}$$

Furthermore, it can be proved (Friedman, 1976) that the optimal exercise policies (σ^*, ζ^*) are defined by

$$\sigma^* = t(A_{\psi_1}), \quad \zeta^* = t(A_{\psi_2}),$$

where

$$A_{\psi_1} = \{(x,t) \mid V(x,t) = \psi_1(x,t)\},$$

$$A_{\psi_2} = \{(x,t) \mid V(x,t) = \psi_2(x,t)\},$$

and $t(A)$ denotes the first hitting time of the set A,

$$t(A) = \inf\{t \mid 0 \leq t \leq T, X_t \in A\}.$$

REMARK The model assumes a continuous coupon payment. The case of discrete coupon dates can be formally included in the model by setting $\kappa(t) = \sum_{i=1}^{N} \kappa_i \delta_{(t-t_i)}$, where κ_i is the coupon paid at time t_i and δ is the Dirac delta function. However, in practice it is better to implement discrete coupons through the so called jump conditions

$$V(S,r,t_i^-) = V(S,r,t_i) + \kappa_i;$$

see, for example, Tavella and Randall (2000).

3. The discrete problem

We follow the method of lines and discretize separately the state variables and then the time. The main advantage of decoupling the discretization procedure is that it makes it easier to combine well developed, numerically efficient methods for each one of the decoupled problems. We present in this section a combined finite element method for the state variables coupled with an explicit-implicit Runge–Kutta method of proved efficiency for convection-diffusion equations. The time integrator has other interesting properties, in particular it gives fast guaranteed convergence of the nonlinear discrete problem arising after the discretization of (5.7).

The discretization of the state variables consists in two steps: Localization and regularization, and finite element approximation.

3.1 Localization and regularization

The solution of (5.7) can be approximated by means of a sequence of problems posed over bounded increasing domains. More precisely, let us consider a sequence $\Omega_k = (0, S_k) \times (0, r_k) \subset \Omega$ with

$$\lim_{k\to\infty} S_k = \infty, \qquad \lim_{k\to\infty} r_k = \infty.$$

For each k, the auxiliary domain Ω_k is called the computational domain.

Let $V^k(x,t)$ be the solution of the localized problem

$$
\begin{aligned}
&\frac{\partial V^k}{\partial t} - LV^k - rV^k + \kappa \geq 0, \qquad \psi_2 < V^k \leq \psi_1, \qquad (S,r) \in \Omega_k,\\
&\frac{\partial V^k}{\partial t} - LV^k - rV^k + \kappa \leq 0, \qquad \psi_2 \leq V^k < \psi_1, \qquad (S,r) \in \Omega_k,\\
&\frac{\partial V^k}{\partial t} - LV^k - rV^k + \kappa = 0, \qquad \psi_2 < V^k < \psi_1, \qquad (S,r) \in \Omega_k,\\
&\qquad V^k(S,r,T) = \psi_2(S,r,T), \quad (S,r) \in \Omega_k,
\end{aligned}
\tag{5.8}
$$

together with the supplementary boundary conditions

$$
\begin{aligned}
V(S, r_k, t) &= \psi_2(S, r_k, t), \quad 0 < S < S_k,\\
V(S_k, r, t) &= \psi_1(S_k, r, t), \quad 0 < r < r_k.
\end{aligned}
\tag{5.9}
$$

We note that the artificial boundary conditions (5.9) are essentially arbitrary, yet financially reasonable. For $nS \geq \mathrm{CP}(t)$ the bond will likely be called back. Otherwise, the holder could convert it, clearly resulting in a not optimal issuer policy. Then choosing $S_k > \mathrm{CP}(t)$, $0 \leq t \leq T$, the appropriate boundary condition is $V(S_k, r, t) = \mathrm{CP}(t) = \psi_1(S_k, r, t)$. For an exceedingly high interest rate, the straight bond component will be small. Then $V(S, r_k, t) = \psi_2(S, r_k, t)$ for r_k big enough. Other boundary conditions are possible. We refer for example to Tavella and Randall (2000) for a discussion of the different possibilities. From Friedman (1976) (see also Jaillet et al., 1990; Kangro and Nicolaides, 2000; Marcozzi, 2001) it can be shown that

$$
\lim_{k\to\infty} \max_{t\in[0,T]} \|V(\cdot,t) - V^k(\cdot,t)\|_{\overline{\Omega}_A} = 0, \tag{5.10}
$$

where $\Omega_A \subset \Omega$ is any given fixed bounded approximation domain.

In the next step we regularize the problem (5.8) – (5.9) by penalization. To this end, for $\epsilon > 0$ we look for $V^{k,\epsilon}$ solving the penalty problem

$$
\begin{aligned}
&\frac{\partial V^{k,\epsilon}}{\partial t} - LV^{k,\epsilon} - rV^{k,\epsilon} - \frac{1}{\epsilon}\beta(V^{k,\epsilon}) + \kappa = 0, \quad (S,r) \in \Omega_k,\\
&\qquad V^{k,\epsilon}(S,r,T) = \psi_2(S,r,T), \qquad (S,r) \in \Omega_k,\\
&\qquad V^{k,\epsilon}(S,r_k,t) = \psi_2(S,r_k,t), \qquad 0 < S < S_k,\\
&\qquad V^{k,\epsilon}(S_k,r,t) = \psi_1(S_k,r,t), \qquad 0 < r < r_k,
\end{aligned}
\tag{5.11}
$$

where

$$
\beta(U) = \max(U - \psi_1, 0) + \min(U - \psi_2, 0). \tag{5.12}
$$

We have the following convergence result (see Friedman, 1976; Nochetto, 1988):

$$\psi_2 - C\epsilon \leq V^{k,\epsilon}(S,r,t) \leq \psi_1 + C\epsilon, \quad (S,r) \in \Omega_k, \quad t \in [0,T], \tag{5.13}$$

$$\lim_{k\to\infty} \max_{t\in[0,T]} \|V(\cdot,t) - V^{k,\epsilon}(\cdot,t)\|_{\overline{\Omega}_A} \leq C\epsilon. \tag{5.14}$$

3.2 Finite element approximation

Let us consider a family of partitions

$$\mathcal{P} = \{Q_{ij}\}_{i,j=1}^{J_S,J_r}, \quad Q_{ij} = (S_{i-1},S_i) \times (r_{j-1},r_j)$$

of the computational domain Ω_k, with

$$\bigcup_{i,j} \overline{Q}_{ij} = \overline{\Omega}_k.$$

For technical reasons, we suppose that the family of partitions is regular and quasiuniform. That is, there exist constants γ_1 and γ_2, independent of the partition $\mathcal{P}$, such that

$$\max_{i,j} \frac{h_{ij}}{\rho_{ij}} \leq \gamma_0, \quad \max_{i,j} \frac{h}{h_{ij}} \leq \gamma_1,$$

where $h_{ij} = \max(S_i - S_{i-1}, r_j - r_{j-1})$, $\rho_{ij} = \min(S_i - S_{i-1}, r_j - r_{j-1})$ and $h = h(\mathcal{P}) = \max_{ij} h_{ij}$.

For each partition $\mathcal{P}$ we consider the space of test functions

$$W_h = \{\phi : \text{continuous}, \phi|_{Q_{ij}} \text{ is a bilinear polynomial}\}$$
$$W_h = \{\phi \in C(\Omega_k) \mid \phi|_{Q_{ij}} \in \mathbb{P}_1\},$$

where $\mathbb{P}_1$ is the set of polynomials

$$\mathbb{P}_1 = \text{span}\{S^n r^m, 0 \leq n,m \leq 1\}.$$

The functions $\phi_{ij} \in W_h$, $0 \leq i \leq J_S + 1$, $0 \leq j \leq J_r + 1$, defined by

$$\phi_{ij}(S_n,r_m) = \delta_{in}\delta_{jm} = \begin{cases} 1, & \text{if } i = n \text{ and } j = m, \\ 0, & \text{if } i \neq n \text{ or } j \neq m, \end{cases}$$

are a base of the vectorial space W_h with the following convenient property

$$v_h(S,r) = \sum_{i,j=0}^{J_S,J_r} v_h(S_i,r_j)\phi_{ij}(S,r), \quad \forall v_h \in W_h.$$

We remark that each function $v_h \in W_h$ is determined by its nodal values. The nodal values $v_h(S_i, r_j)$ are the degrees of freedom of the finite element discretization. From now on, we will denote by $\{x_\nu\}_{\nu=1}^J$, $J = (J_S+1)(J_r+1)$, the ordered set of nodes, using, for example, the natural lexicographical order. We will also order the functions so that

$$\phi_\nu(x_\mu) = \delta_{\mu\nu}, \quad \nu, \mu = 1, \dots, J.$$

The semidiscrete finite element approximation u_h to the value function $V^{k,\epsilon}$ consists in finding a time dependent function $u_h\colon [0,T] \to W_h$ satisfying the discrete boundary and final conditions

$$\begin{aligned} u_h(S_i, r_k, t) &= \psi_2(S_i, r_k, t) = \min\bigl(\max(nS_i, \mathrm{PP}(t)), \mathrm{CP}(t)\bigr), \\ u_h(S_k, r_j, t) &= \psi_1(S_k, r_j, t) = \mathrm{CP}(t), \\ u_h(S_i, r_j, T) &= \psi_2(S_i, r_j, T) = \min\bigl(\max(nS_i, \mathrm{PP}(T), \mathrm{Par}), \mathrm{CP}(T)\bigr), \end{aligned}$$

for $0 \le t < T$, $0 \le i \le J_S$, $0 \le j \le J_r$, such that

$$\left(\frac{\partial u_h}{\partial t}, \varphi_h\right) - a(u_h, \varphi_h) - (ru_h, \varphi_h) - \frac{1}{\epsilon}(\beta(u_h), \varphi_h)_h + (\kappa, \varphi_h) = 0, \quad (5.15)$$

for all $\varphi_h \in W_h$ with $\varphi_h(S_k, r) = \varphi_h(S, r_k) = 0$. Here $(\cdot,\cdot)$ denotes the $L^2(\Omega_k)$ inner product and the bilinear form $a(\cdot,\cdot)$ is the weak form of the characteristic operator

$$a(v, w) = \int_{\Omega_k} \nabla w^T A \nabla v \, dS\, dr - \int_{\Omega_k} B^T \nabla v w \, dS\, dr,$$

with A and B the matrices

$$A = \begin{pmatrix} \frac{1}{2}\sigma_S^2 S^2 & \frac{1}{2}\rho\sigma_S\sigma_r S r^{1/2} \\ \frac{1}{2}\rho\sigma_S\sigma_r S r^{1/2} & \frac{1}{2}\sigma_r^2 r \end{pmatrix},$$

$$B = \begin{pmatrix} (r-D)S - \sigma^2 S - \frac{1}{4}\rho\sigma_S\sigma_r S r^{-1/2} \\ a - br - \frac{1}{2}\sigma_r^2 - \frac{1}{2}\rho\sigma_S\sigma_r r^{1/2} \end{pmatrix}.$$

Finally, $(\cdot,\cdot)_h$ denotes the discrete inner product that uses the so-called vertex quadrature

$$(v, w)_h = \sum_{\nu=1}^{J} v(x_\nu) w(x_\nu) \int_{\Omega_k} \phi_\nu(S, r)\, dS\, dr.$$

The variational equations (5.15) are equivalent to the following system of ordinary differential equations

$$\mathbf{M}\frac{d\boldsymbol{U}_h}{d\tau} + \mathbf{K}\boldsymbol{U}_h + \mathbf{C}\boldsymbol{U}_h + \mathbf{M}_r\boldsymbol{U}_h + \epsilon^{-1}\boldsymbol{\beta}(\boldsymbol{U}_h) = \boldsymbol{\kappa}_h, \quad (5.16)$$

where $\tau = T - t$, $\boldsymbol{U}_h(\tau) = [U_1(\tau), \ldots, U_J(\tau)]$, is the vector containing the (unknown) nodal values of the approximate finite element solution, $\boldsymbol{\kappa}_h = [(\kappa, \phi_\nu)]_{\nu=1}^J$, and

$$\boldsymbol{\beta}(\boldsymbol{U}_h) = [(\beta(u_h), \phi_\nu)_h]_{\nu=1}^J = \left[\beta(u_h(x_\nu)) \int_{\Omega_k} \phi_\nu(S, r)\, dS\, dr\right]_{\nu=1}^J.$$

The mass, $\mathbf{M}$, stiffness, $\mathbf{K}$, convection, $\mathbf{C}$ and reaction $\mathbf{M}_r$ are defined by

$$\mathbf{M} = \left(\int_{\Omega_k} \phi_\mu \phi_\nu \, dS\, dr\right)_{\nu,\mu=1}^J, \qquad \mathbf{K} = \left(\int_{\Omega_k} \nabla\phi_\mu^T A \nabla\phi_\nu \, dS\, dr\right)_{\nu,\mu=1}^J,$$

$$\mathbf{C} = \left(\int_{\Omega_k} B^T \nabla\phi_\mu \phi_\nu \, dS\, dr\right)_{\nu,\mu=1}^J, \quad \mathbf{M}_r = \left(\int_{\Omega_k} r\phi_\mu \phi_\nu \, dS\, dr\right)_{\nu,\mu=1}^J.$$

Equation (5.15) defines an order 2 approximation, so that taking into account (5.14)

$$\lim_{k\to\infty} \max_{t\in[0,T]} \|V(\cdot, t) - u_h(\cdot, t)\|_{\overline{\Omega}_A} = \mathcal{O}(\epsilon + h^2) \tag{5.17}$$

3.3 Implicit-explicit time discretization

The next step is to solve the system of ordinary differential equations (5.16) by means of an appropriate time integrator. As it is well known in the numerical analysis literature, explicit time integrators are usually inefficient when applied to the time integration of semidiscretizations of parabolic partial differential equations, because of the severe time step restrictions that must be imposed for stability reasons. On the other hand, fully implicit time integrators require the numerical solution of implicit nonlinear algebraic equations. In the case of (5.16), the non-smooth nonlinear term $\boldsymbol{\beta}(\boldsymbol{U}_h)$ together with the convective term $\mathbf{C}\boldsymbol{U}_h$ can make this task somewhat difficult and expensive. A compromise alternative is to resort to the so called implicit-explicit Runge–Kutta time integrators which use different methods for the different terms in (5.16) rolled into a single composite method so that the final scheme can be efficiently implemented.

Let us start by writing (5.16) in the form

$$\mathbf{M}\frac{d\boldsymbol{U}_h}{d\tau} = \mathbf{L}(\boldsymbol{U}_h) + \mathbf{N}(\boldsymbol{U}_h), \tag{5.18}$$

where

$$\mathbf{L}(\boldsymbol{U}_h) = -\mathbf{K}\boldsymbol{U}_h - \epsilon^{-1}\boldsymbol{\beta}(\boldsymbol{U}_h),$$
$$\mathbf{N}(\boldsymbol{U}_h) = -\mathbf{C}\boldsymbol{U}_h - \mathbf{M}_r\boldsymbol{U}_h + \boldsymbol{\kappa}_h.$$

Let $\Delta t > 0$ be a positive parameter and $\tau_n = n\Delta t$, $n = 0, 1, \ldots, T/h$. A time integrator for (5.18) looks for an approximation $\boldsymbol{U}_h^n$ to $u_h(\tau_n)$ with $\boldsymbol{U}_h^0 = u_h(0)$. In an implicit-explicit Runge–Kutta method, the equations describing the step $\tau_n \mapsto \tau_{n+1}$ take the form

$$\mathbf{M}\boldsymbol{Y}_1 = \mathbf{M}\boldsymbol{U}_h^n, \tag{5.19}$$

$$\mathbf{M}\boldsymbol{Y}_i = \mathbf{M}\boldsymbol{U}_h^n + \Delta t a_{ii}\mathbf{L}(\boldsymbol{Y}_i) + \Delta t\Bigg(\sum_{j=2}^{i-1} a_{ij}\mathbf{L}(\boldsymbol{Y}_j) + \sum_{j=1}^{i-1} \hat{a}_{i,j}\mathbf{N}(\boldsymbol{Y}_j)\Bigg), \quad 2 \le i \le s+1, \tag{5.20}$$

$$\mathbf{M}\boldsymbol{U}_h^{n+1} = \mathbf{M}\boldsymbol{U}_h^n + \Delta t\Bigg(\sum_{i=2}^{s+1} b_i\mathbf{L}(\boldsymbol{Y}_i) + \sum_{i=1}^{s+1} \hat{b}_i\mathbf{N}(\boldsymbol{Y}_i)\Bigg), \tag{5.21}$$

where $\boldsymbol{Y}_i$ denotes the (auxiliary) internal stages of the method. The coefficients of the method, that is, the matrices $\mathbf{A} = (a_{ij})$, $\hat{\mathbf{A}} = (\hat{a}_{ij})$ and the vectors $\boldsymbol{b}^T = (b_i)$ and $\hat{\boldsymbol{b}}^T = (\hat{b}_i)$, are computed as to satisfy the so-called order conditions (to a certain attainable order depending on the number of stages $s+1$) and some stability restrictions. We refer to Calvo et al. (2001) (see also Hairer and Wanner, 1991) for a review of the order conditions and a study of the stability properties of implicit-explicit Runge–Kutta methods. Several efficient implicit-explicit Runge–Kutta methods exist in the literature, see Ascher et al. (1997) and Kennedy and Carpenter (2003) where an exhaustive comparison among different possibilities are reported.

At each stage of the method a nonlinear system of algebraic equations of the form

$$(\mathbf{M} + \Delta t a_{ii}\mathbf{K})\boldsymbol{Y}_i + \Delta t a_{ii}\epsilon^{-1}\boldsymbol{\beta}(\boldsymbol{Y}_i) = \boldsymbol{G}_i(\boldsymbol{Y}_1, \ldots, \boldsymbol{Y}_{i-1}) \tag{5.22}$$

has to be solved. To this end we propose to use the following fixed point Newton-like iteration: Given an initial iterate $\boldsymbol{Y}^0$, for $k = 0, 1, \ldots,$

$$\begin{aligned}(\mathbf{M} + \Delta t a_{ii}\mathbf{K} + \Delta t a_{ii}\epsilon^{-1}\frac{\partial\boldsymbol{\beta}_1}{\partial\boldsymbol{Y}}(\boldsymbol{Y}_i^k) + \Delta t a_{ii}\epsilon^{-1}\frac{\partial\boldsymbol{\beta}_2}{\partial\boldsymbol{Y}}(\boldsymbol{Y}_i^k))\boldsymbol{Y}_i^{k+1} \\ = \boldsymbol{G}_i + \Delta t a_{ii}\epsilon^{-1}\frac{\partial\boldsymbol{\beta}_1}{\partial\boldsymbol{Y}}(\boldsymbol{Y}_i^k)\boldsymbol{\psi}_1 + \Delta t a_{ii}\epsilon^{-1}\frac{\partial\boldsymbol{\beta}_2}{\partial\boldsymbol{Y}}(\boldsymbol{Y}_i^k)\boldsymbol{\psi}_2,\end{aligned} \tag{5.23}$$

where $\boldsymbol{\beta}_1(\boldsymbol{Y}) = \max(\boldsymbol{Y} - \boldsymbol{\psi}_1, 0)$, $\boldsymbol{\beta}_2(\boldsymbol{Y}) = \min(\boldsymbol{Y} - \boldsymbol{\psi}_2, 0)$, so that $\boldsymbol{\beta}(\boldsymbol{Y}) = \boldsymbol{\beta}_1(\boldsymbol{Y}) + \boldsymbol{\beta}_2(\boldsymbol{Y})$. The matrices $\partial\boldsymbol{\beta}_\nu(\boldsymbol{Y})/\partial\boldsymbol{Y}$ are the diagonal matrices

$$\frac{\partial\boldsymbol{\beta}_1}{\partial\boldsymbol{Y}}(\boldsymbol{Y}_i^k)_{jj} = \begin{cases} 1, & \text{if } (\boldsymbol{Y}_i^k)_j > \boldsymbol{\psi}_{1j}, \\ 0, & \text{if } (\boldsymbol{Y}_i^k)_j \le \boldsymbol{\psi}_{1j}, \end{cases},$$

$$\frac{\partial \beta_2}{\partial \boldsymbol{Y}}(\boldsymbol{Y}_i^k)_{jj} = \begin{cases} 1, & \text{if } (\boldsymbol{Y}_i^k)_j < \psi_{2j}, \\ 0, & \text{if } (\boldsymbol{Y}_i^k)_j \geq \psi_{2j}. \end{cases}$$

We have the following convergence result

THEOREM 5.1 *The fixed point iteration* (5.23) *converges in a finite number of steps to the unique solution of* (5.22).

Proof. We first observe that $M + \theta K$, $\theta = a_{ii}\Delta t$, is a positive definite matrix and that

$$(\boldsymbol{V}_h - \boldsymbol{W}_h)^T(\boldsymbol{\beta}(\boldsymbol{V}_h) - \boldsymbol{\beta}(\boldsymbol{W}_h)) \geq 0, \quad \forall \boldsymbol{V}_h, \boldsymbol{W}_h \in \mathbb{R}^J.$$

Using the Brouwer's fixed point theorem (cf. Lions, 1969, p. 53) is easy to show that equation (5.22) has a unique solution.

In order to prove the convergence of the iteration, we subtract (5.23) from (5.22) to get

$$\begin{aligned} (M + \theta K)(\boldsymbol{Y}_i^{k+1} - \boldsymbol{Y}_i) &+ \frac{\theta}{\epsilon}\sum_{\nu=1}^{2}\frac{\partial \beta_\nu}{\partial \boldsymbol{Y}}(\boldsymbol{Y}_i^k)(\boldsymbol{Y}_i^{k+1} - \boldsymbol{Y}_i) \\ &= \frac{\theta}{\epsilon}\sum_{\nu=1}^{2}\left[\frac{\partial \beta_\nu}{\partial \boldsymbol{Y}}(\boldsymbol{Y}_i) - \frac{\partial \beta_\nu}{\partial \boldsymbol{Y}}(\boldsymbol{Y}_i^k)\right](\boldsymbol{Y}_i - \psi_\nu), \quad (5.24) \end{aligned}$$

where we have used that

$$\beta_\nu(\boldsymbol{Y}_i) = \frac{\partial \beta_\nu}{\partial \boldsymbol{Y}}(\boldsymbol{Y}_i)(\boldsymbol{Y}_i - \psi_\nu), \quad \nu = 1, 2.$$

We observe that

$$\begin{aligned} &(\boldsymbol{Y}_i^{k+1} - \boldsymbol{Y}_i)^T\frac{\partial \beta_\nu}{\partial \boldsymbol{Y}}(\boldsymbol{Y}_i^k)(\boldsymbol{Y}_i^{k+1} - \boldsymbol{Y}_i) \geq 0, && \nu = 1, 2, \\ &\left\|\left[\frac{\partial \beta_\nu}{\partial \boldsymbol{Y}}(\boldsymbol{Y}_i) - \frac{\partial \beta_\nu}{\partial \boldsymbol{Y}}(\boldsymbol{Y}_i^k)\right](\boldsymbol{Y}_i - \psi_\nu)\right\| \leq \|\boldsymbol{Y}_i - \psi_\nu\|, && \nu = 1, 2. \end{aligned}$$

Then, taking the scalar product of (5.24) with $\boldsymbol{Y}_i^{k+1} - \boldsymbol{Y}_i$ and using the Cauchy – Schwarz inequality, we have

$$\|\boldsymbol{Y}_i^{k+1} - \boldsymbol{Y}_i\| \leq C\frac{\theta}{\epsilon}\sum_{\nu=1}^{2}\|\boldsymbol{Y}_i - \psi_\nu\|,$$

for some constant $C > 0$. The convergence of the sequence $\{\boldsymbol{Y}_i^k\}_{k=1}^{\infty}$ follows from the fact that, being a bounded sequence, its only possible accumulation point is precisely the unique solution of (5.22).

We finish the proof showing that the limit $\boldsymbol{Y}_i$ is attained in a finite number of steps. Let $J_\nu = \{j : 1 \le j \le J, \boldsymbol{Y}_{ij} \neq \boldsymbol{\psi}_{\nu j}\}$, $\nu = 1, 2$. Let $k_0 = \max(k_1, k_2)$, where k_ν, $\nu = 1, 2$, is the first index such that

$$|\boldsymbol{Y}_{ij}^k - \boldsymbol{Y}_{ij}| < |\boldsymbol{Y}_{ij} - \boldsymbol{\psi}_{\nu j}|, \quad \forall j \in J_\nu.$$

We have that

$$\operatorname{sign}(\boldsymbol{Y}_{ij}^{k_0} - \boldsymbol{\psi}_{\nu j}) = \operatorname{sign}(\boldsymbol{Y}_{ij} - \boldsymbol{\psi}_{\nu j}), \quad \forall j \in J_\nu, \quad \nu = 1, 2,$$

and, consequently,

$$\frac{\partial \boldsymbol{\beta}_\nu}{\partial \boldsymbol{Y}}(\boldsymbol{Y}_i)_{jj} = \frac{\partial \boldsymbol{\beta}_\nu}{\partial \boldsymbol{Y}}(\boldsymbol{Y}_i^{k_0})_{jj}, \quad \forall j \in J_\nu, \quad \nu = 1, 2.$$

Examining the right hand side of (5.24) we conclude that

$$(M + \theta K)(\boldsymbol{Y}_i^{k_0+1} - \boldsymbol{Y}_i) + \frac{\theta}{\epsilon} \sum_{\nu=1}^{2} \frac{\partial \boldsymbol{\beta}_\nu}{\partial \boldsymbol{Y}}(\boldsymbol{Y}_i^{k_0})(\boldsymbol{Y}_i^{k_0+1} - \boldsymbol{Y}_i) = 0.$$

Taking into account that the matrix

$$M + \theta K + \frac{\theta}{\epsilon} \sum_{\nu=1}^{2} \frac{\partial \boldsymbol{\beta}_\nu}{\partial \boldsymbol{Y}}(\boldsymbol{Y}_i^{k_0}),$$

being positive definite, is not singular, we conclude that $\boldsymbol{Y}_i^{k_0+1} = \boldsymbol{Y}_i$. Therefore, the iteration scheme (5.23) converges, in at most, $k_0 + 1$ steps. □

4. Numerical experiments

In this section we consider the implicit-explicit Runge–Kutta third order method (LIRK3) with $s + 1 = 4$ stages constructed in Calvo et al. (2001).

The implicit part of the method is based on the well-known L-stable, third order SDIRK (see Hairer and Wanner, 1991) and uses the simplifying assumptions

$$c_i = \sum_{j=2}^{i} a_{ij} = \sum_{j=2}^{i-1} \hat{a}_{ij}, \quad b_i = \hat{b}_i.$$

The method has quasi-optimal stability properties when applied to equations of convection-diffusion type, see Calvo et al. (2001). For the reader's convenience we have listed in the appendix the coefficients of the method.

We have implemented the scheme in variable-step mode, so that the time step is automatically chosen by the code depending on an estimation of the local errors. To this end, we have considered the second order formula

$$\mathbf{M}\widetilde{\boldsymbol{U}}_h^{n+1} = \mathbf{M}\boldsymbol{U}_h^n + \Delta t\Big(b_2\big(\mathbf{L}(\boldsymbol{Y}_2) + \mathbf{N}(\boldsymbol{Y}_2)\big) + b_3\big(\mathbf{L}(\boldsymbol{Y}_3) + \mathbf{N}(\boldsymbol{Y}_3)\big) \\ + b_4\big(\mathbf{L}(\widetilde{\boldsymbol{U}}_h^{n+1}) + \mathbf{N}(\boldsymbol{Y}_4)\big)\Big),$$

where $\boldsymbol{Y}_2$, $\boldsymbol{Y}_3$ and $\boldsymbol{Y}_4$ are the internal stages of the third order scheme. The second order approximation $\widetilde{\boldsymbol{U}}_h^{n+1}$ can be interpreted as the solution generated with a second order implicit-explicit Runge–Kutta method with an additional stage $\boldsymbol{Y}_5 = \widetilde{\boldsymbol{U}}_h^{n+1}$ defined by the coefficients $a_{5,i} = \hat{a}_{5,i} = b_i$, $1 \le i \le 3$, $a_{5,4} = \hat{a}_{5,5} = 0$, $a_{5,5} = \hat{a}_{5,4} = b_4$.

Each time a new approximation $\boldsymbol{U}_h^{n+1}$ is computed, the local error is estimated by

$$\mathrm{ERR} = \|\boldsymbol{U}_h^{n+1} - \widetilde{\boldsymbol{U}}_h^{n+1}\|_\infty.$$

The step is accepted if $\mathrm{ERR} \le \mathrm{TOL}$, where TOL is the precision required by the user. If $\mathrm{ERR} > \mathrm{TOL}$ the step is rejected and the computation is restarted from the previously accepted approximation using a smaller time step. In both cases the new time step size is selected according to the rule

$$\Delta t_{new} = \min\left(\mathrm{hlim}, \Delta t_{\mathrm{old}} \min\left(\mathrm{FACMAX}, \mathrm{FAC}\left(\frac{\mathrm{TOL}}{\mathrm{ERR}}\right)^{1/3}\right)\right), \quad (5.25)$$

where hlim is the maximum admissible step size and FACMAX and FAC are safety factors that limit the variations in step size in order to make the code more robust.

Although the convergence of the iteration scheme (5.22) is guaranteed by Theorem 5.1, in practice it is necessary to control the cost of the solution of the nonlinear systems. Therefore, we have decided to adopt a conservative policy and limit the maximum number of iterations in each stage. Iteration (5.23) is stopped when

$$\max \frac{|Y_j^{k+1} - Y_j^k|}{\max(1, |Y_j^k|)} \le 10^{-3}\mathrm{TOL},$$

where Y_j^k, $j = 1, \ldots,$ denote the components of the iterant $\boldsymbol{Y}^k$ in (5.23). If, in the computation of one stage, the nonlinear iteration has not converged after four iterations, the full time step is rejected, the computation restarted with time step halved and the maximum number of

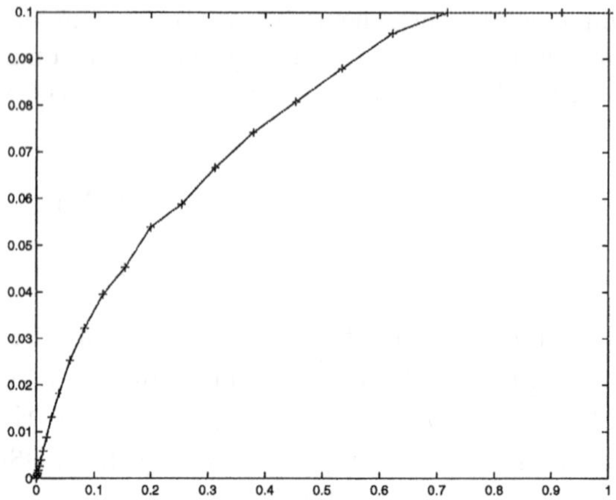

Figure 5.1. Time step selection history. MAXITER = 5.

iterations allowed is increased by one unit until no further rejections are found. In practice a relatively small number of iterations (four or five) is enough to guarantee the convergence of (5.23), see below.

In order to illustrate the method we present some numerical results for the following contract and parameters specifications: $\omega_S = 0.35$, $\omega_r = 0.75$, $\rho = -0.3$, $a = 0.04$, $b = 0.08$, CP $= 1.5$, PP $= 0.5$, $D = 0$, $\kappa = 0$. The expiration date is $T = 1$. For practical reasons it is convenient to normalize asset and bond prices so that the face value of the bond is Par $= 1$ and the conversion ratio is $n = 1$. In all the numerical experiments we have taken $\Omega_k = (0,2) \times (0,1)$. For this computational domain the error caused by the artificial boundary conditions were found to be negligible compared with errors caused by the discretization procedure.

Figure 5.1 shows the time step history for a single run using a grid with 32 nodes in each direction and setting TOL $= 10^{-3}$ and $\epsilon = 10^{-5}$. The horizontal axis represent time and the vertical axis represent the size of the step taken. As we can see, the code selects small time steps at the beginning of the computation and smoothly increments the time step as the computation proceeds. We remark that the final payoff has only piecewise smooth derivatives although it is smoother for $\tau > 0$, or equivalently for $0 \leq t < T$, due to the parabolic character of the regularized equation (5.11). The small initial steps are the response of the code to the lack of regularity at $t = T$. Note that no special procedure is needed to deal with nonsmooth initial conditions as compared with other time integrators of common use, see Forsyth and Vetzal (2002).

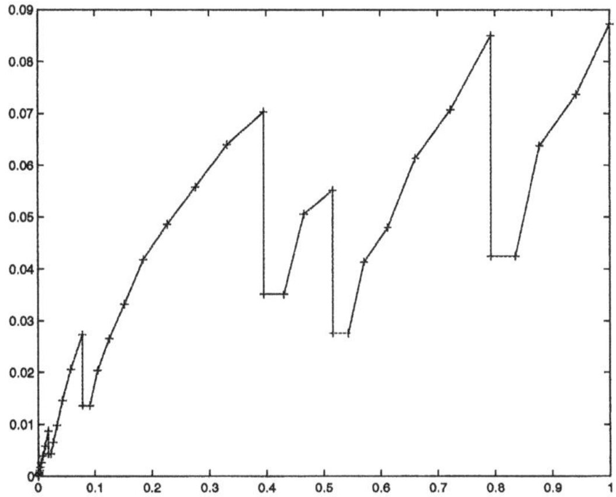

Figure 5.2. Time step selection history. MAXITER = 4.

Once the solution has been smoothed, the code increments the time step until a maximum predetermined time step is reached, $\Delta t = 0.1$ in the experiment show in Figure 5.1, or a default in the convergence of the nonlinear iteration is detected. This can happen if a excessively small value of the parameter MAXITER is set. In this experiment we use MAXITER $= 5$ and as we can see the code never rejects a time step by default in the nonlinear iteration.

In Figure 5.2 we have used MAXITER $= 4$. This time the code rejects 5 times the predicted time step. Each time it automatically reduces the time step, see Figure 5.2 near $\tau = 0.4$ for example, and continues the time integration increasing again the time step. The time step history was found to depend only on the number of nodes in the state discretization, being independent of both the penalty parameter and tolerance in the time discretization, see Table 5.1 below.

In the next test we have checked the behaviour of the method with respect to the penalty parameter. We have monitored the maximum relative error in enforcing the early exercise constraint by the penalty method by means of the quantity

$$\text{AMERR} = \max\left(\frac{\max(\psi_2 - u_h, 0)}{\max(1, \psi_2)} + \frac{\max(u_h - \psi_1, 0)}{\max(1, \psi_1)}\right) \tag{5.26}$$

Table 5.1 shows the results obtained for several values of the penalty parameter, ϵ, tolerance of the time integrator, TOL, and number of nodes in the finite element approximation, Nodes (number of nodes in each dimension). We observe that the size of AMERR is proportional

Table 5.1. Behaviour with respect the penalty parameter.

ϵ	Nodes	TOL	AMERR	Ratio	Steps	ITER
10^{-2}	16	10^{-2}	$1.30\ 10^{-3}$	⋆⋆⋆	24	3
10^{-2}	32	10^{-2}	$1.61\ 10^{-3}$	0.81	24	4
10^{-2}	64	10^{-2}	$2.30\ 10^{-3}$	0.70	24	5
10^{-3}	16	10^{-3}	$2.97\ 10^{-4}$	⋆⋆⋆	30	3
10^{-3}	32	10^{-3}	$4.00\ 10^{-4}$	0.74	30	4
10^{-3}	64	10^{-3}	$4.05\ 10^{-4}$	0.99	30	5
10^{-4}	16	10^{-4}	$2.02\ 10^{-5}$	⋆⋆⋆	41	3
10^{-4}	32	10^{-4}	$2.47\ 10^{-5}$	0.82	43	4
10^{-4}	64	10^{-4}	$3.35\ 10^{-5}$	0.74	44	5
10^{-2}	16	10^{-2}	$1.30\ 10^{-3}$	⋆⋆⋆	24	2
10^{-3}	16	10^{-2}	$1.71\ 10^{-4}$	7.60	24	3
10^{-4}	16	10^{-2}	$2.08\ 10^{-5}$	8.22	24	3
10^{-2}	32	10^{-3}	$1.60\ 10^{-3}$	⋆⋆⋆	30	4
10^{-3}	32	10^{-3}	$2.47\ 10^{-4}$	6.48	30	4
10^{-4}	32	10^{-3}	$3.46\ 10^{-5}$	7.14	30	4
10^{-2}	64	10^{-4}	$2.31\ 10^{-3}$	⋆⋆⋆	44	4
10^{-3}	64	10^{-4}	$2.85\ 10^{-4}$	8.11	44	5
10^{-4}	64	10^{-4}	$3.53\ 10^{-5}$	8.08	44	5

Table 5.2. Time integrator accuracy.

		$r = 0.1$, $S = 1.11$		$r = 0.15$, $S = 1.11$	
TOL	**STEPS**	**Difference**	**Ratio**	**Difference**	**Ratio**
10^{-2}	16	$1.88\ 10^{-5}$	⋆⋆⋆	$1.87\ 10^{-5}$	⋆⋆⋆
10^{-3}	28	$2.19\ 10^{-6}$	8.58	$3.22\ 10^{-6}$	5.81
10^{-4}	44	$3.10\ 10^{-7}$	7.06	$3.80\ 10^{-7}$	8.47

to ϵ, in good agreement with (5.17). An interesting property of the penalty method is that the number of iterations needed to achieve a given error grows slowly with the number of degrees of freedom in the discretization being independent of TOL and ϵ. Furthermore, the error is nearly independent of the discretization parameters, TOL and Nodes.

Note, that, as a consequence of the strong stability properties of the time integrator, the number of time steps is independent of the penalization parameter and of the number of nodes in the finite element mesh, being only dependent of the accuracy desired in the time integration. This is an important quality of an efficient numerical integration for partial differential equations.

In order to check the accuracy of the time integrator in this application we have performed several runs for different values of the parameter TOL. We present the results in Table 5.2. The number of nodes was set to be Nodes = 100 in each variable so that the finite element error

Table 5.3. Finite element discretization accuracy.

	$r = 0.125$, $S = 0.5$		$r = 0.19$, $S = 0.5$	
Nodes	**Difference**	**Ratio**	**Difference**	**Ratio**
16	$1.76\ 10^{-3}$	$\star\star\star$	$1.83\ 10^{-3}$	$\star\star\star$
32	$6.18\ 10^{-4}$	2.85	$6.17\ 10^{-4}$	2.96
64	$1.71\ 10^{-4}$	3.61	$1.68\ 10^{-4}$	3.67

is negligible in the reported experiments. The penalty parameter was $\epsilon = \text{TOL}/10$. We have measured the errors in two particular points of the computational domain far from the artificial boundary conditions region of influence. The column Difference shows the difference between the approximation and a reference solution computed with $\text{TOL} = 10^{-5}$ and can be considered an indicator of the error due to the temporal discretization. The column ratio shows the ratio between two consecutive errors. We observe that the errors are proportional to the tolerance showing a good performance of the step control procedure. A very rapid convergence is observed as shown by the high values in the Ratio column. Each time TOL is reduced, the error is reduced by the same order of magnitude whereas only a relative small increment of the number of steps in observed. The conclusion is that in spite of the lack of regularity of the solution of (5.8) the use of a stiffly accurate, high order time integrator results in a rapid convergence with a moderate increment in the cost of the computation, giving a very efficient procedure.

The accuracy of the finite element discretization has been checked in the next experiment. The results are presented in Table 5.3. This time we fixed the parameters $TOL = 10^{-5}$ and $\epsilon = 10^{-6}$ and ran the code for several values of Nodes. The errors are measured with respect to a reference solution computed with Nodes $= 100$. They are shown in the column Difference. As in the previous experiment, the column Ratio contains the ratio between two consecutive runs. As we can see, this ratio approaches 4 corresponding to a second order discretization. Furthermore, for reasonable values of Nodes, the finite element error is significantly small showing that the finite element approach blended with an efficient time discretization results in a competitive numerical approach for the valuation of complex multidimensional financial products such as the two factor convertible bond model.

As a final illustration we present in Figure 5.3 the surface $V(S, r, 0)$ of values for the bond in this example. As it is well known, the value function is decreasing with increasing values of the spot interest rate and increasing with the asset price. We remark that a larger computational domain results in larger values of $V(S, r, 0)$. This value tends to stabilize

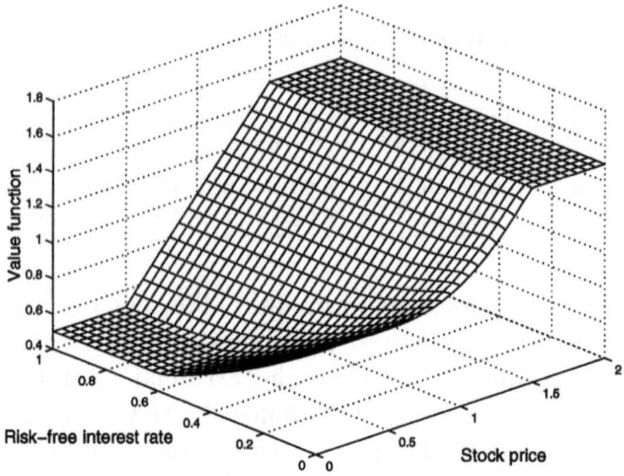

Figure 5.3. The surface of bond values.

thanks to the early exercise constraints. In practice, some trial and error experimentation is needed for each particular contract. This clearly is a drawback of the method shared with the rest of valuation methods based on the partial differential equations approach. How to choose the computational domain and what kind of artificial boundary condition has to be imposed is again an open subject.

Appendix: The coefficients of LIRK3

We shall write the coefficients of the method in compact form using the Butcher tableau (Hairer and Wanner, 1991)

$$\begin{array}{c|c|c} \mathbf{c} & \mathbf{A} & \widehat{\mathbf{A}} \\ \hline & b^T & \hat{b}^T \end{array}.$$

LIRK3 has $s+1=4$ step, three of them implicit. The implicit part of the method (left part of the Bucher tableau) is based on the third order SDIRK of Hairer and Wanner (1991). The coefficients of the explicit part of the method (right part of the Bucher tableau) has been computed to optimize the stability properties in Calvo et al. (2001). The coefficents of the method are:

$$\begin{array}{c|cccc|cccc} 0 & 0 & & & & 0 & & & \\ \gamma & 0 & \gamma & & & \gamma & 0 & & \\ \frac{1+\gamma}{2} & 0 & \frac{1-\gamma}{2} & \gamma & & \frac{1+\gamma}{2}-\varsigma & \varsigma & 0 & \\ 1 & 0 & b_2 & b_3 & \gamma & 0 & 1-\xi & \xi & 0 \\ \hline & 0 & b_2 & b_3 & \gamma & 0 & b_2 & b_3 & \gamma \end{array},$$

where γ is the middle root of $6x^3 - 18x^2 + 9x - 1 = 0$ and

$$b_2 = -\tfrac{3}{2}\gamma^2 + 4\gamma - \tfrac{1}{4}, \qquad b_3 = \tfrac{3}{2}\gamma^2 - 5\gamma + \tfrac{5}{4},$$
$$\varsigma = (\tfrac{1}{3} - 2\gamma^2 - 2b_3\xi\gamma)/\gamma(1-\gamma), \qquad \xi = -\frac{7}{20}.$$

Acknowledgments Research partially supported by DGI-MCYT, project BFM2001-2138 (cofinanced by FEDER funds) and by JCYL, project VA112/02. This research was completed while the author was visiting professor at GERAD and HEC Montréal.

References

Ascher, U.M., Ruuth, S.J., and Spiteri, R.J. (1997). Implicit-explicit Runge – Kutta methods for time-dependent partial differential equations. *Applied Numerical Mathematics*, 25:151 – 167.

Barone-Adesi, G. Bermudez, A., and Hatgioannides, J. (2003). Two factor convertible bonds valuation using the method of characteristic/finite elements. *Journal of Economic Dynamics and Control*, 27:1801 – 1831.

Ben-Ameur, H., Breton, M., Karoui, L. and L'Ecuyer, P. (2004). A Dynamic Programming Approach for Pricing Options Embedded in Bonds. *Les Cahiers du GERAD*, G–2004–35.

Brennan, M.J. and Schwarz, E.S. (1977). Savings bonds, retractable bonds and callable bonds. *Journal of Financial Economics*, 5:67 – 88.

Calvo, M.P., de Frutos, J., and Novo, J. (2001). Linearly implicit Runge – Kutta methods for advection-reaction-diffusion equations. *Applied Numerical Mathematics*, 37:535 – 549.

Cox, J.C., Ingersoll, J.E. and Ross, S.A. (1985). A theory of the term structure of interest rates. *Econometrica*, 53:285 – 407.

Elliot, R.J. and Kopp, P.E. (1999). *Mathematics of Financial Markets.* Springer Verlag, New York.

Fosyth, P.A. and Vetzal, K.R. (2002). Quadratic convergence for valuing options using a penalty method. *SIAM Journal on Scientific Computing*, 23:2095 – 2122.

Friedman, A. (1976). *Stochastic Differential Equations and Applications.* Academic Press, New York.

de Frutos, J. (2004). Implicit-explicit Runge – Kutta methods for financial derivatives pricing models. Forthcoming in *European Journal of Operation Research.*

d'Halluin, Y., Forsyth, P.A., Vetzal, K.R., and Labahn, G. (2001). A numerical PDE approach for pricing callable bonds. *Applied Mathematical Finance*, 8:49 – 77.

Hairer, E. and Wanner, G. (1991). *Solving Ordinary Differential Equations. II. Stiff and Differential-Algebraic Problems.* Springer Verlag,

New York.

Hull, J. and White, A. (1990). Pricing interest-rate derivative securities. *Review of Financial Studies*, 3:573–592.

Jaillet, A., Lamberton, D., and Lapeyre, B. (1990). Variational inequalities and the pricing of American options. *Acta Applicandae Mathematicae*, 21:263–289.

Jiang, X. and Nochetto, R.H. (1994). Effect of numerical integration for elliptic obstacle problems. *Numerische Mathematik*, 67:501–512.

Kangro, K. and Nicolaides, R. (2000). Far field conditions for Black–Scholes equations. *SIAM Journal on Numerical Analysis*, 38:1357–1368.

Kennedy, C.A. and Carpenter, M.H. (2003). Additive Runge–Kutta schemes for convection-diffusion-reaction equations. *Applied Numerical Mathematics*, 44:131–181.

Lions, J.L. (1969). *Quelques méthodes de résolution des problèmes aux limites non linéaires.* Dunod, Paris.

Marcozzi, M.D. (2001). On the approximation of optimal stopping problems with applications to financial mathematics. *SIAM Journal on Scientific Computing*, 22:1865–1884.

Nochetto, R.H. (1988). Sharp L^∞-error estimates for semilinear elliptic problems with free boundaries. *Numerische Mathematik*, 54:243–255.

Tavella, D. and Randall, C. (2000). *Pricing Financial Instruments. The Finite Difference Method.* John Wiley & Sons, New York.

Wilmott, P. (1998). *Derivatives.* John Wiley & Sons, New York.

Chapter 6

ON NUMERICAL METHODS AND THE VALUATION OF AMERICAN OPTIONS

Mondher Bellalah

Abstract We study the valuation of index options in a stochastic interest rate economy with a composite volatility. We generalize Black and Scholes type models by including stochastic interest rates and proposing a decomposition of the underlying index volatility. We use the Crank–Nicholson numerical scheme in two space dimensions and extend the Alternating Direction Implicit method for the valuation of American options. We also provide an efficient algorithm and simulate option values.

1. Introduction

Since options on the spot equity index, futures and options on futures are based on the same underlying stock index, their prices must be related. If their prices do not obey the inter market relationships, then the relative mispricing, often documented in empirical studies,[1] should be instantaneously corrected given the high degree of sophistication of market participants. In this chapter, we use some of the ideas underlying these models with the observed behavior of the volatility and interest rates for the valuation of long term options.

This work makes two contributions to the pricing of short and long term options. The first concerns the decomposition of the index price volatility which is useful in the valuation of long term options for which the impact of interest rates fluctuations is more important when compared to short term options. The second contribution is an efficient

[1]Several studies report mispricing of index options. See for example Nayar and Lee (1993), Bellalah (1991), Briys-Bellalah et al. (1998).

method for approximating boundary conditions when numerical schemes as the Alternating Direction Implicit, ADI[2] are used in solving parabolic equations. An extension of the ADI is used and a θ-scheme of the implicit type is adopted (for $\theta = \frac{1}{2}$). A computationally simple algorithm, unconditionally stable and convergent is provided. The interest of the method lies in the speed of convergence of the numerical scheme and the simplicity of the solution method. The algorithm can be used for several other problems in option pricing theory with two or more state variables.

The outline for this chapter is as follows. Section 2 reports the effects of the interest rates volatility on the volatility of stocks. It reviews the principal results on which this research is based. Using the principal results in the literature, a two-state model is derived in Section 3 for the valuation of American long term index options and index futures options. Section 4 presents a stable and convergent numerical scheme for the American index options and index futures options. Simulations are run and comparisons are made with respect to previous studies. We also show the impact of interest rate volatility on the early exercise of American options.

2. The relationship between interest rate volatility and the underlying asset volatility

Empirical evidence shows that there exists a relationship between stock prices, interest rates and inflation.[3] Fama and French (1993) identify common risk factors in the returns on stocks and bonds. They show that stock returns have shared variation due to the stock market factors and that they are associated to bond returns through shared variation in bond market factors.

Copeland and Stapleton (1985), Boquist et al. (1975), Lanstein and Sharpe (1978) and Weinstein (1981) highlight the importance of the interest rate by implementing and transposing the familiar concepts in bond valuation to the pricing of stocks.

These studies rely on the assumption that the variance of the rate of returns on the market portfolio is a function of the variations in conditional expectations regarding cash-flows, the variance of interest rates and the covariance between these variables. Since it is extremely difficult to establish the exact relationship between interest rates and the expected cash-flows, it is often assumed that these variables are indepen-

[2]See McKee and Mitchell (1970).

[3]See for example Copeland and Stapleton (1985) and Peterson and Peterson (1994).

dent. Under this assumption, it is possible to decompose the variance of the market portfolio into a proportion ϑ corresponding to the variance of cash flows and a proportion $(1 - \vartheta)$ resulting from variations in interest rates.

We briefly review the models in Ramaswamy and Sundaresan (1985) and Brenner et al. (1987) (hereafter respectively RS and BCS). In the RS model, the dynamics of the index price, S, are given by the following equation:

$$dS = [\alpha S - \delta S]\, dt + \sigma_S S\, dz_S \tag{6.1}$$

where:

α: the instantaneous expected return on S,
δ: the dividend yield on the stock index,
σ_S: the instantaneous expected standard deviation of returns on S,
dz_S: the increment of a Wiener process.

The dynamics of the spot interest rates are given by the familiar square root process which has correlation ρ with dz_S, i.e, $\text{cov}(dz_S, dz_r) = \rho\, dt$. In the BCS model, the effect of the volatility of interest rates is explicitely taken into account. The dynamics of the index price are given by the following equation :

$$dS = [\alpha S - \delta S]\, dt + (\sigma_I + \nu\sigma_r) S\, dz_S \tag{6.2}$$

where δ stands for the dividend yield on the index price, σ_I is the specific index volatility, σ_r is the interest rate volatility and ν is a coefficient which transmits the effect of interest rates volatility to the index volatility. The dynamics of the interest rate r are given by an Ornstein–Uhlenbeck process where $\text{cov}(dz_S, dz_r) = \rho\, dt$.

3. The model and the main results

Our model is based on six assumptions.

ASSUMPTION 3.1 *Assets are traded in "frictionless" markets with no taxes or transaction costs.*

ASSUMPTION 3.2 *Assets are traded continuously in order to allow for investors to rebalance their portfolios instantaneously.*

ASSUMPTION 3.3 *There are no restrictions on short sales and borrowing and lending rates are equal.*

ASSUMPTION 3.4 *The local expectations hypothesis, hereafter L-EH, of Cox et al. (1981, 1985) (hereafter CIR) applies at each instant of time.*

The L-EH is appealing since it allows the derivation of contingent claim valuation equations without a risk premium on the interest rate. In fact, since the L-EH hypothesis allows the construction of hedging portfolios which are "locally" riskless (by using a discount-free riskless bond, B), it is possible to give valuation equations without restrictions on the preferences of the investors. Also, the L-EH takes into account the absence of profitable riskless arbitrage. Using the L-EH is equivalent to assuming that the expected instantaneous return on a coupon-paying bond (independently of its time to maturity) is equal to the spot rate $r(t)$ on a bond maturing instantaneously, i.e.:

$$E_t[dB/B] = r(t)dt \tag{6.3}$$

where E_t is the mathematical expectation conditional on all the available information at time t.

ASSUMPTION 3.5 *The dynamics of the short interest rates are described by the familiar square root process:*[4]

$$dr(t) = \kappa[\mu - r]\, dt + \sigma_r \sqrt{r}\, dz_r. \tag{6.4}$$

In this expression, $\kappa[\mu - r]$ corresponds to the mean reverting drift pulling the short interest rate toward its long-term value μ where κ defines the speed of the adjustment. It is convenient to note that the square root process is more suitable than the Ornstein – Uhlenbeck process because it does not allow for negative interest rates, among other reasons. The choice of this process rather than that used in BCS is based on the fact that the critics addressed to arbitrage models like the Vasicek (1977) model do not apply to the CIR intertemporal general equilibrium term structure model.

ASSUMPTION 3.6 *The dynamics of the stock index or the underlying commodity are described by the following equation:*

$$dS = (\alpha S - \delta S)\, dt + (\sigma_S + \nu\sigma_r\sqrt{r})S\, dz_S \tag{6.5}$$

where dz_S has correlation ρ with dz_r, i.e, $\text{cov}(dz_S, dz_r) = \rho\, dt$.

This formulation is similar in spirit to that in BCS. In the above formulation, αS stands for the expected instantaneous relative price change of the underlying commodity asset. When there are no arbitrage opportunities, the assumption of a constant proportional carrying cost implies

[4]This process was used in Cox, Ingersoll, and Ross (1985) among others.

that, $F = Se^{bT}$ where F is the futures price, $b = r - \delta$ is the cost of carrying the commodity and T is the time to maturity.

For a non-dividend-paying asset, $b = r$ and for a dividend-paying asset, $b = r - \delta$. The volatility of the underlying index is given by $\sigma_S + \nu\sigma_r\sqrt{r}$. It is composed of a specific volatility σ_S, the interest rate volatility σ_r and a coefficient ν which transmits the effect of interest rates volatility to the index volatility. Hence, for a given level of the interest rate volatility, variations in the level of interest rates induces variations in the volatility of the stock index. Since the two markets are not completely independent, it is plausible that the rise in volatility in one market affects the volatility in the other market. This effect is transmitted through the coefficient ν. Also, for a given level of the interest rate, a rise in its volatility affects the volatility of the index. This decomposition is important for long term options because it shows the effect of interest rates on the probability of early exercise.

We denote by $U(S, r, t)$ the option value as a function of the two underlying state variables and time. This function stands for C and P which are used later for the option value of a call or a put. Applying Ito's lemma under the assumptions 3.1 to 3.6 and using the standard hedging arguments, it is possible to construct a locally riskless portfolio with a riskless bond and the underlying stock index. At equilibrium, the expected rate of return on this portfolio under the L-EH must be the short riskless interest rate and, under the free boundary formulation, the option price must obey the following partial differential equation in the continuation region:

$$\frac{1}{2}(\sigma_S + \nu\sigma_r\sqrt{r})^2 S^2 \frac{\partial^2 U}{\partial S^2} + \frac{1}{2}\rho\sigma_r S(\sigma_S + \nu\sigma_r\sqrt{r})\sqrt{r}\frac{\partial^2 U}{\partial S \partial r} + \frac{1}{2} r\sigma_r^2 \frac{\partial^2 U}{\partial r^2} + bS\frac{\partial U}{\partial S} + \kappa(\mu - r)\frac{\partial U}{\partial r} - rU + \frac{\partial U}{\partial t} = 0. \quad (6.6)$$

If one conserves the assumptions 3.1 to 3.5 and uses the following dynamics for the index price in the assumption 3.6:

$$dS = bS\,dt + \sigma_I S\,dz_S \quad (6.7)$$

where σ_I refers to the total index volatility rather than its specific volatility, then the PDE becomes:

$$\frac{1}{2}\sigma_I^2 S^2 \frac{\partial^2 U}{\partial S^2} + \rho\sigma_r S\sigma_I\sqrt{r}\frac{\partial^2 U}{\partial S \partial r} + \frac{1}{2} r\sigma_r^2 \frac{\partial^2 U}{\partial r^2} + bS\frac{\partial U}{\partial S} + \kappa(\mu - r)\frac{\partial U}{\partial r} - rU + \frac{\partial U}{\partial t} = 0 \quad (6.8)$$

which is equation (6.6) for which $(\sigma_I + \nu\sigma_r\sqrt{r})$ is replaced by σ_I. Note that when $\mu = r$ and $\sigma_r = 0$, this equation reduces to the commodity equation in Merton (1973). When $\mu = r = b$ and $\sigma_r = 0$, it becomes the Black and Scholes (1973) equation. When $\mu = r$, $\sigma_r = 0$ and $b = 0$, it becomes the Black (1976) equation for commodity futures options.

Denote by $\mathcal{R}$ the continuation region defined by $\mathcal{R} = \{(S,r,t) \in [0,\infty[\times[0,\infty[\times[0,T[|\ C(S,r,T) > (S-K)^+\}$ and $\partial\mathcal{C}$ its frontier expressed in terms of the underlying asset price S. $\partial\mathcal{C}$ is the optimal stopping boundary. To find solutions for an American stock index call option with a strike price K and a maturity date T, the PDE (6) must be solved under the following boundary conditions:

$$\begin{aligned} C(S,r,T) &= (S-K)^+ \\ C(S,r,t)|_{\partial\mathcal{R}} &= (S-K)^+ \\ \frac{\partial C(S,r,t)}{\partial S}|_{\partial\mathcal{R}} &= 1. \end{aligned} \tag{6.9}$$

The last condition is the usual "smooth fit" principle. These conditions are similar to those in BCS and can be justified using probabilistic arguments as in Myneni (1992) and Chesney et al. (1993).

Denote by $\mathcal{R}'$ the continuation region defined by $\mathcal{R}' = \{(S,r,t) \in [0,\infty[\times[0,\infty[\times[0,T[|P(S,r,T) > (K-S)^+\}$ and $\partial\mathcal{R}'$ its frontier expressed in terms of the underlying asset price S. An American stock index put option with a strike price K and a maturity date T must satisfy the PDE (6.6) subject to the following boundary conditions:

$$\begin{aligned} P(S,r,T) &= (K-S)^+ \\ P(S,r,t)|_{\partial\mathcal{R}'} &= (K-S)^+ \\ \frac{\partial P(S,r,t)}{\partial S}|_{\partial\mathcal{R}'} &= -1. \end{aligned} \tag{6.10}$$

The characterization of the optimal exercise boundary with two states variables is more complicated than in the usual case with just one variable.

4. The solution method: numerical solutions and simulations

In this section, the PDE is discretized on a grid with respect to the two space-variables S, r and time t. The Crank–Nicholson scheme is used and some simulations are ran. The numerical scheme is a θ-scheme of the implicit type for which $\theta = \frac{1}{2}$. It is centered in space and in time. It is unconditionally stable and convergent.

4.1 Numerical results

The time to maturity $(T-t)$ is divided into N time intervals of length k. The option value is calculated at time $(s-k)$ in a recursive way as a function of its value at instant s with $t \leq s \leq T$. The instant $s = T$ corresponds to the option's maturity date.

The underlying index price and the interest rate are divided into M intervals of size h. The state variables are considered within the intervals $[0, S^*]$ and $[0, r^*]$. Note that the larger M and N, the closer is the numerical solution of the discrete system to the real solution of the PDE.[5] Hence, using:

$$\begin{aligned} S &= ih \quad && \text{for } 0 \leq i \leq M \\ r &= jh \quad && \text{for } 0 \leq j \leq M \\ t &= nk \quad && \text{for } 0 \leq n \leq N, \end{aligned} \tag{6.11}$$

the option value is represented by a three-dimensional array, $U(S,r,t) = U(ih, jh, nk) = U^n(i,j)$. At each time step, $s = T - nk$, the first and second derivatives of S and r and the time derivative in (2.6) are approximated using the central differences :

$$\begin{aligned} \frac{\partial U^n(i,j)}{\partial S} &= \frac{U^n(i+1,j) - U^n(i-1,j)}{2h} \\ \frac{\partial U^n(i,j)}{\partial r} &= \frac{U^n(i,j+1) - U^n(i,j-1)}{2h} \\ \frac{\partial^2 U^n(i,j)}{\partial S^2} &= \frac{U^n(i-1,j) - 2U^n(i,j) + U^n(i+1,j)}{h^2} \\ \frac{\partial^2 U^n(i,j)}{\partial r^2} &= \frac{U^n(i,j-1) - 2U^n(i,j) + U^n(i,j+1)}{h^2} \\ \frac{\partial^2 U^n(i,j)}{\partial S \partial r} &= \frac{U^n(i+1,j+1) - U^n(i-1,j+1)}{4h^2} \\ &\quad + \frac{-U^n(i+1,j-1) + U^n(i-1,j-1)}{4h^2} \\ \frac{\partial U^n(i,j)}{\partial t} &= \frac{U^n(i,j) - U^(n - \frac{1}{2})(i,j)}{k/2}. \end{aligned}$$

[5]The derivatives may be also approximated using an explicit or an implicit difference scheme, but for some well-known reasons, the scheme adopted has many desirable properties when compared to other numerical methods. See for example Bellalah (1990) and Briys-Bellalah et al. (1998) among others.

Define the operators H_S, H_r, $H_S H_r$, δ_S^2, δ_r^2, $\delta_S^2\delta_r^2$ as:

$$\begin{aligned}
H_S H_r U^n(i,j) &= H_S[U^n(i,j+1) - U^n(i,j-1)] \\
&= U^n(i+1,j+1) - U^n(i-1,j+1) \\
&\quad - U^n(i+1,j-1) + U^n(i-1,j-1) \\
\delta_S^2 U^{n+1}(i,j) &= U^{n+1}(i+1,j) - 2U^{n+1}(i,j) + U^{n+1}(i-1,j) \\
\delta_r^2 U^{n+1}(i,j) &= U^{n+1}(i,j+1) - 2U^{n+1}(i,j) + U^{n+1}(i,j-1) \\
\delta_S^2\delta_r^2 U^n(i,j) &= U^n(i+1,j+1) - 2U^n(i,j+1) + U^n(i-1,j+1) \\
&\quad - 2U^n(i+1,j) + 4U^n(i,j) - 2U^n(i-1,j) \\
&\quad + U^n(i+1,j-1) - 2U^n(i,j-1) + U^n(i-1,j-1).
\end{aligned}$$

If we replace the derivatives by their values, the PDE (6.6) can be approximated for each instant $s = T - (n - \frac{1}{2})k$ at points $S = ih$ and $r = jh$ by the following system

$$\begin{aligned}
&[1 - \tfrac{1}{2}A\delta_S^2 - \tfrac{1}{2}B\delta_r^2 - \tfrac{1}{8}CH_rH_S - \tfrac{1}{4}DH_S - \tfrac{1}{4}EH_r]U^n(i,j) \\
&\quad = [\tfrac{1}{2}A\delta_S^2 + \tfrac{1}{2}B\delta_r^2 - \tfrac{1}{8}CH_rH_S + \tfrac{1}{4}DH_S + \tfrac{1}{4}EH_r + F]U^{n-1}(i,j)
\end{aligned}$$

with:

$$\begin{aligned}
A &= \frac{(\sigma_I + \nu\sigma_r\sqrt{jh})^2(i^2k)}{2G} & B &= \frac{\sigma_r^2 jk}{2hG} \\
C &= \frac{\rho\sigma_r i(\sigma_I\sqrt{jh} + \nu\sigma_r jh)k}{hG} & D &= \frac{(bih)k}{hG} \\
E &= \frac{\kappa(\mu - jh)k}{hG} & F &= \frac{1 - (jhk/2)}{G} \\
G &= 1 + \frac{1}{2}jhk,
\end{aligned}$$

$1 \le i \le M-1$ and $1 \le j \le M-1$.

It is possible to show that this system of $(M-1)^2$ equations may be solved in two steps, given a value of n. For each i, it presents $(M-1)$ equations with $(M+1)$ unknowns for $0 \le i \le M$. After calculating the values $U^{n*}(i+1, j-1)$, the second step implies to solve a system of $(M-1)$ equations with $(M+1)$ unknowns for $0 \le j \le M$. This method must be repeated N times for $0 \le j \le M$.

Until now, the ADI scheme shows no particular problems. The approximation of the boundary condition when the interest rate is zero poses a serious problem and makes the difference between our method and the numerical schemes reported in the financial literature. The main difficulty consists in preserving the properties of the numerical scheme, i.e., the tridiagonal structure of the matrix, the stability and the speed of convergence. This is our main contribution to numerical analysis and represents our extension of the ADI to the valuation of derivative assets in two or more dimensions. In particular, a straightforward ADI is not stable and speed of convergence is affected.

When the interest rate r is zero, i.e; when $j = 0$, the PDE becomes:

$$\frac{1}{2}\sigma_I^2 S^2 \frac{\partial^2 U}{\partial S^2} + \kappa\mu \frac{\partial U}{\partial r} + bS \frac{\partial U}{\partial S} + \frac{\partial U}{\partial t} = 0. \tag{6.12}$$

This PDE is also discretized by the Crank–Nicholson scheme, centered in the space, except for the term $\partial U/\partial r$ which is treated explicitely and "decentered inside the scheme". Hence, all the terms are of the second order, except this latter term which is of a first order in time and of a second order in space.

This approximation accelerates the speed of convergence and reduces the computation time. The following discretization is used:

$$\frac{\partial U}{\partial r} = \left[\frac{3U^n(i,0) - 4U^n(i,1) + U^n(i,2)}{2h}\right] = \left[\frac{H *_r U^{n-1}(i,0)}{2h}\right]$$

which gives:

$$[1 - \tfrac{1}{2}A'\delta_S^2 - \tfrac{1}{4}B'H_S]U^n(i,0) = [1 + \tfrac{1}{2}A'\delta_S^2 + \tfrac{1}{4}B'H_S + \tfrac{1}{2}C'H*_r]U^{n-1}(i,0)$$

with:

$$A' = \frac{\sigma_I^2(i^2k)}{2} \qquad B' = \frac{(bih)k}{h} \qquad C' = \frac{\kappa\mu k}{h}$$

The algorithm is available upon request.

4.2 Results and implications

Tables 6.1 to 6.6 present numerical results for in the money, at the money and out of the money American index options using different parameter values for the dynamics of the underlying index and interest rates. In order to facilitate comparisons between standard and non-standard option pricing models, the choice of the parameters is done with respect to some empirical studies and is in accordance with the BCS results.

Using 500 iterations in the space and 100 iterations in time, index option prices are evaluated for different levels of interest rates and two levels of the interest rate volatility parameter, $\sigma_r = 0.10$ and $\sigma_r = 0.15$. For example, when σ_r varies from 0.10 to 0.15, Table 6.1 reveals insignificant differences between out of the money call values. This result

Table 6.1. Simulation of American Out-of-the-money Call Option Prices with a composite volatility for $S/K = 0.9$, $\rho = 0.2$, $\mu = 0.08$, $\delta = 0.05$ $\kappa = 0.5$, $\sigma_I = 0.15$, $\nu = 4$, $h = 0.002$, $k = 0.001$, $M = 500$, $N = 100$

σ_r/r	$r = 0.02$	$r = 0.04$	$r = 0.06$	$r = 0.08$	$r = 0.1$	$r = 0.12$	$r = 0.14$	$r = 0.16$
$\sigma_r = 0.10$	0.26733	0.26735	0.26740	0.26742	0.26748	0.26754	0.26760	0.26900
$\sigma_r = 0.15$	0.26901	0.27131	0.27310	0.2740	0.2752	0.2754	0.2763	0.2801
d_p	0.00167	0.00396	0.0057	0.0065	0.0077	0.0078	0.0087	0.011
p_p	0.0062	0.0248	0.0213	0.0246	0.0288	0.0293	0.0325	0.0408

- **d_p and p_p stand respectively for the absolute and relative differences between option prices.**

Table 6.2. Simulation of American At-The-Money Call Option prices for $S/K = 1$, $\rho = 0.2$, $\mu = 0.08$, $\delta = 0.05$ $\kappa = 0.5$, $\sigma_I = 0.15$, $\nu = 4$, $h = 0.002$, $k = 0.001$, $M = 500$, $N = 100$

σ_r/r	$r = 0.02$	$r = 0.04$	$r = 0.06$	$r = 0.08$	$r = 0.1$	$r = 0.12$	$r = 0.14$	$r = 0.16$
$\sigma_r = 0.10$	0.5028	0.5030	0.5033	0.5036	0.5038	0.5048	0.5050	0.5063
$\sigma_r = 0.15$	0.5142	0.5145	0.5149	0.5252	0.5269	0.5282	0.5396	0.5409
d_p	0.0114	0.0115	0.0116	0.0216	0.0231	0.0234	0.0346	0.0348
p_p	0.0226	0.0228	0.023	0.0428	0.0458	0.046	0.0685	0.0686

Table 6.3. Simulation of American In-The-Money Call Option Values for $S/K = 1.1$, $\rho = 0.2$, $\mu = 0.08$, $\delta = 0.05$ $\kappa = 0.5$, $\sigma_I = 0.15$, $\nu = 4$, $h = 0.002$, $k = 0.001$, $M = 500$, $N = 100$

σ_r/r	$r = 0.02$	$r = 0.04$	$r = 0.06$	$r = 0.08$	$r = 0.1$	$r = 0.12$	$r = 0.14$	$r = 0.16$
$\sigma_r = 0.10$	0.9244	0.9257	0.9287	0.93238	0.9359	0.93956	0.94316	0.94675
$\sigma_r = 0.15$	0.9253	0.9267	0.9298	0.93369	0.9461	0.94979	0.95346	0.95714
d_p	0.0009	0.0010	0.0011	0.0013	0.0102	0.01023	0.0103	0.01039
p_p	0.0009	0.0010	0.0011	0.0014	0.0108	0.0108	0.0109	0.0109

Table 6.4. Simulation of American In-The-Money Put Option Values for $S/K = 0.9$, $\rho = 0.2$, $\mu = 0.08$, $\delta = 0.05$ $\kappa = 0.5$, $\sigma_I = 0.15$, $\nu = 4$, $h = 0.002$, $k = 0.001$, $M = 500$, $N = 100$

σ_r/r	$r = 0.02$	$r = 0.04$	$r = 0.06$	$r = 0.08$	$r = 0.1$	$r = 0.12$	$r = 0.14$	$r = 0.16$
$\sigma_r = 0.10$	0.8145	0.81719	0.81972	0.82197	0.82405	0.82600	0.82785	0.82962
$\sigma_r = 0.15$	0.81786	0.82303	0.82739	0.83132	0.83497	0.83840	0.84167	0.84481
d_p	0.0033	0.0058	0.0076	0.0093	0.0109	0.0124	0.0138	0.0151
p_p	0.0040	0.0070	0.0090	0.0113	0.0132	0.0147	0.0166	0.0183

Table 6.5. Simulation of American At-The-Money Put Option Values for $S/K = 1$, $\rho = 0.2$, $\mu = 0.08$, $\delta = 0.05$ $\kappa = 0.5$, $\sigma_I = 0.15$, $\nu = 4$, $h = 0.002$, $k = 0.001$, $M = 500$, $N = 100$

σ_r/r	$r = 0.02$	$r = 0.04$	$r = 0.06$	$r = 0.08$	$r = 0.1$	$r = 0.12$	$r = 0.14$	$r = 0.16$
$\sigma_r = 0.10$	0.40502	0.40618	0.40695	0.40777	0.40843	0.40909	0.40971	0.41030
$\sigma_r = 0.15$	0.40631	0.41828	0.41956	0.43188	0.44228	0.45421	0.45527	0.45728
d_p	0.00129	0.0119	0.0126	0.0241	0.0338	0.0451	0.0455	0.0469
p_p	0.0020	0.0292	0.0309	0.0590	0.0828	0.1102	0.1112	0.1145

Table 6.6. Simulation of American Out of the money Put Option Values for $S/K = 1.1$, $\rho = 0.2$, $\mu = 0.08$, $\delta = 0.05$ $\kappa = 0.5$, $\sigma_I = 0.15$, $\nu = 4$, $h = 0.002$, $k = 0.001$, $M = 500$, $N = 100$

σ_r/r	$r = 0.02$	$r = 0.04$	$r = 0.06$	$r = 0.08$	$r = 0.1$	$r = 0.12$	$r = 0.14$	$r = 0.16$
$\sigma_r = 0.10$	0.2000	0.2008	0.2011	0.2014	0.2018	0.2023	0.2028	0.2034
$\sigma_r = 0.15$	0.2040	0.2050	0.2065	0.2082	0.2102	0.2129	0.2160	0.2202
d_p	0.0040	0.0042	0.0054	0.0068	0.0084	0.0106	0.0132	0.0168
p_p	0.0200	0.0209	0.0260	0.0337	0.0416	0.0523	0.0650	0.0825

is expected since out of the money calls are less sensitive to the interest rate and its volatility than at the money options.

The differences reported in Table 6.2 for at the money calls are more important than those in Table 6.1. The maximum difference between option values is 3.47 percent corresponding to nearly 6.86 percent of the option value. Also, the minimum difference is 1.14 percent corresponding to 2.26 percent of the option value. Table 6.3 shows a maximum difference of 1.039 percent and a minimum difference of 0.09 percent corresponding respectively to nearly 1.09 and 0.09 percent of the in the money call price.

Using the same comparisons, the maximum difference in Table 6.4 represents 1.83 percent of the option value and the minimum difference is 0.4 percent of the in the money put price. For at the money put options, the maximum difference in Table 6.5 corresponds to 11.45 percent of the option price and the minimum difference is 0.2 percent of the put price. For out of the money put options, the maximum difference in Table 6.6 is 8.25 percent and the minimum difference is 2 percent of the put price.

The impact of the composite volatility and stochastic interest rates seem to be significant on American at the money call and put option values. This effect is more important for put options and may trigger early exercise of index puts. The effect reported here is greater than that in standard models and is less than that in BCS. While the negligible effect in standard models is intuitive, the effect in the BCS model may be due to the process of interest rates chosen, allowing for negative interest rates. Also, the numerical scheme presented here is more efficient than those presented in previous studies. Empirical tests can be conducted in order to test if the parameters are statistically stable and if option prices are close to market prices.

5. Conclusion

Our option valuation model for American index options is similar in spirit to that used in BCS, except for the process describing the dynamics of interest rates and for the solution method. The index price volatility depends on its specific volatility and on the interest rate volatility. This model is motivated by the results of empirical and theoretical studies regarding the market index, as opposed to a single stock and by the relative mispricing of long term index options.

It is possible to use finite difference methods to get American option values. We extend the classic ADI method based on the Crank–Nicholson scheme in two space dimensions and provide an efficient, stable and convergent algorithm for the pricing of these options. Some numerical recipes are used to reduce the computation-time. The algorithm reduces to solving tridiagonal systems and may be used to handle other complex problems in financial economics. The solution method is quite general and can be applied to any option valuation problem in the presence of two state variables. Our option prices lie between those reported in standard models as the RS's model and those in BCS. The results indicate the significant effect of interest rates and the volatility on the pricing and the early exercise of long term index options.

Acknowledgements We thank Richard Roll, Darell Duffie, Bertrand Jacquillat and the participants at the seminar conferences at the University of Paris-Dauphine and Cergy-Pontoise for their helpful comments on earlier drafts of this chapter.

References

Black, F. (1976). The pricing of commodity contracts. *Journal of Financial Economics*, 3:167–179.

Black, F. and Scholes, M. (1973). The pricing of options and corporate liabilities. *Journal of Political Economy*, 81:637–654.

Bellalah, M. (1990). *Quatre essais pour l'évaluation des options sur indices et sur contrats à terme d'indice.* Doctorat de l'Université de Paris-Dauphine.

Bellalah, M. (1991). *Gestion quantitative du portefeuille et nouveaux marchés financiers.* Éditions Nathan.

Bellalah, M. (1996). Les tests empiriques des modèles d'options sur indices et des options de taux d'intérêt sur la place de Paris. Working chapter, THEMA, Universite de Cergy, France.

Boquist, J., Racette, G., and Schlarbaum, G. (1975). Duration and risk assessment for bonds and common stocks. *Journal of Finance*, 30:1360 – 1365.

Brenner, M., Courtadon, G., and M. Subrahmanyam, M. (1985). Options on the spot and options on the futures. *Journal of Finance*, 40:1303 – 1317.

Brenner, M., Courtadon, G., and Subrahmanyam, M. (1987). The Valuation of Stock Index Options. Working chapter, June.

Briys, E., Bellalah, M., Mai, H.M., and de Varenne, F. (1998). *Options, Futures and Other Exotics.* John Wiley & Sons.

Carr, P., Jarrow, R., and Myneni, R. (1992). Alternative characterization of American put options. *Mathematical Finance*, 2:87 – 106.

Chesney, M., Elliott, J., and Gibson, R. (1993). Analytical solutions for the pricing of American bond and yield options. *Mathematical Finance*, 3:277 – 294.

Copeland, S. and Stapleton, R. (1985). Inflation, Interest Rate Risk and the Variance of Common Stock Prices. Working chapter, Graduate School of Business Administration.

Cox, J., Ingersoll, J., and Ross, S. (1981). A re-examination of traditional hypotheses about the term structure of interest rates, *Journal of Finance*, 36:769 – 799.

Cox, J., Ingersoll, J., and Ross, S. (1985). A theory of the term structure of interest rates. *Econometrica*, 53:385 – 407.

Fama, E. and French, K.R. (1993). Common risk factors in the returns on stocks and bonds. *Journal of Financial Economics*, 33:3 – 56.

Harrison, J.M. and Kreps, D.M. (1979). Martingales and arbitrage in multi-period security markets. *Journal of Economic Theory*, 20:381 – 408.

Karatzas, I. (1988). On the pricing of American options. *Applied Mathematics and Optimization*, 17:37 – 60.

Lanstein, R. and Sharpe, W. (1978). Duration and security risk. *Journal of Financial and Quantitative Analysis*, 13:653 – 668.

McKee, S. and Mitchell, R. (1970). Alternating direction implicit methods for parabolic equations in two dimensions with a mixed derivative. *The Computer Journal*, 13:81 – 86.

Merton, R.C. (1973). Theory of rational option pricing. *Bell Journal of Economics and Management Science*, 4:141 – 183

Myneni, R. (1992). The pricing of the American option. *Annals of Applied Probability*, 2:1 – 23.

Nayar, N. and Lee, H. (1993). A transaction data analysis of arbitrage between index options and undex futures. *Journal of Futures Markets*, 8:889 – 902.

Peterson, D. and Peterson, P. (1994). Variance increases following large stock distributions: The role of changing bid-ask spreads and true variances. *Journal of Banking and Finance*, 18:199 – 206.

Ramaswamy, K. and Sundaresan, S. (1985). The valuation of options on futures contracts. *Journal of Finance*, 5:1319 – 1341.

Scott, L. (1987). Option pricing when the variance changes randomly: Theory, estimation and application. *Journal of Financial and Quantitative Analysis*, 22:419 – 438.

Vasicek, O. (1977). A equilibrium characterization of the term structure. *Journal of Financial Economics*, 5:177 – 188.

Weinstein, M. (1981). The systematic risk of corporate bonds. *Journal of Financial and Quantitative Analysis*, 16:257 – 278.

Chapter 7

VALUING AMERICAN CONTINGENT CLAIMS WHEN TIME TO MATURITY IS UNCERTAIN

Tony Berrada

Abstract In this chapter we show how to use the early exercise premium decomposition to value american option with uncertain maturity. We provide two examples where the valuation of such product appears natural, Employee Stock Options and Real Options. We discuss through a numerical example, how the optimal exercise boundary and the option value are affected by the uncertainty in the maturity, and document significant effects.

1. Introduction

American options are contracts which are actively traded on most financial markets. They allow the holder to exercise his rights on or before the maturity. The valuation problem of this type of contract has been extensively studied in the literature, and though there is no analytical solution, numerical techniques have reached very satisfying levels of speed and accuracy (for a review of numerical methods see Broadie and Detemple, 1996). The concept of American option applies to a wide range of situations outside of the financial markets. The theory of real options considers capital budgeting as an optimal timing of investment opportunities, and uses standard financial option theory to determine optimal operating policies (see Dixit and Pyndick, 1994, for a review on real options). Example abound in corporate finance, when considering optimal default decisions (see, e.g., Leland, 1994).

In these applications the maturity of the option is in general assumed fixed or infinite (this allows computation of analytical solutions), we propose to relax this assumption and study the impact of stochastic maturity on the value of the contingent claim and the optimal exercise boundary. This problem has been considered in the literature by Carr (1998) for a specific class of distribution (exponential) which yields a time independent exercise boundary. This allows one to obtain quasi analytical formula, and it is then possible to approximate the value of a fixed maturity American option by letting the variance of the maturity go to zero. This methodology is known as randomization. Also, El Karoui and Martellini (2001) describe a general framework for the existence of an equivalent martingale measure when the time horizon is uncertain.

We use distributions which are function of time, and rely on numerical methods to obtain the time dependent exercise boundary. We then consider two applications of the concept. We first look at a real option model and discuss the shape of the exercise boundary and its implication for the optimal operating policies, focusing on the impact of uncertainty in the maturity. We then consider the valuation of Employee Stock Options, the maturity of which depends both on the employment length of the holder and the contractual expiration date. The latter constitutes an upper bound to the distribution of the maturity and the former is in general stochastic. The rest of the chapter is organized as follows. In Section 2 we develop the valuation methodology, in particular we consider the backward integral equation leading to the optimal exercise boundary. This implies the computation of European contingent claim with stochastic maturity, which we consider in detail in Section 2.1. In Section 3.1 we investigate the applicability of the concept to real options situation, while in Section 3.2 we consider the valuation of Employee Stock Options and compare the results with the accounting standard regulations. We conclude and propose further extensions in Section 4.

2. Valuation methodology

In this section we will consider the valuation of an American call option with random maturity. We will use the early exercise premium decomposition and propose an extension to allow for random maturity.

Let us define a probability space by the triplet $(\Omega, \mathcal{F}, \mathcal{Q})$ and a $\mathcal{Q}$-Brownian motions W_t. The filtration is the natural filtration of the Brownian motion, $\mathcal{F}^{W_t}$, enlarged to incorporate the occurrence of the maturity. All subsequent process and expectations are taken with respect to that filtration, which implies that at any point in time t the agent is able to assess whether the maturity has occurred at time $s \leq t$. It is assumed that $\mathcal{Q}$ is the equivalent martingale measure (EMM). El Karoui and Martellini (2001) have shown that in the presence of timing risk, there exist an infinity of EMMs, which depend on the market price of timing risk. An equilibrium model is needed to establish such a price and define a unique EMM. Throughout the chapter we assume that the timing risk is diversifiable, namely that the price of timing risk is zero. In that context (since markets are otherwise complete) a unique EMM exists and allows to determine the price of the contingent claim.[1] The underlying process S_t (under $\mathcal{Q}$) is described by the stochastic differential equation

$$\begin{aligned} \frac{dS_t}{S_t} &= (r - \delta)\, dt + \sigma\, dW_t \\ S_0 &= s \end{aligned} \tag{7.1}$$

where r, δ and σ are constants. The economic interpretation of the parameters will vary with the specific applications, and will be exposed in details in Section 3. We are interested in finding the value and optimal exercise boundary of an American contingent claim written on S_t, with stochastic maturity, denoted $C^{\mathrm{A}}(S_t, t)$. The conditional distribution of the maturity, T, is a function of time only; in particular it is independent of W_t. We assume that T is bounded above by $\overline{T}$ and below by 0, and its density function at time t is denoted $g(t, T)$.

The early exercise premium decomposition, introduced by El Karoui and Karatzas (1991) and Myneni (1992), allows to write the value of an American call option, $C^{\mathrm{a}}(S_t, t)$ with strike K and maturity T as

$$C^{\mathrm{a}}(S_t, t) = C^{\mathrm{e}}(S_t, t) + E_t\left[\int_t^T e^{-r(v-t)}[\delta S_v - rK]1_{\{S_v > B_v\}}\, dv\right] \tag{7.2}$$

where $C^{\mathrm{e}}(S_t, t)$ is a European call option with identical characteristics. B_t denotes the optimal exercise boundary and $1_{\{S_v > B_v\}}$ is an indicator function which takes value 1 when the underlying is superior to the boundary. A simple extension of that formula allows to introduce the stochastic nature of the maturity.[2] The early exercise premium decomposition for an American call option with stochastic maturity is given by

$$\begin{aligned} C^{\mathrm{A}}(S_t, t) &= C^{\mathrm{E}}(S_t, t) \\ &\quad + E_t\left[\int_t^{\overline{T}} e^{-r(v-t)}[\delta S_v - rK]1_{\{S_v > B_v, T > v\}}\, dv\right] \end{aligned} \tag{7.3}$$

where $C^{\mathrm{E}}(S_t, t)$ is a European call option with stochastic maturity and $1_{\{S_v > B_v, T > v\}}$ is an indicator function which takes a value 1 when the underlying is superior to the boundary and the maturity has not been

[1] Alternatively, one could consider risk neutrality with respect to timing risk.

[2] I thank Jérôme Detemple for suggesting this approach.

reached at time v. Recall that the distribution of T is independent of S_t, therefore we have

$$C^{\mathrm{A}}(S_t,t) = C^{\mathrm{E}}(S_t,t) + E_t\left[\int_t^{\overline{T}} e^{-r(v-t)}[\delta S_v - rK]1_{\{S_v>B_v\}}1_{\{T>v\}}\,dv\right] \quad (7.4)$$

which, for the stochastic process under consideration, yields

$$C^{\mathrm{A}}(S_t,t) = C^{\mathrm{E}}(S_t,t) + \int_t^{\overline{T}} \Big(\delta S_t e^{-\delta(s-t)} N\big(d_2(S_t,B_s,s-t)\big) - rKe^{-r(s-t)}N\big(d_3(S_t,B_s,s-t)\big)\Big) \times \Pr[T \geq s]\,ds \quad (7.5)$$

where $\Pr[T > s]$ depends on the density function of T. The boundary $B(t)$ is the solution of the backward integral equation

$$B_t - K = C^{\mathrm{E}}(B_t,t) + \int_t^{\overline{T}} \Big(\delta B_t e^{-\delta(s-t)} N\big(d_2(B_t,B_s,s-t)\big) - rKe^{-r(s-t)}N\big(d_3(B_t,B_s,s-t)\big)\Big) \times \Pr[T \geq s]\,ds \quad (7.6)$$

$$B_T = \max\left\{K, \frac{r}{\delta}K\right\}$$

where

$$d_2(B_t,B_s,s-t) = \frac{\log(B_t/B_s) + (r-\delta-\sigma^2/2)(s-t)}{\sigma\sqrt{s-t}}$$
$$d_3(B_t,B_s,s-t) = d_2(B_t,B_s,s-t) - \sigma\sqrt{s-t}. \quad (7.7)$$

Although these equations are fairly explicit, the backward integral equation for the exercise boundary (7.6) must be solved using numerical techniques. To do so we must discretize the problem and solve the equation piecewise. In our numerical example, we will assume that the boundary is linear in time over the discrete interval. Once the approximate exercise boundary is obtained, it is used in equation (7.5) to compute the value of the American option with random maturity.

2.1 Valuation of the European call with stochastic maturity

In order to compute the optimal exercise boundary and the American option value, we have to first provide a methodology to obtain a value for the European option with stochastic maturity. We use a modified version of the Feinman-Kac theorem provided by Dynkin (1965). We will first present the problem solved by Dynkin and then show that the valuation of a European option with stochastic maturity is equivalent (originally Dynkin's demonstration was for a family of Itô processes, for simplicity we consider here the case of a single Itô process).

Define an Itô process $X(t)$ with drift $\mu(X,t)$ and volatility $\sigma(X,t)$ and initial value X_0 given. Consider T a random stopping time in the interval $[0,\infty)$. Define the function $V(X,t)$ by

$$V(X,t) = E_{X,T}\left[\int_t^T e^{-\int_t^s \Phi(u)\,du} u(X,s)\,ds + e^{-\int_t^T \Phi(u)\,du} f(X,T)\right] \quad (7.8)$$

where the expectation is taken over X and T, $\Phi(s)$ can be seen as a discount factor, $u(X,s)$ is a cashflow, and $f(X,T)$ is the final payoff function. Under certain regularity conditions $V(t)$ is well defined and solves the following PDE:

$$\frac{\partial V(X,t)}{\partial t} + \frac{\partial V(X,t)}{\partial X}\mu(X,t) + \frac{1}{2}\frac{\partial^2 V(X,t)}{\partial X^2}\sigma^2(X,t) - \Phi(t)V(X,t) + u(X,t) = 0 \quad (7.9)$$

subject to the following boundary condition:

$$V(X,T) = f(X,t); \quad (7.10)$$

note also that $V(X,t)$ is unique. Using standard arbitrage argument (Black and Scholes, 1973) we can show that $C^{\mathrm{E}}(S_t,t)$ solves the following partial differential equation

$$\frac{\partial C^{\mathrm{E}}(S_t,t)}{\partial t} + \frac{\partial C^{\mathrm{E}}(S_t,t)}{\partial S}(r-\delta)S_t + \frac{1}{2}\frac{\partial^2 C^{\mathrm{E}}(S_t,t)}{\partial V^2}\sigma^2 S_t^2 - rC^{\mathrm{E}}(S_t,t) = 0 \quad (7.11)$$

with random boundary

$$C^{\mathrm{E}}(S_T,T) = \max[(S_T - K),0] \quad (7.12)$$

which is equivalent to Dynkin's problem, with $u(X,t)$ set equal to zero, since holding the option yield no intermediate payments. After simplifying we therefore obtain

$$C^{\mathrm{E}}(S_t,t) = \int_t^{\overline{T}} C^{\mathrm{e}}(S_t,t;K,x)g(x,t)\,dx \quad (7.13)$$

where $C^e(S_t, t; K, x)$ is a European call option with strike K and fixed maturity x.[3] Equation (7.13) is then used in equation (7.6) and (7.5) to obtain the exercise boundary and the value of the American option with random maturity.

3. Applications

In this section we will consider two examples of American contingent claims with random maturity. We will first discuss the case of real options and then study the valuation of employee stock options. To obtain numerical values we will make use of equations (7.6) and (7.5).

3.1 Real options

3.1.1 Context. An implicit assumption in the original approach to real options (Macdonald and Siegel, 1986) is the absolute market power of the holder of the investment opportunity. The decision to invest is taken optimally only if there are no other agents with a potential impact on the investment opportunity availability. However, we know that this assumption is usually not verified. Economic agents traditionally interact in a competitive world where decision are not always taken independently but rather try to incorporate other agents' actions, hence the introduction of competition aspects in the real option field. Lambrecht and Perraudin (1997) model the situation by analyzing the optimal timing decision in a two agent setting where the action of one agent has an impact on the other agent's payoff. They show the equivalence with an optimal stopping time problem and provide a closed form solution for a general type of payoff. Schwartz and Moon (1994) tackle the issue in a different way: in their model for R&D valuation they introduce a jump process in the dynamic of the project value, and thus allow the R&D project value to drop suddenly to zero because of concurrent activity. It is also possible to use a reduced form model, by concentrating on one agent decision, taking as exogenous the action of other agents.[4] We assume that all uncertainty coming from other agents' activity can be summed up in the structure of the maturity of the investment opportunity. Another argument closely related to the competition issue concerns technological changes. Consider a firm which has an opportunity to invest in a product using a particular technology, the product in question would become obsolete if a new technology became available

[3] There is no distinction between $C^e(S_t, t; K, x)$ and $C^e(S_t, t)$, the former is used to enhance the dependence on the maturity x.

[4] To consider the problem this way, we must also assume that agents are price takers.

and the investment opportunity would then be lost. The managers of a firm involved in such an industry clearly have an idea of how long it would take for the new technology to be operational, but here again the maturity is not certain. Furthermore, even if we consider a problem with a structure such that the maturity should be fixed, it might be difficult to evaluate it. We could therefore consider the case of random maturity as a consequence of estimation errors. It is often the case in project valuation that the data is relatively scarce and not always perfectly reliable. One could also consider the case of project linked to R&D activity, such as developing a technical or human support to a particular research project. The opportunity of adding resources is available only as long as the research project is itself being conducted. Typically one does not have a perfect evaluation of the development period of an R&D project.

3.1.2 Numerical example. In this example we are interested in looking at the difference in the optimal operating policies when a stochastic maturity is introduced. We compare the value of the investment opportunities with fixed and stochastic maturity; the American option with fixed maturity will be denoted as the "benchmark" case.

When considering real options, the parameter δ stands for an implicit dividend yield, i.e., a difference in return from holding a perfectly correlated traded asset instead of the true underlying real asset (for a discussion see Dixit and Pyndick, 1994). We consider two type of bounded distribution over the interval $[a; b]$,namely uniform and triangular distribution. The density for the uniform distribution is given by

$$f(x) = \frac{1}{b-a}. \tag{7.14}$$

The triangular distribution is often used when little data is available but the mean, upper and lower limit can be approximated. The density function is given by

$$\begin{aligned} f(x) &= \frac{2(x-a)}{(b-a)(c-a)} \qquad a \leq x \leq c \\ f(x) &= \frac{2(b-x)}{(b-a)(b-c)} \qquad c < x \leq b. \end{aligned} \tag{7.15}$$

For both distributions we set $a = 0$ and $b = \overline{T}$. In the triangular distribution, c determines the mean of the distribution given by $(a + b + c)/3$. Figure 7.1 and 7.2 display the optimal exercise boundary for the triangular and uniform distribution respectively, for upper bounds ranging from 0.1 to 2. Figure 7.3)displays the optimal exercise boundary for the fixed maturity benchmark.

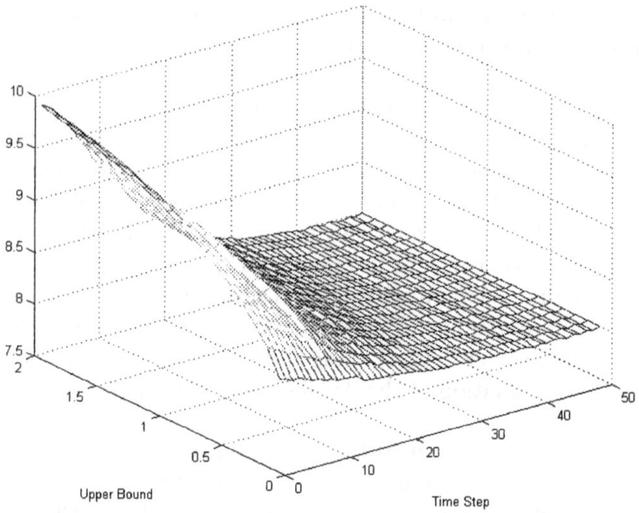

Figure 7.1. Optimal exercise boundary when considering the triangular distribution. We use 50 time steps for the numerical procedure. $r = 0.05$, $\delta = 0.06$, $\sigma = 0.2$ and $K = 8$.

The uniform distribution exercise boundary displays a concavity similar to the benchmark boundary. It is however larger in general as depicted in Figure 7.4, in particular when the upper bound becomes large.

Real options project typically have long maturity (usually several years), and it appears that for this type of situation the uniform distribution tends to increase the exercise boundary and induce, therefore, to invest later in the project. For the triangular distribution the effect is opposite, as we can see in Figure 7.5: the exercise boundary is always below the benchmark case. It also displays an unusual convexity, and will induce an earlier exercise than the uniform assumption, and the benchmark case.

We now turn to the value of the investment opportunity (i.e. the option) under the three different maturity assumptions. Table 3.1 provides valuation for various upper bounds to the maturity. We can see that in all cases the introduction of a stochastic maturity, for both distributions, lowers the value of the investment opportunity. This result is expected since by adding the possible occurrence of the maturity at an earlier date, we reduce the flexibility inherent in the investment project. The shape of the distribution has a greater impact on the optimal exercise policy than on the value of the investment opportunity: the uniform and triangular distribution assumptions yield very close valuations.

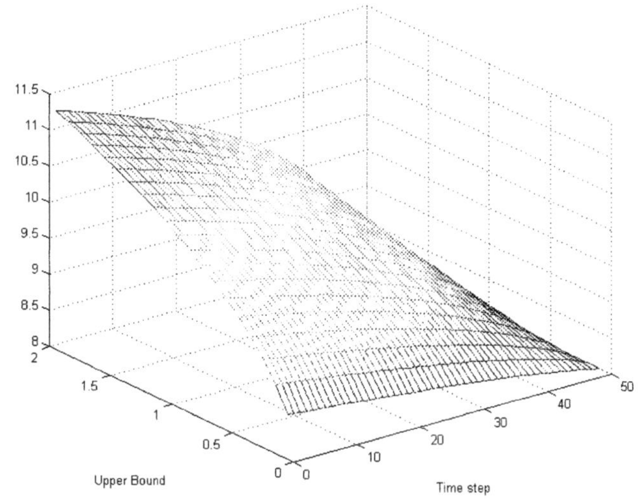

Figure 7.2. Optimal exercise boundary when considering the uniform distribution. We use 50 time steps for the numerical procedure. $r = 0.05$, $\delta = 0.06$, $\sigma = 0.2$ and $K = 8$.

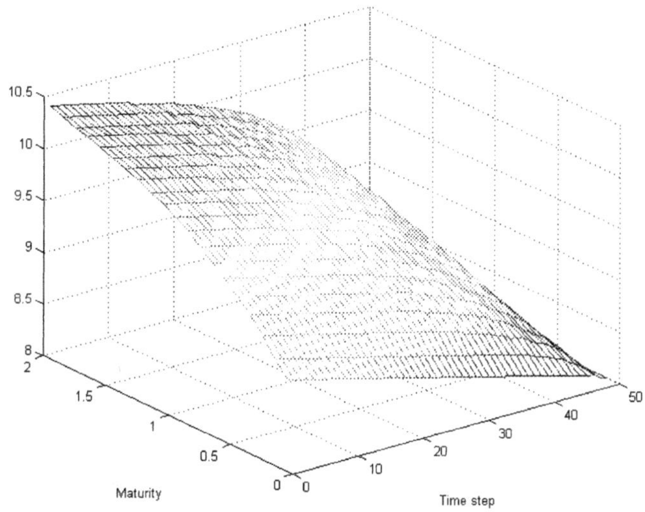

Figure 7.3. Optimal exercise boundary when considering the benchmark fixed maturity. We use 50 time steps for the numerical procedure. $r = 0.05$, $\delta = 0.06$, $\sigma = 0.2$ and $K = 8$.

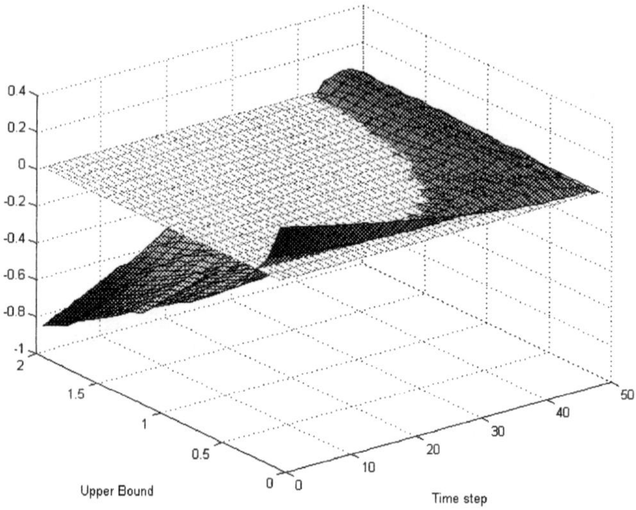

Figure 7.4. Difference between the uniform and benchmark exercise boundary. A positive value implies that the uniform exercise boundary is below the benchmark.

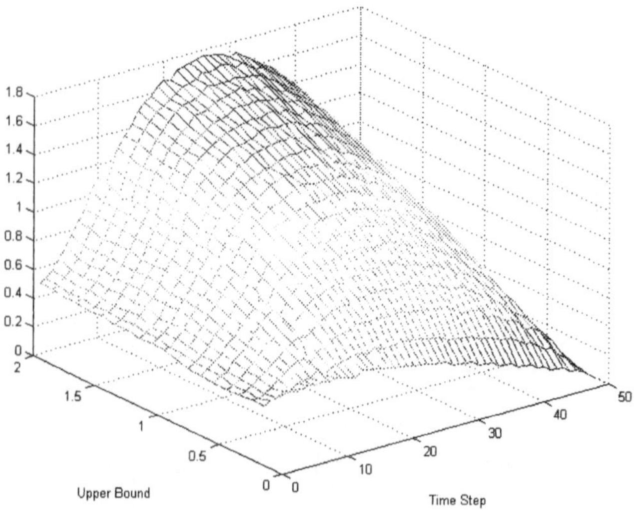

Figure 7.5. Difference between the triangular and benchmark exercise boundary. A positive value implies that the triangular exercise boundary is below the benchmark.

Table 7.1. Investment opportunity for different distribution assumptions. $S(0) = 8$

	Upper Bound				
	0.1	0.5	1	1.5	2
Triangular	0.14	0.30	0.41	0.49	0.55
Uniform	0.13	0.28	0.39	0.46	0.53
Benchmark	0.28	0.42	0.57	0.66	0.73

Notice that if the uncertainty about the maturity could be reduced by adding any kind of managerial support,[5] the cost of this support should be compared to the increase in value of the option.

3.2 Employee Stock Options

3.2.1 Context. It is now a common practice to offer Employee Stock Options (ESO) as a part of a remuneration package. ESO are similar to traded stock options in most aspects, but display some specific particularities. The holders of the ESO are not allowed to sell them and are also restricted in their trading of the underlying security. As pointed out in Huddart (1997), usage of traditional arbitrage argument may be difficult in the valuation of ESO because of the trading restrictions. Another distinct characteristic of ESO is that their maturity is bounded above by the contractual features, but is in fact stochastic, since the employee may leave the company (intentionally or not) at any time from the date he is granted the ESO. Statement of Financial Accounting Standards no. 123 suggests that ESO should be evaluated using a standard option pricing models with maturity equal to the expected exercise date (based on historical experience). If we assume that the trading restrictions are insignificant and focus solely on the maturity issue, then the SFAS no. 123 assumes that

$$C^{\mathrm{e}}(S_t, t; K, T_m) = C^{\mathrm{A}}(S_t, t; K, \overline{T}) \tag{7.16}$$

where T_m is the expected exercise date, i.e. the expected first passage time of S_t at the boundary B_t. There are no apparent reasons for this relationship to hold in general, and it might be the case that the SFAS recommendation leads to over/under valuation of the ESO. Note that the underlying asset in this problem is the stock price.

[5]We mean by this any type of support, wether hardware or data acquisition or hiring new staff with higher expertise.

3.2.2 Numerical example. We consider here a numerical example for the valuation of the ESO. We must first define the distribution of the maturity T. We first note that it is defined over the interval $[0;\overline{T}]$ where $\overline{T}$ is the contractual expiration date of the ESO. Denote $D \in [0,\infty)$ the date at which the employee leaves the firm. D is a random variable, and we assume that it is independent of W_t. We can express the maturity as

$$T = \min[D, \overline{T}]l. \tag{7.17}$$

This implies that the cumulative distribution function (CDF) of the maturity will in general be discontinuous. We will however assume as a simplified example that the CDF is indeed continuous and displays a sharp positive slope near the upper bound. Namely we consider CDF of the form

$$F(t) = \frac{A + (t-B)^C}{D} \tag{7.18}$$

where the constant parameters A, B, C and D are chosen to adequately describe the CDF of the maturity of a ESO.[6] Namely we would like to consider shapes as depicted in Figure 7.6.

Here the contractual expiration date is set at 5 years. The shape capture the fact that the probability of the employee leaving the company is initially high (trial period), then lower and finally there is a sharp increase when getting close to $\overline{T}$. The parameters of the underlying security are set to: $r = 0.05$, $\delta = 0.06$, $S_0 = 10$, $K = 10$.

We use numerical simulations to obtain the value of the expected exercise time T_m. Note that T_m is defined in our example as the expected value of the first hitting time of the boundary B_t conditional on early exercise. Figure 7.7 displays the distribution of the first passage at the optimal exercise boundary for $\sigma = 0.32$. Note that to perform this simulation we have set the drift of the stock price process to $\mu = 0.09$, since we are computing the expected passage time in the original probability and not in the risk neutral measure. The following results are robust in nature to changes in μ.

Figure 7.8 displays the optimal exercise boundary for the holder of the ESO as a function of time and volatility of the underlying. The exercise boundary does not display the usual concavity: it is first convex on its first part and then concave. This is due to the high early probability

[6] Notice that our approximation uses a continuous distribution, which has a smoothing effect on the exercise boundary. The use of a discontinuous distribution could imply discontinuities in the exercise boundary as well.

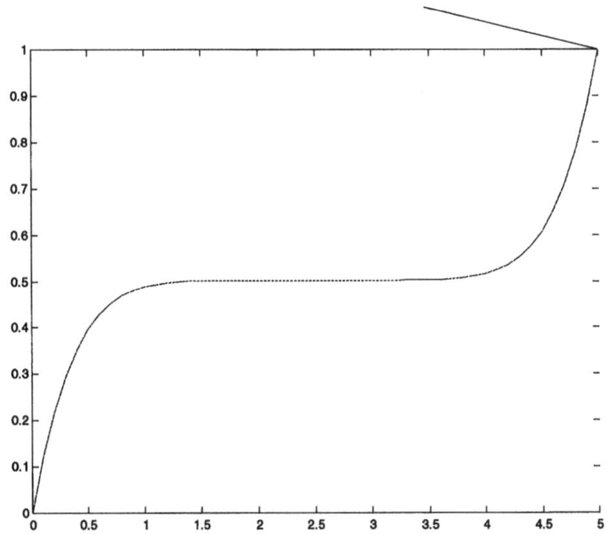

Figure 7.6. Exemple of a CDF for the maturity of an Employee Stock Option.

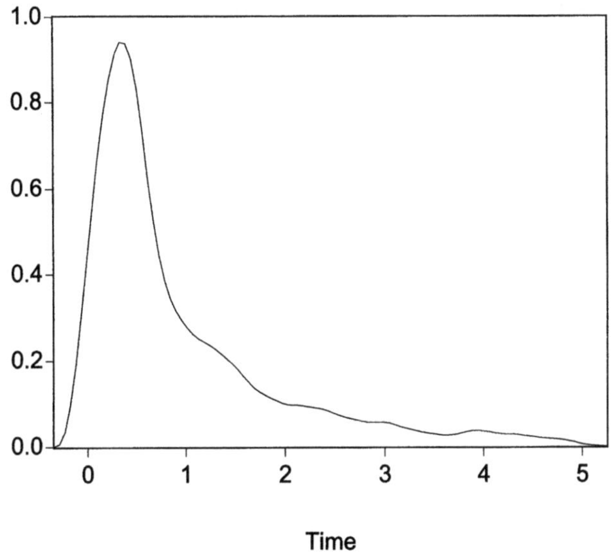

Figure 7.7. Kernel density of the first passage at the optimal exercise boundary for $\sigma = 0.32$.

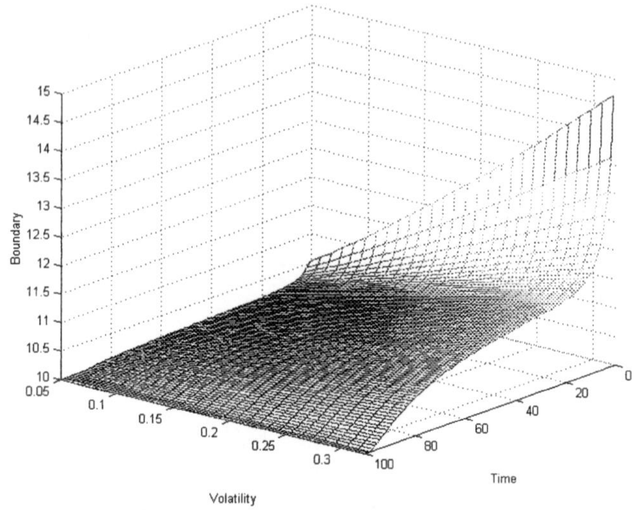

Figure 7.8. Optimal exercise boundary as a function of time and volatility of the underlying. The boundary is obtained by numerical evaluation of the backward integral equation given in Section 2. We use here 100 steps.

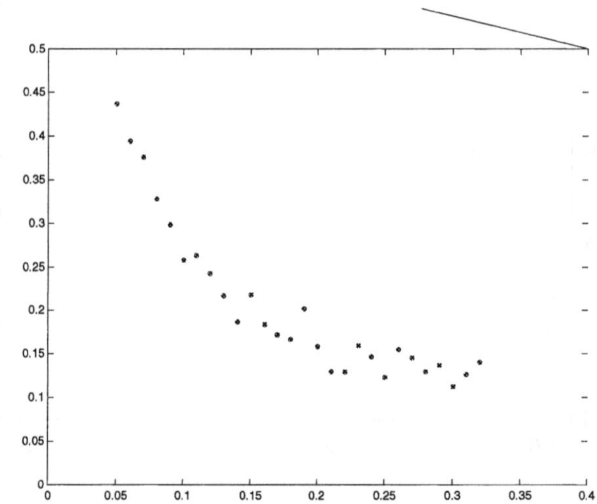

Figure 7.9. Relative error, computed as $(C^{\mathrm{A}}(S_t,t) - C^{\mathrm{e}}(S_t,t;K,T_m))/C^{\mathrm{A}}(S_t,t)$ for the entire range of σ $\{0.05; 0.32\}$

of occurrence of the maturity. As expected, the boundary is increasing with volatility.

In Figure 7.9, we consider the evaluation error E, defined as

$$E = \frac{C^{\mathrm{A}}(S_t, t) - C^{\mathrm{e}}(S_t, t; K, T_m)}{C^{\mathrm{A}}(S_t, t)},$$

as a function of volatility of the underlying. It appears that for our set of parameters (and for the entire range for σ) the error term is positive. The proposed accounting standard seems to undervalue the ESO in a significant way. The average error over the range of σ is of 20.5 %. Since the goal of a balance sheet is to accurately reflect the expenses and profit made by a firm and ESO constitute an important part of the remuneration of employee, it might be useful to consider the random nature of the maturity of the ESO. In particular, firm with consequent human capital and in early stages of development may display benefits which are much higher than the actual profit.

4. Conclusion

In this chapter we have considered the implication of stochastic maturity for the valuation of American contingent claims. We have shown how to use the early exercise premium decomposition to derive a backward integral equation which gives the value of the contingent claim as a solution. It is also possible to obtain in that manner the optimal exercise boundary. Both results must be obtained numerically. We have provided two applications of the methodology. First we have considered real options. In that setting we have shown why it is natural to consider a stochastic maturity and we have studied what this consideration implies for the optimal operating policies. The impact of the stochastic maturity depends on the choice of the distribution function and parameters. In general the option value is lowered by the introduction of the random maturity. The changes affecting the optimal operating policies differ in our 2 examples. The uniform distribution implies an exercise at a latter date (for most parameters choices) and the triangular distribution implies an earlier exercise than the fixed maturity benchmark.

We have also studied the valuation of ESO, and seen how the consideration of stochastic maturity could imply large deviations from the accounting standard rule for the pricing of such product. In general we have found that (in our setting) the FASA no. 123 tends to undervalue the Employee Stock Options, and that the valuation error could be as high as 40% for some selected parameters (low variance of the underlying). However others characteristics of the Employee Stock Options, especially when endowed to executive, have strong impact on the value and early exercise decisions, and the stochastic maturity should be added to these known particularities to obtain a satisfactory valuation model.

Acknowledgements I thank Marc Chesney, Jérôme Detemple, Rajna Gibson Henri Loubergé, Ernst-Ludwig Von Thadden as well as participants to the 3rd International Conference on Real Options at NIAS, the CEPR Conference on Capital Markets at The University Catholique de Louvain, the 1999 AFFI meeting and the 1999 European Finance Association meeting.

References

Black, F. and Scholes, M. (1973). The pricing of options and corporate liabilities. *Journal of Political Economy*, 81:637 – 54.

Broadie, M. and Detemple, J. (1996). American option valuation: New bounds, approximations, and a comparison of existing methods. *Review of Financial Studies*, 9:1211 – 1250.

Carr, P. (1998). Randomization and the American put. *Review of Financial Studies*, 11:597 – 626.

Dixit, A.K. and Pindyck, R.S. (1994). *Investment under Uncertainty.* Princeton University Press.

Dynkin, E.B. (1965). *Markov Processes*, Volumes I and II. Springer-Verlag.

El Karoui, N. and Karatzas, I. (1991). A new approach to the Skorohod problem and its application. *Stochastics and Stochastics Reports*, 34:57 – 82.

El Karoui, N. and Martellini, L. (2001). *Dynamic Asset Pricing Theory with Uncertain Time-Horizon.* Working paper. Marshall School of Business, USC.

Huddart, S. (1998). Patterns of stock option exercise in the United States. In: J. Carpenter and D. Yermack (eds.), *Executive Compensation and Shareholder Value*, pp. 115 – 142. Kluwer Academic Publishers, Norwell, MA.

Lambrecht, B. and Perraudin, W. (1997). *Real Options and Preemption.* Working paper. IFR, Birbeck College, London.

Leland, H. (1994). Corporate debt value, bond covenants, and optimal capital structure. *Journal of Finance*, 49:1213 – 1252.

Myeni, R. (1992). The pricing of American options, *The Annals of Probability*, 2:1 – 23.

Schwartz, E. and Moon (1994). *Evaluating research and development investments.* Working paper. John E. Anderson Graduate School of Management, UCLA.

Chapter 8

FOREIGN DIRECT INVESTMENT: THE INCENTIVE TO EXPROPRIATE AND THE COST OF EXPROPRIATION RISK

Ephraim Clark

Abstract This chapter examines the firm's cost of expropriation risk in a framework that links it to the government's incentive to expropriate. Using standard methods of stochastic calculus, the value of expropriation to the government is modeled as a function of the value of the Foreign Direct Investment, which fluctuates randomly over time. The cost of expropriation risk to the firm is modeled as the value of an insurance policy that pays off all net losses resulting from expropriation. It is shown that the firm's cost of expropriation risk depends on how the host government perceives the cost it will incur in the expropriation. Incomplete information brings out the give and take between government and firm found in the game theoretic models.

1. Introduction

Foreign direct investments are typically exposed to two types of risk that are absent from purely domestic investments, that is, currency risk and political risk. Currency risk refers to variations in project cash flows generated by variations in exchange rates. Political risk is a broad concept that refers to variations in project cash flows generated by the particularities of the host country's political, economic and social organization. It can originate from many diverse factors such as overall economic performance, political change, social upheavals or government decrees. Recent growth in foreign direct investment (FDI) and the sometimes radical evolution of political, economic, and social systems worldwide has accentuated the need for rigorous and theoretically sound procedures for integrating political risk in the financial decision making of multinational corporations.

Expropriation is the most dramatic form of political risk.[1] Although rare in recent years, the threat of expropriation remains a major source of risk in the process of capital budgeting for FDI. Kobrin (1984) and Kennedy (1992) argue that expropriation will become more likely as substantial portions of Least Developed Countries economies revert to foreign ownership. Minor (1994) concurs, although he sees significant expropriation activity as unlikely for the forseeable future. The United Nations' World Investment Report (1993) echoes these arguments and warns of a possible reversal of the privatization trend as the influence of short term imperatives recedes and governments seek to regain greater control over decision-making, especially if economic growth remains weak, foreign direct investment proves to be a disappointment in transferring technology and skills or if world markets are closed by protectionism.

In this chapter, I follow the Clark (2003, 1997) framework for estimating the firm's cost of expropriation risk and integrating the estimate in the capital budgeting process. The expropriation decision is modeled as an American style option and as such can be interpreted in the well known terms of contingent claims analysis. I show that besides the value of the investment itself, the expected growth of the investment, and its volatility, the firm's cost of expropriation risk depends on how the government perceives the costs it will incur if it decides to exercise its option to expropriate.

The outstanding literature on the expropriation phenomenon emphasizes the conflict between government and firm in models of one time yes-no decisions presented from the government's perspective where risk arises from information asymmetries. In Eaton and Gersovitz (1984), for example, expropriation risk is related to the particular uncertainty regarding the host country's endowment in management skills. In Andersson (1989), expropriation risk depends on the number of foreign firms in the country where the firm and host country benefit from complete information, and expropriation, which is always successful, results from the host country randomly selecting its victims from a large number of potential targets. Besides the limited treatment of expropriation risk for the firm, by considering only successful outcomes, Eaton and Gersovitz and Andersson also ignore host country risk associated with unsuccess-

[1] In this chapter expropriation is defined as forced divestment of equity ownership of a foreign direct investor, including nationalization and confiscation as in Kobrin (1984) and Minor (1994).

ful expropriations. Raff (1992) considers the possibility of unsuccessful expropriations but ignores the uncertainty associated with stochastic movements in the value of the assets themselves. In his model, the host country knows its own endowment in managerial skills and the sole uncertainty stems from its incomplete information about the firm's technology that is only resolved after the expropriation is carried out. Thus, there is a risk that the expropriation will be unsuccessful and overall welfare will be reduced. Expropriation risk for the firm depends on the probability for the host country that if it does expropriate it will be able to capture a share of the firm's rent.

In this chapter we show how government uncertainty about expropriation costs can be incorporated in the capital budgeting process. The model is based on the insight that when a firm makes a foreign direct investment, it effectively issues an American style call option that gives the government the right to expropriate its assets. The government will choose to exercise the option according to how it perceives the net gain to be realized through exercise. The net gain is equal to the value of the expropriated assets less the costs associated with expropriation. These costs depend on the practical international limits on unilateral sovereign decrees, the country's endowment in managerial skills, and the firm's ability to shield itself from the nefarious effects of government interference. They include direct and indirect compensation payments to the firm and a higher cost of foreign capital due to reduced investor confidence as well as losses of production and marketing know-how due to the elimination of the parent company.

Recognizing the implicit option that it effectively issues the host government when it invests, the firm evaluates the cost of this expropriation risk as the value of an insurance policy that pays off all net losses resulting from expropriation. Net losses are equal to the value of the expropriated assets less direct and indirect compensation by the host government, political risk insurance claims and any other value such as trademarks, patents, clients, know-how, etc. that can be salvaged from the investment. I show that the value of the insurance policy depends on how the host government perceives the cost it will incur in the expropriation. Incomplete information brings out the give and take between government and firm found in the game theoretic models. An important element in the system is the fact that the cost of expropriation to the government and the firm's compensation and salvage value are likely to be different.

This model I propose includes dividends and continuous exercise. It identifies the key variable as government's perceived cost of expropriation, rather than the real cost of expropriation. It also brings out the fact that the value of the government's option to expropriate can differ, in fact, is likely to differ, from the firm's cost of expropriation risk.

The rest of the chapter is organized as follows. Section 2 develops the model and the analytical framework. Section 3 shows how the model can be applied and brings out the role of perceived costs in the pricing problem. Section 4 contains the concluding remarks.

2. The model

2.1 The value of the option to expropriate

The right of a government to expropriate or nationalize a foreign firm's assets, derived from the generally accepted concept of national sovereignty, is essentially an option and, consequently, can be valued as such. Let $x(t)$ follow geometric Brownian motion and represent the value of the local dividend paying subsidiary in the absence of possible expropriation with an infinite time horizon[2] and a required rate of return, R:

$$dx(t) = \alpha x(t)\,dt + \sigma x(t)\,dz(t) \tag{8.1}$$

where

α : the firm's growth rate,
$dz(t)$: a Wiener process with zero mean and variance equal to dt,
σ^2 : the variance parameter of the percentage change of $x(t)$.
The instantaneous dividend rate or convenience yield is equal to $R - \alpha = \psi$.

Letting $Y = Y\big(x(t)\big)$ represent the value of the option to expropriate or nationalize, following the usual steps of setting up a riskless hedge consisting of one unit of the option and $-Y'(x)$ units of the investment and applying Ito's lemma gives the following differential equation:

$$\frac{1}{2}\sigma^2 x(t)^2 Y''\big(x(t)\big) + Y'(\big(x(t)\big)(r-\phi)x(t) - rY\big(x(t)\big) = 0. \tag{8.2}$$

The solution to (8.2) is

$$Y = A_1 x(t)^{\gamma_1} + A_2 x(t)\gamma_2 \tag{8.3}$$

[2]The typical direct investment involves setting up a subsidiary in the host country or purchasing all or part of an already existing company. Legislation in most countries is such that either there is no specified life span for a company or when the life span is specified, such as in France, it can be renewed indefinitely. Consequently, the typical direct investment can be viewed as a perpetual claim. Many direct investments, of course, do have a specified contractual life span. When this is the case, Y is a function of time as well as of the value of the investment. The consequences of this on the value of the option depend on the particular conditions for terminating the investment on the specified date. Mahajan (1990), for example, looks at the particular case where the government's option to exercise is limited to the project's termination date.

where $\gamma_1 > 1$ (under the assumption that $\phi > 0$) and $\gamma_2 < 0$ are the roots to the quadratic equation in γ:

$$\frac{\sigma^2}{2}\gamma^2 + \left(r - \phi - \frac{\sigma^2}{2}\right)\gamma - r = 0$$

$$\gamma_1, \gamma_2 = \frac{-(r - \phi - \sigma^2/2) \pm \sqrt{(r - \phi - \sigma^2/2)^2 + 2\sigma^2 r}}{\sigma^2}.$$

The constants A_1 and A_2 in (8.3) depend on the boundary conditions. The first boundary condition is straightforward. When the value of the firm is zero, the option to expropriate has no value:

$$Y(0) = 0. \tag{8.4}$$

This condition implies that $A_2 = 0$.

Let $\Omega(x(t))$ represent the net value that the government receives when it expropriates. This will be equal to the value of the firm less the indemnities and other costs associated with their action. Let C represent these indemnities and costs so that:

$$\Omega(x(t)) = x(t) - C.$$

There will be a level of x, designated by x^*, where it will be optimal for the government to act. At values of x lower than x^*, the value of the right to expropriate will be higher than the net value of the expropriation and, consequently, it will be in the government's interest to put off expropriation until the net value of the expropriation is at least as high as the value of the right to expropriate that must be surrendered. At the boundary, then, the value of the right to expropriate is just equal to the net value to be obtained through expropriation:

$$Y(x^*(t)) = x^*(t) - C. \tag{8.5}$$

The smooth pasting condition that makes it possible to find x^* jointly with the function $Y(x(t))$ is:

$$Y'(x(t)) = \Omega'(x(t)) = 1 \tag{8.6}$$

and the solution to (8.2) is:

$$Y = A_1 x(t)^{\gamma_1} \tag{8.7}$$

where

$$x^* = C\frac{\gamma_1}{\gamma_1 - 1}$$

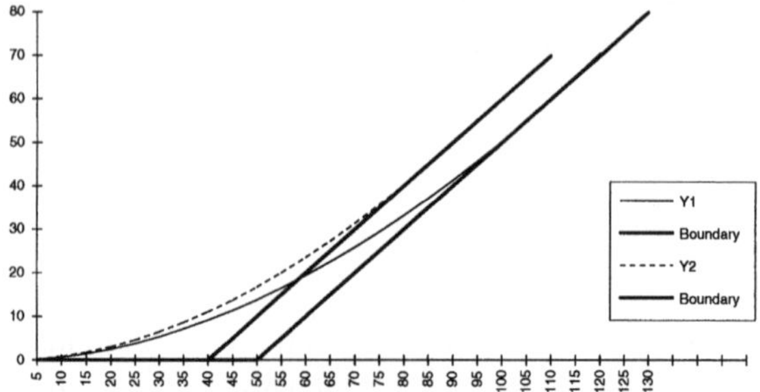

Figure 8.1. $r - \psi = 0.015$, $\sigma^2 = 0.04$, $r = 0.06$, $C = \$40$ and $C = \$50$

and

$$A_1 = \frac{C}{\gamma_1 - 1}\left[C\frac{\gamma_1}{\gamma_1 - 1}\right]^{-\gamma_1}$$

found by solving (8.5) and (8.6) simultaneously.

Figure 8.1 shows $Y(x)$ for $r - \psi = 0.015$, $\sigma^2 = 0.04$, $r = 0.06$, $C = 40$ and $C = 50$. The tangency point of $Y(x)$ with $x - C$ gives the critical value x^* where it is optimal for the authorities to expropriate. It also shows that larger values of C lower the value of the right to expropriate and raise the critical value x^*. Companies have long known and acted on this principle by taking actions that raise the costs of expropriation. However, in the model presented above, high expropriation costs in themselves are insufficient to deter expropriation. Since the initiative for expropriation comes from the government, deterrence can only be achieved if these costs are apparent to the government. An underestimation of the expropriation costs on the part of the government would lower the perceived x^* and raise the probability of government action. Thus, we rejoin Raff's (1992) conclusion that incomplete information about the cost of expropriation may induce a host country to expropriate even when other policy instruments are available.

2.2 The cost of expropriation risk

The cost of expropriation risk to the foreign firm can be measured as the value of an insurance policy that would cover any losses arising from expropriation. Losses are equal to $x - c$, where c represents any compensation paid in lieu of indemnities for the expropriation plus any other value such as trademarks, clients, patents, etc., that can be salvaged from the investment. Although C, the cost of expropriation to the government, and c, the firm's compensation and salvage value, can be equal, in practice, the two are likely to be different. Government losses in the form of a higher cost for foreign capital due to lower confidence and higher risk, for example, will not accrue to the firm nor will many of the losses associated with host country shortcomings in management, production, and marketing know-how.

Let V represent the value of an insurance policy covering the firm against its losses arising from the expropriation so that when losses occur, they are reimbursed by the insurance. Thus, V is a function of the exposure to losses arising from expropriation:

$V = V(x(t))$ = value of the insurance policy covering the investment against losses arising from expropriation.

Following the same steps as above and applying Ito's lemma gives the following differential equation

$$\frac{1}{2}\sigma^2 x(t)^2 V''(x(t)) + V'(x(t))\alpha x(t) - rV(x(t)) = 0 \tag{8.8}$$

with solution

$$V(x(t)) = B_1 x(t)^{\gamma_1} + B_2 x(t)^{\gamma_2} \tag{8.9}$$

where $\gamma_1 > 1$ (because $r > \alpha$) and $\gamma_2 < 0$ are the roots to the quadratic equation in γ that we saw above.

The only potential differences between (8.3) and (8.9) occur in the constants B_1 and B_2, which depend on the boundary conditions. The first boundary condition is the same. When the value of the investment is zero, the insurance policy has no value:

$$V(0) = 0. \tag{8.10}$$

This condition implies that $B_2 = 0$. The second boundary condition, however, is different. When the government expropriates at x^*, the parent receives $x^* - c$, the value of the loss less any compensation and salvage value. Thus:

$$B_1 = (x^* - c)x^{*-\gamma_1}$$

and

$$V(x(t)) = B_1 x(t)^{\gamma_1}. \tag{8.11}$$

From (8.7) and (8.11) we can see that the value of the option to expropriate and the value of the insurance policy covering losses arising from expropriation differ only in so far as C and c are concerned. When they are equal, $A_1 = B_1$ and valuing the insurance policy boils down to valuing the option to expropriate. When $C \neq c$, the values of the two assets are different. However, x^* depends on C as shown in (8.5) and (8.6). Consequently, determining the value of the insurance policy requires an evaluation of the value of the option to expropriate.

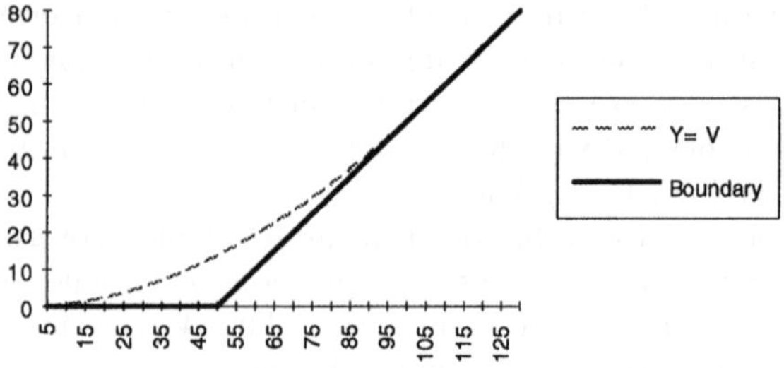

Figure 8.2. $c = C$. $r - \psi = 0.015$, $\sigma^2 = 0.04$, $r = 0.06$, $C = \$50$ and $C = \$40$

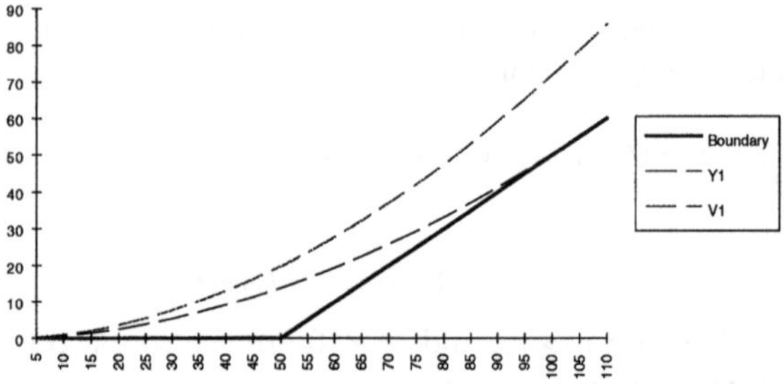

Figure 8.3. $c = 25 < C = 50$. $r - \psi = 0.015$, $\sigma^2 = 0.04$, $r = 0.06$, $C = \$50$ and $C = \$40$

3. Applying the model

3.1 Complete information

When information is complete, both host country and firm know the true values of C and c before and after the FDI is undertaken. Three situations are possible: $c = C$, $c > C$, and $c < C$. When $c = C$, the values of $Y(x(t))$ and $V(x(t))$ are equal; when $c > C$, $Y(x(t)) > V(x(t))$; when $c < C$, $Y(x(t)) < V(x(t))$. Figures 8.2, 8.3, and 8.4 show the values of $Y(x(t))$ and $V(x(t))$ for different values of x, for $c = C = 50$ as in figure 8.2, $c = 25 < C = 50$ as in figure 8.3, and $c = 75 > C = 50$ as in figure 8.4.

In this context expropriation and investment decisions are straightforward. Consider the following information:

Cost of investment $=$ \$45 million
Net present value $=$ \$50 million
$x_0 =$ \$95 million, the initial outlay plus the NPV.

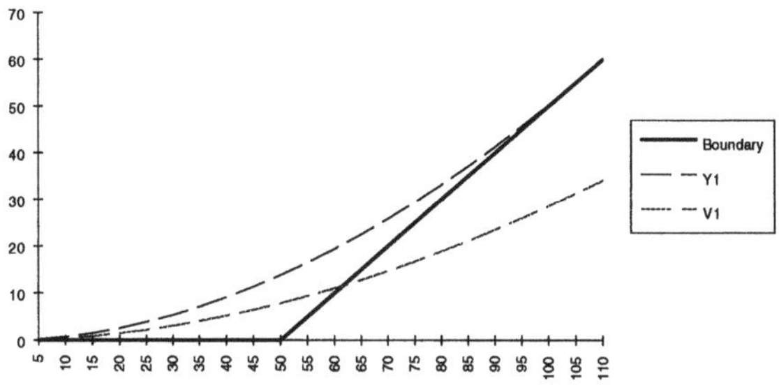

Figure 8.4. $c = 75 > C = 50$. $r - \psi = 0.015$, $\sigma^2 = 0.04$, $r = 0.06$, $C = \$50$ and $C = \$40$

The government always expropriates at the optimal moment, i.e., at $x = x^*$. Using the values of the parameters above, when $c = C = 50$, the value of the insurance policy is \$45.68 million and $x^* = \$108.03$ million. The firm's position can be considered as a portfolio of a long position in the investment and a short position in the insurance policy. Thus, following Clark (1997), if it undertakes the FDI, its net position will be equal to the NPV of the FDI less the value of the insurance policy, which it effectively issues free of charge when it undertakes the investment:

$$\begin{aligned}\text{Overall NPV} &= \text{Project NPV} - \text{Value of insurance policy}\\ &= \$50 - \$45.68 = \$4.32 \text{ million.}\end{aligned}$$

Since the NPV of the overall position is positive, the firm undertakes the investment. When $c = 25 < C = 50$, the value of the insurance policy is \$65.36 million and the firm's net position is: $\$50 - \$65.36 = -\$15.36$. Since the NPV of the overall position is negative, the FDI is not undertaken. When $c = 75 > C = 50$, the value of the insurance policy is \$26.00 million, the firm's net position is: $\$50 - \$26.00 = \$24.00$, and since the NPV of the overall position is positive, the firm undertakes the investment. Table 8.1 summarizes these outcomes.

Table 8.1. Outcomes with different levels of "c" with complete information

	$c = C = 50$	$c = 75 > C = 50$	$c = 25 < C = 50$
x^*	\$108.03	\$108.03	\$108.03
$Y(x(t))$	\$45.68	\$45.68	\$45.68
$V(x(t))$	\$45.68	\$26.00	\$65.36
Decision	Invest	Invest	Don't Invest
$r - \varphi = 0.015$, $\sigma^2 = 0.04$, $r = 0.06$			

3.2 Incomplete information

When information is incomplete, the situation is more complicated. Three cases come to mind: (1) when the firm has private information and the host country doesn't; (2) when the host country has private information and the firm doesn't; (3) when both have private information. In these scenarios, which are likely to obtain in practice, C becomes a perceived cost rather than an actual cost from the standpoint of one or both parties. As we will see, the firm must base its analysis of the cost of expropriation risk on how it thinks the government perceives its expropriation costs rather than on what those costs actually are.

Consider case 1 where the host government and the firm both know the amount of compensation that will be paid but only the firm knows how much will be lost due to the elimination of the firm. Going back to Figure 8.1, we can see that if the host government underestimates the cost, it will expropriate too soon. If it overestimates the cost, it will expropriate too late or not at all. In both instances it loses value but the firm's position depends on whether or not it accurately estimates what the host government perceives its costs to be.

Consider an investment with the same parameter values as above with an initial outlay of \$45 million, $x_0 = \$80$ million and NPV = \$35 million. Suppose that the government believes that the cost of expropriation will be a \$50 million compensation payment whereas the firm knows that the host government will be obliged to make an additional outlay of \$75 million to compensate for the absence of its management, production, and marketing know-how. Thus, the true cost is \$50+\$75 = \$125 million and $x^* = \$270.08$ million. If, however, the government acts on its mistaken belief that the cost is only the \$50 million compensation payment, it will exercise when $x^* = \$108.03$ million. Thus it will make a loss of \$16.97 million (\$108.03 − \$125 = −\$16.97 million) and the expropriation, when it happens, will be unsuccessful for the host government. The firm's position, however, depends on how it estimates the value of the insurance policy. From equation (8.11) we know the value of the insurance policy depends on when the host government actually exercises, which in this case is at $x^* = \$108.03$ million and $V = \$45.68$. Thus the overall NPV of the project is negative:

$$\begin{aligned}\text{Overall NPV} &= \text{Project NPV} - \text{Value of insurance policy}\\ &= \$50 - \$45.68 = \$4.32 \text{ million.}\end{aligned}$$

The firm should not undertake the project. However, the cost of the insurance policy is only \$31.47 million when $C = \$125$. If the firm mistakenly used this figure it would be seriously underestimating the expropriation risk, which would make the overall NPV positive and the project acceptable: $50 – $31.47 = $18.53 million.[3]

Thus, the cost to the firm of expropriation risk revolves around the perceived costs to the government if it undertakes expropriation. When the firm has private information about these costs, it has a strong incentive in making clear to the host government the actual levels of losses at stake. In fact, besides making the actual costs of expropriation clear to the government, it also has an interest in taking steps to raise these costs. Internationally integrated production, purchasing and marketing structures and control of technology and human resources are some of the more effective measures that have been undertaken. The government, on the other hand, has the incentive to take steps that lower the cost of expropriation. Covenants related to what has become known as "good citizen" policy such as technology transfers and local sourcing and management training are some of the most obvious examples of measures of this type.

In case 2 only the government has private information. For example, both firm and host government know how much will be lost to the host government due to the elimination of the firm but only the host government knows how much it will lose through compensation payments. In this case, expropriation is never unsuccessful because the government always expropriates at the optimal moment. Hence, the host country's position is different from that of case 1. The firm's position, however, is similar to that of case 1 because of the uncertainty surrounding the exercise price of the government's option to expropriate. In case 1, the uncertainty for the firm was related to whether or not the host country knows the true cost of expropriation while in case 2 the uncertainty is linked to what the expropriation costs really are. The consequences for the firm are the same. In deciding whether or not to invest, the firm must estimate C in order to evaluate the cost of expropriation risk. If the firm overestimates C, the value of the insurance policy will be underestimated and bad investments may be undertaken. If it underestimates C, the value of the insurance policy will be overestimated and good investments may be dropped.

[3] One way to account for uncertainty about the government's perception of its true expropriation costs is to set up a probability distribution for each possible level of C and then estimate the expected value of the insurance policy. By setting up a probability distribution, we can also get a Raff-like model of expropriation with asymmetric information. A simpler, alternative method involves taking the expected value of C and using it in the evaluation of the insurance policy. Because of Jensen's inequality and the convexity of the function, the value of the insurance policy calculated in this way will be lower than the former method.

In case 3 where both host government and firm possess private information concerning the cost of expropriation, the host government can make unsuccessful expropriations and the firm can make bad decisions, investing when it should not and not investing when it should.

In conclusion, then, we can say that the perceived cost of expropriation to the government determines the firm's actual cost of expropriation risk. An accurate estimate of this cost on the part of the firm requires an accurate estimate of what the government perceives its expropriation costs to be.

4. Conclusion

This chapter examines the firm's cost of expropriation risk in a framework that links it to the government's incentive to expropriate. Following Clark (2003, 1997), the value of expropriation to the government is modeled as a call option whose underlying is the value of the FDI, which fluctuates randomly over time. The cost of expropriation risk to the firm is modeled as the value of an insurance policy that pays off all net losses resulting from expropriation. It is shown that the firm's cost of expropriation risk depends on how the host government perceives the cost it will incur in the expropriation. This leads to two conclusions. First of all, the political risk analysis should focus on the government's perception of the costs it will incur if it decides to expropriate. Secondly, the firm should take measures that influence government perceptions so that these costs are not under-estimated.

References

Andersson, T. (1989). *Foreign Direct Investment in Competing Host Countries.* Doctoral Dissertation, Stockholm School of Economics.

Brewer, T.L. (1992). An issue area approach to the analysis of MNE government relations. *Journal of International Business Studies*, 2:295–309.

Clark, E. (1997). Valuing political risk. *Journal of International Money and Finance*, 16:477–490.

Clark, E. (2002). *International Finance*, 2nd edition. International Thomson Learning, London.

Clark, E. (2003). Pricing the cost of expropriation risk. *Review of International Economics*, 11:412–422.

Eaton, J. and Gersovitz, M. (1984). A theory of expropriation and deviations from perfect capital mobility. *Economic Journal*, 94:16–40.

Kennedy, C.R. (1992). *Relations Between Transnational Corporations and Governments of Host Countries: A Look to the Future.* Transnational Corporations.

Kobrin, S.J. (1984). Expropriations as an attempt to control foreign affiliates, 1960 – 1979. *International Studies Quarterly*, 28(3):329 – 348.

Mahajan, A. (1990). Pricing expropriation risk. *Financial Management*, 19:77 – 86.

Minor, M.S. (1994). The demise of expropriation as an instrument of LDC policy, 1980 – 1992. *Journal of International Business Studies*, 25(1):177 – 188.

Raff, H. (1992). A model of expropriation with asymmetric information. *Journal of International Economics*, 33:245 – 265.

Saunders, A. (1986). The determinants of country risk. *Studies in Banking and Finance*, 3:2 – 38.

Shapiro, A.C. (1978). Capital budgeting for the multinational corporation. *Financial Management*, 7:7 – 16.

Stonehill, A. and Nathanson, L. (1968). Capital budgeting and the multinational corporation. *California Management Review*, 4:39 – 54.

United Nations (1993). *World Investment Report*, p. 17. United Nations, New York.

Williams, M.L. (1975). The extent and significance of the nationalization of foreign owned assets in developing countries. *Oxford Economic Papers*, 27:260.

Chapter 9

EXACT MULTIVARIATE TESTS OF ASSET PRICING MODELS WITH STABLE ASYMMETRIC DISTRIBUTIONS

Marie-Claude Beaulieu
Jean-Marie Dufour
Lynda Khalaf

Abstract In this chapter, we propose exact inference procedures for asset pricing models that can be formulated in the framework of a multivariate linear regression (CAPM), allowing for stable error distributions. The normality assumption on the distribution of stock returns is usually rejected in empirical studies, due to excess kurtosis and asymmetry. To model such data, we propose a comprehensive statistical approach which allows for alternative — possibly asymmetric — heavy tailed distributions without the use of large-sample approximations. The methods suggested are based on Monte Carlo test techniques. Goodness-of-fit tests are formally incorporated to ensure that the error distributions considered are empirically sustainable, from which exact confidence sets for the unknown tail area and asymmetry parameters of the stable error distribution are derived. Tests for the efficiency of the market portfolio (zero intercepts) which explicitly allow for the presence of (unknown) nuisance parameter in the stable error distribution are derived. The methods proposed are applied to monthly returns on 12 portfolios of the New York Stock Exchange over the period 1926 – 1995 (5 year subperiods). We find that stable possibly skewed distributions provide statistically significant improvement in goodness-of-fit and lead to fewer rejections of the efficiency hypothesis.

1. Introduction

An important problem in empirical finance consists in testing the efficiency of a market portfolio by assessing the statistical significance of the intercepts of a multivariate linear regression (MLR) on asset returns (the capital asset pricing model (CAPM)); see MacKinlay (1987), Jobson and Korkie (1989), Gibbons et al. (1989), Shanken (1996), Campbell et al. (1997, Chapters 5 and 6), Stewart (1997), and Fama and French (2003). Traditional statistical theory supplies a reliable distributional theory mainly in the case where the disturbances in the model follow a Gaussian distribution; see, for example, Anderson (1984, Chapters 8 and 13) and Rao (1973, Chapter 8). However, in financial data, the Gaussian assumption is typically inappropriate, because asset returns often exhibit excess kurtosis and asymmetries; see, for example, Fama (1965), Baillie and Bollerslev (1989), Beaulieu (1998), and Dufour et al. (2003). Further, asymptotic approximations aimed at relaxing the Gaussian assumption tend to be unreliable in multivariate models such as those considered in CAPM applications, especially when the number of equations (or assets) is not small; see Campbell et al. (1997, Chapter 5), Gibbons et al. (1989), Shanken (1996, Section 3.4.2), and Dufour and Khalaf (2002b). Consequently, it is important from an inference viewpoint that we approach this problem from a finite sample perspective.[1]

In recent work (Dufour et al., 2003; Beaulieu et al., 2004), we considered this problem by developing exact efficiency tests of the market portfolio in the case where the CAPM disturbances follow t distributions or normal mixtures. In particular, we observed that: (i) monthly returns reject multivariate normality conclusively, and (ii) CAPM tests based on the assumption of elliptical errors yield less rejections than those based on the (erroneous) normality assumption. The latter result obtains if the (unknown) parameters underlying the elliptical error distribution are formally accounted for.[2] Indeed, the whole issue centers on the uncertainty associated with unknown (nuisance) parameters, one of the main difficulties which complicate the development of exact tests. This analysis was however restricted to symmetric error distributions.

In the present chapter, we consider distributional models that can accommodate more pronounced skewness and kurtosis. Specifically, we study the case where the disturbances in a CAPM regression can follow stable possibly asymmetric distributions. Our results reveal notable dif-

[1] For more general discussions of the importance of developing finite-sample statistical procedures, see Dufour (1997, 2003).

[2] Concerning normality tests, our procedures achieve size control exactly, so test rejections cannot be spurious by construction. Concerning tests on intercepts, we formally demonstrate location-scale invariance of the commonly used procedures for the context at hand. Since the normal distribution is completely defined by its mean and variance, nuisance parameter-free test procedures can easily be derived. Non-normal distributions raise further nuisance parameter problems; examples include the number of degrees of freedom, for a multivariate Student t distribution, and the probability-of-mixing and scale-ratio parameters for normal mixtures.

ferences with respect to the mainstream elliptical framework. Besides being consistent with optimization arguments underlying the CAPM (see Samuelson, 1967), the family of stable distributions is entailed by various central limit arguments in probability theory (as an alternative to the Gaussian distribution) and has often been suggested as a useful model for return and price distributions in finance; see, for example, Mandelbrot (1963), Ibragimov and Linnik (1975), Zolotarev (1986), Cambanis et al. (1991), Samorodnitsky and Taqqu (1994), Embrechts et al. (1997), Rachev et al. (1999a,b), Uchaikin and Zolotarev (1999), Adler et al. (2000), Mittnik et al. (2000), Rachev and Mittnik (2000), and Meerschaert and Scheffler (2001). One should note, however, that tests and confidence sets which have been proposed for inference on such models are almost always based on asymptotic approximations that can easily be unreliable. Further, standard regularity conditions and asymptotic distributional theory may easily not apply to such distributions (for example, because of heavy tails).

To obtain finite-sample inference for such models, we combine several techniques. *First*, we obtain finite-sample joint confidence sets for the unknown parameters of the stable distribution (i.e., the tail thickness α_s and the asymmetry β_s) through the "inversion" of goodness-of-fit tests based on multivariate kurtosis and skewness coefficients computed from model residuals. *Second*, in view of the complicated distribution of these statistics, we exploit invariance properties of the goodness-of-fit statistics to implement the corresponding tests as finite-sample Monte Carlo (MC) tests (as proposed in Dufour et al., 2003). *Thirdly*, using general results from Dufour and Khalaf (2002b) on hypothesis testing in multivariate linear regressions with non-Gaussian disturbances, we note that finite-sample standard LR-type efficiency tests can easily be obtained as soon as the parameters (α_s, β_s) of the stable error distribution are specified, again through the application of the MC test technique. *Fourth*, we exploit a two-stage confidence technique proposed in Dufour (1990), Dufour and Kiviet (1996, 1998), and Dufour et al. (1998b) to derive efficiency tests that formally take into account the uncertainty of the stable distribution parameters (α_s, β_s) by maximizing the MC p-values associated with different nuisance parameter values (α_s, β_s) over a confidence set for the latter built as described in the first step above (with an appropriately selected level).

The technique of MC tests — which plays a crucial role in our approach — is an exact simulation-based inference procedure originally proposed by Dwass (1957) and Barnard (1963). It is related to the parametric bootstrap in the sense that the distribution of the test statistic is simulated under the null hypothesis. When the latter does not involve unknown nuisance parameters, the MC test method controls the size of the procedure perfectly, while bootstrap methods are justified only by asymptotic arguments. The finite-sample theory that underlies MC tests allows one to implement test statistics with very complicated distributions (as long as they can be simulated) and does not require establishing a limit distribution as the sample size goes to infinity (or even the existence of such a distribution). It is easy to see that this feature can be quite convenient when dealing with stable distributions under which standard central limit theorems may not apply. The contrast is even more important when test statistics involve nuisance parameters. Here we use extensions of this MC test technique that allow for the presence of nuisance parameters. The level of the test can be controlled in finite samples as soon as the null distribution of the test statistic can be simulated once the values of the nuisance parameters are set.[3] This is clearly not the case in bootstrapping, where bootstrap samples are drawn after setting the unknown nuisance parameters at some "consistent" estimate. For further discussion of Monte Carlo test methods, see, for example, Dufour (2002), Dufour and Khalaf (2001, 2002a,b, 2003), Dufour and Kiviet (1996, 1998), Kiviet and Dufour (1997), Dufour et al. (1998a, 2004, 2003), and Beaulieu et al. (2004). Since bootstrap-type procedures are gaining popularity in finance (see, e.g., Li and Maddala, 1996), we emphasize the importance of using such procedures correctly.

We show that the proposed approach is both practical and useful from an empirical viewpoint by applying it to monthly returns on 12 portfolios of the New York Stock Exchange over the period 1926 – 1995 (5 year subperiods). Among other things we find that heavy-tailed skewed distributions provide statistically significant improvement in goodness-of-fit and lead to fewer rejections of the efficiency hypothesis. Our results show clearly that the introduction of an asymmetric distribution instead of an elliptical distribution yields noteworthy changes in the decision regarding the efficiency hypothesis of the market portfolio. In our opinion this is an important finding since CAPM rejections are often attributed to the presence of excess kurtosis in stock returns. Further, inference on the tail thickness parameter α_s appears to be more precise than inference on the asymmetry parameter β_s.

The chapter is organized as follows. Section 2 describe the model and test problem studied. In Section 3, we describe the existing test procedures and we show how extensions allowing for nonnormal distributions

[3]In nuisance parameter dependent problems, a test is *exact* at level α if the largest rejection probability over the nuisance parameter space consistent with the null hypothesis is not greater than α (see Lehmann, 1986, Sections 3.1 and 3.5).

are obtained. In Section 4 we report the empirical results. Section 5 concludes and discusses extensions to other asset pricing tests.

2. Framework

The framework we consider here is the same one as in Beaulieu et al. (2004):

$$r_{it} = a_i + b_i \tilde{r}_{\mathrm{M}t} + u_{it}, \quad t = 1, \ldots, T, i = 1, \ldots, n, \tag{9.1}$$

where $r_{it} = R_{it} - R_t^F$, $\tilde{r}_{\mathrm{M}t} = \tilde{R}_{\mathrm{M}t} - R_t^F$, R^F is the riskless rate of return, R_{it}, $i = 1, \ldots, n$, are returns on n securities for period t, $\tilde{R}_{\mathrm{M}t}$ is the return on the market portfolio, and u_{it} is a random disturbance.[4] In this context, the CAPM entails the following efficiency restrictions:

$$H_{\mathrm{CAPM}} : a_i = 0, \quad i = 1, \ldots, n, \tag{9.2}$$

i.e., the intercepts a_i are jointly equal to zero (Gibbons et al., 1989).

The above model can be cast in matrix form as a MLR model:

$$Y = XB + U \tag{9.3}$$

where $Y = [Y_1, \ldots, Y_n]$ is a $T \times n$ matrix of dependent variables, X is a $T \times k$ full-column rank matrix of regressors, and

$$U = [U_1, \ldots, U_n] = [V_1, \ldots, V_T]' \tag{9.4}$$

is a $T \times n$ matrix of random disturbances. Specifically, to get (9.1), we set:

$$Y = [r_1, \ldots, r_n], \quad X = [\iota_T, \tilde{r}_{\mathrm{M}}], \quad \iota_T = (1, \ldots, 1)', \tag{9.5}$$

$$r_i = (r_{1i}, \ldots, r_{Ti})', \quad \tilde{r}_{\mathrm{M}} = (\tilde{r}_{1\mathrm{M}}, \ldots, \tilde{r}_{T\mathrm{M}})'. \tag{9.6}$$

Further, in the matrix setup, the mean-variance efficiency restriction H_{CAPM} belongs to the class of so-called *uniform linear* (UL) restrictions, i.e., it has the form

$$H_0 : HB = D \tag{9.7}$$

where H is an $h \times k$ matrix of rank h. H_{CAPM} corresponds to the case where $h = 1$, $H = (1, 0)$ and $D = 0$.

In general, asset pricing models impose further restrictions on the error distributions. In particular, the standard CAPM obtains assuming that

$$V_1, \ldots, V_T \overset{\text{i.i.d.}}{\sim} N[0, \Sigma] \tag{9.8}$$

[4] For convenience, we focus here on the single beta case. For some discussion of the multi-beta CAPM, see Beaulieu et al. (2004).

or elliptically symmetric (Ingersoll, 1987); for recent references, see Hodgson et al. (2002), Vorkink (2003), Hodgson and Vorkink (2003), and the references cited therein. We consider the more general case

$$V_t = JW_t, \quad t = 1, \ldots, T, \tag{9.9}$$

where J is an unknown nonsingular matrix, $W_t = (W_{1t}, \ldots, W_{nt})'$ is a $n \times 1$ random vector, and the distribution of $w = \text{vec}(W_1, \ldots, W_T)$ conditional on X is either: (i) completely specified (hence, free of nuisance parameters), or (ii) partially specified up to an unknown nuisance-parameter. We call w the vector of *normalized disturbances* and its distribution the *normalized disturbance distribution.* When W_t has an identity covariance matrix, i.e.,

$$\mathsf{E}[W_t W_t'] = I_n, \tag{9.10}$$

the matrix $\Sigma = JJ'$ is the covariance matrix of V_t, so that $\det(\Sigma) \neq 0$. Note that the assumption (9.10) will not be needed in the sequel. No further regularity conditions are required for most of the statistical procedures proposed below, not even the existence of second moments.

In Beaulieu et al. (2004), we focused on multivariate t distributions and normal mixtures, which we denote $\mathcal{F}_1(W)$ and $\mathcal{F}_2(W)$ respectively, and define as follows:

$$W \sim \mathcal{F}_1(W; \kappa) \iff W_t = Z_{1t}/(Z_{2t}/\kappa)^{1/2}, \tag{9.11}$$

where Z_{1t} is multivariate normal $(0, I_n)$ and Z_{2t} is a $\chi^2(\kappa)$ variate independent from Z_{1t};

$$W \sim \mathcal{F}_2(W; \pi, \omega) \iff W_t = \pi Z_{1t} + (1 - \pi) Z_{3t}, \tag{9.12}$$

where Z_{3t} is multivariate normal $(0, \omega I_n)$ and is independent from Z_{1t}, and $0 < \pi < 1$.

In the present chapter, we extend our empirical investigation to asymmetric stable distributions

$$W \sim \mathcal{F}_s(W; \alpha_s, \beta_s) \iff W_{ti} \overset{\text{i.i.d.}}{\sim} S(\alpha_s, \beta_s), \quad i = 1, \ldots, n, \tag{9.13}$$

where $S(\alpha_s, \beta_s)$ represents the stable distribution with the tail thickness α_s, skewness parameter β_s, location parameter zero and scale parameter one. In view of the presence of a regression model (9.1) and the J matrix in (9.9), the location and scale parameters of W_t can be set to zero and one without loss of generality (and for identification purposes). As it is well known, a simple closed-form expression is not available for stable distributions (except in special cases) but there is one for the characteristic function $\phi(t)$: if $S \sim S(\alpha_s, \beta_s)$,

$$\begin{aligned}\ln \phi(t) &= \ln \mathsf{E}[\exp(itS)] \\ &= \begin{cases} -|t|^{\alpha_s}[1 - i\beta_s \operatorname{sgn}(t) \tan(\pi\alpha_s/2)], & \text{for } \alpha_s \neq 1, \\ -|t|[1 + i\beta_s(2/\pi) \operatorname{sgn}(t) \ln |t|], & \text{for } \alpha_s = 1, \end{cases}\end{aligned}$$

where $0 < \alpha_s \leq 2$ and $-1 \leq \beta_s \leq 1$, and sgn(t) is the sign function, i.e.,

$$\operatorname{sgn}(t) = \begin{cases} 1, & \text{if } t > 0, \\ 0, & \text{if } t = 0, \\ -1, & \text{if } t < 0; \end{cases} \tag{9.14}$$

see Rachev and Mittnik (2000, Chapter 2), Samorodnitsky and Taqqu (1994, Chapter 1). Note also that random variables with stable distributions can easily be simulated; see Chambers et al. (1976) and Weron (1996).

For further reference, we use the following notation:

$$W \sim \mathcal{F}_i(W;\nu), i = 1, 2, \tag{9.15}$$

where ν is the vector of nuisance parameters in the distribution of W, for example

$$\begin{aligned}\nu &= \kappa, & &\text{if } W_t \text{ satisfies (9.11)}, \\ &= (\pi, \omega), & &\text{if } W_t \text{ satisfies (9.12)}, \\ &= (\alpha_s, \beta_s), & &\text{if } W_t \text{ satisfies (9.13)}.\end{aligned}$$

In the sequel, we shall focus on the third case where $\nu = (\alpha_s, \beta_s)$ may be unknown.[5]

3. Statistical method

As in Gibbons et al. (1989), the statistic we use to test H_{CAPM} in (9.2) is the Gaussian quasi maximum likelihood (QMLE) based criterion:

$$\text{LR} = T \ln(\Lambda), \quad \Lambda = |\widehat{\Sigma}_{\text{CAPM}}|/|\widehat{\Sigma}|, \tag{9.16}$$

where $\widehat{\Sigma} = \widehat{U}'\widehat{U}/T$, $\widehat{U} = Y - X\widehat{B}$, $\widehat{B} = (X'X)^{-1}X'Y$ and $\widehat{\Sigma}_{\text{CAPM}}$ is the Gaussian QMLE under H_{CAPM}. In Beaulieu et al. (2004), we derive the

[5] For a theoretical discussion of the CAPM with stable Paretian laws, see Samuelson (1967). For discussions of the class of return distributions compatible with the CAPM, see Ross (1978); Chamberlain (1983), Ingersoll (1987, Chapter 4), Nielsen (1990), Allingham (1991), Berk (1997) and Dachraoui and Dionne (2003).

exact null distribution of the latter statistic under (9.1) and (9.9). This result is reproduced here for convenience.

THEOREM 9.1 *Under* (9.1), (9.2) *and* (9.9), *the* LR *statistic defined by* (9.16) *is distributed like*

$$T \ln(|W'MW|/|W'M_0W|), \tag{9.17}$$

where

$$M = I - X(X'X)^{-1}X', \tag{9.18}$$

$$M_0 = M + X(X'X)^{-1}H'[H(X'X)^{-1}H']^{-1}H(X'X)^{-1}X', \tag{9.19}$$

$$X = [\iota_T, \tilde{r}_{\mathrm{M}}], \quad \tilde{r}_{\mathrm{M}} = (\tilde{r}_{1\mathrm{M}}, \ldots, \tilde{r}_{T\mathrm{M}})', \tag{9.20}$$

H is the row vector $(1, 0)$, *and* $W = [W_1, \ldots, W_T]'$ *is defined by* (9.9).

We exploit two results regarding this distribution, the first one being a special case of the latter. First, Theorem 9.1 leads to Gibbons et al.'s (1989) results. Specifically, when errors are Gaussian,

$$\frac{T-s-n}{n}(\Lambda - 1) \sim F(n, T-s-n),$$

which yields Hotelling's T^2 test proposed by MacKinlay (1987) and Gibbons et al. (1989). Second, under the general assumption (9.9), the null distribution of (9.16) does not depend on B and Σ and may thus easily be simulated if draws from the distribution of $W_1, \ldots, W_T$ are available. This entails that a Monte Carlo exact test procedure (Dufour, 2002) may be easily applied based on LR. The general simulation-based algorithm which allows to obtain a MC size-correct exact p-value for all hypotheses conforming with (9.9) and (9.15) is presented in Beaulieu et al. (2004) and may be summarized as follows.

Given ν in (9.15), generate N *i.i.d.* draws from the distribution of $W_1, \ldots, W_T$; on applying (9.17), these yield N simulated values of the test statistic. The exact Monte Carlo p-value is then calculated from the rank of the observed LR [denoted by LR_0] relative to the simulated ones:

$$\hat{p}_N(\mathrm{LR}_0 \mid \nu) = \frac{N\widehat{G}_N(S_0) + 1}{N + 1} \tag{9.21}$$

where $N\widehat{G}_N(\mathrm{LR}_0)$ is the number of simulated criteria not smaller than LR_0.

In Beaulieu et al. (2004) we also consider testing H_{CAPM} (9.2) in the context of

$$r_{it} = a_i + \sum_{j=1}^{s} b_{ji}\tilde{r}_{jt} + u_{it}, \quad t = 1, \ldots, T, \ i = 1, \ldots, n, \tag{9.22}$$

where $\tilde{r}_{jt} = \tilde{R}_{jt} - R_t^F$ and $\tilde{R}_{jt}$, $j = 1, \ldots, s$, are returns on s benchmark portfolios. In this case, the null distribution of the statistic defined by (9.16) obtains as in Theorem 9.1 where

$$X = [\iota_T, \tilde{r}_1, \ldots, \tilde{r}_s], \quad \tilde{r}_j = (\tilde{r}_{1j}, \ldots, \tilde{r}_{Tj})' \tag{9.23}$$

and H is the $(s+1)$-dimensional row vector $(1, 0, \ldots, 0)$.

Let us now extend the above results to the unknown distributional parameter case for the error families of interest, namely (9.15). The α-level procedure adopted in Beaulieu et al. (2004) (based on Dufour 1990 and Dufour and Kiviet 1996) involves two stages: (1) build an exact confidence set (denoted $\mathcal{C}(Y)$) for ν, with level $1-\alpha_1$; (2) maximize the p-value function $\hat{p}_N(LR_0|\nu)$ in (9.21) over-all values of ν in the latter confidence set; then compare the latter maximal p-value with α_2 where $\alpha = \alpha_1 + \alpha_2$.[6] Formally, the test we denote *maximized MC* (MMC) *test*, is significant if

$$Q_U(\nu) \leq \alpha_2 \tag{9.24}$$

where

$$Q_U(\nu) = \sup_{\nu \in \mathcal{C}(Y)} \hat{p}_N(LR_0 \mid \nu). \tag{9.25}$$

To obtain $\mathcal{C}(Y)$, we proceed by "inverting" a goodness-of-fit (GF) test for the null hypothesis (9.15) where $\nu = \nu_0$ for known ν_0, as proposed in Dufour et al. (2003). The GF test statistic is based on the following excess skewness and kurtosis criteria:

$$\text{ESK}(\nu_0) = |\,\text{SK} - \overline{\text{SK}}(\nu_0)|, \tag{9.26}$$

$$\text{EKU}(\nu_0) = |\,\text{KU} - \overline{\text{KU}}(\nu_0)|, \tag{9.27}$$

where SK and KU are the well known multivariate measures (see Mardia, 1970):

$$\text{SK} = \frac{1}{T^2} \sum_{t=1}^{T} \sum_{i=1}^{T} \hat{d}_{ii}^3, \tag{9.28}$$

$$\text{KU} = \frac{1}{T} \sum_{t=1}^{T} \hat{d}_{tt}^2, \tag{9.29}$$

$\hat{d}_{it}$ are the elements of the matrix $\widehat{D} = \widehat{U}(\widehat{U}'\widehat{U})^{-1}\widehat{U}'$ and $\overline{\text{SK}}(\nu_0)$ and $\overline{\text{KU}}(\nu_0)$ are simulation-based estimates of the expected SK and KU given

[6] In the empirical section, we use $\alpha_1 = \alpha_2 = \alpha/2$.

by (9.15). Given ν_0, these may be obtained by drawing N_0 samples of T observations from (9.15), and then computing the corresponding average measures of skewness and kurtosis.[7] Specifically, we use the combined criterion

$$\text{CSK} = 1 - \min\{\hat{p}(\text{ESK}(\nu_0) \mid \nu_0), \hat{p}(\text{EKU}(\nu_0) \mid \nu_0))\}, \tag{9.30}$$

where $\hat{p}_N(\text{ESK}(\nu_0) \mid \nu_0)$ and $\hat{p}_N(\text{EKU}(\nu_0) \mid \nu_0)$ are MC p-values based on $\text{ESK}(\nu_0)$ and $\text{EKU}(\nu_0)$.[8] The intuition underlying this combined criterion is to reject the null hypothesis if at least one of the individual tests is significant; for convenience, we subtract the minimum p-value from one to obtain a right-sided test. The MC test technique is once again applied to obtain a test based on the combined statistic; details of the algorithm can be found in Dufour et al. (2003) and Beaulieu et al. (2004). For further reference on such combined tests, see Dufour and Khalaf (2002a) and Dufour et al. (2004).

4. Empirical analysis

Our empirical analysis focuses on testing (9.2) in the context of (9.1) with different distributional assumptions on stock market returns. We use nominal monthly returns over the period going from January 1926 to December 1995, obtained from the University of Chicago's Center for Research in Security Prices (CRSP). As in Breeden et al. (1989), our data include 12 portfolios of New York Stock Exchange (NYSE) firms grouped by standard two-digit industrial classification (SIC). Table 9.1 provides a list of the different sectors used as well as the SIC codes included in the analysis.[9] For each month the industry portfolios comprise those firms for which the return, price per common share and number of shares outstanding are recorded by CRSP. Furthermore, portfolios are value-weighted in each month. In order to assess the testable implications of the asset pricing models, we proxy the market return with the value-weighted NYSE returns, also available from CRSP. The risk-free rate is proxied by the one-month Treasury Bill rate, also from CRSP.

Our results are summarized in Tables 9.2 – 9.4. All MC tests were applied with $N = 999$ replications. As usual in this literature, we es-

[7] For the Gaussian case, one may use $\overline{\text{SK}} = 0$ and $\overline{\text{KU}} = n(n+2)$; see Mardia (1970).

[8] In Beaulieu et al. (2004), we demonstrate that these criteria are pivotal, i.e., under (9.15), their null distribution does not depend on B and Σ and thus may easily be simulated if draws from the distribution of $W_1, \ldots, W_T$ are available. Hence the MC p-values $\hat{p}_N(\text{ESK}(\nu_0) \mid \nu_0)$ and $\hat{p}_N(\text{EKU}(\nu_0) \mid \nu_0)$ can be obtained following the same simulation technique underlying $\hat{p}_N(\text{LR}_0 \mid \nu)$; see (9.21).

[9] As in Breeden et al. (1989), firms with SIC code 39 (Miscellaneous manufacturing industries) are excluded from the dataset for portfolio formation.

Table 9.1. Portfolio definitions

Portfolio number	Industry Name	Two-digit SIC codes
1	Petroleum	13, 29
2	Finance and real estate	60 – 69
3	Consumer durables	25, 30, 36, 37, 50, 55, 57
4	Basic industries	10, 12, 14, 24, 26, 28, 33
5	Food and tobacco	1, 20, 21, 54
6	Construction	15 – 17, 32, 52
7	Capital goods	34, 35, 38
8	Transportation	40 – 42, 44, 45, 47
9	Utilities	46, 48, 49
10	Textile and trade	22, 23, 31, 51, 53, 56, 59
11	Services	72, 73, 75, 80, 82, 89
12	Leisure	27, 58, 70, 78, 79

Note. This table presents portfolios according to their number and sector as well as the SIC codes included in each portfolio using the same classification as Breeden et al. (1989).

timate and test the model over intervals of 5 years.[10] In columns (1), (2), (6), (8) and (9) of Table 9.2, we present the LR and its asymptotic $\chi^2(n)$ p-value (p_∞), and stable errors based on maximal MC p-values (Q_U). For comparison purposes, we also report [in columns (3) – (4)] the Gaussian based MC p-value $p_{\mathcal{N}}$ and the Student t MMC p-value (Q_U) from Beaulieu et al. (2004). The confidence sets $\mathcal{C}(Y)$ for the nuisance parameters appear in columns (5), (7) and (10). To simplify the presentation, the confidence region is summarized as follows: we present the confidence sets for α_s given $\beta_s = 0$, and the union of the confidence sets for α_s given $\beta_s \neq 0$. These results allow one to compare rejection decisions across different distributional assumptions for the returns of the 12 portfolios.

Our empirical evidence shows the following. In general, asymptotic p-values are quite often spuriously significant (e.g., 1941 – 55). Furthermore, non-Gaussian based maximal p-values exceed the Gaussian-based p-value. Note however that the results of exact goodness-of-fit tests (available from Dufour et al., 2003) indicate that normality is definitively rejected except in 1961 – 65 and 1991 – 95.

As emphasized in Beaulieu et al. (2004), it is "easier" to reject the testable implications under normality, and any symmetric error considered. Indeed, at the 5% significance level, we find ten rejections of the

[10]Note that we also ran the analysis using ten year subperiods and that our results were not significantly affected.

Table 9.2. CAPM tests

	(1)	(2)	(3)	(4)	(5)	(6)	(7)	(8)	(9)	(10)
				Student t		Stable symmetric $\beta_s = 0$		Stable asymmetric		
								$\beta_s > 0$	$\beta_s < 0$	$\beta_s \neq 0$
Sample	QLR	p_∞	$p_\mathcal{N}$	Q_U	$C(Y)$	Q_U	$C(Y)$	Q_U	Q_U	$C(Y)$
1927–30	16.10	.187	.364	.357	3–12	.367	1.38–1.96	.927	.941	1.44–1.94
1931–35	16.26	.180	.313	.322	3–8	.298	1.34–1.92	.926	.925	1.42–1.92
1936–40	16.02	.190	.319	.333	4–26	.316	1.56–1.98	.737	.764	1.56–1.98
1941–45	25.87	.011	.045	.049	≥ 5	.031	1.58–1.98	.324	.285	1.56–1.98
1946–50	37.20	.000	.003	.004	4–26	.002	1.56–1.98	.108	.082	1.56–1.98
1951–55	36.51	.000	.004	.005	5–31	.001	1.56–1.98	.084	.048	1.56–1.98
1956–60	43.84	.000	.002	.002	≥ 5	.001	1.56–1.98	.032	.014	1.58–1.98
1961–65	39.10	.000	.002	.002	≥ 7	.001	1.66–2.00	.044	.020	1.20–1.99
1966–70	36.79	.000	.003	.003	≥ 5	.001	1.56–1.98	.116	.044	1.58–1.99
1971–75	21.09	.049	.120	.129	4–24	.111	1.56–1.98	.566	.596	1.56–1.98
1976–80	28.37	.005	.023	.026	4–17	.017	1.50–1.98	.425	.329	1.50–1.98
1981–85	27.19	.007	.033	.035	5–34	.023	1.56–1.98	.324	.309	1.56–1.98
1986–90	35.75	.001	.003	.005	≥ 5	.004	1.62–2.00	.086	.058	1.63–1.99
1991–95	16.75	.159	.299	.305	≥ 15	.287	1.68–2.00	.473	.477	1.70–1.99

Note. Column (1) presents the quasi-LR statistic defined in (9.16) to test H_{CAPM} (see (9.2)); columns (2), (3), (4), (6), (8) and (9) are the associated p-values using, respectively, the asymptotic $\chi^2(n)$ distribution, the pivotal statistics based MC test method imposing multivariate normal regression errors, an MMC confidence set based method imposing, in turn, multivariate $t(\kappa)$ errors, symmetric stable and asymmetric stable errors, which yields the largest MC p-value for all nuisance parameters within the specified confidence sets. The latter are reported in columns (5), (7) and (10); for convenience, for the asymmetric stable case, we present the union of the confidence sets for α_s given $\beta_s \neq 0$. October 1987 and January returns are excluded from the dataset.

null hypothesis for the asymptotic $\chi^2(11)$ test, nine for the MC p-values under normality, eight under a symmetric stable error distribution, and just two rejections (1956–60, 1961–65) with left-skewed (negative β_s) asymmetric stable errors; no rejections are noted with right-skewed (positive β_s) asymmetric stable errors. Note that our MC tests under non-normal errors are joint tests for nuisance parameters consistent with the data and the efficiency hypothesis. Since we used $\alpha_1 = 0.025$ for the construction of the confidence set, to establish a fair comparison with the MC p-values under the normality assumption or the asymptotic p-values, we must refer the p-values for the efficiency tests under the Student and

Table 9.3. Supremum p-values for various positive skewness measures

β_s	0	.3	.4	.5	.6	.7	.9	.99
1927−30	.367	.540	.665	.777	.759	.798	.888	.927
1931−35	.298	.549	.640	.744	.876	.919	.907	.926
1936−40	.316	.395	.456	.521	.538	.639	.688	.737
1941−45	.031	.052	.070	.096	.129	.170	.276	.324
1946−50	.002	.004	.006	.010	.017	.034	.080	.108
1951−55	.001	.003	.004	.007	.018	.030	.058	.084
1956−60	.001	.002	.002	.002	.003	.006	.020	.032
1961−65	.002	.002	.002	.002	.003	.008	.017	.044
1966−70	.001	.002	.009	.010	.021	.034	.080	.116
1971−75	.011	.154	.199	.246	.299	.362	.490	.566
1976−80	.017	.033	.063	.106	.166	.197	.418	.425
1981−85	.023	.043	.052	.079	.116	.164	.277	.324
1986−90	.004	.006	.010	.013	.019	.022	.063	.086
1991−95	.287	.296	.307	.324	.358	.388	.443	.473

Note. Numbers shown are p-values associated with our efficiency test using an MMC confidence set based method imposing asymmetric stable errors, which yields, given the specific $\beta_s > 0$, the largest MC p-value for all α_s within the specified confidence sets. The latter are reported in Table 9.2. October 1987 and January returns are excluded from the dataset.

the mixtures of normals distributions to 2.5%.[11]

An important issue here concerns the effect of asymmetries. Consider for instance the subperiods 1941−45, 1976−80 and 1981−85. With Student t errors, the p-values for these subperiods are not significant since they exceed 2.5%, yet they remain below 5%. Although we emphasize the importance of accounting for the joint characteristic of our null hypothesis, this result remains empirically notable. The results of the symmetric stable errors are not substantially different from those of the elliptical distributions. This result is interesting since it is often postulated that extreme kurtosis may affect the CAPM test. However, when asymmetries are introduced, the p-values are definitively larger and not significant.

The results for the stable distribution differ in one important aspect from the case of elliptical errors. Interestingly, we have observed that the MC p-values increase almost monotonically with β_s and decrease almost

[11]In this regard, we emphasize that the 2.5% level allotted to the distributional GF pre-test should not be perceived as an efficiency loss. From an empirical perspective, considering a distribution which is not supported by the data is clearly uninteresting; consequently, disregarding the joint characteristic of the null hypothesis (beside the fact that it is a statistical error) causes flawed and misleading decisions.

Table 9.4. Supremum p-values for various negative skewness measures

β_s	0	-1	$-.3$	$-.5$	$-.7$	$-.9$	$-.99$
1927 – 30	.367	.363	.539	.758	.830	.929	.941
1931 – 35	.298	.330	.517	.761	.906	.918	.925
1936 – 40	.316	.320	.408	.563	.651	.764	.740
1941 – 45	.031	.340	.039	.077	.152	.233	.285
1946 – 50	.002	.002	.002	.006	.026	.050	.082
1951 – 55	.001	.001	.002	.009	.028	.048	.038
1956 – 60	.001	.002	.001	.002	.002	.014	.010
1961 – 65	.001	.002	.002	.002	.004	.012	.020
1966 – 70	.001	.002	.002	.008	.014	.032	.044
1971 – 75	.011	.110	.146	.257	.382	.545	.596
1976 – 80	.017	.017	.024	.073	.149	.281	.329
1981 – 85	.023	.025	.033	.079	.128	.309	.285
1986 – 90	.004	.004	.005	.014	.020	.043	.058
1991 – 95	.287	.283	.297	.346	.355	.405	.477

Note. Numbers shown are p-values associated with our efficiency test using an MMC confidence set based method imposing asymmetric stable errors, which yields, given the specific $\beta_s < 0$, the largest MC p-value for all α_s within the specified confidence sets. The latter are reported in Table 9.2. October 1987 and January returns are excluded from the dataset.

monotonically with α_s (for $\beta_s > 0$ and $\alpha_s < 2$); recall that $\beta_s = 0$ and $\alpha_s = 2$ lead to the Gaussian distribution. In other words, the MC test is *less likely to reject* the no-abnormal returns null hypothesis *the more pronounced skewness and kurtosis* are modelled into the underlying regression errors. Furthermore, quite regularly, throughout our data set, the maximal p-value corresponds to the error distribution whose parameters are the smallest α_s and the largest β_s not rejected by our GF test. This monotonicity with respect to nuisance parameters (which we did not observe under elliptical errors) is notable. Of course, it also emphasizes the importance of our two-step test procedures which allows to rule out the values of α_s and β_s not supported by the data.

A simulation study conducted on the power of these GF tests (not reported here, but available from the authors upon request) reveals that while α_s is well estimated, the precision of the estimation of β_s raises further challenges. To the best of our knowledge however, the inference procedures we apply in this chapter are the only exact ones available to date. Here we show that the difficulty in estimating the skewness parameter has crucial implications for asset pricing tests. This result provides motivation to pursue research on exact approaches to the estimation of stable laws.

5. Conclusion

In this chapter, we have proposed likelihood based exact asset-pricing tests allowing for high-dimensional non-Gaussian and nonregular distributional frameworks. We specifically illustrate how to deal in finite samples with elliptical and stable errors with possibly unknown parameters. The tests suggested were applied to an efficiency problem in a standard asset pricing model framework with CRSP data.

Our empirical analysis reveals that abnormal returns are less prevalent when skewness is empirically allowed for; in addition, the effects of extreme kurtosis in the errors on test p-values are less marked than the effects of skewness. We view these results as a motivation for assessing the skewness corrected versions of the CAPM (introduced by Kraus and Litzenberger, 1976, among others). The regression model with stable errors provides an initial framework to assess asset pricing anomalies by modelling skewness via *unobservables.* Other skewness-justified approaches include: (i) extra pricing factors (see Fama and French, 1993, 1995; Harvey and Siddique, 2000) added to the regression, or (ii) the two-factor regression model of Barone-Adesi (1985) and Barone-Adesi et al. (2004a,b). To the best of our knowledge, the three-moments CAPM has been tested with procedures which are only asymptotically valid, even under normality. Our framework easily allows one to deal with multi-factor models; however, Barone-Adesi's (1985) model and its recent modification analyzed by Barone-Adesi et al. (2004a), Barone-Adesi et al. (2004b) impose nonlinear constraints. The latter empirical tests have not been reconsidered to date with reliable finite sample techniques. The development of exact versions of these tests and of alternative versions which correct for skewness is an appealing idea for future research.

References

Adler, R., Feldman, R., and Taqqu, M.S., eds. (2000). *A Practical Guide to Heavy Tails: Statistical Techniques for Analyzing Heavy Tailed Distributions.* Birkaüser, Boston.

Allingham, M. (1991). Existence theorems in the capital asset pricing model. *Econometrica*, 59:1169 – 1174.

Anderson, T.W. (1984). *An Introduction to Multivariate Statistical Analysis*, 2nd edition. John Wiley & Sons, New York.

Baillie, R. and Bollerslev, T. (1989). The message in daily exchange rates: A conditional variance tale. *Journal of Business and Economic Statistics*, 7:297 – 305.

Barnard, G.A. (1963). Comment on "The spectral analysis of point processes" by M.S. Bartlett. *Journal of the Royal Statistical Society,*

Series B, 25:294.

Barone-Adesi, G. (1985). Arbitrage equilibrium with skewed asset returns, *Journal of Financial and Quantitative Analysis*, 20(3):299 – 313.

Barone-Adesi, G., Gagliardini, P., and Urga, G. (2004a). A test of the homogeneity hypothesis on asset pricing models. In: E. Jurczenkoand B. Maillett (eds.), *Multi-Moment CAPM and Related Topics.* Springer-Verlag, Berlin.

Barone-Adesi, G., Gagliardini, P., and Urga, G. (2004b). Testing asset pricing models with coskewness. Forthcoming in *Journal of Business and Economic Statistics.*

Beaulieu, M.-C. (1998). Time to maturity in the basis of stock market indices: Evidence from the S&P 500 and the MMI. *Journal of Empirical Finance*, 5:177 – 195.

Beaulieu, M.-C., Dufour, J.-M., and Khalaf, L. (2004). *Multivariate Tests of Mean-Variance Efficiency with Possibly Non-Gaussian Errors: An Exact Simulation-Based Approach.* Working paper, Département d'économique, Université Laval, and CIREQ, Université de Montréal.

Berk, J.B. (1997). Necessary conditions for the CAPM. *Journal of Economic Theory*, 73:245 – 257.

Breeden, D.T., Gibbons, M., and Litzenberger, R.H. (1989). Empirical tests of the consumption based CAPM. *Journal of Finance*, 44;231 – 262.

Cambanis, S., Samorodnitsky, G., and Taqqu, M.S., eds. (1991). *Stable Processes and Related Topics: A Selection of Papers from MSI Workshop.* Birkhaüser, Boston.

Campbell, J.Y., Lo, A.W., and MacKinlay, A.C. (1997). *The Econometrics of Financial Markets.* Princeton University Press, Princeton.

Chamberlain, G. (1983). A characterization of the distributions that imply mean-variance utility functions. *Journal of Economic Theory*, 29:185 – 201.

Chambers, J.M., Mallows, C.L., and Stuck, B.W. (1976). A method for simulating stable random variables. *Journal of the American Statistical Association*, 71:340 – 344. Correction, 82:704, 83:581.

Dachraoui, K. and Dionne, G. (2003). *Conditions Ensuring the Separability of Asset Demand by all Risk Averse Investors.* Working paper, Risk Management Chair, HEC Montréal, Canada.

Dufour, J.-M. (1990). Exact tests and confidence sets in linear regressions with autocorrelated errors. *Econometrica*, 58:475 – 494.

Dufour, J.-M. (1997). Some impossibility theorems in econometrics, with applications to structural and dynamic models. *Econometrica*, 65:1365 – 1389.

Dufour, J.-M. (2002). Monte Carlo tests with nuisance parameters: A general approach to finite-sample inference and nonstandard asymptotics in econometrics. Forthcoming in *Journal of Econometrics.*

Dufour, J.-M. (2003). Identification, weak instruments and statistical inference in econometrics. *Canadian Journal of Economics*, 36(4):767–808.

Dufour, J.-M., Farhat, A., Gardiol, L., and Khalaf, L. (1998a). Simulation-based finite sample normality tests in linear regressions. *The Econometrics Journal*, 1:154–173.

Dufour, J.-M., Hallin, M., and Mizera, I. (1998b). Generalized runs tests for heteroskedastic time series. *Journal of Nonparametric Statistics*, 9:39–86.

Dufour, J.-M. and Khalaf, L. (2001). Monte Carlo test methods in econometrics. In: B. Baltagi (ed.), *Companion to Theoretical Econometrics*, pp. 494–519. Blackwell Companions to Contemporary Economics, Basil Blackwell, Oxford.

Dufour, J.-M. and Khalaf, L. (2002a). Exact tests for contemporaneous correlation of disturbances in seemingly unrelated regressions. *Journal of Econometrics*, 106(1):143–170.

Dufour, J.-M. and Khalaf, L. (2002b). Simulation based finite and large sample tests in multivariate regressions. *Journal of Econometrics*, 111(2):303–322.

Dufour, J.-M. and Khalaf, L. (2003). Finite sample tests in seemingly unrelated regressions, In: D.E.A. Giles (ed.), *Computer-Aided Econometrics*, pp. 11–35. Marcel Dekker, New York.

Dufour, J.-M., Khalaf, L. and Beaulieu, M.-C. (2003). Exact skewness-kurtosis tests for multivariate normality and goodness-of-fit in multivariate regressions with application to asset pricing models. *Oxford Bulletin of Economics and Statistics*, 65:891–906.

Dufour, J.-M., Khalaf, L., Bernard, J.-T., and Genest, I. (2004). Simulation-based finite-sample tests for heteroskedasticity and ARCH effects. *Journal of Econometrics*, 122(2):317–347.

Dufour, J.-M. and Kiviet, J.F. (1996). Exact tests for structural change in first-order dynamic models. *Journal of Econometrics* 70:39–68.

Dufour, J.-M. and Kiviet, J.F. (1998). Exact inference methods for first-order autoregressive distributed lag models. *Econometrica*, 66:79–104.

Dwass, M. (1957). Modified randomization tests for nonparametric hypotheses. *Annals of Mathematical Statistics*, 28:181–187.

Embrechts, P., Klüppelberg, C. and Mikosch, T. (1997). *Modelling Extremal Events for Insurance and Finance.* Springer-Verlag, Berlin.

Fama, E.F. (1965). The behaviour of stock prices. *Journal of Business*, 60:401–424.

Fama, E.F. and French, K.R. (1993). Common risk factors in the returns on stocks and bonds. *Journal of Financial Economics*, 33:3 – 56.

Fama, E.F. and French, K.R. (1995). Size and book-to-market factors in earnings and returns. *The Journal of Finance*, 50:131 – 155.

Fama, E.F. and French, K.R. (2003). *The CAPM: Theory and Evidence.* Working paper, Center for Research in Security Prices, The University of Chicago, Chicago, and Amos Tuck School of Business, Dartmouth College, Hanover, NH.

Gibbons, M.R., Ross, S.A., and Shanken, J. (1989). A test of the efficiency of a given portfolio. *Econometrica*, 57:1121 – 1152.

Harvey, C.R. and Siddique, A. (2000). Conditional skewness in asset pricing tests. *The Journal of Finance*, 55:1263 – 1295.

Hodgson, D.J., Linton, O., and Vorkink, K. (2002). Testing the capital asset pricing model efficiently under elliptical symmetry: A semiparametric approach. *Journal of Applied Econometrics*, 17;617 – 639.

Hodgson, D.J. and Vorkink, K. (2003). Efficient estimation of conditional asset pricing models. *Journal of Business and Economic Statistics*, 21:269 – 283.

Ibragimov, I.A. and Linnik, Y.V. (1975). *Independent and Stationary Sequences of Random Variables.* Wolters-Nordhoff, Groningen.

Ingersoll, J. (1987). *Theory of Financial Decision Making.* Rowman & Littlefield, NJ.

Jobson, J.D. and Korkie, B. (1989). A performance interpretation of multivariate tests of asset set intersection, spanning, and mean-variance efficiency. *Journal of Financial and Quantitative Analysis*, 24:185 – 204.

Kiviet, J.F. and Dufour, J.-M. (1997). Exact tests in single equation autoregressive distributed lag models. *Journal of Econometrics*, 80:325 – 353.

Kraus, A. and Litzenberger, R. (1976). Skewness preference and the valuation of risk assets. *Journal of Finance*, 31:1085 – 1100.

Lehmann, E.L. (1986). *Testing Statistical Hypotheses*, 2nd edition. John Wiley & Sons, New York.

Li, H. and Maddala, G.S. (1996). Bootstrapping time series models. *Econometric Reviews*, 15:115 – 158.

MacKinlay, A.C. (1987). On multivariate tests of the Capital Asset Pricing Model. *Journal of Financial Economics*, 18:341 – 372.

Mandelbrot, B. (1963). The variation of certain speculative prices. *Journal of Business*, 36:394 – 419.

Mardia, K.V. (1970). Measures of multivariate skewness and kurtosis with applications. *Biometrika*, 57:519 – 530.

Meerschaert, M.M. and Scheffler, H.-P. (2001). *Limit Distributions for Sums of Independent Random Vectors: Heavy Tails in Theory and Practice.* John Wiley & Sons, New York.

Mittnik, S., Paolella, M. and Rachev, S. (2000). Stable paretian modeling in finance: Some empirical and theoretical aspects. In Adler et al. (2000).

Nielsen, L.T. (1990). Existence of equilibrium in CAPM. *Journal of Economic Theory* 52:223 – 231.

Rachev, S., Kim, J.-R., and Mittnik, S. (1999a). Stable paretian econometrics, Part I. *The Mathematical Scientist* 24:24 – 55.

Rachev, S., Kim, J.-R., and Mittnik, S. (1999b). Stable paretian econometrics. Part II. *The Mathematical Scientist*, 24:113 – 127.

Rachev, S. and Mittnik, S. (2000). *Stable Paretian Models in Finance.* John Wiley & Sons, New York.

Rao, C.R. (1973). *Linear Statistical Inference and its Applications*, 2nd edition. John Wiley & Sons, New York.

Ross, S.A. (1978). Mutual fund separation in financial theory — The separating distributions. *Journal of Economic Theory*, 17:254 – 286.

Samorodnitsky, G. and Taqqu, M.S. (1994). *Stable Non-Gaussian Random Processes: Stochastic Models with Infinite Variance.* Chapman & Hall, New York.

Samuelson, P. (1967). On multivariate tests of the Capital Asset Pricing Model. *Journal of Financial and Quantitative Analysis*, 2:107 – 122.

Shanken, J. (1996). Statistical methods in tests of portfolio efficiency: A synthesis. In: G.S. Maddala and C.R. Rao (eds.), *Handbook of Statistics 14: Statistical Methods in Finance*, pp. 693 – 711. North-Holland, Amsterdam.

Stewart, K.G. (1997). Exact testing in multivariate regression. *Econometric Reviews*, 16:321 – 352.

Uchaikin, V.V. and Zolotarev, V.M. (1999). *Chance and Stability. Stable Distributions and Their Applications.* VSP, Zeist, The Netherlands.

Vorkink, K. (2003). Return distributions and improved tests of asset pricing models. *The Review of Financial Studies*, 16(3):845 – 874.

Weron, R. (1996). On the Chambers – Mallows – Stuck method for simulating skewed stable random variables. *Statistics and Probability Letters*, 28:165 – 171.

Zolotarev, V.M. (1986). *One-Dimensional Stable Distributions.* Vol. 65 of *Translations of Mathematical Monographs*, American Mathematical Society, Providence, RI.

Chapter 10

A STOCHASTIC DISCOUNT FACTOR-BASED APPROACH FOR FIXED-INCOME MUTUAL FUND PERFORMANCE EVALUATION

Mohamed A. Ayadi
Lawrence Kryzanowski

Abstract A general asset pricing framework is used to derive a conditional non-linear asset pricing kernel that accounts efficiently for time variation in expected returns and risk, and is suitable to perform (un)conditional evaluations of fixed-weight and dynamic investment strategies. The negative abnormal unconditional performance of Canadian fixed-income mutual funds over the period 1985 – 2000 weakly improves with conditioning. The unconditional-based superior performance of larger over smaller funds that weakens with limited conditioning is somewhat alleviated with an expansion of the conditioning set.

1. Introduction

Performance measurement and evaluation of actively managed funds have received wide interest in the academic literature and among practitioners. However, most of the academic attention focuses on equity and not bond (fixed-income) mutual funds.[1] This alternative category of funds is important considering the increasing number of fixed-income funds and the growth in their total assets under management over the last fifteen years.

The majority of the papers in the bond fund literature rely on traditional single- to multi-factor asset pricing models adapted to bond

[1]For example, see Jensen (1968, 1969); Lehmann and Modest (1987); Grinblatt and Titman (1989, 1993, 1994); Chen and Knez (1996); Kryzanowski et al. (1994, 1997, 1998); Ferson and Schadt (1996); Carhart (1997); Christopherson et al. (1998), and Farnsworth et al. (2002).

pricing.[2] The performance metrics are obtained by comparing the portfolio's average excess return to that implied by the selected model for the same level of risk. These models also fail to deliver reliable measures of performance and sometimes generate misleading inferences. This is caused essentially by problems related to estimation bias due to the presence of timing information (Dybvig and Ross, 1985; Admati and Ross, 1985; Grinblatt and Titman, 1989) and to the choice and efficiency of the chosen benchmarks where rankings can change with the use of different benchmarks (Roll, 1978). These problems led to the development of an asset pricing model-free measure to assess portfolio performance.

This alternative methodology relies on the general asset-pricing framework or GAPF based on the stochastic discount factor or SDF representation of asset prices. According to Harrison and Kreps (1979), this methodology requires weaker market conditions of either the law of one price or no arbitrage conditions. The GAPF implies that any gross return discounted by a market-wide random variable has a constant conditional expectation. The GAPF nests all common (un)conditional asset pricing models such as the CAPM, APT, ICAPM, Multifactor Models, CCAPM, or Option Models, depending on the specification of the stochastic discount factor. Moreover, the GAPF allows for an integration of the role of conditioning information with different structures (Hansen and Richard, 1987).

Grinblatt and Titman (1989) initially apply the GAP framework to evaluate the performance of stock mutual funds via their positive period weighting measure or PPWM where the SDF is the marginal utility

[2]For example, Cornell and Green (1991) use a two-factor model reflecting movements in interest rates and stock prices to study the performance of U.S. high-yield bond funds. They conclude that the risk-adjusted returns of bond funds are well explained by this two-factor model. Blake et al. (1993) use (non)linear single- and multi-factor models to conduct the first rigorous test of the performance of U.S. bond funds. They find that the underperformance of bond funds net-of-expenses is robust. Lee (1994) uses several mean-variance efficient benchmark model specifications to assess the performance of a large sample of U.S. bond funds. Lee finds that a multi-factor model with medium- and short-term bond and stock market indices as factors is the most appropriate for performance evaluation, and that bond fund managers do not exhibit any superior abilities after expenses. Elton et al. (1995) use a relative pricing APT model, which is based on a few bond indices and unanticipated changes in macroeconomic variables, to evaluate bond fund performance. Elton et al. report negative risk-adjusted performance that is comparable to the level of transaction costs. Detzler (1999) reports evidence of underperformance for global bond funds but her framework stems from unconditional single and multi-index benchmark models and fails to account for the time-variation in the expected returns of international bonds (Harvey et al., 2002). Ayadi and Kryzanowski (2004) find that the unconditional risk-adjusted performance of Canadian fixed-income mutual funds is negative, deteriorates with partial and full conditionings, and is sensitive to the choice of the return-generating process. The use of a full conditional five-factor model best describes the return generating process of Canadian fixed-income funds.

of the return on an efficient portfolio.[3] However, this methodology has rarely been applied to the performance evaluation of fixed-income mutual funds. To illustrate, He et al. (1999) test the performance of a small sample of corporate bond mutual funds using the non-parametric (un)conditional models of Hansen and Jagannathan (1991) and Chen and Knez (1996). Kang (1997) adapts the numeraire portfolio approach of Long (1990) to evaluate the performance of U.S. government and corporate bond funds and concludes that the numeraire-denominated abnormal returns after expenses are negative and similar to the Jensen alpha estimates. Using extended SDF representations of continuous-time term structure models, Ferson et al. (2004) report evidence of conditional underperformance over the period 1985 – 1999 for U.S. fixed-income funds, and that a two-factor affine model outperforms a single factor model. Most of these papers use existing asset pricing kernels that are not adapted to performance evaluation where realizations may be negative, adopt simple linear conditioning information integration between the unconditional and conditional pricing kernels, and/or employ unconditional average returns.

Thus, given these limitations in the existing literature, this chapter has two major objectives. The first major objective is to introduce a conditional asset-pricing kernel adapted to performance evaluation that efficiently accounts for the time variation in expected returns and risk, and does not rely on the linear information scaling used in most SDF-based performance tests reported in the literature. This SDF depends on some parameters and on the returns on an efficient portfolio, and satisfies some regularity conditions. This approach has the advantage of not being dependent on any asset pricing model or any distributional assumptions. The proposed SDF is efficient by construction, given that it prices all of the benchmarks and assets. The proposed SDF is further differentiated from most existing SDF models because it has a unique structure that reflects nonlinear interdependences between its unconditional and conditional versions caused essentially by the time-variability in the optimal risky asset allocation. The framework also is suitable for performing unconditional evaluations of fixed-weight strategies and (un)conditional evaluations of dynamic strategies.[4]

[3]Subsequent tests on stock equity mutual funds are developed by Glosten and Jagannathan (1994); Grinblatt and Titman (1994); Chen and Knez (1996); Kryzanowski and Lalancette (1996); Goldbaum (1999); Dahlquist and Soderlind (1999); Farnsworth et al. (2002), and Ayadi and Kryzanowski (2005).

[4]See Ayadi and Kryzanowski (2005) for an application to Canadian equity mutual funds.

The second major objective is to develop the appropriate empirical framework for the estimation of the performance measures. We advocate the use of a flexible estimation methodology using the (un)conditional Generalized Method of Moments or GMM of Hansen (1982). We construct the empirical performance measures and their associated tests, and use this methodology to assess the performance of a comprehensive sample of Canadian fixed-income mutual funds over the period 1985–2000. The GMM system is estimated consecutively using a one-step method and the excess returns for each individual fund or each portfolio of funds and the set of bond passive portfolios.

The main finding is that the measured unconditional performance of fund managers is negative. The performance statistics weakly improve with conditioning, which suggests that the time-variation in the conditional risky asset allocation used herein appears to have a greater impact on conditional performance than the common linear information scaling applied in most SDF-based performance tests. While the unconditional performance estimates are similar when the averages of the individual fund performances are compared against the average performances of the portfolios of all funds, the tests of significance for the latter are more reliable since the latter reflect the contemporaneous correlations in the returns among the individual funds. In contrast, the former assumes that the performances of individual funds are independent contemporaneously of each other. With limited conditioning, the performance statistics based on all individual funds are higher than those based on portfolios of the funds, and the superior performance of larger over smaller funds is weakened (enhanced) in a comparison of size- versus equal-weighted portfolios of funds, when the assessment relies on portfolios of funds (individual funds). These results may be due to an increased nonlinearity in the risk adjustment for the limited conditional pricing kernel. Furthermore, an expansion of the conditioning information set seems to alleviate the impact of the conditional pricing kernel on the size-based statistics.

The remainder of the chapter is organized as follows: Section 2 presents the general asset-pricing framework. In Section 3, we derive the asset-pricing kernel in the presence of time-varying returns. A (un)conditional portfolio performance evaluation using the developed normalized pricing operator is conducted in Section 4. In Section 5, we develop and explain the econometric methodology and the construction of the tests. Section 6 introduces the sample and the data used herein. Section 7 presents and discusses the main empirical results. Finally, Section 8 summarizes the findings and discusses their implications.

2. General asset pricing framework or GAPF

The fundamental theorem in asset pricing theory states that the price of a security is determined by the conditional expectations of its discounted future payoffs in frictionless markets. The stochastic discount factor or SDF is a random variable that reflects the fundamental economy-wide sources of risk.[5] The basic asset pricing equation, using gross returns, is written as:

$$E_t(M_{t+1}R_{i,t+1}) = 1, \quad \text{all } i = 1, \ldots, N. \tag{10.1}$$

The conditional expectation is defined with respect to the sub-sigma field on the set of states of nature, Ω_t, which represents the information available to investors at time t. $R_{i,t+1}$ is the gross return (payoff divided by price) of asset i at time $t+1$, and M_{t+1} is the stochastic discount factor or the pricing kernel.[6] The prices, payoffs and discount factors can be real or nominal, and the general assumption is that the asset payoffs have finite second moments. As shown by Luttmer (1996), (10.1) becomes an inequality when transaction costs or any other market frictions are introduced.

If $r_{i,t+1} \equiv R_{i,t+1} - R_{f,t+1}$ is defined as an excess return, it has a zero price. The pricing equation then becomes:

$$E_t(M_{t+1}r_{i,t+1}) = 0, \quad \text{all } i = 1, \ldots, N. \tag{10.2}$$

The SDF representation integrates both the absolute and the relative pricing approaches and has several advantages. First, the SDF is general and convenient for pricing stocks, bonds, derivatives and real assets. Second, the SDF representation is simple and flexible in that it nests all asset-pricing models by introducing explicit assumptions on the functional form of the pricing kernel and on the payoff distributions. Third, the SDF representation leads to a reliable analysis of passively and actively managed portfolios by providing robust measures by avoiding the limitations of the traditional models. Fourth, by construction, the SDF representation offers a suitable framework when performing econometric tests of such models using the GMM approach of Hansen (1982). Fifth,

---

[5] It is a generalization of the standard discount factor under uncertainty, which is stochastic because it varies across the states of nature.

[6] The SDF has various other names such as the intertemporal marginal rate of substitution in the consumption-based model, the equivalent martingale measure for allowing the change of measure from the actual or objective probabilities to the risk-neutral probabilities, or the state price density when the Arrow–Debreu or state-contingent price is scaled by the associated state probability.

the SDF representation accommodates conditioning information and exploits its implications and the predictions of the underlying model in a simple way.

3. Time-varying returns and asset pricing kernels

When investment opportunities are time-varying, the stochastic discount factors or the period weights can be interpreted as the conditional marginal utilities of an investor with isoelastic preferences described by a power utility function that exhibits constant relative risk aversion (CRRA) given by:

$$U(W_t) = \frac{1}{1-\gamma} W_t^{1-\gamma},$$

where W_t is the level of wealth at t, and γ is the relative risk aversion coefficient. In a single-period model, the uninformed investor who holds the benchmark portfolio (the risky asset) maximizes the conditional expectation of the utility of his terminal wealth:

$$E[U(W_{t+1}) \mid \Omega_t]. \tag{10.3}$$

The conditional expectation is based upon the information set Ω_t.

The investor with such preferences decides on the fraction δ_t of wealth to allocate to the risky asset and any remaining wealth is invested in a risk-free security. The return on wealth is given by:

$$R_{w,t+1} = \delta_t r_{B,t+1} + R_{f,t+1}, \tag{10.4}$$

where:

$r_{B,t+1}$: the excess return on the benchmark portfolio from t to $t+1$;

$R_{f,t+1}$: the gross risk-free rate from t to $t+1$ that is known one period in advance at time t; and

δ_t: is the proportion of total wealth invested in the benchmark portfolio.

The optimal risky asset allocation or portfolio policy is no longer a constant parameter when asset returns are predictable. Fama and French (1988, 1989); Ferson and Harvey (1991); Bekaert and Hodrick (1992); Schwert (1989), and Kandel and Stambaugh (1996), among others, document evidence of significant return predictability for long and short horizons, where the means and variances of asset returns are time-varying and depend on some key variables such as lagged returns, dividend yield, term structure variables, and interest rate variables. Moreover, more recent papers by Brennan et al. (1997); Campbell and Viceira (1999); Brandt (1999), and Aît-Sahalia and Brandt (2001) invoke different assumptions on the intertemporal preferences of investors and on stock return dynamics. They show that the optimal portfolio weight is a function of the state variable(s) that forecast the expected returns when stock returns are predictable. It follows that the optimal portfolio weight is a random variable measurable with respect to the set of state or conditioning variables and is consistent with a conditional Euler equation:[7]

$$\delta_t \equiv \delta(\Omega_t). \tag{10.5}$$

Thus, considering a constant optimal portfolio weight when returns are predictable affects the construction of any measure based on this variable, and distorts inferences related to the use of such a measure. In addition, the functional form and the parameterization of the optimal portfolio allocation depend on the relationship between asset returns and the predicting variables.[8]

Assuming initial wealth at time t equals one, the conditional optimization problem as in Brandt (1999); Ferson and Siegel (2001), and Aît-Sahalia and Brandt (2001) for the uninformed investor is:

$$\delta_t^* = \arg\max_{\delta_t} E[U(\delta_t r_{B,t+1} + R_{f,t+1}) \mid \Omega_t]. \tag{10.6}$$

The first order condition gives the conditional Euler equation:

$$E[(\delta_t r_{B,t+1} + R_{f,t+1})^{-\gamma} r_{B,t+1} \mid \Omega_t] = 0. \tag{10.7}$$

Now define, $M_{t+1}^c \equiv (\delta_t r_{B,t+1} + R_{f,t+1})^{-\gamma}$, which is a strictly positive conditional stochastic discount factor consistent with the no-arbitrage principle. This ensures that, if a particular fund has a higher positive payoff than another fund, then it must have a higher positive performance. Grinblatt and Titman (1989) and Chen and Knez (1996) stress the importance of this positivity property in providing reliable performance measures.[9,10] M_{t+1}^c can be normalized such that:

$$m_{t+1}^c \equiv \frac{M_{t+1}^c}{E_t(M_{t+1}^c)} = M_{t+1}^c R_{f,t+1}. \tag{10.8}$$

[7]See Ayadi and Kryzanowski (2004) for a proof that the optimal risky asset allocation is a nonlinear function of the first and second conditional moments of asset returns.

[8]Brandt (1999) conducts a standard non-parametric estimation of the time-varying portfolio choice using four conditioning variables; namely, dividend yield, default premium, term premium, and lagged excess return.

[9]In this sense, the traditional Jensen alpha is implied by the CAPM pricing kernel when the positivity condition is not satisfied everywhere (Dybvig and Ross, 1985).

[10]In general, when the pricing kernel can be negative with certain positive probability, a truncation is adopted. The truncation provides a similar representation to that for an option on a payoff with a zero strike price.

Then $E_t(m^c_{t+1}) = 1$. This scaling is more convenient and is consistent with the original derivation of the PPWM of Grinblatt and Titman (1989) and Cumby and Glen (1990). The new conditional normalized pricing kernel plays a central role in the construction of the portfolio performance measure. The unconditional normalized pricing kernel is given by:

$$m^u_{t+1} \equiv \frac{M^u_{t+1}}{E(M^u_{t+1})} = M^u_{t+1} R_{f,t+1}, \tag{10.9}$$

where δ is a constant parameter. Then $E(m^u_{t+1}) = 1$.

Let α^i_t, $i = (u, c)$, be the (un)conditional portfolio performance measure depending on the use of the appropriate SDF. It is an admissible positive performance measure with respect to the Chen and Knez (1996) definition.[11] If $r_{y,t+1}$ is the excess return on any particular portfolio y, then:

$$\alpha^u_t = E(m^u_{t+1} r_{y,t+1}) = E(r_{y,t+1}) + \mathrm{Cov}(m^u_{t+1}, r_{y,t+1}), \tag{10.10}$$

$$\alpha^c_t = E_t(m^c_{t+1} r_{y,t+1}) = E_t(r_{y,t+1}) + \mathrm{Cov}_t(m^c_{t+1}, r_{y,t+1}). \tag{10.11}$$

It follows that the expected performance measure reflects an average value plus an adjustment for the riskiness of the portfolio measured by the covariance of its excess return with the appropriate normalized pricing kernel.

4. Performance evaluation of passively and actively managed portfolios

4.1 Unconditional framework

When uninformed investors do not incorporate public information, the portfolio weights are fixed or constant. The gross return on such a portfolio is: $R_{p,t+1} = w' R_{1,t+1}$, with $w' 1_N = 1$, R_1 being a N-vector of gross security returns, and 1_N being a N-vector of ones. We assume that the portfolio weights w are chosen one period before. The corresponding unconditional performance measure is:

$$\alpha^u_t = E(m^u_{t+1} r_{p,t+1}) = E(m^u_{t+1} R_{p,t+1}) - R_{f,t+1} = 0, \tag{10.12}$$

$$m^u_{t+1} \equiv m(r_{B,t+1}, \delta).$$

It follows that the risk-adjusted return on the passive portfolio held by the uninformed investor is equal to the risk-free rate. The parameters

[11] According to Chen and Knez (1996), a performance measure is admissible when it satisfies four minimal conditions: it assigns zero performance to each portfolio in the defined reference set, and it is linear, continuous, and nontrivial.

of m^u_{t+1} are chosen such that $E(m^u_{t+1} r_{B,t+1}) = 0$. If $r_{B,t+1}$ is of dimension K, then $E(m^u_{t+1} r_{B,t+1}) = 0_K$ and $E(m^u_{t+1}) = 1$. Informed investors, such as possibly some mutual fund managers, trade based on some private information or signals implying non-constant weights for their portfolios.[12,13] The gross return on an actively managed portfolio is given by:

$$R_{a,t+1} = w(\Omega^a_t)' R_{1,t+1}, \quad \text{with } w(\Omega^a_t)' 1_N = 1,$$

where Ω^p and Ω^a represent public and private information sets, respectively.

The unconditional performance measure is given by:

$$\begin{aligned} \alpha^u_t = E(m^u_{t+1} r_{a,t+1}) &= E(m^u_{t+1} R_{a,t+1}) - R_{f,t+1} \\ &= E(w(\Omega^a_t)' m^u_{t+1} R_{1,t+1}) - R_{f,t+1}. \end{aligned} \tag{10.13}$$

When informed investors optimally exploit their private information or signals, this measure is expected to be strictly positive.

4.2 Conditional framework

When uninformed investors use publicly known information, Ω^p, in constructing their portfolios, the weights are a function of the information variables. The gross return is given by:

$$R_{p,t+1} = w(\Omega^p_t)' R_{1,t+1}, \quad \text{with } w(\Omega^p_t)' 1_N = 1, \text{ and } \Omega^p_t \subset \Omega^a_t.$$

Consistent with the semi-strong form of the efficient market hypothesis, the conditional SDF prices the portfolio such that:

$$\alpha^c_t = E_t(m^c_{t+1} r_{p,t+1}) = E_t(m^c_{t+1} R_{p,t+1}) - R_{f,t+1} = 0, \tag{10.14}$$

$$m^c_{t+1} \equiv m(r_{B,t+1}, \Omega^p_t, \delta).$$

To model the conditioning information, define $Z_t \in \Omega^p_t$, where Z_t is a L-vector of conditioning variables containing unity as its first element. These conditional expectations are analysed by creating general managed portfolios, and then examining the implications for the unconditional expectations as in Cochrane (1996).

Hansen and Singleton (1982) and Hansen and Richard (1987) propose including the conditioning information by scaling the original returns by

[12]The information may either concern individual stocks and/or the overall market.

[13]There is no restriction on the weight function. It may be nonlinear including any option-like trading strategies (Merton, 1981; Glosten and Jagannathan, 1994).

the instruments.[14] This simple multiplicative approach implies linear trading strategies and does not require the specification of the conditional moments. This approach allows one to uncover an additional implication of the conditional SDF model that is not captured by the simple application of the law of iterated expectations. These scaled returns can be interpreted as payoffs to managed portfolios or conditional assets. The payoff space is expanded to NL dimensions to represent the number of trading strategies available to uninformed investors.[15]

The conditional performance measure can be written as:

$$\alpha_t^c = E_t(m_{t+1}^c R_{1,t+1}) \otimes Z_t - R_{f,t+1} 1_N \otimes Z_t = 0 \tag{10.15}$$

$$E_t(m_{t+1}^c) Z_t = Z_t. \tag{10.16}$$

Assuming stationarity and applying the law of iterated expectations yields:

$$E[m_{t+1}^c (R_{1,t+1} \otimes Z_t)] = E(R_{f,t+1} 1_N \otimes Z_t), \tag{10.17}$$

$$E(m_{t+1}^c Z_t) = E(Z_t), \tag{10.18}$$

where $\otimes$ is the Kronecker product obtained by multiplying every asset return by every instrument. These two conditions ensure that the conditional mean of the pricing kernel is one, and that these managed portfolios are correctly priced. The conditional normalized pricing kernel is only able to price any asset or portfolio whose returns are attainable from dynamic trading strategies of the original N assets (i.e., asset returns scaled with the instruments) with respect to the defined conditioning information set.

The conditional performance for the actively managed portfolio is given by:

$$\alpha_t^c = E_t(m_{t+1}^c r_{a,t+1}) = E_t(m_{t+1}^c R_{a,t+1}) - R_{f,t+1}. \tag{10.19}$$

[14] Bekaert and Liu (2004) propose that the conditioning information be integrated into the conditional pricing kernel model by determining the optimal scaling factor or the functional form of the conditioning information. These authors argue that the multiplicative model is not necessarily optimal in terms of exploiting the conditioning information and in providing the greatest lower bound. However, at the empirical level, this approach has a notable limitation in that the optimal scaling factor depends on the first and second conditional moments of the distribution of asset returns leading to an increasing number of parameters to be estimated and different parameterization of the conditional asset-pricing kernel. All of this leads to the need to estimate a complex system of equations.

[15] The intuition underlying the multiplicative approach is closely related to the evidence for returns predictability, where some prespecified variables predict asset returns. Such evidence potentially improves the risk-return tradeoffs available to uninformed investors, unlike the time-invariant risk-return tradeoff. Bekaert and Hodrick (1992); Cochrane (1996), and Bekaert and Liu (2004) show that scaling the original returns by the appropriate instruments improves or sharpens the Hansen–Jagannathan lower bound on the pricing kernel when conditioning information is accounted for.

This conditional test determines whether the private information or signal contains useful information beyond that available publicly, and whether or not this information has been used profitably.

5. Econometric methodology and construction of the tests

In this section, the empirical framework for the estimation of the performance measures and for the tests of the different hypotheses and specifications using Hansen's (1982) generalized method of moments (GMM) is detailed. Important issues associated with the estimation procedure and the optimal weighting or distance matrix also are dealt with.

5.1 The general methodology

The estimation of performance of actively managed portfolios (such as mutual funds) is based on a one-step method using a GMM system approach. The one-step method jointly and simultaneously estimates the normalized pricing kernel parameters and the performance measures by augmenting the number of moment conditions in the initial system with the actively managed fund(s) or portfolio(s) of funds.

Here, the *one-step estimation is repeated using the excess returns for each individual fund or each portfolio of funds and the set of three passive portfolios.*[16] This multivariate framework incorporates all of the cross-equation correlations. By construction, such estimations account for the restriction on the mean of the normalized (un)conditional pricing kernels,[17] which Dahlquist and Soderlind (1999) and Farnsworth et al. (2002) show is important in order to obtain reliable estimates.

We now present the general steps and expressions leading primarily to the general case of conditional GMM estimation relevant for the conditional evaluation of dynamic trading-based portfolios. The unconditional GMM estimation is trivially obtained as a special case.

Let $\theta \equiv (\delta\, \gamma)'$ be the vector of unknown SDF parameters to be estimated. Our model implies the following conditional moment restriction:

$$E_t[m^c(r_{B,t+1}, Z_t, \theta_0) r_{p,t+1}] = 0_N \tag{10.20}$$

[16]Farnsworth et al. (2002) show that the performance estimates and associated standard errors are invariant to the number of actively managed individual funds or portfolios of funds in the GMM system. Thus, a system, which is estimated simultaneously for each fund or portfolio of funds with the passive portfolios, is equivalent to an extended system with several funds or portfolios of funds. Such a system setup limits the number of moment conditions and controls the saturation ratios associated with the estimations.

[17]The means of the normalized and non normalized pricing kernels are equal to one and the inverse of the gross return on the risk-free asset, respectively.

such that $E_t[m^c(r_{B,t+1}, Z_t, \theta_0)] = 1$. Now define

$$u_{t+1}^c = m^c(r_{B,t+1}, Z_t, \theta) r_{p,t+1} \equiv u(r_{B,t+1}, r_{p,t+1}, Z_t, \theta)$$

as a N-vector of residuals or pricing errors, which depend on the set of unknown parameters, the excess returns on the benchmark portfolio(s), the conditioning variables, and the excess returns on passive trading strategy-based portfolios.

Assume that the dimensions of the benchmark excess return and the conditioning variables are K and L, respectively. Then, the dimension of the vector of unknown parameters is $(KL+1)$. We then have:

$$E_t[u(r_{B,t+1}, r_{p,t+1}, Z_t, \theta_0)] = E[u(r_{B,t+1}, r_{p,t+1}, Z_t, \theta_0)] = 0_N. \quad (10.21)$$

Define $h(r_{B,t+1}, r_{p,t+1}, Z_t, \theta) = u_{t+1}^c \otimes Z_t = u(r_{B,t+1}, r_{p,t+1}, Z_t, \theta) \otimes Z_t$. Our conditional and unconditional moment restrictions can be written as:[18]

$$E_t[h(r_{B,t+1}, r_{p,t+1}, Z_t, \theta_0)] = E[h(r_{B,t+1}, r_{p,t+1}, Z_t, \theta_0)] = 0_{NL}, \quad (10.22)$$

$$E_t[m^c(r_{B,t+1}, Z_t, \theta_0) Z_t - Z_t] = E[m^c(r_{B,t+1}, Z_t, \theta_0) Z_t - Z_t] = 0_L. \quad (10.23)$$

Because the model is overidentified, the GMM system is estimated by setting the $(KL+1)$ linear combinations of the NL moment conditions equal to zero. When the system estimation of the performance measures is completed in one step, the number of moment conditions $(L(N+1))$ and the number of unknown parameters $(KL+2)$ is augmented.

Following Hansen (1982), the GMM estimator is obtained by selecting $\hat{\theta}_T$ that minimizes the sample quadratic form J_T given by:[19]

$$J_T(\theta) \equiv g_T(\theta)' W_T g_T(\theta), \quad (10.24)$$

where W_T is a symmetrical and nonsingular positive semi-definite $NL \times NL$ weighting matrix and $g_T(\theta)$ is given by:

$$g_T(\theta) = \frac{1}{T} \sum_{t=1}^{T} h(r_{B,t+1}, r_{p,t+1}, Z_t, \theta). \quad (10.25)$$

[18]Some technical assumptions are required for the consistency (strict stationarity and ergodicity of the process underlying the observable variables) and for the identification of the model. The variable h must have a nonsingular population (un)conditional covariance matrix, and the (un)conditional expectations of the first derivatives of h must have a full raw rank. See Hansen (1982) and Gallant and White (1988) for more details.

[19]Under some regularity conditions, Hansen (1982) shows that the GMM estimator is consistent and asymptotically normal for any fixed weighting matrix.

Let $J_T(\hat{\theta}_T)$ be the minimized value of the sample quadratic form.[20] When the optimal weighting matrix or the inverse of the variance-covariance matrix of the orthogonality conditions is used, $TJ_T(\hat{\theta})$ has an asymptotic standard central chi-square distribution with $((N-K)L-1)$ degrees of freedom. This is the well-known Hansen J_T-statistic. This estimation can handle the assumption that the vector of disturbances exhibits non-normality, conditional heteroskedasticity, and/or serial correlation even with unknown form.

5.2 The estimation procedure and the optimal weighting matrix

The estimates of the portfolio performance measure are obtained by minimizing the GMM criterion function constructed from a set of moment conditions in the system. This requires a consistent estimate of the weighting matrix that is a general function of the true parameters at least in the efficient case. The dominant approach in the literature is the iterative procedure suggested by Ferson and Foerster (1994).[21]

Hansen (1982) proves that the GMM estimator is asymptotically efficient when the weighting matrix is chosen to be the inverse of the variance-covariance matrix of the moment conditions.[22]

To estimate the optimal weighing matrix and to calculate the asymptotic standard errors for the GMM estimates, a consistent estimate of the empirical variance-covariance matrix of the moments is required. This variance-covariance matrix is defined as the zero-frequency spectral density of the pricing errors vector $h(r_{B,t+1}, r_{p,t+1}, Z_t, \theta_0)$. A consistent estimate of this spectral density is used herein to construct a heteroskedastic and autocorrelation consistent (HAC) or robust variance-covariance matrix in the presence of heteroskedasticity and autocorrelation of unknown forms (Priestley, 1981). Chen and Knez (1996); Kryzanowski et al. (1997); Dahlquist and Soderlind (1999), Farnsworth et al. (2002), and Ayadi and Kryzanowski (2005, 2004) construct robust t-statistics for their estimates of performance by using the modified Bartlett kernel

[20] Jagannathan and Wang (1996) show that T times the minimized GMM criterion function is asymptotically distributed as a weighted sum of central chi-squared random variables.

[21] This consists of updating the weighting matrix based on a previous step estimation of the parameters, and then updating the estimator. This is repeated until convergence for a prespecified criterion and for a large number of steps. Ferson and Foerster (1994) and Cochrane (1996) find that this iterative approach has better small sample properties than the two-step procedure, and is robust to small variations in the model specifications.

[22] The choice of the weighting matrix only affects the efficiency of the GMM estimator. Newey (1993) shows that the estimator's consistency only depends on the correct specification of the residuals and the information or conditioning variables.

proposed by Newey and West (1987a) to construct a robust estimator for the variance-covariance matrix.[23]

6. Sample and data

6.1 Mutual fund and benchmark returns

Two different samples of Canadian fixed-income funds are carefully constructed over the period from March 1985 through February 2000 using information from the Financial Post mutual fund database augmented by Financial Post quarterly reports, individual fund reports, and specific fund news in the financial press. The first sample consists of 162 fixed-income funds that still exist at the end of February 2000. This sample includes 108 government funds, 28 corporate funds, 21 mortgage funds, and 5 high-yield funds. The non-surviving funds sample is smaller with 72 funds. Potential mergers and name changes are accounted for in constructing the two samples. The investment objectives of the terminated funds are government securities (46), followed by corporate (11), mortgage (13), and high-yield (2) securities. The monthly returns for each fund are given by the monthly changes in the net asset values per share (NAVPS), and are adjusted for all distributions. Fund size is proxied by total net asset (TNA) value. The samples of surviving and of terminated funds allow for a comprehensive analysis of Canadian fixed-income fund performance and an assessment of the impact of survivorship bias across performance models and metrics, and across cross-sections of funds classified by investment objectives. As in Ferson et al. (2004), only fixed-income funds are considered for the tests of abnormal performance since a fixed-income based-asset pricing kernel cannot price or be used to evaluate the performance of non-fixed-income funds. The SC Universe bond index (i.e., a broad Canadian bond index) is used as the benchmark variable because it contains 900 marketable Canadian bonds with terms to maturity longer than 1 year. The average term is 9 years, and the average duration is 5.5 years.

Some summary statistics on the surviving funds are presented in Table 10.1. Panel A of Table 10.1 reports statistics on the cross-sectional distribution by investment objective and for all of the 162 surviving funds. The average annual fund returns over the 111 month period vary from 1.07% for Industrial Alliance bond 2 fund to 10.92% for SSQ bond fund, and have a cross-sectional mean of 7.13%. The fund annual volatilities or standard deviations range from 0.53% for Synergy Canadian ST

[23] The higher-order sample autocovariances are downweighted using linear declining weights, and those with order exceeding a certain parameter receive zero weight.

income fund to 7.96% for Spectrum United LT bond fund. The annual average mean and volatility of the return on the Scotia Universe bond index are 10.54% and 2.26%, respectively, over the same time period.

Summary statistics for equal- and size-weighted portfolios of funds grouped by each of four investment objectives (deemed sub-sector portfolios) and for all of the surviving funds are reported in Panel B of Table 10.1. The number of funds in each sub-sector portfolio is time varying as individual funds entered and exited over the studied time period. The size-weighted portfolio of government funds and the equal-weighted portfolio of mortgage funds exhibit the highest and the lowest uncondi-

Table 10.1. Summary statistics for the returns and entries and exits of the surviving and non-surviving fixed-income funds

This table reports summary statistics for the returns (in %) and fund attributes for Canadian fixed-income funds using monthly data from March 1985 through February 2000. The prefixes EW and SW refer to equal- and size-weighted portfolios of funds, respectively. Panel A provides the statistics on the distribution of various return parameter estimates for three cross-sections based on investment objectives and for all funds (including the five high-yield funds). N is the number of surviving funds as of the end of February 2000. Panel B reports some statistics on the returns and number of time-series observations per fund (T) for four equal- and four size-weighted portfolios of funds for the samples of surviving and non-surviving funds. The numbers of non-surviving funds over the study period are 46 (government), 11 (corporate), 13 (mortgage) and 72 (All, including 2 high-yield funds). Panel C reports the number of funds at the end of each year for the period of March 1985 to February 2000, and the number of funds that enter and exit during each year. The attrition rate (%) is given by the number of exiting funds divided by the number of funds at the end of the year. Survived funds are funds still in existence at the end of March 2000. The mortality rate (%) is computed as one minus the number of survived funds divided by the number of funds at the end of the year.

Panel A: Individual surviving mutual funds

Fund Group	Statistics	Mean	Std. Dev.	Min.	Max.	Skewness	Kurtosis
Government	Mean	0.603	1.534	−4.023	4.859	0.040	1.132
($N = 108$)	Std. Dev.	0.176	0.366	1.948	1.375	0.539	2.093
	Median	0.641	1.595	−4.314	4.805	−0.061	0.663
Corporate	Mean	0.562	1.400	−3.344	4.363	0.031	1.123
($N = 28$)	Std. Dev.	0.183	0.442	1.648	1.535	0.561	1.760
	Median	0.569	1.486	−2.605	4.467	0.206	0.566
Mortgage	Mean	0.576	0.850	−2.511	3.099	−0.428	2.662
($N = 21$)	Std. Dev.	0.139	0.194	0.951	0.810	0.627	1.941
	Median	0.644	0.804	−2.547	3.212	−0.314	2.480
All	Mean	0.594	1.424	−3.746	4.526	−0.030	1.377
($N = 162$)	Std. Dev.	0.172	0.424	1.864	1.453	0.572	2.092
	Median	0.636	1.483	−3.891	4.459	−0.067	0.756

Table 10.1 (continued).

Panel B: Portfolios of surviving and of non-surviving funds based on fund investment objectives

Objective	Surviving Funds				Non-surviving Funds			
	Mean	Std. Dev.	Min.	Max.	Mean	Std. Dev.	Min.	Max.
Government, T	112		29	180	71		2	152
Ret. EW	0.750	1.528	−4.422	4.507	0.679	1.537	−4.356	4.676
Ret. SW	0.766	1.593	−4.624	4.968	0.745	1.655	−4.406	5.304
Corporate, T	100		26	180	86		3	158
Ret. EW	0.735	1.492	−3.843	4.344	0.750	1.557	−4.462	5.868
Ret. SW	0.759	1.630	−4.420	4.972	0.764	1.651	−4.543	6.095
Mortgage, T	131		38	180	131		62	180
Ret. EW	0.684	0.718	−2.592	2.256	0.632	0.769	−2.821	2.446
Ret. SW	0.692	0.750	−2.503	2.306	0.641	0.733	−2.870	2.096
High-Yield, T	53		40	64	13		13	13
Ret. EW	0.739	1.354	−3.968	3.415	0.134	1.189	−3.396	2.063
Ret. SW	0.713	1.307	−3.865	3.268	0.134	1.189	−3.396	2.063
All, T	111		26	180	83		2	180
Ret. EW	0.735	1.339	−4.030	4.119	0.671	1.205	−3.950	3.849
Ret. SW	0.748	1.327	−4.063	3.865	0.692	1.087	−3.759	3.594

Panel C: Annual fund entries and exits

Year/Statistic	Entry	Exit	Year End	Survived	Attrition Rate	Mortality Rate
1985	–	–	59	46	–	22.03
1986	7	0	66	52	0.00	21.21
1987	14	0	80	63	0.00	21.25
1988	12	0	92	73	0.00	20.65
1989	15	0	107	85	0.00	20.56
1990	6	1	112	91	0.89	18.75
1991	6	2	116	96	1.72	17.24
1992	10	0	126	106	0.00	15.87
1993	13	0	139	117	0.00	15.83
1994	30	0	169	142	0.00	15.98
1995	18	3	184	153	1.63	16.85
1996	17	19	182	170	10.44	6.59
1997	18	3	197	186	1.52	5.58
1998	3	7	193	189	3.63	2.07
1999	5	5	193	193	2.59	0.00

tional mean returns of 9.19% and 8.20% per annum, respectively. The size-weighted portfolio of corporate bond funds has the highest unconditional volatility of 5.65% per annum, and the equal-weighted portfolio of mortgage funds has the lowest unconditional volatility of 2.49% per annum. The average annual returns on portfolios of all funds are 8.82% and 8.98% using equal- and size-weighted structures, respectively. For all but the high-yield portfolios, the unconditional mean returns and volatilities of the size-weighted portfolios are higher than those of the equal-weighted portfolios.

Similar information for portfolios of terminated funds is provided in Panel B of Table 10.1. For the major fund classifications (government, corporate, and mortgage), the mean return and volatility statistics are higher and lower than those obtained with the surviving funds, respectively, with the exception of the equal-weighted portfolio of corporate bond funds. The average annual returns for portfolios of all funds are 8.05% and 8.30% using equal- and size-weightings, respectively. Given the nature of these funds, the minimum, maximum, and average numbers of observations for the 72 individual funds across the four fund classifications are smaller, which leads to an average sample length of approximately seven years.

6.2 Fund survivals and mortalities

The two constructed samples include virtually all of the fixed-income funds that existed in Canada between 1985 and 2000. The samples mirror the evolution of the Canadian bond fund market over this period of time. The annual entry and exit of both funds and the corresponding estimates of attrition and mortality rates are reported in Panel C of Table 10.1. The attrition rate, which reflects the percentage of funds that are left in the sample at each point in time, ranges between 0% and 10.44% and averages 1.60%. These figures are somewhat similar (with more variability) that those obtained for the U.S. equity mutual fund market. Elton et al. (1996) find an attrition rate of 2.3% that varies across the fund groupings. Carhart et al. (2002) use a comprehensive sample of funds over a long time period of 1962-1995 and estimate an attrition rate between 0.5% and 8.6% with an average of 3.6%. However, our average rate is lower than the 9.37% reported by Dahlquist et al. (2000) for Swedish bond funds. Our sample exhibits a mortality rate that is decreasing over the sample period. Nevertheless, more than 20% of the funds that existed at the beginning of the sample period are terminated by the end of the studied period.[24] The number of funds increases by more than three times over the studied time period.

[24]The attrition rate in 1996 appears to be anomalous. Most of the fund terminations resulted from fund integrations following fund family acquisitions by Spectrum United from United Financial Management and by Mutual Life from Prudential Assurance (the Strata family) in 1995. Others resulted from fund consolidations of similar funds existing prior to further fund

6.3 Information variables

For the conditional models, four instrumental variables are used based on their predictive power uncovered in studies of bond return predictability.[25] They are drawn from Statistics Canada's CANSIM database and are the lagged values of TB1 or the one-month Treasury bill rate (Fama and French, 1989; Ilmanen, 1995; Balduzzi and Robotti, 2001), DEF or the default premium as measured by the yield spread between the long-term corporate McLeod, Young, Weir bond index and long-term government of Canada bonds (Chang and Huang, 1990; Fama and French, 1989, 1993; Kirby, 1997; Aît-Sahalia and Brandt, 2001), TERM or the slope of the term structure as measured by the yield spread between long-term government of Canada bonds and the one period lagged three-month Treasury bill rate (Chang and Huang, 1990; Fama and French, 1989, 1993; Ilmanen, 1995; Kirby, 1997; Aît-Sahalia and Brandt, 2001), and REALG or the real return on long-term government bonds measured by the difference between the yield on the long-term government bond (5 to 10 years) and the inflation rate lagged by one month (Ilmanen, 1995). Since the first three instruments exhibit high degrees of persistence, they have been stochastically detrended by subtracting a moving average over a period of two months. This follows the approach of Campbell (1991); Ferson et al. (2004), and Ayadi and Kryzanowski (2004). The unreported analysis of predictability for bond indices and portfolios of funds based on the stochastically detrended instruments shows that the default premium (DEF) is highly significant in all regressions while the yield on the one-month Treasury bill (TB1), the slope of the term structure (TERM), and the real return on the LT government bond (REALG) are weakly significant. To keep the dimension of the estimated system manageable, the subsequent empirical analysis only uses DEF or DEF and REALG in the estimation of the performance measures. To allow for a simple interpretation of the estimated coefficients, the variables are demeaned in the conditional tests, as in Ferson and Schadt (1996).

Descriptive statistics and autocorrelations, and a correlation analysis of these variables are provided in Panels A and B of Table 10.2, respectively. The correlations between all of the instruments range from −0.36 to 0.04.

---

acquisitions within the same mutual fund family, particularly among the Spectrum family of funds.

[25]Similar inferences result from tests using several other conditioning variables, such as inflation rate, yield spread between the three-month T-bill and the one-month T-bill, yield spread between the six-month T-bill and the one-month T-bill, real yield on one-month T-bill, an equal-weighted stock index, and a dummy variable for the month of January.

Table 10.2. Summary statistics for the instrumental variables, bond indices, and factors.

This table reports the summary statistics for the monthly returns of the instrumental variables, bond indices, and factors. TB1 is the yield on one-month Treasury bills in % per month. TERM is the yield spread between long Canadas and the one period lagged 3-month Treasury bill rate in % per month. DEF is the default premium measured by the yield spread between the long-term corporate bond (McLeod, Young, Weir bond index) and long Canadas in % per month. REALG is the difference between the long-maturity (5 − 10 years) government bond yield and the inflation rate lagged by one month in % per month. The first three instruments are stochastically detrended by subtracting a moving average over a period of two months. The bond indices and factors are the Scotia Capital universe bond index (SCUN), the Scotia Capital government bond index (SCGOVT), and the Scotia Capital corporate bond index (SCCORP). Panel A reports various statistics for all variables, including autocorrelation coefficients of order 1, 3, 6 and 12. Panel B presents the correlation matrix of instruments. Panel C presents the correlation matrix of bond indices and factors. The data cover the period from March 1985 to February 2000, for a total of 180 observations.

Panel A: Descriptive statistics and autocorrelations

Variable	Mean	Median	Std. Dev.	Min.	Max.	Skew.	Kurt.
TB1	−0.0040	−0.0060	0.051	−0.2088	0.2342	0.634	7.229
DEF	0.0002	0.0000	0.007	−0.0217	0.0413	1.035	10.056
TERM	0.0000	0.0040	0.054	−0.2150	0.1704	−0.617	5.077
REALG	0.2291	0.1997	0.310	−0.6863	2.5913	2.448	20.515
SCUN	0.8787	0.9031	6.576	−4.8235	1.7852	0.012	3.461
SCGOVT	0.8948	0.9463	1.820	−4.9653	6.5710	−0.023	3.403
SCCORP	0.9208	1.0500	1.742	−4.9476	5.4148	−0.099	3.174

Variable	ρ_1	ρ_3	ρ_6	ρ_{12}
TB1	0.499	−0.046	−0.004	−0.059
DEF	0.308	−0.008	−0.218	0.109
TERM	0.308	−0.074	−0.087	−0.073
REALG	0.038	0.170	0.074	0.397
SCUN	0.066	0.016	−0.047	0.051
SCGOVT	0.064	0.003	−0.051	0.045
SCCORP	0.108	−0.014	−0.005	0.032

Panel B: Correlation matrix of instruments

Variable	TB1	DEF	TERM	REALG
TB1	1.00			
DEF	−0.07	1.00		
TERM	−0.36	−0.15	1.00	
REALG	−0.06	−0.09	0.04	1.00

Table 10.2 (continued).

Panel C: Correlation matrix of bond indices and factors

Portfolio	SCUN	SCGOVT	SCCORP
SCUN	1.00		
SCGOVT	0.98	1.00	
SCCORP	0.98	0.98	1.00

6.4 Passive strategies

Passive (basis or reference) assets must reflect the investment opportunity sets of investors and portfolio managers. In the empirical implementation of the performance measures, the type and the number of assets to be considered are important issues. In effect, assets included must be consistent with the type of funds (essentially fixed-income) under consideration. We use three bond indexes representing passive buy and hold fixed-income strategies and reflecting the Canadian domestic bond and mortgage markets. The SC Universe bond index is naturally used because our model correctly prices the benchmark return. Similarly, two bond indices related to government and corporate bond issues with complete maturity structures are retained. All of these indices and factors are obtained from Datastream.

Descriptive statistics and autocorrelations, and a correlation analysis of these variables are provided in Panels A and C of Table 10.2, respectively. All three bond fund index categories have correlations of 0.98.

6.5 Optimal risky asset allocation specifications

In a conditional setting, the optimal risky asset allocation of the uninformed investor is a function of the conditional moments of asset returns. We assume that these conditional moments are linear in the state variables. Hence two linear specifications are adopted and integrated into the construction of the performance measures; namely:[26]

$$\delta_t = Z_t' \delta, \tag{10.26}$$

where δ is a vector of unknown parameters, and Z_t is a vector of instruments (including a constant) with a dimension equal to two or three depending on whether the set of conditioning variables includes DEF only or both DEF and REALG. When an unconditional evaluation is conducted, the uninformed investor's portfolio policy is a constant.

[26] Aît-Sahalia and Brandt (2001) use a single linear index to characterize the relationship between the portfolio weight and the state variables.

7. Empirical performance results

The performance of portfolios of funds[27] and of individual funds[28] are examined using the (un)conditional pricing kernel models. We test the sensitivity of the performance metrics to conditioning information.

7.1 Evaluation of unconditional performance

The performance results for the equal- and size-weighted portfolios of mutual funds are summarized in Table 10.3. Based on Panel A, all equal-weighted portfolios have consistently negative and significant abnormal performance with the exception of the mortgage and high-yield portfolios. The alpha of a portfolio of all funds is −0.1011% per month, and the portfolio of government funds contributes the most to this performance with a highly significant alpha of 0.1177%. The same analyses conducted on the size-weighted portfolios of funds produces comparable results. The alphas of the portfolios of government funds and of corporate funds are highly significant at −0.1006% and −0.1143%, respectively. The alpha of the size-weighted portfolio of all funds is −0.0758% per month, which is significantly higher than the alpha of the equal-weighted portfolio of all funds. The superior performance of large funds is only confirmed for the government fund portfolio.[29] The performance tests are augmented by conducting a joint test of the restriction that all alphas are jointly zero across equations by using a GMM estimation of a system that includes the four portfolios of funds based on investment objectives. The test largely rejects the proposed hypothesis for the two types of portfolios (equal- and size-weighted) due to the negative alphas of the government and corporate fund groups.

The cross-sectional average performance of individual funds is summarized in Panel A of Table 10.4. The results are somewhat consistent with those reported for portfolios of funds. The performance point estimates improve except for the size-weighted portfolio of corporate funds and the high yield group. The equal- and size-weighted cross-sectional average alphas are −0.0845% and −0.0413% per month. They are essentially

[27]Equal- and size-weighted portfolios of funds based on investment objectives and for all funds provide evidence on potential size effects in performance. These portfolios can be interpreted as funds-of-funds, since they represent diversified investments that do not suffer from the most common criticism of funds-of-funds that they add an extra layer of costs. Other constructions could be based on industry or geographic sector investment themes.

[28]Our analysis of individual funds is conducted on all funds with at least 60 monthly observations given the increasing dimension of the extended conditional pricing kernel model.

[29]Based on unreported test results, the hypothesis that the alphas of the equal- and size-weighted portfolios for the corporate, mortgage, and high-yield groups are equal cannot be rejected at the 10% level.

Table 10.3. Performance measures for the portfolios of funds using the (un)conditional pricing kernel models.

This table reports the performance measures (α in %) per investment objective using the unconditional pricing kernel for the two selected benchmarks. The default premium (DEF) and the real yield on long-maturity government bonds (REALG) are used as instrumental variables. Simultaneous system estimation, consisting of the three bond passive portfolios and each portfolio of managed funds, is conducted using the GMM method. All represents the statistics of the portfolios of all funds. Size is defined as the total net asset value of the fund. The Scotia Capital universe bond index is used as the benchmark variable. The J-Statistic is the minimized value of the sample quadratic form constructed using the moment conditions and the optimal weighting matrix. Wald corresponds to the p-value based on the Newey and West (1987b) test of the marginal significance of the one conditioning variable and the two conditioning variables for the limited conditional model and extended conditional model, respectively. Monthly data are used from March 1985 through February 2000, for a total of 180 observations per portfolio of funds.

Fund Category	**Equal-weighted portfolios of funds**			**Size-weighted portfolios of funds**		
	α	p-value	Wald	α	p-value	Wald
Panel A: Unconditional pricing kernel						
Government	−0.1177	0.00		−0.1006	0.00	
Corporate	−0.1118	0.00		−0.1143	0.00	
Mortgage	−0.0283	0.42		−0.0166	0.64	
High-yield	0.1377	0.42		0.1295	0.43	
All	−0.1011	0.00		−0.0758	0.00	
J-Stat	0.0205			0.0205		
Panel B: Conditional pricing kernel with DEF as instrumental variable						
Government	−0.1141	0.00	0.03	−0.0996	0.00	0.01
Corporate	−0.1042	0.00	0.03	−0.1051	0.00	0.02
Mortgage	−0.0313	0.40	0.00	−0.0332	0.36	0.01
High-yield	0.2738	0.07	0.01	0.2803	0.06	0.01
All	−0.0985	0.00	0.03	−0.0811	0.00	0.01
J-Stat	0.0344			0.0485		
Panel C: Conditional pricing kernel with DEF and REALG as instrumental variables						
Government	−0.1134	0.00	0.00	−0.1008	0.00	0.00
Corporate	−0.1040	0.00	0.00	−0.1065	0.00	0.04
Mortgage	−0.0248	0.48	0.00	−0.0254	0.46	0.00
High-yield	0.2385	0.08	0.01	0.2501	0.05	0.01
All	−0.0917	0.00	0.00	−0.0702	0.00	0.00
J-Stat	0.0223			0.0281		

caused by the negative performance of the government and corporate fund cross-sections. The comparison between these cross-sectional averages of individual performances and the performance of portfolios of all funds suggests similar inferences with comparable alpha point estimates and the consistent superior relative performance of larger versus smaller funds for the government and aggregate groups. However, the p-values associated with the performances of portfolios of funds are superior and more reliable than those obtained from a cross-sectional averaging of the individual standard errors. This evidence contradicts with the unreported results obtained using cross-sections of individual surviving funds only. This suggests a consistently strong performance of larger terminated funds over smaller ones, which may be driven by consolidation in the industry.

To better understand the sources of the negative average performance, the distribution of the p-values for all funds and per fund grouping is examined for the two benchmarks using heteroskedasticity and autocorrelation consistent t-statistics. Based on Table 10.5, less than 22% of the funds have p-values less than 5%, and none of the funds exhibit significant positive performance. There are 27 government funds and 9 corporate funds with negative and significant alphas. The p-values based on the Bonferroni inequality indicate that the negative extreme t-statistics are significant for all funds and across all major fund categories, and that none of the Bonferroni p-values associated with the maximum t-statistics are significant.[30] This rejects the joint hypothesis of zero alphas.

The overall performance inferences for the unconditional pricing kernel model are similar to those reported by Blake et al. (1993); Lee (1994); Elton et al. (1995), and Kang (1997) for U.S. bond mutual funds, by Dahlquist et al. (2000) for Swedish bond mutual funds, and with those reported by Ayadi and Kryzanowski (2004) for Canadian bond funds for the same period using linear factor models. This negative and significant unconditional performance may reflect the presence of private and/or public information correlated with future returns. A conditional performance evaluation controlling for the effects of public information is necessary to better assess whether the performance of our sample is due to the inferior abilities of its managers.

[30] This test uses the maximum or the minimum one-tailed p-value from the t-statistic distribution for all funds and fund groupings multiplied by the corresponding number of funds.

Table 10.4. Average summary statistics of the performance measures for individual funds using the (un)conditional pricing kernel models.

This table reports summary statistics of the average performance measures (α in %) per investment objective based on individual fund performances using the (un)conditional pricing kernel models. The default premium (DEF) and the real yield on long-maturity government bond (REALG) are used as instrumental variables. Simultaneous GMM system estimation is conducted for each individual fund together with the three passive bond portfolios. All represents the equal- or the size-weighted averages of the performances of all of the individual funds. The Scotia Capital universe bond index is used as the benchmark variable. Size is defined as the total net asset value of the fund. Monthly data are used from March 1985 through February 2000, for a maximum of 180 observations per fund.

Fund Category	**Using equal-weighted averages over each of the funds in the respective fund category**		**Using size-weighted averages over each of the funds in the respective fund category**	
	α	*p*-val	α	*p*-val
Panel A: Unconditional pricing kernel				
Government	−0.1007	0.38	−0.0455	0.67
Corporate	−0.1080	0.23	−0.1153	0.11
Mortgage	−0.0236	0.74	−0.0058	0.93
High-yield	0.1237	0.48	0.1018	0.56
All	−0.0845	0.41	−0.0413	0.66
Panel B: Conditional pricing kernel with DEF as the instrument				
Government	−0.1067	0.66	−0.0252	0.89
Corporate	−0.0892	0.59	−0.1112	0.36
Mortgage	0.0783	0.63	0.0901	0.59
High-yield	0.2162	0.23	0.1936	0.29
All	−0.0654	0.76	−0.0048	0.98
Panel C: Conditional pricing kernel with DEF and REALG as the instruments				
Government	−0.0718	0.44	−0.0281	0.76
Corporate	−0.0853	0.28	−0.0914	0.15
Mortgage	−0.0247	0.67	−0.0306	0.57
High-yield	0.0883	0.50	0.0867	0.50
All	−0.0629	0.46	−0.0331	0.68

7.2 Evaluation of conditional performance

The conditional model is estimated using two specifications for the conditioning structure in order to assess the sensitivity of the performance measures to the conditional specification. The first specification considers only the default premium, while the second considers both the default premium and the real yield on long-maturity government bonds. To assess the validity of the conditional approach, Wald tests (Newey

Table 10.5. Summary statistics for the cross-sections of individual fund performance estimates based on the (un)conditional pricing kernel models.

This table presents summary statistics for the various cross-sections of individual fund performance measures based on the (un)conditional pricing kernel models for each fund category and for all funds. The two used instrumental variables are the lagged values of the default premium (DEF) and the real yield on long-maturity government bonds (REALG). Only the funds with at least 60 observations are considered. All of the p-values are adjusted for serial correlation and heteroskedasticity (Newey and West, 1987a). The number of funds in each group is given in Table 10.1. Information related to the funds with significant performances at the 5% level and with positive or negative significant performances is provided in this table. The Bonferroni p-values are the minimum and the maximum one-tailed p-values from the t-distribution across all funds and all fund groupings, multiplied by the defined number of funds.

Fund Group	**% funds $p < 5\%$**	**# funds $\alpha > 0$ & $p < 5\%$**	**# funds $\alpha < 0$ & $p < 5\%$**	**Bonferroni p**	
				Max.	**Min.**
Panel A: Unconditional pricing kernel					
Government	24.32	0	27	1.00	0.00
Corporate	37.50	0	9	1.00	0.00
Mortgage	3.13	0	1	1.00	0.00
High-yield	0.00	0	0	0.25	0.77
All	21.89	0	37	1.00	0.00
Panel B: Conditional pricing kernel with DEF as the instrumental variable					
Government	13.51	0	15	1.00	0.00
Corporate	25.00	0	6	1.00	0.00
Mortgage	6.25	1	1	0.77	0.01
High-yield	0.00	0	0	0.10	0.44
All	13.61	1	22	1.00	0.00
Panel C: Conditional pricing kernel with DEF and REALG as the instrumental variables					
Government	31.53	1	34	1.00	0.00
Corporate	25.00	0	6	1.00	0.00
Mortgage	9.38	0	3	1.00	0.00
High-yield	0.00	0	0	0.47	0.52
All	26.04	1	43	1.00	0.00

and West, 1987b) are conducted on the coefficients of the time-varying deltas.

7.2.1 Conditioning with the default premium only. When the conditional asset pricing kernel model with DEF as the only instrumental variable is used, the risk-adjusted performance remains negative and significant for the government, corporate and aggregate portfolios of funds. Only the high-yield portfolios display positive and significant alphas. These performance metrics show some improvement over the unconditional ones except for the mortgage portfolios and the size-weighted portfolio of all funds. To illustrate, the alphas of equal-weighted portfolios of government funds and all of the funds are −0.1141% and −0.0985% per month, respectively (see Panel B in Table 10.3). These statistics are significantly lower than those achieved with similar size-weighted portfolios, which preserves the unconditional based superior performance of larger funds over smaller ones. However, the magnitude of this differential in performance decreases with conditioning information. Overall, this realized negative performance is smaller than the average monthly management fees of 0.1205%, which implies weak positive performance pre-expenses. Moreover, the joint test on all four alphas in a GMM system for the two sets of portfolios is largely rejected for all the conditional benchmark models. These results are consistent with those obtained for Canadian and US equity funds by Kryzanowski et al. (1997) and Ferson and Schadt (1996), respectively. But they are inconsistent with the findings of Ayadi and Kryzanowski (2005, 2004) for Canadian equity and bond funds where the inclusion of conditioning information moves their performance statistics towards worse performance.[31]

The Wald tests conducted on the marginal contribution of the predetermined information variables in the conditional risky asset allocation specification are highly significant for all of the portfolios of funds. The Wald statistics also reject the hypothesis that the coefficient associated with the default premium in the time-varying delta structure is zero for all of the portfolios of funds.[32]

An analysis of the cross-sectional average performances of the individual funds reported in Table 10.4 preserves the inferences about the effect of conditioning (see Table 10.4). The simple average conditional alpha is still negative at −0.0654% but now is superior to the unconditional estimate of −0.0845%. The performance improvement is widely observed except for the mortgage group and the size-weighted average of all funds. This result could be caused by the relatively good but still negative conditional performance of some large government and corporate bond funds. Moreover, in contrast to the portfolio of funds-based evidence, the performance superiority of larger over smaller funds is enhanced with limited conditionings. When compared to the performance

[31] Ayadi and Kryzanowski (2005) find that the measured performance becomes negative with conditioning over the period 1989 – 1999 using a fully conditional and nonlinear asset pricing kernel framework. Christopherson et al. (1998) also find such deterioration in performance using a partial conditional CAPM and style index benchmarks for U.S. pension funds.

[32] Unreported results emit similar conclusions based on the individual fund performance tests. The hypothesis of no time-variation in the delta coefficient is rejected for over 81% of the funds at the 10% level of significance for the limited conditioning-based kernel model.

of portfolios of funds, these cross-sectional averages of conditional individual performances remain superior (except for the high-yield group and the size-weighted statistics of the corporate fund group). Furthermore, these differences are higher than the unconditional ones and are maximized with the size-weighted statistics.[33] This result could be explained by the increasing nonlinearity in the risk adjustment with the conditional pricing kernel.

The distributions of the p-values for the cross-sections of alpha estimates that are adjusted for serial correlation and heteroskedasticity are reported in Panel B of Table 10.5. The number of funds with positive (negative) and significant alphas is 1 (22), which reflects an improvement compared to 0 (37) positive (negative) and significant alphas using the unconditional specification. This last observation tends to support our previous argument that the poor performance of a certain number of funds is driving the weak average conditional performance. All of the Bonferroni p-values are significant for the minimum t-statistics except for those associated with high-yield funds. This rejects the joint hypothesis of zero conditional alphas.

Overall, the conditional alphas indicate that fund performance weakly improves, which implies that fund managers still underperform the market, once we control for conditional information effects. This confirms the conclusions of He et al. (1999); Dahlquist et al. (2000), and Ayadi and Kryzanowski (2004) for U.S., Swedish, and Canadian bond funds, respectively.

7.2.2 Conditioning with the default premium and real yield on LT government bonds. Based on the results reported in Panel C of Table 10.3, the performance values of the portfolios of funds remains negative with mixed changes in the point estimates when the information set is expanded to two instruments. For example, the alphas of the size-weighted portfolio of government and corporate funds and the two portfolios of high-yield funds deteriorate with increasing conditioning. The alpha for the equal-weighted portfolio of all funds is -0.0917% per month, which is significantly smaller than -0.0702% per month for its size-weighted counterpart. This performance superiority is also observed for the portfolios of government funds but is somewhat alleviated with extended conditioning. The Wald tests validate the conditional approach in that the Wald statistics reject the null hypothesis

[33] This result persists when the cross-sectional averages are compared to the performances of restricted portfolios including funds for which at least 60 monthly observations are used to compute the individual performance averages.

of no time-variation in the optimal allocation of risky assets for all portfolios except for the mortgage group.[34] Finally, the joint tests on the nullity of the alphas of the four portfolios conducted in a GMM system are largely rejected.

Based on Panel C of Table 10.4, the cross-sectional averages of the performances of the individual funds support the conclusions reached previously for the portfolios of funds. There are mixed changes in the performance estimates for the equal- and size-weighted statistics. The superior performance of larger over smaller funds is enhanced with the full conditional model. Moreover, the differences between the cross-sectional averages of the performances of individual funds and the performances of portfolios of funds are weakly sensitive to the extension of the information set.

Based on Panel C of Table 10.5, 43 funds have significant and negative alphas for the full conditional model to 37 and 22 funds using the unconditional and partial conditional estimations with one-instrument, respectively. The number of significant and positive alphas remains unchanged at one. These figures are essentially caused by the negative performance of the government funds. In addition, the Bonferroni conservative p-values are significant for the minimum extreme t-statistics for most cross-sections, which rejects the joint hypothesis of zero conditional alphas against the alternative that at least one alpha is negative.

The overall results indicate that fund managers experience greater difficulty in realizing excess returns when public information, such as the default premium and the real yield on long-maturity government bonds, are integrated into the construction of the asset pricing kernel and the performance measures. This finding are somewhat consistent with the conclusions of Ayadi and Kryzanowski (2004) and partially confirms the theoretical conclusions of Chen and Knez (1996) who advocate that performance results can change in either direction in the presence of conditioning information, due to the presence of an infinite number of admissible (un)conditional stochastic discount factors.

8. Conclusion

This chapter uses the general asset-pricing or SDF framework to derive an asset-pricing kernel that is relevant for evaluating the performance of actively managed portfolios. Our approach reflects the predictability of asset returns and accounts for conditioning information. Three per-

[34]Unreported results of the tests on individual funds indicate similar evidence where the hypothesis that all the coefficients in the time-varying delta are jointly zero is rejected (at the 10% level of significance) for more than 77% of all of the funds.

formance measures are constructed and are related to the unconditional evaluation of fixed-weight strategies, and unconditional and conditional evaluations of dynamic strategies. The appropriate empirical framework to estimate and implement the proposed performance measures and their associated tests using the GMM method is developed.

All of the estimations are conducted on a comprehensive sample of surviving and non-surviving Canadian fixed-income mutual funds. The results indicate that performance is negative and weakly improves with conditioning information. The unconditional-based superior performance of larger over smaller funds, which weakened with limited conditioning, is somewhat alleviated with an expansion of the conditioning set.

Our approach may be extended in various directions, such as using a *continuous* stochastic discount factor methodology adapted to the pricing of fixed-income securities, to examine potential relationships between the performance measures and some business cycle indicators to better determine if the performance of active portfolio management differs during periods of expansion and contraction, assessing the market timing behavior of bond fund mangers, and identifying the determinants of fund flows based on several fund characteristics. These alternative directions are left for future work.

Acknowledgements Financial support from Faculty of Business of Brock University, BUAF (Brock University Advancement Fund), Ned Goodman Chair in Investment Finance, CIRPÉE_FCAR (Fonds pour la formation des Chercheurs et l'Aide à la Recherche), IFM2 and SSHRC (Social Sciences and Humanities Research Council of Canada) are gratefully acknowledged.

References

Admati, A.R. and Ross, S.A. (1985). Measuring investment performance in a rational expectations equilibrium model. *Journal of Business*, 58:1 – 26.

Aît-Sahalia, Y. and Brandt, M.W. (2001). Variable selection and portfolio choice. *Journal of Finance*, 56:1297 – 1351.

Ayadi, M.A. and Kryzanowski, L. (2005). Portfolio performance measurement using APM-free kernels models. *Journal of Banking and Finance*, 29:623 – 659.

Ayadi, M.A. and Kryzanowski, L. (2004). *Performance of Canadian Fixed-Income Mutual Funds*. Working paper, Concordia University.

Balduzzi, P. and Robotti, C. (2001). *Minimum-Variance Kernels, Economic Risk Premia, and Tests of Multi-Beta Models.* Working paper, Boston College.

Bekaert, G. and Hodrick, R.J. (1992). Characterizing predictable components in excess returns on equity and foreign exchange markets. *Journal of Finance*, 47:467 – 509.

Bekaert, G. and Liu, J. (2004). Conditioning information and variance bounds on pricing kernels. *Review of Financial Studies*, 17:379 – 404.

Blake, C.R., Elton, E.J., and Gruber, M.J. (1993). The performance of bond mutual funds. *Journal of Business*, 66:371 – 403.

Brandt, M.W. (1999). Estimating portfolio and consumption choice: a conditional Euler equations approach. *Journal of Finance*, 54:1609 – 1645.

Brennan, M.J., Schwartz, E.S., and Lagnado, R. (1997). Strategic asset allocation. *Journal of Economic Dynamics and Control*, 21:1377 – 1403.

Campbell, J.Y. (1991). A variance decomposition for stock return. *The Economic Journal*, 101:157 – 179.

Campbell, J.Y. and Viceira, L.M. (1999). Consumption and portfolio decisions when expected returns are time-varying. *Quarterly Journal of Economics*, 114:433 – 495.

Carhart, M. (1997). On persistence in mutual fund performance. *Journal of Finance*, 52:57 – 82.

Carhart, M., Carpenter, J., Lynch, A.W., and Musto, D.K. (2002). Mutual fund survivorship. *Review of Financial Studies*, 15:1439 – 1463.

Chang, E. and Huang, R. (1990). Time-varying return and risk in the corporate bond market. *Journal of Financial and Quantitative Analysis*, 25:323 – 340.

Chen, Z. and Knez, P.J. (1996). Portfolio performance measurement: theory and applications. *Review of Financial Studies*, 9:511 – 555.

Christopherson, J.A., Ferson, W.E., and Glassman, D.A. (1998). Conditioning manager alphas on economic information: another look at the persistence of performance. *Review of Financial Studies*, 11:111 – 142.

Cochrane, J.H. (1996). A cross-sectional test of an investment-based asset pricing model. *Journal of Political Economy*, 104:572 – 621.

Cornell, B. and Green, K. (1991). The investment performance of low-grade bond funds. *Journal of Finance*, 46:29 – 48.

Cumby, R.E. and Glen, J.D. (1990). Evaluating the performance of international mutual funds. *Journal of Finance*, 45:497 – 521.

Dahlquist, M., Engtsrom, S., and Soderlind, P. (2000). Performance and characteristics of Swedish mutual funds. *Journal of Financial and Quantitative Analysis*, 35:409 – 423.

Dahlquist, M. and Soderlind, P. (1999). Evaluating portfolio performance with stochastic discount factors. *Journal of Business*, 72:347–384.

Detzler, M.E. (1999). The performance of global bond mutual funds. *Journal of Banking and Finance*, 23:1195–1217.

Dybvig, P.H. and Ross, S.A. (1985). Performance measurement using differential information and a security market line. *Journal of Finance*, 40:483–496.

Elton, E.J., Gruber, M.J., and Blake, C.R. (1995). Fundamental economic variables, expected returns, and bond fund performance. *Journal of Finance*, 50:1229–1256.

Elton, E.J., Gruber, M.J., and Blake, C.R. (1996). Survivorship bias and mutual fund performance. *Review of Financial Studies*, 9:1097–1120.

Fama, E.F. and French, K.R. (1988). Dividend yields and expected stock returns. *Journal of Financial Economics*, 22:3–25.

Fama, E.F. and French, K.R. (1989). Business conditions and expected returns on stocks and bonds. *Journal of Financial Economics*, 25:23–49.

Fama, E.F. and French, K.R. (1993). Common risk factors in the returns on stocks and bonds. *Journal of Financial Economics*, 33:3–56.

Farnsworth, H., Ferson, W.E., Jackson, D., and Todd, S. (2002). Performance evaluation with stochastic discount factors. *Journal of Business*, 75:473–503.

Ferson, W.E. and Foerster, S.R. (1994). Small sample properties of the GMM in tests of conditional asset pricing models. *Journal of Financial Economics*, 36:29–55.

Ferson, W.E. and Harvey, C.R. (1991). The variation of economic risk premia. *Journal of Political Economy*, 99:385–415.

Ferson, W.E., Kisgen, D., and Henry, T. (2004). *Evaluating Government Bond Fund Performance with Stochastic Discount Factors.* Working paper, Boston College.

Ferson, W.E., Sarkissian, S., and Simin, T. (2003). Is stock return predictability spurious. *Journal of Investment Management*, 1:1–10.

Ferson, W.E. and Schadt, R. (1996). Measuring fund strategy and performance in changing economic conditions. *Journal of Finance*, 51:425–461.

Ferson, W.E. and Siegel, A.F. (2001). The efficient use of conditioning information in portfolios. *Journal of Finance*, 56:967–982.

Gallant, A.R. and White, H. (1988). *A Unified Theory of Estimation and Inference for Nonlinear Dynamic Models.* Basil Blackwell, New York.

Glosten, L. and Jagannathan, R. (1994). A contingent claims approach to performance evaluation. *Journal of Empirical Finance*, 1:133 – 166.

Goldbaum, D. (1999). A nonparametric examination of market information: application to technical trading rules. *Journal of Empirical Finance*, 6:59 – 85.

Grinblatt, M. and Titman, S. (1989). Portfolio performance evaluation: old issues and new insights. *Review of Financial Studies*, 2:393 – 422.

Grinblatt, M. and Titman, S. (1993). Performance measurement without benchmarks: an examination of mutual fund returns. *Journal of Business*, 66:47 – 68.

Grinblatt, M. and Titman, S. (1994). A study of monthly mutual funds returns and performance evaluation techniques. *Journal of Financial and Quantitative Analysis*, 29:419 – 444.

Hansen, L.P. (1982). Large sample properties of generalized method of moments estimators. *Econometrica*, 50:1029 – 1054.

Hansen, L.P. and Jagannathan, R. (1991). Implications of security market data for models of dynamic economies. *Journal of Political Economy*, 99:225 – 262.

Hansen, L.P. and Richard, S.F. (1987). The role of conditioning information in deducing testable restrictions implied by dynamic asset pricing models. *Econometrica*, 55:587 – 613.

Hansen, L.P. and Singleton, K.J. (1982). Generalized instrumental variable estimation of nonlinear rational expectations models. *Econometrica*, 50:1269 – 1286.

Harrison, M. and Kreps, D. (1979). Martingales and arbitrage in multiperiod security markets. *Journal of Economic Theory*, 20:381 – 408.

Harvey, C.R., Solnik, B., and Zhou, G. (2002). What determine expected international returns? *Annals of Economics and Finance*, 3:249 – 298.

He, J., Ng, L., and Zhang, C. (1999). Asset pricing specification errors and performance evaluation. *European Finance Review*, 3:205 – 232.

Ilmanen, A. (1995) Time-varying expected returns in international bond markets. *Journal of Finance*, 50:481 – 506.

Jagannathan, R. and Wang, Z. (1996) The conditional CAPM and the cross-section of expected returns. *Journal of Finance*, 51:3 – 35.

Jensen, M.C. (1968). The performance of mutual funds in the period 1945 – 1964. *Journal of Finance*, 23:385 – 346.

Jensen, M.C. (1969). Risk, the pricing of assets and the evaluation of investment portfolios. *Journal of Business*, 50:549 – 572.

Kandel, S., and Stambaugh, R.F. (1996). On the predictability of stock returns: an asset allocation perspective. *Journal of Finance*, 51:385 – 424.

Kang, J. (1997). *The Numeraire Portfolio Approach to Bond Mutual Fund Performance Evaluation.* Working paper, University of Rochester.

Kirby, C. (1997). Measuring the predictable variation in stock and bond returns. *Review of Financial Studies*, 3:579 – 630.

Kryzanowski, L. and Lalancette, S. (1996). *Conditional Performance Evaluation of Portfolios with Linear and Nonlinear Payoffs.* Working paper, Concordia University.

Kryzanowski, L., Lalancette, S., and To, M.C. (1994). Performance attribution using a multivariate intertemporal asset pricing model with one state variable. *Canadian Journal of Administrative Sciences*, 11:75 – 85.

Kryzanowski, L., Lalancette, S., and To, M.C. (1997). Performance attribution using an APT with prespecified macrofactors and time-varying risk premia and betas. *Journal of Financial and Quantitative Analysis*, 32:205 – 224.

Kryzanowski, L., Lalancette, S., and To, M.C. (1998). Benchmark invariancy, seasonality, and APM-free portfolio performance measures. *Review of Quantitative Finance and Accounting*, 10:75 – 94.

Lee, S. (1994). *The Evaluation of Bond Mutual Fund Performance.* Working paper, University of New York at Buffalo.

Lehmann, B.N. and Modest, D.M. (1987). Mutual funds performance evaluation: a comparison of benchmarks and benchmarks comparisons. *Journal of Finance*, 42:233 – 265.

Long, J.B., Jr. (1990). The numeraire portfolio. *Journal of Financial Economics*, 26:29 – 69.

Luttmer, E.G.L. (1996). Asset pricing in economies with frictions. *Econometrica*, 64:1439 – 1467.

Merton, R.C. (1981). On market timing and investment performance I: an equilibrium theory of market forecasts. *Journal of Business*, 54:363 – 406.

Newey, W.K. (1993). Efficient estimation of models with conditional moment restriction. *Handbook of Statistics*, 11:419 – 445.

Newey, W.K. and West, K.D. (1987a). A simple positive semi-definite heteroskedasticity and autocorrelation consistent covariance matrix. *Econometrica*, 55:703 – 708.

Newey, W.K. and West, K.D. (1987b). Hypothesis testing with efficient method of moments estimation. *International Economic Review*, 28:777 – 787.

Priestley, M.B. (1981). *Spectral Analysis and Time Series.* Academic Press, New York.

Roll, R. (1978). Ambiguity when performance is measured by the security market line. *Journal of Finance*, 38:1051 – 1069.

Schwert, G.W. (1989). Why does stock market volatility change over time? *Journal of Finance*, 44:1115 – 1153.

Chapter 11

PORTFOLIO SELECTION WITH SKEWNESS

Phelim Boyle
Brian Ding

Abstract Konno et al. (1993) proposed a method for incorporating skewness into the portfolio optimization problem. This paper extends their technique and proposes a modification which leads to portfolios with improved characteristics. The model is then used to analyze the potential for put options to increase the skewness of portfolios. This strategy is tested with historical returns on a portfolio of TSE stocks. Compared to the Konno et al. (1993) approach our resulting portfolio has higher skewness and lower variance ; with expected return being equal.

1. Introduction

The traditional approach to portfolio selection is due to Markowitz (1952). He showed how to select optimal portfolios when the investor only cares about expected return and variance. The Markowitz approach can be readily formulated as a quadratic programming problem.

His analysis was confined to the first two moments of the return distributions of the securities analyzed. However, in recent years there has been a huge increase in the use of derivatives by portfolio managers and corporate investors. Many derivatives, specifically options, have one-sided return characteristics. The traditional Markowitz approach is incapable of handling this dimension of risk. Thus, in order to analyze the efficiency of these derivatives, it is not enough to rely on the first two moments of the return distribution. One of the advantages of options is that they can be used to increase the skewness of a portfolio. It is well known that investors prefer high skewness of the return distribution if other things are equal.

Konno et al. (1993) presented an algorithm which took skewness into account in the portfolio optimization problem. They formulated the problem as the maximization of skewness subject to a fixed expected return and fixed variance. Because the resulting problem is highly non-convex, they used a linear approximation for both the quadratic term and the cubic term. In our approach, we keep the quadratic term unchanged and only use a linear approximation for the cubic term. Thus we replace the problem with a simpler quadratic programming problem.

The underlying theory in use in these models is that of expected utility. Kahneman and Tversky (1979) presented a critique of expected utility theory. They formulated an alternative model called prospect theory. Levy and Levy (2004) have applied prospect theory results to portfolio theory where there is diversification between assets. Under certain conditions, they show that the prospect theory efficient set is a subset of the mean-variance efficiency frontier. Also, the prospect theory inefficient set is a small low variance, low mean subset of mean-variance efficiency frontier. The interested reader is referred to Levy and Levy (2004).

Sun and Yan (2003) have shown that optimally selected portfolios in the Japanese and US markets have shown persistence in their skewness characteristics. This further validates the idea that skewness is an important factor when forming optimal portfolios.

Portfolio selection methods which include moments higher than the first two have assumed greater importance because of the growth of hedge funds. Hedge fund returns tend to exhibit significant skewness and kurtosis. One approach to optimally select a portfolio including hedge funds is to devise a portfolio selection technique that uses more than just the first two moments. Davies et al. (2004) use polynomial goal programming to incorporate investor preferences for skewness and kurtosis.

The layout of this paper is as follows. In Section 2 we describe the Konno et al. (1993) approach. In Section 3 we describe our approach and explain how it can be implemented. In Section 4 we report some numerical results. These results are based on historical returns on a portfolio of TSE stocks. First we compare our method with the Konno et al. (1993) method and show that it generates improved results both in term of higher skewness and lower variance. Then we demonstrate how our method can be used to pick optimal portfolios when the available investments consist of common stocks and put options. The introduction of put options serves to reduce the variance and increase the skewness of the optimal portfolio. The algorithm selects which put options are optimal in a given situation.

2. The Konno, Shirakawa and Yamazaki approach

In this section, we review the mean-absolute deviation-skewness portfolio optimization model developed by Konno et al. (1993). The purpose of the model is to maximize the third moment while the variance and the expected return are fixed. Before presenting the model, we need some notation.

Let R_j be the random variable representing the rate of return of the asset S_j $(j = 1, \cdots, n)$, and let x_j be the proportion invested in S_j. The rate of return of the portfolio $x = (x_1, \cdots, x_n)$ is given by

$$R(x) = \sum_{j=1}^{n} R_j x_j. \tag{11.1}$$

Let

$$\begin{aligned} r_j &= E[R_j], \\ \sigma_{ij} &= E[(R_i - r_i)(R_j - r_j)], \\ \gamma_{ijk} &= E[(R_i - r_i)(R_j - r_j)(R_k - r_k)]. \end{aligned} \tag{11.2}$$

The original model suggested by Konno et al. (1993) is as follows:

$$\begin{aligned} \text{maximize} \quad & \sum_{i=1}^{n}\sum_{j=1}^{n}\sum_{k=1}^{n} \gamma_{ijk} x_i x_j x_k, \\ \text{subject to} \quad & \sum_{i=1}^{n}\sum_{j=1}^{n} \sigma_{ij} x_i x_j = \sigma^2, \\ & \sum_{j=1}^{n} r_j x_j = r, \\ & \sum_{j=1}^{n} x_j = 1, \;\; x_j \geq 0, j = 1, \cdots, n, \end{aligned} \tag{11.3}$$

where r and σ are input parameters.

Problem (11.3) is a nonconvex maximization problem. The global maximum cannot be calculated by current state of the art nonlinear programming algorithms. Therefore we require some kind of approximation to convert Problem (11.3) into a tractable problem. First, Problem (11.3) is transformed into the following problem

$$\begin{aligned}
\text{maximize} \quad & -E[| \sum_{j=1}^{n} R_j x_j - \rho_1 \; |_-] - \alpha E[| \sum_{j=1}^{n} R_j x_j - \rho_2 \; |_-], \\
\text{subject to} \quad & E[| \sum_{j=1}^{n} (R_j - r_j) x_j \; |] \leq w, \\
& \sum_{j=1}^{n} r_j x_j = r, \\
& \sum_{j=1}^{n} x_j = 1, \; j = 1, \cdots, n,
\end{aligned} \tag{11.4}$$

where α,w, ρ_1, ρ_2 are parameters with $\alpha, w > 0$ and $\rho_1, \rho_2 < 0$, and $| \cdot |_-$ is a function defined by

$$| v |_- = \begin{cases} 0, \text{ if } v \geq 0 \\ -v, \text{ if } v < 0. \end{cases}$$

The expressions

$$E[| \sum_{j=1}^{n} (R_j - r_j) x_j \; |] \leq w$$

and

$$-E[| \sum_{j=1}^{n} R_j x_j - \rho_1 \; |_-] - \alpha E[| \sum_{j=1}^{n} R_j x_j - \rho_2 \; |_-]$$

are used to approximate the quadratic constraint and the objective function in Problem (11.3), respectively. Let r_{ij} be the realization of S_j at time i ($i = 1, \cdots, m$; $j = 1, \cdots, n$), then we have

$$E[| \sum_{j=1}^{n} (R_j - r_j) x_j \; |] = \frac{1}{m} \sum_{i=1}^{m} | \sum_{j=1}^{n} (r_{ij} - r_j) x_j \; |,$$

$$E[| \sum_{j=1}^{n} R_j x_j - \rho_1 \; |_-] = \frac{1}{m} \sum_{i=1}^{m} | \sum_{j=1}^{n} (r_{ij} - r_j) x_j - \rho_1 \; |_-$$

and

$$E[| \sum_{j=1}^{n} R_j x_j - \rho_2 \; |_-] = \frac{1}{m} \sum_{i=1}^{m} | \sum_{j=1}^{n} (r_{ij} - r_j) x_j - \rho_2 \; |_-$$

Now, by introducing some new variables, it can be shown that Problem (11.4) is equivalent to

$$
\begin{aligned}
\text{minimize} \quad & \sum_{i=1}^{m} u_i + \alpha \sum_{i=1}^{m} v_i, \\
\text{subject to} \quad & u_i + \sum_{j=1}^{n} r_{ij} x_j \geq \rho_1, \; i = 1, \cdots, m, \\
& v_i + \sum_{j=1}^{n} r_{ij} x_j \geq \rho_2, \; i = 1, \cdots, m, \\
& \xi_i - \eta_i - \sum_{j=1}^{n} r_{ij} x_j = r, \; i = 1, \cdots, m, \\
& \sum_{j=1}^{n} r_j x_j = r, \\
& \sum_{i=1}^{m} (\xi_i + \eta_i) \leq w, \\
& \sum_{j=1}^{n} x_j = 1, \; x_j \geq 0, \; j = 1, \cdots, n, \\
& u_i \geq 0, v_i \geq 0, \xi_i \geq 0, \eta_i \geq 0, \\
& i = 1, \cdots, m
\end{aligned}
\tag{11.5}
$$

The problem depicted in (11.5) is called the mean-absolute deviation-skewness portfolio optimization model by Konno et al. (1993) and they claim that it can be used to generate portfolios with large skewness and low variance. We will investigate the efficiency of their algorithm using numerical tests in Section 4.

3. A new approach

In this section, we present our approach to compute a high third moment (or skewness) based on a given portfolio: the *base portfolio.* The base portfolio may be computed by either the mean-variance model or the model discussed in Section 2. As we have seen in Section 2, Konno et al. used linear approximations for the variance and the third moment in order to get a high third moment while keeping the variance in a reasonable range. The difference between our approach and the Konno et al. (1993) approach is that our approach only makes a linear approximation for the third moment and this linear approximation is based on the base portfolio. For different base portfolios the linear approximation can be different.

Since r_{ij} is the realization of R_j at time period i ($i = 1, \cdots, m$), we have the following realizations for each given portfolio $x \in R^n$

$$\sum_{j=1}^{n} r_{1j}x_j, \sum_{j=1}^{n} r_{2j}x_j, \cdots, \sum_{j=1}^{n} r_{mj}x_j.$$

Let r_x be the average return for this portfolio, then the third moment can be approximated as follows:

$$\frac{1}{m}\left[\Big(\sum_{j=1}^{n} r_{1j}x_j - r_x\Big)^3 + \cdots + \Big(\sum_{j=1}^{n} r_{mj}x_j - r_x\Big)^3\right] \tag{11.6}$$

Now since

$$\begin{aligned} r_x =& \frac{1}{m}\left[\sum_{j=1}^{n} r_{1j}x_j + \cdots + \sum_{j=1}^{n} r_{mj}x_j\right] \\ =& \frac{1}{m}\sum_{j=1}^{n}\Big(\sum_{i=1}^{m} r_{ij}\Big)x_j = \sum_{j=1}^{n} r_j x_j, \end{aligned}$$

Problem (11.6) can be written as

$$\frac{1}{m}\left[\Big(\sum_{j=1}^{n}(r_{1j} - r_j)x_j\Big)^3 + \cdots + \Big(\sum_{j=1}^{n}(r_{mj} - r_j)x_j\Big)^3\right].$$

Let

$$\hat{r}_{ij} = r_{ij} - r_j, \ i = 1, \cdots, m; \ j = 1, \cdots, n.$$

Then Problem (11.6) can be simplified to

$$\frac{1}{m}\left[\Big(\sum_{j=1}^{n}\hat{r}_{1j}x_j\Big)^3 + \cdots + \Big(\sum_{j=1}^{n}\hat{r}_{mj}x_j\Big)^3\right]. \tag{11.7}$$

Now, let us consider how to approximate Problem (11.7) locally. In doing so, let us consider the cubic function t^3, where t is a real number. For a fixed point t_0, if $\epsilon > 0$ is a small number, then t^3 on $[t_0 - \epsilon, t_0 + \epsilon]$ can be approximated by the following linear function

$$(t_0 - \epsilon)^3 + [(t_0 + \epsilon)^2 + t_0^2 - \epsilon^2 + (t_0 - \epsilon)^2](t - t_0 + \epsilon).$$

Now, suppose that we have a base portfolio x^*. The idea is to obtain a new portfolio x "close to x^*" such that the new portfolio will have a high third moment (or skewness) with a reasonably low variance. We proceed as follows. Let

$$\alpha_i = \sum_{j=1}^{n} \hat{r}_{ij} x_j^*, \; i = 1, \cdots, m$$

and let $\epsilon > 0$ be a small number, then

$$\Big(\sum_{j=1}^{n} \hat{r}_{1j} x_j\Big)^3 + \cdots + \Big(\sum_{j=1}^{n} \hat{r}_{mj} x_j\Big)^3 \tag{11.8}$$

can be approximated by

$$\sum_{i=1}^{m} \bigg((\alpha_i - \epsilon)^3 + \Big((\alpha_i + \epsilon)^2 + \alpha_i^2 - \epsilon^2 + (\alpha_i - \epsilon)^2 \Big) \Big(\sum_{j=1}^{n} \hat{r}_{ij} x_j - \alpha_i + \epsilon \Big) \bigg) \tag{11.9}$$

when x satisfies the following inequalities:

$$\alpha_i - \epsilon \leq \sum_{j=1}^{n} \hat{r}_{ij} x_j \leq \alpha_i + \epsilon, \; i = 1, \cdots, m. \tag{11.10}$$

Therefore, if x satisfies Problem (11.10), we can maximize Equation (11.8) by maximizing (ignore all constant terms in Problem (11.9))

$$\sum_{i=1}^{m} \Big((\alpha_i + \epsilon)^2 + \alpha_i^2 - \epsilon^2 + (\alpha_i - \epsilon)^2 \Big) \Big(\sum_{j=1}^{n} \hat{r}_{ij} x_j \Big)$$

$$= \sum_{j=1}^{n} \bigg(\sum_{i=1}^{m} \Big((\alpha_i + \epsilon)^2 + \alpha_i^2 - \epsilon^2 + (\alpha_i - \epsilon)^2 \Big) \hat{r}_{ij} \bigg) x_j = \sum_{j=1}^{n} c_j x_j,$$

where

$$c_j = \bigg(\sum_{i=1}^{m} \Big((\alpha_i + \epsilon)^2 + \alpha_i^2 - \epsilon^2 + (\alpha_i - \epsilon)^2 \Big) \hat{r}_{ij} \bigg), \; j = 1, \cdots, n.$$

Let

$$\beta = \sum_{j=1}^{n} c_j x_j^*$$

and r be the fixed return which we hope to achieve. Then we can formulate the following problem

$$\begin{aligned}
\text{minimize} \quad & \sum_{k=1}^{n}\sum_{j=1}^{n}\sigma_{kj}x_k x_j, \\
\text{subject to} \quad & x_1 + \cdots + x_n = 1, \\
& r_1 x_1 + \cdots + r_n x_n = r, \\
& \alpha_i - \epsilon \le \sum_{j=1}^{n}\hat{r}_{ij}x_j \le \alpha_i + \epsilon, \; i = 1, \cdots, m, \\
& \sum_{j=1}^{n} c_j x_j \ge \beta + \delta, \\
& x_j \ge 0, \; j = 1, \cdots, n,
\end{aligned} \tag{11.11}$$

where δ is a small positive number or zero.

We will now explain in intuitive terms why Problem (11.11) can be used to get a high third moment (or skewness) and a relatively lower variance from a base portfolio and how Problem (11.11) can be implemented in a repeated fashion

From Problems (11.8)-(11.10) and the definition of c_j, we know that $\sum_{j=1}^{n} c_j x_j$ is increasing if and only if the third moment is increasing provided x satisfies Problem (11.10). So, if Problem (11.11) is feasible for some $\delta > 0$, then the third moment can be increased by a certain amount for any feasible solution. Therefore an optimal solution of Problem (11.11) will increase the third moment by a certain amount and keep the variance as low as possible. Now, suppose x^1 is an optimal solution of Problem (11.11) and we are still not satisfied with this portfolio, then we can replace x^* by x^1 and compute α_j, c_j and β. From these new α_j, c_j and β, a new version of Problem (11.11) can be formulated and an optimal solution x^2 can be obtained. Assume that this process has been repeated k times and from the kth portfolio x^k, a new version of Problem (11.11) is formulated. If this new version of Problem (11.11) is feasible only for a very small number δ, then we should stop the process as the third moment can hardly be improved further. Also we can restrict the increase in the variance with respect to the original portfolio or iterations of the process. For example, we may stop the process when the variance is increased by say 20 or 40 percent.

From the above discussion, we know that the third moment will always be increased when Problem (11.11) is implemented, but we don't know if the variance will be increased or not. In fact, both situations can happen. So, if Problem (11.11) is implemented and the variance is decreasing, then the new portfolio will give a high skewness. Of course, it is possible to get an increase in skewness even if the variance is increasing. In fact, when Problem (11.11) is repeated, we can monitor the skewness at each step. Therefore, if we are only interested in high skewness, we can select the portfolio with the highest skewness after we apply Problem (11.11) several times.

Before concluding this section, we show that Problem (11.11) can be simplified under certain conditions. In doing so, we assume that the base portfolio x^* is available and its variance is small (say, less than 0.1). Based on this portfolio, if δ is small and we use Problem (11.11) to get a new portfolio, then the variance of the new portfolio will also be small. This implies that the inequalities in Problem (11.10) or most of them will be satisfied by the new portfolio. So, we may ignore the inequality constraints in Problem (11.10), that is, solve the following problem

$$\begin{aligned} \text{minimize} \quad & \sum_{k=1}^{n}\sum_{j=1}^{n} \sigma_{kj} x_k x_j, \\ \text{subject to} \quad & x_1 + \cdots + x_n = 1, \\ & r_1 x_1 + \cdots + r_n x_n = r, \\ & \sum_{j=1}^{n} c_j x_j \geq \beta + \delta, \\ & x_j \geq 0, \; j = 1, \cdots, n, \end{aligned} \tag{11.12}$$

Obviously, Problem (11.12) is much simpler than (11.11), especially when m is large.

4. Numerical results

In this section, we report the results of the numerical experiments using the historical data from the Toronto Stock Exchange. We use five years monthly data with portfolios ranging from 90 to 180 stocks over the period 1990 to 1994. We are interested in comparing the numerical solutions of our approach and the approach developed by Konno et al. (1993) to see if they generate solutions with large skewness.

First we implement the Konno et al. (1993) algorithm. The parameters of Problem (11.5) are chosen as follows: $(\alpha, \rho_1, \rho_2) = (1.0, r - 1.0, r - 2.0)$. Readers may refer to Konno et al. (1993) for details. When r is given, w is chosen as the smallest value such that Problem (11.5) is feasible. The parameters of Problem (11.11) are chosen as follows: $(\epsilon, \delta) = (0.2, 0.0003)$. We will implement Problem (11.11) based on the portfolio computed using the mean-variance model and Problem (11.5), respectively. The portfolios in Table 11.1, 11.2, 11.3 and 11.4 are computed from a universe of 90 stocks.

In Tables 11.1 and 11.2, the given expected return 0.006676 corresponds to the equally weighted portfolio of the 90 stocks. In Table 11.1, our approach is implemented based on the mean-variance portfolio and the process is repeated six times. Compared to the mean-variance portfolio, our approach gives a larger skewness, but the variance also increases. In Table 11.2, our approach is implemented based on the Konno et al. (1993) portfolio and the procedure is repeated four times. Compared to the Konno et al. (1993) portfolio, our approach not only gives a larger third moment and skewness, but also gives a lower variance.

In Tables 11.3 and 11.4, we choose an expected return which is double the previous one. The numerical solutions are quite similar to those in Tables 11.1 and 11.2, that is, our approach generates a portfolio with a larger third moment, (larger skewness) and a relatively lower variance. For a fixed return, if we are only interested in generating portfolios with larger skewness and lower variance, then Tables 11.1 to 11.4 tell us that starting from the mean-variance portfolio or the Konno et al. (1993) portfolio will generate virtually the same portfolio (i.e., the proportions in each stock are almost the same).

We also implemented Problem (11.12) on the same set of data, and obtained identical solutions.

We now consider how the algorithm works in the presence of put options. We used the empirical distribution of returns to generate a sequence of put option returns in the case of each stock. For each stock we computed the volatility of the stock over the 5 year period. At the start of each month we computed the current price of the one-month, at-the-money put option using our estimate of the volatility. Because the put option is at the money we can use the following estimate of its Black Scholes price[1]

$$\text{Put price} = \frac{S\sigma\sqrt{T}}{\sqrt{2\pi}},$$

where S is the current stock price, σ is the volatility p.a. and $T = 1/12$, the time to expiration. Because we are only interested in the return on the option we can normalize the stock price to one unit at the start of each month. To find the return on the option we compute the stock value at the end of each month from the actual historical distribution,

[1] For details see Boyle and Ananthananarayanan (1979).

Table 11.1. Comparison of Stock Portfolios Generated by the Mean Variance Approach and Our Method

	Mean Variance Approach	*Our Approach*
Return	0.006676	0.006676
Variance	0.000363	0.000639
Third moment	-0.000003	0.000032
Skewness	-0.428784	2.012495
Number of iterations	not applicable	6

Table 11.2. Comparison of Stock Portfolios Generated by the Konno et al. (1993) Approach and Our Method

	Konno et al. (1993) Approach	*Our Approach*
Return	0.006676	0.006676
Variance	0.000714	0.000642
Third moment	0.000009	0.000033
Skewness	0.462865	2.006694
Number of iterations	not applicable	4

i.e. we multiply the initial stock price (one unit) by the one plus realized rate of return on the stock over the following month.
We compare this with the strike price to see if the option is in the money or not. From this information we can get the one month return on the put option. By using the one month in the money options we minimize

Table 11.3. Comparison of Stock Portfolios Generated by the Mean Variance Approach and Our Method

	Mean Variance Approach	*Our Approach*
Return	0.013352	0.013352
Variance	0.000510	0.000862
Third moment	-0.00003	0.000052
Skewness	-0.286527	2.051597
The number of iterations	not applicable	10

Table 11.4. Comparison of Stock Portfolios Generated by the Konno et al. (1993) Approach and Our Method

	Konno et al. (1993) Approach	*Our Approach*
Return	0.013352	0.013352
Variance	0.000877	0.000866
Third moment	0.00000003	0.000053
Skewness	-0.001178	2.067632
The number of iterations	not applicable	10

option pricing errors. In this way we obtain a sequence of 60 put option returns in respect to each stock. These put options are then considered as new assets. We rerun the optimization algorithm with these put options included in the universe. Table 11.5 and Table 11.6 give the results when the put options are included. Notice that in Table 11.5, the variance is

Table 11.5. Comparison of Portfolios of Stocks and Put Options Generated by the Mean Variance Approach and Our Method

	Mean Variance Approach	*Our Approach*
Return	0.014	0.014
Variance	3.743538×10^{-8}	0.000357
Third moment	2.206382×10^{-12}	0.00005
Skewness	0.304613	7.443167
Number of iterations	not applicable	3

Table 11.6. Comparison of Portfolios of Stocks and Put Options Generated by the Konno et al. (1993) Approach and Our Method

	Konno et al. (1993) Approach	*Our Approach*
Return	0.014	0.014
Variance	0.001857	0.000998
Third moment	0.000137	0.000202
Skewness	1.710552	6.405756
Number of iterations	not applicable	5

virtually zero for the mean variance portfolio, while our new approach generates a portfolio with a higher variance and much higher skewness.

5. Conclusion

In this paper we proposed a new algorithm for determining optimal portfolios when the investor cares about skewness as well as expected return and variance. We implemented this algorithm using empirical data and showed it is preferable to existing methods. This approach should be of interest to portfolio managers who want to select optimal portfolios which include options. Managers of pension funds and mutual funds are increasing their usage of derivative instruments. Many of the traditional tools used for portfolio optimization are not well suited to deal with portfolios that include derivatives. This paper provides a practical method to select optimal portfolios by maximizing the expected return and skewness while minimizing the variance.

Acknowledgments The authors wish to thank Ali Jina for diligent research assistance. Phelim Boyle acknowledges research support from the Natural Sciences and Engineering Council of Canada.

References

Boyle, Phelim P. and Ananthananarayanan, A.L. (1979). The impact of variance estimation in option valuation models. *Journal of Financial Economics*, 6:375–388.

Davies, R. J., Kat H. M., and Lu, S. (2004). Fund of Hedge Fund Portfolio Selection: A Multiple Objective Approach. Working paper, Cass Business School, City University, London UK

Kahneman, D. and Tversky A. (1979). Prospect theory: an analysis of decision under risk. *Econometrica*, 47:263–292.

Konno, H., Shirakawa, H., and Yamazaki, H. (1993). A mean-absolute deviation-skewness portfolio optimization model. *Annals of Operations Research*, 45:205–220.

Lee, P.J. (1992). Portfolio selection in the presence of options and the distribution of return of portfolios containing options. *3rd AFIR International Colloquium*, 2:691–709.

Markowitz, H. (1952). Portfolio selection. *Journal of Finance*, 7:77-91.

Levy, H. and Levy, M. (2004). Prospect theory and mean-variance analysis. *Review of Financial Studies*, 17:1015–1041.

Sun, Q. and Yan, Y. (2003). Skewness persistence with optimal portfolio selection. *Journal of Banking and Finance*, 27:1111–1121.

Chapter 12

CONTINUOUS MIN-MAX APPROACH FOR SINGLE PERIOD PORTFOLIO SELECTION PROBLEM

Nalan Gülpınar
Berç Rustem

Abstract In this chapter, we introduce continuous min-max approach for single period portfolio selection problem. The min-max optimization is performed over various single-period scenarios of risk and a return range, relative to benchmark. The optimal investment strategy is obtained using robust worst-case analysis. This evaluates the portfolio corresponding to the best performance, simultaneously with the worst-case. Therefore, the resulting strategy is robust in that it has the best lower bound performance which can only improve if any scenario, other than the worst-case, is realized.

1. Introduction

In financial portfolio management, the maximization of return for a level of risk is the accepted approach to decision making. A classical example is the single-period mean-variance optimization model in which expected portfolio return is maximized and risk measured by the variance of portfolio return is minimized Markowitz (1952). The mean-variance framework is based on a single forecast of return and risk. In reality, however, it is often difficult or impossible to rely on a single forecast. There are different rival risk and return estimates, or scenarios.

The inaccuracy in forecasting can be addressed through the specification of rival scenarios. These are used with forecast pooling using stochastic programming; for example see Kall (1994); Lawrence, Edmunson and O'Connor (1986); Makridakis and Winkler (1983). Robust pooling using min-max has been introduced by Rustem, Becker and Marty (2000) and Rustem and Howe (2002). A min-max algorithm for stochastic programs based on bundle method is discussed by Breton and Hachem (1995). This is closer to the multi-stage model in Gülpınar and Rustem (2004) where a discrete min-max model is considered.

Min-max optimization is more robust to the realization of worst-case scenarios than considering a single scenario or an arbitrary pooling of scenarios. It is suitable for situations which need protection against risk of adopting the investment strategy based on the wrong scenario. There are two min-max models; discrete and continuous. The discrete min-max approach determines the optimal investment strategy in view of all specified discrete rival scenarios simultaneously, rather than any single scenario. Its disadvantage is that it requires the specification of a number of discrete scenarios. An alternative approach that addresses the specification of the return forecast in terms of a range given by upper and lower bounds is the continuous min-max. The continuous min-max strategy provides a guaranteed optimal performance in view of continuum of scenarios varying between upper and lower bounds. Thus, there are an infinite number of future scenarios in the continuous min-max framework.

In this chapter, we present a continuous min-max model for robust portfolio optimization based on worst-case analysis. The classical Markowitz framework is extended to the continuous min-max with upper and lower bounds on the return scenarios and various rival risk scenarios. The min-max model integrates benchmark relative computations in view of scalable (not fixed) transaction costs. Robustness arises from the non-inferiority of the worst-case optimal (min-max) strategy. We use the model for investment problems and evaluate the ex-ante performance of the strategy.

The rest of the chapter is organized as follows. In Section 2, we describe the mean-variance optimization model. The discrete and continuous min-max models are introduced in Section 3. The computational results are presented in Section 4.

Notation

A full description of our notation is given in Table 12.1. All quantities in boldface represent vectors in $\mathbb{R}^n$ unless otherwise noted. The transpose of a vector or matrix is denoted with the symbol $'$.

2. Single period mean-variance optimization

The single period mean-variance optimization model considers a portfolio of n assets defined in terms of a set of weights w_i for $i = 1, \ldots, n$,

Table 12.1. Notation

T	planning horizon
n	number of investment assets.
$\mathbf{r}$	vector of return values for the n assets.
$\mathbf{w}$	decision vector indicating asset balances.
$\overline{\mathbf{w}}$	market benchmark.
$\Lambda_i \in \mathbb{R}^{n \times n}$	covariance matrices associated with return values, for $i = 1, \ldots, I$
$\mathbf{p}$	current portfolio position.
$\mathbf{c_b}$	vector of unit transaction costs for buying.
$\mathbf{c_s}$	vector of unit transaction costs for selling.
$\mathbf{b}$	decision vector of "buy" transaction volumes.
$\mathbf{s}$	decision vector of "sell" transaction volumes.
$\mathbf{e}$	$\equiv (1, 1, 1, \ldots, 1)'$
α, δ	risk aversion parameters
μ	worst-case return
ν	worst-case risk
H	Hessian matrix

which sum to unity. In other words, the initial budget is normalized to 1.

$$\mathbf{e}'\mathbf{w} = 1 \tag{12.1}$$

If the investor currently has holdings of assets $1, \ldots, n$, then vector $\mathbf{p}$ (scaled so that $\mathbf{e}'\mathbf{p} = 1$) represents his current position. If the investor currently has no holdings (wishing to buy), then $\mathbf{p} = \mathbf{0}$. The allocation of the initial budget of 1 can be represented with the following constraints:

$$\mathbf{p} + \mathbf{b} - \mathbf{s} = \mathbf{w} \tag{12.2}$$

Let τ represent the transaction costs incurred by moving to strategy $\mathbf{w}$ from current position $\mathbf{p}$, subject to costs $\mathbf{c_b}$, $\mathbf{c_s}$. The transaction cost of the purchase or sale is formulated as

$$\mathbf{c_b}'\mathbf{b} + \mathbf{c_s}'\mathbf{s} = \tau \tag{12.3}$$

The expected portfolio return $E[R_p]$ on an investment is formulated as $E[R_p] = (\mathbf{w} - \overline{\mathbf{w}})'\mathbf{r}$. Risk is measured as the variance of the portfolio return relative to the benchmark $\overline{\mathbf{w}}$ and formulated as $(\mathbf{w}-\overline{\mathbf{w}})'\Lambda_i(\mathbf{w}-\overline{\mathbf{w}})$.

Buy and sell variables for any asset cannot be both nonzero— otherwise, more money is spent on transaction costs than is necessary. In linear programming formulations using the simplex algorithm, this is inherently assured. In the mean-variance framework, requiring quadratic programming solutions, however, it has been observed that common buy and sell variables are often found to be simultaneously and significantly different from zero. This seems to arise from numerical instabilities as well as from the requirement for minimizing risk. In order to solve this problem, we penalize the quantity $\mathbf{b}_i \cdot \mathbf{s}_i$, $\mathbf{b}_i, \mathbf{s}_i \geq 0\ \forall i$, with $\gamma > 0$. Therefore, the single period mean-variance optimization problem can be formulated as the following quadratic programming problem

$$\begin{aligned}
&\min \alpha(\mathbf{w} - \overline{\mathbf{w}})'\Lambda(\mathbf{w} - \overline{\mathbf{w}}) - \left[(\mathbf{w} - \overline{\mathbf{w}})'\mathbf{r} - \tau\right] + \gamma\, \mathbf{b}'\mathbf{s} \\
&\text{s.t.} \\
&\mathbf{e}'\mathbf{w} = 1 \\
&\mathbf{p} + \mathbf{b} - \mathbf{s} = \mathbf{w} \\
&\mathbf{c}_\mathbf{b}'\mathbf{b} + \mathbf{c}_\mathbf{s}'\mathbf{s} = \tau \\
&\mathbf{w}, \mathbf{b}, \mathbf{s} \geq \mathbf{0}
\end{aligned}$$

where the scaling constant α determines the level of risk-aversion optimized for. By sliding from $\alpha = 0$ (total risk-seeking) to $\alpha = \infty$ (total risk aversion), the entire range of efficient investment strategies is obtained.

3. Min-max optimization model for robust decisions

In this section, we summarize the discrete single period min-max problem discussed in Rustem, Becker and Marty (2000) and Rustem and Settergren (2002) and consider the corresponding continuous min-max model.

3.1 Discrete min-max

Let J and I be the total number of rival return and risk scenarios, respectively. Let K denote the number of benchmarks provided. A compact representation of the discrete min-max optimization problem is as follows;

$$\min_{\mathbf{e}'\mathbf{w}=1, \mathbf{w}\geq 0} \{\alpha \cdot \max_{i,k}\{(\mathbf{w} - \overline{\mathbf{w}}_k)'\Lambda_i(\mathbf{w} - \overline{\mathbf{w}}_k)\} - \min_{j,k}\{(\mathbf{w} - \overline{\mathbf{w}}_k)'\mathbf{r}_j - t(\mathbf{w})\}\} \quad (12.4)$$

where $i = 1, \ldots, I$, $j = 1, \ldots, J$ and $k = 1, \ldots, K$. Function $t(\mathbf{w})$ represents the transaction costs incurred by moving to strategy $\mathbf{w}$ from current position $\mathbf{p}$, subject to costs $\mathbf{c}_\mathbf{b}$, $\mathbf{c}_\mathbf{s}$.

In order to solve (12.4) we reformulate it as a quadratically constrained mathematical program:

$$\min \ \alpha\nu - \mu + \gamma\ \mathbf{b}'\mathbf{s}$$

s.t.

$$\begin{aligned} \mathbf{e}'\mathbf{w} &= 1 \\ \mathbf{p} + \mathbf{b} - \mathbf{s} &= \mathbf{w} \\ \mathbf{c}_{\mathbf{b}}'\mathbf{b} + \mathbf{c}_{\mathbf{s}}'\mathbf{s} &= \tau \\ (\mathbf{w} - \overline{\mathbf{w}}_k)'\Lambda_i(\mathbf{w} - \overline{\mathbf{w}}_k) &\le \nu, \qquad i = 1\ldots, I,\ k = 1\ldots, K \\ (\mathbf{w} - \overline{\mathbf{w}}_k)'\mathbf{r}_j - \tau &\ge \mu, \qquad j = 1\ldots, J,\ k = 1\ldots, K \\ \mathbf{w}, \mathbf{b}, \mathbf{s} &\ge \mathbf{0} \end{aligned} \tag{12.5}$$

This yields a total of IK quadratic constraints, $JK + n + 2$ linear constraints, and non-negativity. If $I = 0$ (no risk scenarios provided), then quadratic constraints are omitted and the objective function becomes $\min_{\mathbf{w}} -\mu \equiv \max_{\mathbf{w}} \mu$, which is a purely linear problem. If $J = 0$ (no return scenarios provided), then linear performance constraints are omitted and the objective function becomes simply $\min_{\mathbf{w}} \nu$. If information pertaining to transaction costs is omitted, then the second and third constraints and the variables $\tau, \mathbf{b}, \mathbf{s}$ can be removed. If $K = 1$, then only one benchmark portfolio is considered.

Robustness of discrete worst-case optimization

The robustness of min-max is a basic property arising from the optimality condition of min-max which, in the case of (12.4), is written as

$$\begin{aligned} \Phi(\mathbf{w}_*) \equiv & \min_{\mathbf{e}'\mathbf{w}=1,\mathbf{w}\ge 0} \left\{ \alpha \cdot \max_{i,k}\{(\mathbf{w} - \overline{\mathbf{w}}_k)'\Lambda_i(\mathbf{w} - \overline{\mathbf{w}}_k)\} \right\} \\ & - \min_{\mathbf{e}'\mathbf{w}=1,\mathbf{w}\ge 0} \left\{ \min_{j,k}\{(\mathbf{w} - \overline{\mathbf{w}}_k)'\mathbf{r}_j - t(\mathbf{w})\} \right\} \\ = & \ \alpha \cdot \max_{i,k}\{(\mathbf{w}_* - \overline{\mathbf{w}}_k)'\Lambda_i(\mathbf{w}_* - \overline{\mathbf{w}}_k)\} - \min_{j,k}\{(\mathbf{w}_* - \overline{\mathbf{w}}_k)'\mathbf{r}_j - t(\mathbf{w}_*)\} \\ \ge & \ \alpha \cdot \{(\mathbf{w}_* - \overline{\mathbf{w}}_k)'\Lambda_i(\mathbf{w}_* - \overline{\mathbf{w}}_k)\} - \{(\mathbf{w}_* - \overline{\mathbf{w}}_k)'\mathbf{r}_j - t(\mathbf{w}_*)\}, \forall i, j, k \end{aligned}$$

(see e.g. Rustem and Howe (2002); Demyanov and Malozemov (1974)). Inequality indicates the non-inferiority of the min-max strategy. This means that expected performance is *guaranteed* to be at the level corresponding to the worst case and will *improve* if any scenario other than the worst case is realized.

3.2 Continuous min-max

Assume that the return forecast of assets is defined by the bounds $\mathbf{r}^l \leq \mathbf{r} \leq \mathbf{r}^u$. In view of I rival risk scenarios and a range of return forecasts, the mean-variance optimization problem can be formulated as the following max-min problem

$$\max_{\mathbf{e}'\mathbf{w}=1,\mathbf{w}\geq 0} \left\{ \min_{\mathbf{r}^l\leq\mathbf{r}\leq\mathbf{r}^u} \{(\mathbf{w}-\overline{\mathbf{w}})'\mathbf{r}+\tau\} - \alpha \cdot \min_i \{(\mathbf{w}-\overline{\mathbf{w}})'\Lambda_i(\mathbf{w}-\overline{\mathbf{w}})\} \right\}$$

This can also be formulated as a min-max optimization problem;

$$\min_{\mathbf{e}'\mathbf{w}=1,\mathbf{w}\geq 0} \left\{ \max_{\mathbf{r}^l\leq\mathbf{r}\leq\mathbf{r}^u} -\{(\mathbf{w}-\overline{\mathbf{w}})'\mathbf{r}-\tau\} + \alpha \cdot \max_i \{(\mathbf{w}-\overline{\mathbf{w}})'\Lambda_i(\mathbf{w}-\overline{\mathbf{w}})\} \right\} \tag{12.6}$$

where τ represents the transaction costs. We define

$$\mathbf{x}^+ - \mathbf{x}^- = \mathbf{w} - \overline{\mathbf{w}}$$

so that $\mathbf{x}^+, \mathbf{x}^- \geq 0$ and $\mathbf{x}^+ \cdot \mathbf{x}^- = 0$. Notice that if $\mathbf{w} > \overline{\mathbf{w}}$, then $\mathbf{x}^+ > 0$ and $\mathbf{x}^- = 0$; if $\mathbf{w} < \overline{\mathbf{w}}$, then $\mathbf{x}^+ = 0$ and $\mathbf{x}^- > 0$. Since the expected return of portfolio is a linear function of $\mathbf{r}$, there are worst-case scenarios which are at the lower and the upper bounds of given range: either $x_i^+ r_i^l$ or $x_i^- r_i^u$ is realized. Thus, the min-max problem (12.6) becomes

$$\min_{\mathbf{x}^+,\mathbf{x}^-} \left\{ -\{(\mathbf{x}^-)'\mathbf{r}^u + (\mathbf{x}^+)'\mathbf{r}^l - \tau\} + \alpha \cdot \max_i \{(\mathbf{x}^+-\mathbf{x}^-)'\Lambda_i(\mathbf{x}^+-\mathbf{x}^-)\} \right\}.$$

This is equivalent to the following quadratically constrained mathematical program whose optimal solution provides the worst-case investment strategy.

$$\begin{aligned}
&\min_{\mathbf{x}^+,\mathbf{x}^-} \quad -\{(\mathbf{x}^-)'\mathbf{r}^u + (\mathbf{x}^+)'\mathbf{r}^l - \tau\} + \alpha\nu + \gamma\mathbf{b}'\mathbf{s} + \beta(\mathbf{x}^+)'\mathbf{x}^- \\
&s.t. \\
&\mathbf{e}'\mathbf{w} = 1 \\
&\mathbf{p} + \mathbf{b} - \mathbf{s} = \mathbf{w} \\
&\mathbf{c}_{\mathbf{b}}'\mathbf{b} + \mathbf{c}_{\mathbf{s}}'\mathbf{s} = \tau \\
&\mathbf{x}^+ - \mathbf{x}^- = \mathbf{w} - \overline{\mathbf{w}} \\
&(\mathbf{w}-\overline{\mathbf{w}})'\Lambda_i(\mathbf{w}-\overline{\mathbf{w}}) \leq \nu \qquad i = 1, \ldots, I \\
&\mathbf{w}, \mathbf{b}, \mathbf{s}, \mathbf{x}^+, \mathbf{x}^- \geq \mathbf{0}
\end{aligned} \tag{12.7}$$

where γ and β are penalty terms. The min-max model in (12.7) is numerically unstable with respect to α. An alternative formulation below is somewhat cumbersome but equivalent and numerically stable. Let $\bar{r}$ denote the worst-case portfolio return. Given a required level of expected portfolio return, $\bar{r}$, a min-max optimal portfolio is one that solves the following

(WC_R)

$$\min_{\mathbf{x}^+,\mathbf{x}^-} \; \nu + \gamma \mathbf{b}'\mathbf{s} + \beta(\mathbf{x}^+)'\mathbf{x}^-$$

$s.t.$

$$\mathbf{e}'\mathbf{w} = 1 \tag{12.8}$$

$$\mathbf{p} + \mathbf{b} - \mathbf{s} = \mathbf{w} \tag{12.9}$$

$$\mathbf{c}_\mathbf{b}'\mathbf{b} + \mathbf{c}_\mathbf{s}'\mathbf{s} = \tau \tag{12.10}$$

$$\mathbf{x}^+ - \mathbf{x}^- = \mathbf{w} - \overline{\mathbf{w}} \tag{12.11}$$

$$\mathbf{w}, \mathbf{b}, \mathbf{s}, \mathbf{x}^+, \mathbf{x}^- \geq \mathbf{0} \tag{12.12}$$

$$(\mathbf{x}^-)'\mathbf{r}^u + (\mathbf{x}^+)'\mathbf{r}^l - \tau \geq \bar{r}$$

$$(\mathbf{w} - \overline{\mathbf{w}})'\Lambda_i(\mathbf{w} - \overline{\mathbf{w}}) \leq \nu \qquad i = 1, \ldots, I$$

where the $\bar{r}$ range varies from the solution of linear programming problem

(WC_{LP})

$$\min \; -\left\{(\mathbf{x}^-)'\mathbf{r}^u + (\mathbf{x}^+)'\mathbf{r}^l - \tau\right\} + \gamma \mathbf{b}'\mathbf{s} + \beta(\mathbf{x}^+)'\mathbf{x}^-$$

$s.t.$

Constraints (12.8)–(12.12)

to the value of $\bar{r}$ corresponding to the solution of quadratic programming problem

(WC_{QP})

$$\min \; \nu - \tau + \gamma \; \mathbf{b}'\mathbf{s} + \beta(\mathbf{x}^+)'\mathbf{x}^-$$

$s.t.$

Constraints (12.8)–(12.12)

$$(\mathbf{w} - \overline{\mathbf{w}})'\Lambda_i(\mathbf{w} - \overline{\mathbf{w}}) \leq \nu \qquad i = 1, \ldots, I$$

which provides total risk aversion worst-case investment strategy.

Here, $\mathbf{r}$ is chosen to yield the worst-case return whatever the portfolio decision. In other words, given any choice of $\mathbf{w}$, the corresponding worst-case return is computed. This is in contrast to the saddle point formulation below which computes the best mean-variance optimal decision simultaneously with the worst-case scenario.

Saddle point solution

Consider the min-max problem

$$\min_{\mathbf{e}'\mathbf{w}=1,\mathbf{w}\geq 0} \quad \max_{i=1,\ldots,I,\ \mathbf{r}^l\leq\mathbf{r}\leq\mathbf{r}^u} \left\{-(\mathbf{w}-\overline{\mathbf{w}})'\mathbf{r}+\alpha(\mathbf{w}-\overline{\mathbf{w}})'\Lambda_i(\mathbf{w}-\overline{\mathbf{w}})\right\}. \tag{12.13}$$

Using the equivalence

$$\min_{\mathbf{e}'\mathbf{w}=1,\mathbf{w}\geq 0} \max_{i} \left\{(\mathbf{w}-\overline{\mathbf{w}})'\Lambda_i(\mathbf{w}-\overline{\mathbf{w}})\right\} = \tag{12.14}$$

$$\min_{\mathbf{e}'\mathbf{w}=1,\mathbf{w}\geq 0} \quad \max_{y_i\geq 0,\ \sum_{i=1}^{I} y_i=1} \left\{\sum_{i=1}^{I} y_i(\mathbf{w}-\overline{\mathbf{w}})'\Lambda_i(\mathbf{w}-\overline{\mathbf{w}})\right\}$$

the min-max problem (12.13) can be reformulated as

$$\min_{\mathbf{e}'\mathbf{w}=1,\mathbf{w}\geq 0} \quad \max_{\mathbf{r}^l\leq\mathbf{r}\leq\mathbf{r}^u} \left\{-(\mathbf{w}-\overline{\mathbf{w}})'\mathbf{r}\right\} + \tag{12.15}$$

$$\min_{\mathbf{e}'\mathbf{w}=1,\mathbf{w}\geq 0} \quad \max_{y_i\geq 0,\ \sum_{i=1}^{I} y_i=1} \left\{\alpha\sum_{i=1}^{I} y_i(\mathbf{w}-\overline{\mathbf{w}})'\Lambda_i(\mathbf{w}-\overline{\mathbf{w}})\right\}$$

For illustration purposes we assume that y_i, for $i = 1,\ldots,I$, is fixed such that $y_i \geq 0$ and $\sum_{i=1}^{I} y_i = 1$. It can easily be shown that the solution of (12.15) is a saddle point. For simplicity, we ignore transaction costs and constraints (12.2) and (12.3). We define $\rho = -\mathbf{r}$ and $\mathbf{x} = \mathbf{w} - \overline{\mathbf{w}}$. Therefore, $\mathbf{e}'(\mathbf{w} - \overline{\mathbf{w}}) = \mathbf{e}'\mathbf{x} = c$ and c is a constant. The min-max problem (12.15) can be rewritten as

$$\min_{\mathbf{e}'\mathbf{x}=c} \max_{\rho} \left\{ \rho'\mathbf{x} + \frac{1}{2}\mathbf{x}'H\mathbf{x} \mid \rho^l \leq \rho \leq \rho^u \right\} \tag{12.16}$$

where $\rho^l = -\mathbf{r}^u$, $\rho^u = -\mathbf{r}^l$ and the Hessian matrix with respect to $\mathbf{w}$ is $H = 2\alpha\sum_{i=1}^{I} y_i\Lambda_i$. Let ρ be fixed at the value that maximizes (12.16).

Consider the minimization of (12.16) with respect to $\mathbf{x}$ given the value of ρ. We write Lagrangian function

$$L(\mathbf{x},\pi) = \rho'\mathbf{x} + \frac{1}{2}\mathbf{x}'H\mathbf{x} + (\mathbf{e}'\mathbf{x} - c)\pi$$

and the optimality conditions

$$\begin{aligned} \nabla_{\mathbf{x}} &= \rho + H\mathbf{x} + \mathbf{e}\pi = 0 \\ \nabla_{\pi} &= \mathbf{e}'\mathbf{x} - c = 0 \end{aligned}$$

where π is the multiplier associated with $\mathbf{e}'\mathbf{x} - c = 0$. The minimal point is obtained as

$$\mathbf{x}(\rho) = -PH^{-1}\rho + \mathbf{y}, \quad \pi(\rho) = -(\mathbf{e}'H^{-1}\mathbf{e})^{-1}(\mathbf{e}'H^{-1}\rho + c)$$

where

$$\mathbf{y} = \mathbf{e}'H^{-1}(\mathbf{e}'H^{-1}\mathbf{e})^{-1}c \text{ and } P = \left[I - H^{-1}\mathbf{e}(\mathbf{e}'H^{-1}\mathbf{e})^{-1}\mathbf{e}'\right]$$

Note that PH^{-1} is a symmetric positive semi-definite matrix. Substituting the solution in the min-max problem (12.16), we obtain the following concave quadratic programming problem

$$\max_{\rho}\left\{-\frac{1}{2}\rho'PH^{-1}\rho - \mathbf{y}'P\rho + \mathbf{y}'\rho + \frac{1}{2}\mathbf{y}'H\mathbf{y} \mid \rho^l \leq \rho \leq \rho^u\right\} \quad (12.17)$$

The solution of (12.17) leads to the best mean-variance decision determined *simultaneously* with the worst-case. The min-max problem (12.6) computes the worst-case return for any $\mathbf{w}$. It can be verified that by approximately selecting the corner solution corresponding to the worst-case return given any $\mathbf{w}$, we solve

$$\max_{\mathbf{r}^l \leq \mathbf{r} \leq \mathbf{r}^u} -\mathbf{r}'(\mathbf{w} - \overline{\mathbf{w}}) \quad (12.18)$$

Hence we have the inequality

$$\max_{\mathbf{r}^l \leq \mathbf{r} \leq \mathbf{r}^u} -\mathbf{r}'(\mathbf{w} - \overline{\mathbf{w}}) \geq -\mathbf{r}'(\mathbf{w} - \overline{\mathbf{w}}), \quad \forall \mathbf{r} \in [\mathbf{r}^l, \mathbf{r}^u]$$

The worst-case solution corresponding to the saddle point does not necessarily coincide with the worst-case in (12.18). This is essentially due to the priority given to optimizing risk in (12.13) while the worst-case return is being determined. Thus, in this chapter we are not concerned with solving (12.13). We wish to model the worst-case mean-variance optimization problem so that the worst-case return is determined given any decision $\mathbf{w}$. This is achieved by solving the quadratic optimization problem in (12.7).

4. Computational results

The optimization model (12.7) described in Section 3 was implemented in C++. The nonlinear solver E04UCF, Nag Library, is used to optimize linear and quadratic problems. All computational experiments are carried out on a 3 GHz Pentium 4, running Linux with 1.5GB RAM.

The specification of rival covariance matrices may be realized by considering the data during different periods in the past. This leads to volatility measures corresponding to different historical periods. Thus, by considering subintervals of history, measuring volatility in each one is an effective way of estimating risk scenarios. It is well known that the estimates corresponding to each subperiod can be substantially different, and employing the worst-case scenario arising from this consideration yields a robust strategy. Other covariance estimation methods such as ARCH-GARCH models and bootstrapping are also clearly useful alternatives.

We consider 3 rival risk scenarios which are obtained from the historical data. The first covariance matrix is obtained by an exponential fit of 146 monthly price historical data. For the second and the third risk scenarios we divided the past price data into two parts. Then covariance matrices (corresponding to the second and third rival risk scenarios) are measured from the residuals of the exponential fit of the first part and the second part of the data.

The forecast bounds are determined around the historical mean and the bounds are chosen as (10%$\pm$ standard deviation) for each asset. We compare these forecast bounds with three discrete rival return scenarios within this range. These are selected at the lower bound, upper bound and central mean, and used with the discrete min-max formulation (12.5). We evaluate the performance of the continuous and discrete min-max investment strategies obtained by solving the min-max optimization problems (12.7) and (12.5), respectively, with three rival risk scenarios in terms of worst-case risk-return frontiers. Figure 12.1 presents robustness of continuous min-max (at the top) and discrete min-max (at the bottom).

In order to illustrate the effect of range choice for return forecasts on the min-max models, we kept the upper bound at the same level as (10%+ standard deviation) and change the lower bound to (1%$-$ standard deviation) for each asset. Figure 12.2 illustrates the performance of continuous (at the top) and discrete (at the bottom) min-max approaches and the non-inferiority of continuous and discrete min-max optimization models over three selected rival return scenarios within the

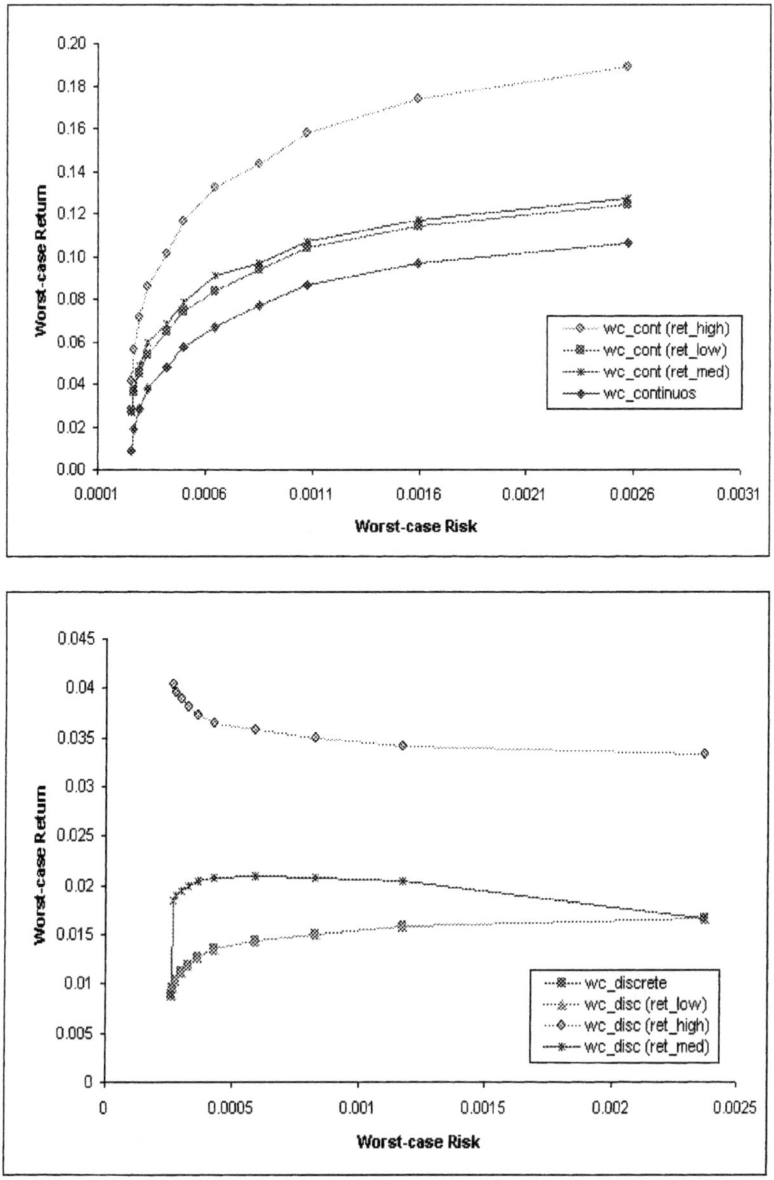

Figure 12.1. Robustness of continuous min-max and discrete min-max at ($r^l = 10\%$-standard deviation).

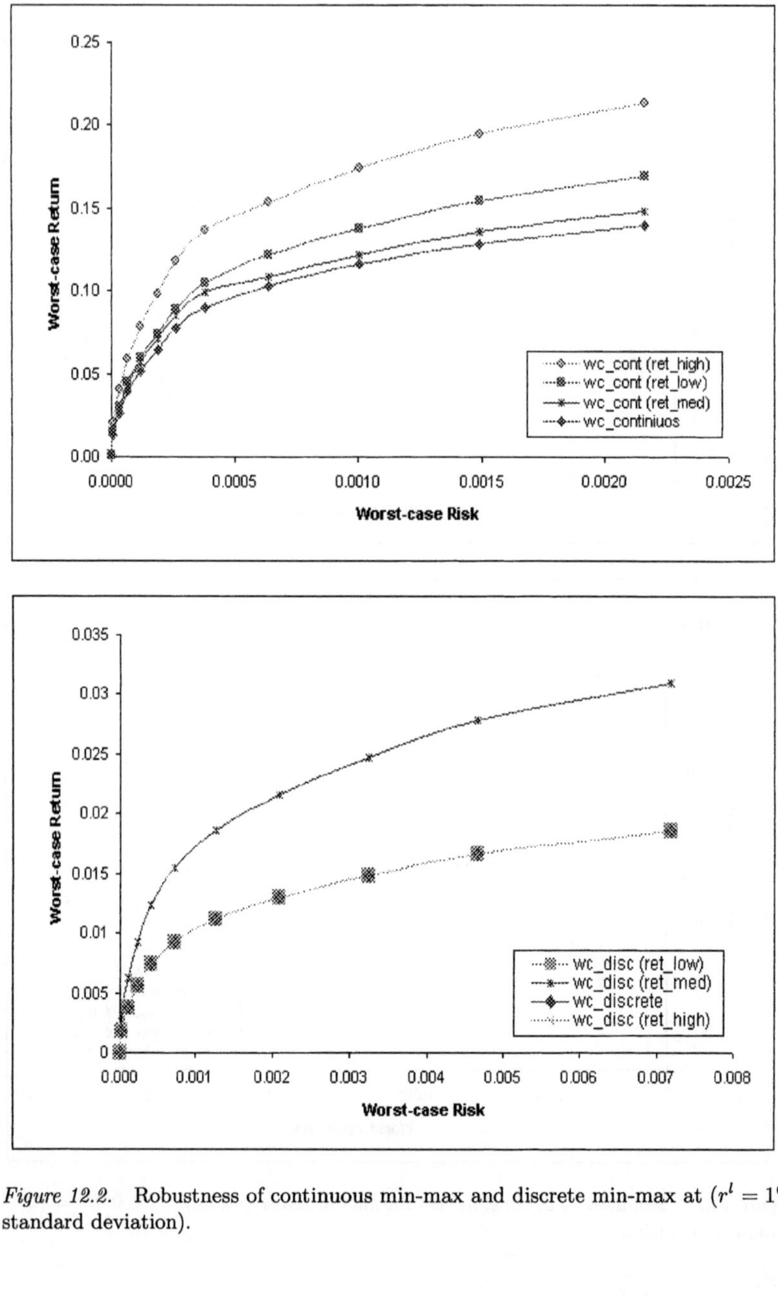

Figure 12.2. Robustness of continuous min-max and discrete min-max at ($r^l = 1\%$-standard deviation).

range of return forecast. Note that in Figure 12.2, the discrete worst-case investment strategy coincides with the efficient frontiers obtained by evaluating the min-max strategy on upper-and-lower-bound based scenarios. In this case, benchmark relative worst-case strategy is adjusted to cover lower-and-upper-bound based scenarios as the rival worst-case.

The impact of transaction costs on the performance of the mean variance models have been investigated by Perold (1984); Konno (1991); Chopra, Hensel and Turner (1993). Here we consider the effect of the transaction cost on the continuous min-max model for single period mean-variance optimization. Table 12.2 presents asset allocation of optimal portfolios $WC_{min}, WC_1, \ldots, WC_9$ and WC_{max} with transaction costs of 0.1% and 0.9%. The total risk-averse and risk-seeking worst-case investment strategies (the lowest and highest points on the worst-case risk-return frontier corresponding to the portfolios WC_{min} and WC_{max}) are obtained by solving (WC_{QP}) and (WC_{LP}) problems, respectively. Varying $\bar{r}$ between the return values corresponding to total risk averse and risk seeking strategies, nine optimal worst-case portfolios $WC_1, \ldots, WC_9$ are found by solving mean-variance optimization problem (WC_R). As expected, Table 12.2 shows less transaction among assets when the transaction cost is increased from 0.1 to 0.9%.

Table 12.2. Asset allocation with transaction cost 0.1% and 0.9%.

Asset	WC_{min}	WC_1	WC_2	WC_3	...	WC_9	WC_{max}
			Transaction cost 0.1%				
1	0.156807	0.155670	0.154524	0.153380	...	-	-
2	0.250823	0.251252	0.251655	0.252058	...	0.364014	0.5
3	0.179654	0.180162	0.180678	0.181193	...	0.345187	-
4	0.219614	0.219933	0.220236	0.220539	...	0.050449	-
5	0.193102	0.192982	0.192907	0.192830	...	0.240349	0.5
			Transaction cost 0.9%				
1	0.1568070	0.1568116	0.1568118	0.1568120	...	0.1568132	0.2
2	0.2508230	0.2507690	0.2507689	0.2507688	...	0.2507678	0.2
3	0.1796540	0.1796584	0.1796583	0.1796583	...	0.1796578	0.2
4	0.2196138	0.2196195	0.2196195	0.2196194	...	0.2196190	0.2
5	0.1931024	0.1931414	0.1931415	0.1931416	...	0.1931422	0.2

The continuous min-max model is also backtested to determine optimal investment strategies for specified levels of risk, and measuring the success of those strategies by their performance with the historical data. We summarize the backtesting procedure below. Further details are given in Gülpınar, Rustem and Settergren (2004).

The historical data consists of monthly prices data of 10 FTSE stocks through the 1990's. At any particular "present" time, the previous t time period of past history is fit to exponential growth curves. Residuals from exponential fit are used to estimate mean and covariance matrices for each asset. The continuous worst-case optimization software is used to find an optimal investment strategy over three risk scenarios and a range of return scenarios. The resulting investment strategy is implemented at "present" prices, and the portfolio value is updated according to "tomorrow's" prices. Then "present" is shifted forward one time period, and the process is repeated. Note that the optimizer can yield the entire range of efficient strategies, from risk-seeking to risk-averse, so the desired risk level is another parameter that needs to be specified during a backtesting experiment. In our computational experiments, we consider 25%, 50%, 75% and 95% risk levels and their results are plotted against index. Different lengths of history such as $t = 30, 70, 100$ are used for the computational experiments in order to show the impact of recent history on robust decision making.

We estimate two sets of risk scenarios in order to show the effect of risk scenarios on the min-max approach. The first set has three prespecified covariance matrices (estimated by considering the whole, first half and the last half of available historical data) and one covariance matrix, estimated from the recent history. The second set has three covariance matrices estimated from historical data up to current time period and dividing the history up to current time into two parts. The second set thus represents a dynamic adjustment of covariance matrices. It can be seen that such adjustment leads to an improvement in performance. The results are presented in Figures 12.3 and 12.4.

Figures 12.3 and 12.4 illustrate a fairly clear ordering of the results of the varying risk strategies by considering short history $t = 30$. The worst-case strategy outperforms in all risk levels apart from 25%. In both cases of $t = 70$ and $t = 100$, the worst-case strategy follows the index closely. In Figure 12.4, we consider the effect of updating the risk scenarios sequentially as backtest progresses. This seems to improve the performance comparing to Figure 12.3.

5. Conclusions

In this chapter, we address the critical issue of forecasting risk and return scenarios in portfolio management. We introduce a continuous min-max model for worst-case analysis of mean-variance portfolio op-

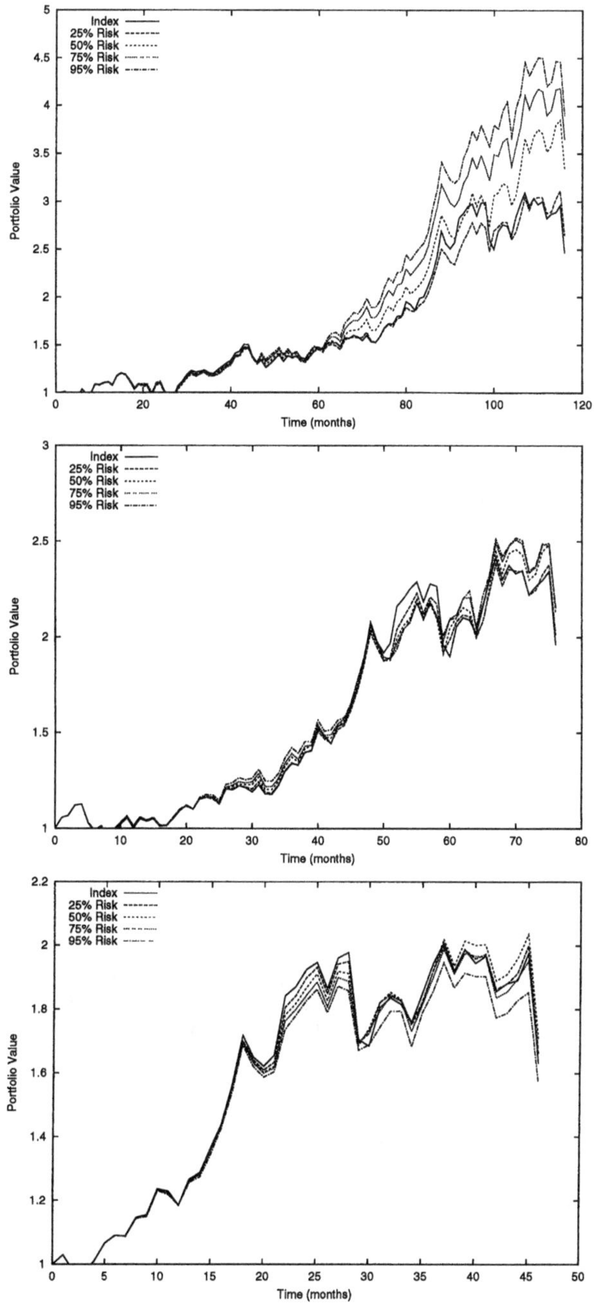

Figure 12.3. Backtesting with 30, 70, 100 history and 3 fixed and 1 dynamic rival risk scenarios.

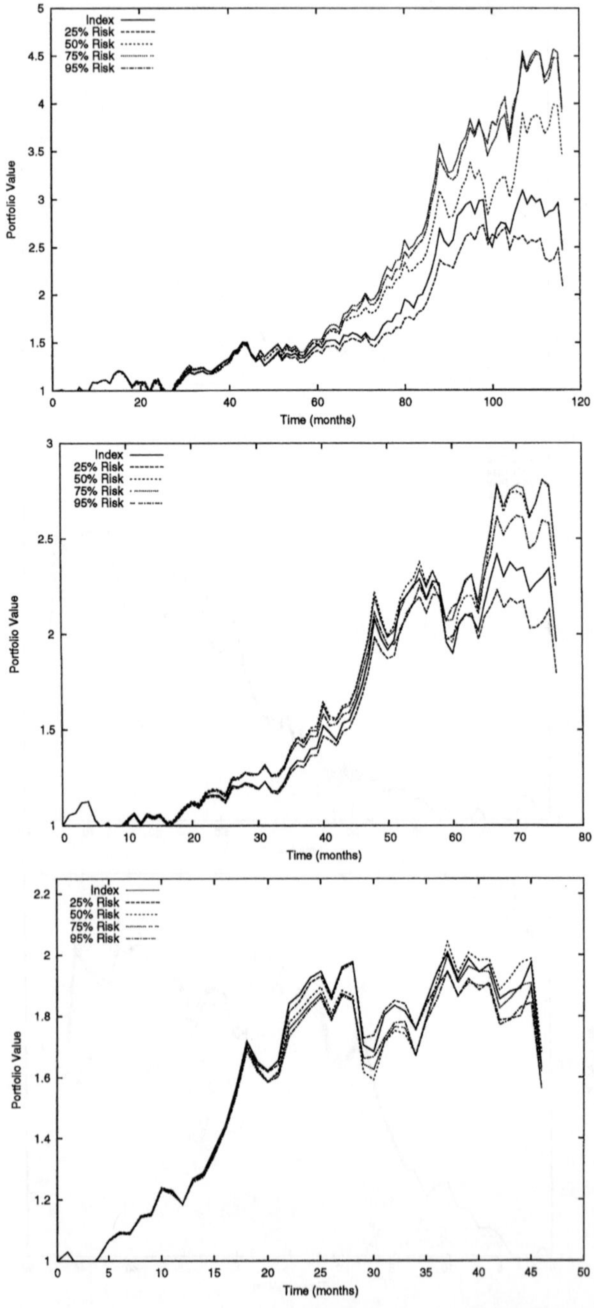

Figure 12.4. Backtesting with 30, 70, 100 history and 3 dynamic rival risk scenarios.

timization. The classical Markowitz framework is extended to a continuous min-max with a range return forecast and rival risk scenarios. This model specifically excludes the saddle point solution since it computes the worst-case return for any investment strategy. This is in contrast with the saddle point solution which computes the optimum mean-variance strategy simultaneously with the worst-case scenario.

Our computational experiments illustrate that the worst-case strategy is robust. The specification of rival risk scenarios and the length of history play important roles on the performance of the worst-case strategy. Out-of-sample backtesting results indicate that relying on long historical data to determine rival risk scenarios tends to give undue emphasis to past volatilities. On the other hand, there are consistent and significant gains to be made by adopting the min-max strategy with a judicious choice of historical data.

Acknowledgments This research was supported by EPSRC grant GR/M41124. The authors are grateful to Michèle Breton for helpful comments.

References

Breton, M. and El Hachem, S. (1995). Algorithms for the solution of stochastic dynamic minimax problems. *Computational Optimization and Applications*, 4:317–345.

Chopra, V.K., Hensel, C.R., and Turner, A.L. (1993). Managing mean-variance inputs: Returns from alternative global investment strategies in the 1980s. *Management Science*, 39(7):845–855.

Demyanov, V.F. and Malozemov, V.N. (1974). *Introduction to Minimax.* John Wiley, New York.

Gülpınar, N., Rustem, B., and Settergren, R. (2004). Optimization and simulation approaches to scenario tree generation. *Journal of Economics Dynamics and Control*, 28(7):1291–1315.

Gülpınar, N. and Rustem, B. (2004). *Worst-case Optimal Robust Decisions for Multi-period Mean-Variance Portfolio Optimization.* Working Paper. Imperial College London.

Kall, P. (1994). *Stochastic Programming.* Wiley, New York.

Konno, H. and Yamazaki, H. (1991). Mean-absolute deviation portfolio optimization model and its applications to Tokyo stock market. *Management Science*, 37(5):519–531.

Lawrence, M.J., Edmunson, R.H., and O'Connor, M.J. (1986). The accuracy of combining judgemental and statistical forecasts. *Management Science*, 32:1521–1532.

Makridakis, S. and Winkler, R. (1983). Average of forecasts: some empirical results. *Management Science*, 29:987 – 996.

Markowitz, H. (1952). Portfolio selection. *Journal of Finance*, 7:77 – 91.

NAG Library, `http://www.nag.co.uk`, The Numerical Algorithms Group, Oxford.

Perold, F.A. (1984). Large scale portfolio optimization. *Management Science*, 30(10):1143 – 1160

Rustem, B., Becker, R., and Marty, W. (2000). Robust min-max portfolio strategies for rival forecast and risk scenarios. *Journal of Economic Dynamics and Control*, 24:1591 – 1623.

Rustem, B. and Howe, M. (2002). *Algorithms for Worst-Case Design and Applications to Risk Management.* Princeton University Press.

Rustem, B. and Settergren, R. (2002). Scenario specification for robust portfolio analysis. In: *Computational Methods in Decision Making, Economics and Finance: Optimization Models*, pp. 75 – 86, Kluwer Academic Publishers.

MIX
Papier aus verantwortungsvollen Quellen
Paper from responsible sources
FSC® C105338

If you have any concerns about our products,
you can contact us on
ProductSafety@springernature.com

In case Publisher is established outside the EU,
the EU authorized representative is:
Springer Nature Customer Service Center GmbH
Europaplatz 3, 69115 Heidelberg, Germany

Printed by Libri Plureos GmbH
in Hamburg, Germany